Improving Literacy Through Home, School, and Community Partnerships

Al Ryanne Gabonada Gatcho
Hunan Institute of Science and Technology, China

Cecille Marie Titar Improgo
Bukidnon State University, Philippines

Merry Ruth Morauda Gutierrez
Philippine Normal University, Philippines

A volume in the Advances
in Educational Marketing,
Administration, and Leadership
(AEMAL) Book Series

Published in the United States of America by
   IGI Global
   Information Science Reference (an imprint of IGI Global)
   701 E. Chocolate Avenue
   Hershey PA, USA 17033
   Tel: 717-533-8845
   Fax: 717-533-8661
   E-mail: cust@igi-global.com
   Web site: http://www.igi-global.com

Library of Congress Cataloging-in-Publication Data

CIP PENDING

Improving Literacy Through Home, School, and Community Partnerships
 Al Ryanne Gatcho, Cecille Marie Improgo, Merry Ruth Gutierrez
   2024 Information Science Reference

ISBN: 9798369317778
eISBN: 9798369317785

This book is published in the IGI Global book series Advances in Educational Marketing,
Administration, and Leadership (AEMAL) (ISSN: 2326-9022; eISSN: 2326-9030)

British Cataloguing in Publication Data
A Cataloguing in Publication record for this book is available from the British Library.

For electronic access to this publication, please contact: eresources@igi-global.com.

Advances in Educational Marketing, Administration, and Leadership (AEMAL) Book Series

ISSN:2326-9022
EISSN:2326-9030

Editor-in-Chief: Siran Mukerji, IGNOU, India

MISSION

With more educational institutions entering into public, higher, and professional education, the educational environment has grown increasingly competitive. With this increase in competitiveness has come the need for a greater focus on leadership within the institutions, on administrative handling of educational matters, and on the marketing of the services offered.

The **Advances in Educational Marketing, Administration, & Leadership (AEMAL) Book Series** strives to provide publications that address all these areas and present trending, current research to assist professionals, administrators, and others involved in the education sector in making their decisions.

COVERAGE

- Educational Marketing Campaigns
- Marketing Theories within Education
- Enrollment Management
- Academic Administration
- Governance in P-12 and Higher Education
- Educational Leadership
- Faculty Administration and Management
- Direct marketing of educational programs
- Educational Management
- Academic Pricing

IGI Global is currently accepting manuscripts for publication within this series. To submit a proposal for a volume in this series, please contact our Acquisition Editors at Acquisitions@igi-global.com or visit: http://www.igi-global.com/publish/.

Titles in this Series

For a list of additional titles in this series, please visit:
http://www.igi-global.com/book-series/advances-educational-marketing-administration-leadership/73677

Minority Women in K-12 Education Leadership Challenges, Resilience, and Support
Annette G. Walters (Independent Researcher, USA)
Information Science Reference • © 2024 • 290pp • H/C (ISBN: 9798369317730) • US $245.00

History and Educational Philosophy for Social Justice and Human Rights
Jahid Siraz Chowdhury (Lincoln University College, Malaysia) Kumarashwaran Vadevelu (Universiti Malaya, Malaysia) A.F.M. Zakaria (Shahjalal University of Science and Technology, Bangladesh) Abdullah Al-Mamun (Sunway University, Malaysia) and Sajib Ahmed (Universiti Malaya, Malaysia)
Information Science Reference • © 2024 • 277pp • H/C (ISBN: 9781668499535) • US $235.00

Exploring Intersectionality and Women in STEM
Luz Idalia Balderas (Tamaulipas Autonomous University, Mexico) Sanju Tiwari (Tamaulipas Autonomous University, Mexico) Elizabeth Verdugo (Pontifícia Universidade Católica do Rio de Janeiro, Brazil) Gina Paola Maestre-Gongora (Universidad de Antioquia, Colombia) and Fernando Ortiz-Rodriguez (Tamaulipas Autonomous University, Mexico)
Information Science Reference • © 2024 • 268pp • H/C (ISBN: 9798369311196) • US $245.00

Revitalizing the Learning Ecosystem for Modern Students
Fatima Al Husseiny (Lebanese International University, Lebanon) and Afzal Sayed Munna (University of Sunderland in London, UK)
Information Science Reference • © 2024 • 242pp • H/C (ISBN: 9798369341032) • US $245.00

Autoethnographic Tactics to Closing the Gap on Educational Attainment
Anika Chanell Thrower (Borough of Manhattan Community College, CUNY, USA) Alex Evangelista (Borough of Manhattan Community College, CUNY, USA) Ruth Baker-Gardner (University of the West Indies, Jamaica) and Hammed Mogaji (Federal University of Bahia, Brazil)
Information Science Reference • © 2024 • 258pp • H/C (ISBN: 9798369310748) • US $230.00

IGI Global
PUBLISHER of TIMELY KNOWLEDGE

701 East Chocolate Avenue, Hershey, PA 17033, USA
Tel: 717-533-8845 x100 • Fax: 717-533-8661
E-Mail: cust@igi-global.com • www.igi-global.com

Table of Contents

Detailed Table of Contents

Chapter 1

 Poonam Anand, University of Bahrain, Bahrain
 Parween Ebrahim, University of Bahrain, Bahrain

The chapter compares the assessment paradigms of summative and formative assessments of English for academic purposes literacies (EAPL) as experienced by teacher candidates in a national pedagogical institute in the Middle East region. EAPL assessments are mapped at different distances utilizing Bronfenbrenner's bioecological model to describe the assessment continuum, which ranges from microsystem to macrosystem, and is defined by the distance from the enacted curriculum. Proximal processes of EAPL formative assessments taking place in the microsystem are ecologically sound in socializing students in their academic discipline. The persistent interactions in the classroom assessment environment enhance the gradual development of academic literacies over time. Teacher candidates encounter tensions that arise between formative and summative assessment paradigms. First, in their teacher training, and second, in their teaching. Similar research findings from other educational contexts have been reported about the tensions between the two types of assessment.

Chapter 2

Bonjovi H. Hajan, Tawi-Tawi College of Technology and Oceanography,
Mindanao State University, Philippines

Clarissa Ayangco-Derramas, Tawi-Tawi College of Technology and
Oceanography, Mindanao State University, Philippines

Wati Sheena M. Bulkia, Tawi-Tawi College of Technology and
Oceanography, Mindanao State University, Philippines

Aljon L. Alpuerto, Tawi-Tawi College of Technology and Oceanography,
Mindanao State University, Philippines

Reading literacy provides a gateway access to other more complex forms of literacies central for navigating the convolution of today's globalized, digital, and data-saturated world. Positioned within this view, this chapter offers a comprehensive literature review of school-community collaboration and literacy education to shed light on facilitators and barriers central to the partnering efforts in the development of reading literacy. Based on the thematic analysis of careful and exhaustive literature reviews, several interesting themes emerged that depict key facilitators and barriers of school-community collaboration in reading education. The chapter, drawing on the authors' critical reflections of the identified themes, charts the future directions of school-community collaboration in the reading education field, shaping the changing landscape of reading education practice, policy, and research.

Chapter 3

M. Serhat Semercioglu, Gumushane University, Turkey

Melek Baba Öztürk, Faculty of Education, Ondokuz Mayis University, Turkey

This section elaborates on the definition, significance, and promotion strategies of civic literacy. The implementation of civic literacy within the context of life skills and social studies courses is extensively discussed, with a focus on the case of Turkey. Emphasizing the importance of integrating the life skills and social studies curriculum in fostering civic literacy, the challenges encountered in practice are also thoroughly examined. Furthermore, the discourse extends to the integration of civic literacy into technology, addressing both the challenges and advantages that citizens may encounter or experience. The role of civic literacy within widely-used social media applications, prevalent in today's technological era, is highlighted. Additionally, the technical application of civic literacy, exemplified by e-government initiatives, is scrutinized through various global instances. The concluding section reflects on the future of civic literacy and civic engagement.

    Hilal Atlar-Yildirim, Independent Researcher, Turkey
    Yıldız Uzuner, Anadolu University, Turkey

Children realize that reading and writing have meaning in spoken and written language development. Over time, they use the sounds in their mother tongue and the letters in their native language alphabet. Early literacy is a combination of verbal language, phonological awareness, alphabetic knowledge, print awareness, concepts related to writing, and the development of scribbles/writings that reflect the child's discovery. In this context, the scope and importance of early literacy and the development of literacy in children with hearing loss are conveyed. Then, the characteristics of the literacy environment, the nature of the experiences, and the views of the family on literacy are presented with examples from the researchers' case studies. Furthermore, an action research example illustrates the role of educator-family collaboration in supporting the early literacy development of children with hearing loss. This chapter presents suggestions to families and teachers to support emergent literacy in daily routines.

    Al Ryanne Gabonada Gatcho, Hunan Institute of Science and
        Technology, China
    Xin Geng Mao, Hunan Institute of Science and Technology, China
    Fu Ting, Hunan Institute of Science and Technology, China

This chapter examines digital technology's impact on early literacy and parental roles. Traditional involvement, like reading and storytelling, now extends to overseeing digital content and using literacy tools. The authors analyze this shift, highlighting the dual role of parents as facilitators in blending digital and traditional literacy. This conceptual analysis underscores the need for parents to navigate digital platforms effectively, ensuring a balance between digital and traditional practices. Challenges include enhancing parental digital literacy for enriched learning experiences. The authors advocate for a collaborative approach among educators, parents, and policymakers to adapt to technological advancements in literacy education, pointing towards the evolving nature of parental guidance in a tech-rich educational environment. This work adds insight into the dynamic parental role in fostering early literacy amidst digital growth.

This policy brief explores the implementation of Aksara Agar Berdaya (AKRAB) in Indonesia. AKRAB seeks to eradicate adult illiteracy in the country believing that literacy creates power for the families and the communities. This paper critically examines the AKRAB program's objectives as well as its implementation challenges and offers a proposal based on the materials visited and analyzed for its enhancement. Drawing on the program's comprehensive analysis, AKRAB 2.0 is proposed, presenting an enhanced version of the program with modifications related to the resolutions deemed to be helpful towards the examined challenges. This brief serves as an insightful resource for policymakers, stakeholders, and interested agents seeking a well-rounded understanding of AKRAB and the action items that it needs for its better implementation.

Chapter 7

Exploring the intersection of technology and community literacy, this reflection chronicles the design and implementation of technology-mediated community literacy (TMCL) programs. It scrutinizes the symbiosis of digital tools and literacy enhancement, addressing challenges like the digital divide and educator resistance. Successes, challenges, and insights from two principal TMCL programs—one for children during COVID-19 and another for adult literacy—are analyzed. Emphasizing core principles such as community engagement and continuous improvement, the chapter outlines future TMCL trajectories influenced by technological advancements and educational policy shifts. Personal reflections offer a vision for TMCL's impact on community literacy.

Chapter 8

Patrícia Dias, ISAG, European Business School and Research Center in Business Science and Tourism (CICET-FCVC), Porto, Portugal

Ana Pinto Borges, ISAG, European Business School and Research Center in Business Science and Tourism (CICET-FCVC), Porto, Portugal & Center for Research in Organizations, Markets and Industrial Management (COMEGI), Porto, Portugal

Elvira Vieira, ISAG, European Business School and Research Center in Business Science and Tourism (CICET-FCVC), Porto, Portugal & IPVC-Polytechnic Institute of Viana do Castelo and Applied Management Research Unit (UNIAG), Instituto Politécnico de Bragança, Portugal

The authors assessed the determinants of the overall financial literacy indicator of higher education students in Portugal and the relationship between the financial literacy indicator and the indicators of resilience and financial well-being. Based on a non-parametric quantitative analysis, the authors used a sample of 469 higher education students. They observed that students present globally more satisfactory indicators compared to the Portuguese population and are influenced by demographic factors such as age, gender, level of education, and income. The results are far from reasonable, especially in the dimension related to knowledge. As also statistically confirmed, there exists a positive and significant relationship between the financial literacy indicator and the indicators of resilience and financial well-being. Therefore, this study adopts a novel approach that intends to link these indicators with higher education students, as there is still a lack of research that addresses the concept of digital financial literacy within this context.

Chapter 9

Simbayi Yafele, University of Johannesburg, South Africa

Literacy-as-social-practice urges inclusive, home-derived pedagogies for marginalised learners. Yet, many global-south universities remain locations of epistemological and monolingual biases that negate students' identities, raising inclusivity-praxis concerns. The study aimed to experiment with translanguaging literacy pedagogy for multilinguals' inclusivity and success by using students' home-based experiences to develop academic reading. Drawing from sociocultural and translanguaging fluidity theories, it seeks alternative localised translanguaging pedagogies to erase literacy-exclusion. Home-culture and language identities become extensions of university literacy learning in an experiment using mixed methods to tackle a reading problem by fluid, translingual, multilingual/cultural practices for inclusivity and success in a 1st-year academic-reading-mediation. Results show success when students' home-derived resources are activated and legitimated for inclusive literacy pedagogy.

Chapter 10

Lemuel-Kim A. Garcia, Department of Education, San Leonardo, Philippines
Ramil Gutierrez Ilustre, Department of Education, San Fernando, Philippines

The researchers implemented Microsoft Reading Progress and Immersive Reader to address the reading problems of students in terms of reading speed and oral reading miscues. Using a true experimental design, it was found that the digital intervention and traditional way of teaching have shown significant improvement on the reading skills of the students. The Reading Progress and Immersive Reading can be considered by the teachers who have numerous workloads because the application can let the students learn reading independently. However, traditional instruction where the teacher is physically guiding the students can not be replaced by the software intervention, despite of its time-consuming-issue. This means that both reading pedagogies have their pros and cons. This enabled the researchers to craft an action plan focused on implementing the application and engaging the stakeholders and parents to address the learning gaps in reading as an education community.

Preface

"Literacy begins at home," a maxim that has echoed through the halls of education for decades, encapsulates a fundamental truth about the origins of learning. This adage underscores the critical role that familial environments play in the early literacy journey of individuals, serving as the initial scaffolding upon which future educational achievements are built. Yet, the profundity of this simple phrase often belies the complexity of the literacy ecosystem. It is within the dynamic interplay between home, school, and community that the literacy narrative of each individual is truly shaped. Despite its evident importance, the synergy among these foundational pillars is frequently undervalued, with concerted efforts to harness their collective potential falling short. The gaps in understanding and operationalizing the collaborative effort required to nurture a literate society are significant and manifold. While homes lay the crucial groundwork and schools aim to amplify these efforts, the broader community's role in reinforcing and extending these literacy practices is pivotal yet inadequately leveraged. This triad's potential to cultivate a rich literacy environment remains partially untapped, obscured by disjointed initiatives and a lack of cohesive strategy. As a result, the path to a truly literate society—where every individual is empowered to navigate the complexities of an increasingly multimedia text-saturated world—remains fraught with challenges. This book aims to delve into these critical issues, highlighting the need for a more integrated approach to literacy that acknowledges the unique contributions of home, school, and community.

At the heart of the struggle to enhance literacy lies a disjointed system, marked by siloed efforts and a fragmented approach to development. This system, with its piecemeal strategies and lack of coordinated action, significantly hampers the seamless progression of literacy from the foundational stages at home, through the formative years in education, to the broadening experiences within the community. Such disconnection not only stymies the potential for comprehensive literacy growth but also creates barriers that are felt most acutely by those from underserved or marginalized backgrounds. The challenge is not merely one of improving individual literacy skills but of weaving these skills into the fabric of daily life in a way that is meaningful, relevant, and accessible to all.

This book is a groundbreaking exploration into the complex factors shaping literacy development, highlighting the significant, yet underutilized, potential of collaboration between homes, schools, and communities. It aims to reveal how these critical sectors can work together to foster a supportive literacy environment, encouraging a shift towards unified and comprehensive literacy strategies that benefit all learners, paving the path to a more inclusive, literate society.

This book offers invaluable insights for a diverse range of stakeholders, from early-career researchers to families, educators, community leaders, and policymakers. For researchers at the outset of their careers, it serves as a vital resource for identifying and addressing the prevalent gaps in literacy development research, guiding their future work towards impactful areas. Families will find guidance on nurturing literacy at home, while educators and community leaders can discover innovative strategies to support literacy through collaboration. Policymakers, too, will gain essential perspectives to shape effective literacy policies. Together, these insights aim to inform and inspire practices, policies, and research initiatives that are crucial for fostering a literate society.

ORGANIZATION OF THE BOOK

Chapter 1: "An Application of Bronfenbrenner's Bioecological Theory to the Assessment of Academic Literacies: Reflections from a Teacher Training College" by Poonam Anand and Parween Ebrahim delves into the comparison between summative and formative assessments of English for academic purposes literacies (EAPL) within a Middle Eastern pedagogical institute. Utilizing Bronfenbrenner's bioecological model, the chapter maps EAPL assessments across various distances within the educational ecosystem. It explores how proximal processes of formative assessments shape students' academic literacy development, highlighting tensions encountered by teacher candidates in navigating formative and summative assessment paradigms.

Chapter 2: "Building a Reading Nation: Insights into School-Community Collaboration" authored by Bonjovi Hajan, Clarissa Ayangco-Derramas, Wati Sheena Bulkia, and Aljon Alpuerto offers a comprehensive literature review on school-community collaboration in literacy education. Through thematic analysis, the chapter identifies facilitators and barriers in this collaborative effort, shaping the future landscape of reading education practice, policy, and research.

Chapter 3: "Civic Literacy and Engagement" by Serhat Semercioglu and Melek Baba Özturk elaborates on civic literacy within the context of Life Skills and Social Studies courses, with a focus on Turkey. The chapter discusses challenges and strategies for integrating civic literacy into technology and social media applications, while also examining the role of civic literacy in e-government initiatives.

Chapter 4: "Early Literacy in Children with Hearing Loss" by Hilal Atlar-Yildirim and Yıldız Uzuner delves into the development of emergent literacy in children with hearing loss. The chapter discusses the components of emergent literacy and explores the role of the literacy environment and family support in fostering early literacy skills in children with hearing loss. Additionally, it presents an action research example highlighting the importance of educator-family collaboration in supporting early literacy development.

Chapter 5: "Early Literacy in the Digital Age: Parental Roles Reimagined" authored by Al Ryanne Gatcho, Xin Geng Mao, and Fu Ting investigates the impact of digital technology on early literacy and parental roles. The chapter analyzes the evolving role of parents in facilitating both digital and traditional literacy practices and advocates for collaborative efforts among educators, parents, and policymakers to adapt to technological advancements in literacy education.

Chapter 6: "Empowering Communities through Literacy: Policy Insights from Indonesia's Akrab Literacy Initiative" by Jeremiah Paul Manuel examines the implementation of the Aksara Agar Berdaya (AKRAB) literacy initiative in Indonesia. The chapter explores the program's objectives, implementation challenges, and proposes enhancements for the future, serving as a valuable resource for policymakers and stakeholders interested in community literacy initiatives.

Chapter 7: "From Consultation to Implementation: Reflective Pathways in Designing Technology-Mediated Community Literacy Programs" by Al Ryanne Gatcho chronicles the design and implementation of Technology-Mediated Community Literacy (TMCL) programs. The chapter discusses successes, challenges, and insights from TMCL programs and outlines future trajectories influenced by technological advancements and educational policy shifts.

Chapter 8: "Literacy, Resilience, and Financial Well-Being in Higher Education Students," by Patrícia Dias, Ana Pinto Borges, and Elvira Vieira assesses the financial literacy, resilience, and financial well-being of higher education students in Portugal. The chapter explores demographic influences on financial literacy and establishes a positive relationship between financial literacy, resilience, and financial well-being, contributing to the understanding of financial literacy within higher education contexts.

Chapter 9: "Reading development in 1st year: Experimenting with translanguaging to connect home ways with university texts" by Simbayi Yafele investigates the use of translanguaging literacy pedagogy for inclusive reading development in first-year university students. The chapter explores alternative translanguaging pedagogies to promote inclusivity and success in academic reading, emphasizing the integration of home-based experiences into university literacy learning.

Chapter 10: "Towards a Literate Community: An Action Plan Using Microsoft's Reading Progress and Immersive Reader" by Lemuel-Kim Garcia and Ramil Ilustre examines the implementation of Microsoft Immersive ReaderTM and Reading

ProgressTM in improving reading literacy among students in the Philippines. The chapter presents findings from experimental design research and discusses the effectiveness of technology-mediated reading interventions in enhancing reading skills, providing insights for educators and policymakers.

IN CONCLUSION

As editors of this comprehensive reference book, we are thrilled to witness the culmination of diverse perspectives, insightful research, and innovative practices that collectively contribute to the overarching goal of fostering literacy through collaborative efforts between home, school, and community.

Through the chapters presented within these pages, readers embark on a journey that traverses the intricate interplay of various factors shaping literacy development, from the foundational role of home environments to the dynamic landscape of digital literacy in the 21st century. Each chapter offers unique insights and practical recommendations, underscoring the importance of holistic approaches to literacy education.

From the exploration of theoretical frameworks like Bronfenbrenner's bioecological theory to the implementation of community literacy initiatives such as AKRAB in Indonesia, this book encapsulates the breadth and depth of efforts aimed at nurturing literate societies. It addresses challenges, celebrates successes, and charts pathways for future endeavors in the realm of literacy education.

As we conclude this preface, we extend our gratitude to the contributors, whose dedication and expertise have enriched this volume immeasurably. We also extend our appreciation to the readers, educators, policymakers, and stakeholders who will engage with this book, trusting that its contents will inspire meaningful dialogue, inform practice, and ignite further research in the pursuit of literacy for all.

May the insights shared within these pages serve as catalysts for transformative action, fostering a world where every individual has the opportunity to unlock the power of literacy and realize their full potential.

Al Ryanne Gabonada Gatcho
Hunan Institute of Science and Technology, China

Cecille Marie Titar Improgo
Bukidnon State University, Philippines

Merry Ruth Morauda Gutierrez
Philippine Normal University, Philippines

Acknowledgment

We begin by extending our deepest gratitude to the chapter contributors, whose exceptional works form the backbone of this volume. It is through their dedication, expertise, and innovative research that this book has been brought to life. Without their contributions, the exploration of such a pivotal subject would not have been possible.

Our thanks also go out to the diligent external reviewers who generously shared their time and expertise. Their keen insights and thorough evaluations have ensured that the content not only meets the high standards set by IGI Global but also remains relevant and compelling within our discipline. Their commitment to excellence has been indispensable in shaping a book that truly advances the field of literacy education.

We are immensely grateful to the IGI Global team for their unwavering support throughout this journey. From the initial conception to the final publication, their belief in the vision of this book has been a constant source of encouragement. Their professionalism, expertise, and guidance have been crucial in bringing this project to fruition.

To our colleagues and friends within the discipline, your shared insights and encouragement have been invaluable. Your willingness to engage in discussions, provide feedback, and offer perspectives has enriched this endeavor in countless ways. This collaborative spirit is what drives our field forward, and we are thankful for your contributions to this collective journey.

Lastly, but most importantly, we owe a profound debt of gratitude to our families. In moments of doubt and exhaustion, your unwavering support and understanding have been our bedrock. You have been the source of strength that fueled our persistence, the quiet comfort that soothed our stressed minds, and the joy that reminded us of the importance of our work. This book is not just a testament to our dedication but a reflection of the love and sacrifice you have generously offered.

Al Ryanne Gabonada Gatcho, Cecille Marie Titar Improgo, and Merry Ruth Morauda Gutierrez

Chapter 1
An Application of Bronfenbrenner's Bioecological Theory to the Assessment of Academic Literacies:
Reflections From a Teacher Training College

Poonam Anand
University of Bahrain, Bahrain

Parween Ebrahim
ⓘ https://orcid.org/0000-0002-4969-0159
University of Bahrain, Bahrain

ABSTRACT

The chapter compares the assessment paradigms of summative and formative assessments of English for academic purposes literacies (EAPL) as experienced by teacher candidates in a national pedagogical institute in the Middle East region. EAPL assessments are mapped at different distances utilizing Bronfenbrenner's bioecological model to describe the assessment continuum, which ranges from microsystem to macrosystem, and is defined by the distance from the enacted curriculum. Proximal processes of EAPL formative assessments taking place in the microsystem are ecologically sound in socializing students in their academic discipline. The persistent interactions in the classroom assessment environment enhance the gradual development of academic literacies over time. Teacher candidates encounter tensions that arise between formative and summative assessment paradigms. First, in their teacher training, and second, in their teaching. Similar research findings from other educational contexts have been reported about the tensions between the two types of assessment.

DOI: 10.4018/979-8-3693-1777-8.ch001

INTRODUCTION

The landscape of higher education has seen a remarkable diversification in its student body, which encompasses linguistic, social, and cultural variation. Thanks to inclusive education and internationalization efforts, most student bodies are increasingly multilingual, which significantly affects the emphasis that universities place on the development of the academic literacy of students, regardless of their linguistic or cultural background. The term academic literacy broadly refers to the range of academic abilities, mostly higher order thinking and learning, which students acquire when starting out in a new academic discipline. Over the past two decades, researchers (Lea & Street, 1998, 2006; Wingate, 2015, 2018) have suggested a shift in academic literacy from discrete, transferable skills to literacy as a textual, social, and contextual practice. A prevalent assumption, albeit questionable, is that students—whether native (L1) or non-native (L2)—enter university equipped with the requisite academic literacy to navigate their degree studies (Murray & Nallaya, 2016; Wingate, 2015, 2018). However, this perception often encapsulates a narrow view of academic literacy, most prominently in English for Academic Purposes (EAP) programs. Many of these programs focus on grammatical accuracy and rhetorical appropriateness in academic writing (Lea, 2017). In this chapter, the authors diverge from this limited perspective and embrace a pluralistic view of academic literacies, which entails the use of multimodal materials to convey meaning, ideas, and knowledge within discipline-specific academia.

Language use and skills learning in English for Academic Purposes Literacies (EAPL) are embedded in the culture of a particular discipline (Anand & Ackley, 2021; Lea & Street, 1998, 2006; Wingate, 2015). Learning to communicate within that discipline is essentially a process of socialization that reflects an emergent understanding of and ability to participate in its traditions of meaning-making. The constituent elements of EAPL proficiency are tripartite, with social, linguistic, and cognitive dimensions which extend beyond literacy in the four-language skills. EAPL moves from culturally applied language skills (e.g., textual analysis or compositional logic) to strategic proficiency in situational and domain specific community exchanges (Parodi, 2010; Bhatia, 2017). Thus, EAPL has a significant third dimension realized in social interactions and negotiations. Assessment of these ecologically sound social interactions, be it the performative, or collaborative is the focus of this chapter's inquiry. Currently, most assessments of English as a second language, or Academic Literacies, EAPL, use textual/verbal performance indicators to measure internal processes that focus on a *monoglossic* view, i.e. language components as separate entities. Such assessments generally do not use measurement tools to assess the external processes. Fewer assessments measure skills related to social processes.

Comprehensive academic literacies demand a *heteroglossic* view of literacies that meld linguistic, cultural, and sociolinguistic abilities in academia.

Prior to embarking on our examination of English for Academic Purposes Literacies (EAPL) assessment in a teacher training institute, we will set the stage by defining some critical terms. We aim to clarify the scope, objectives, and essence of EAPL. As its nomenclature suggests, EAPL entails the instruction, learning, and evaluation of English with a distinct emphasis on academic contexts, all of which assists L2 students in either studying or conducting research in the English language (Fox, 2004; Hamp-Lyons, 2011; Wingate, 2015). Integral to engaging in academic communities are two primary considerations: a) students require comprehension of how knowledge is formulated, presented, and debated across disciplines, alongside linguistic support; and b) academic literacies that encompass reading, writing, and reasoning within any discipline pose challenges for both native and non-native speakers alike (Lea & Street, 2006; Wingate, 2015).

Using a situated stance of reflective practice, this chapter will explore the assessment of EAPL from the perspective of Bronfenbrenner's bioecological theory of human development. More specifically, it focuses on the microsystem and the embedded proximal development processes which posit persistent forms of interaction in the immediate environment (Bronfenbrenner, 1979, 2005). Bioecological theory upholds that within supportive environments, if human relationships are strengthened, it is possible to increase the extent of development and improve positive outcomes. The authors concur with support considerations and strategies for acculturating students into academic literacies through proximal processes. Hence, in our chapter, we look at alternative models for acculturating students into academic literacies. We view Bronfenbrenner's bioecological model through a reflective lens to shed light on the extent to which that model is realized in the constant interactions built into the formative or classroom assessment practices of a pre-university program (PUP) and Bachelor of Education (B.Ed.) program of a bilingual teacher's college in an Arab context. Some of the examples of classroom assessments are group and collaborative projects, oral presentations and self- and/or peer-assessments.

As mentioned at the outset of this chapter, learning to communicate in academia is essentially a *process of socialization*. Cultural norms that are assumed to be understood and are embedded within academic literacies assessment may be unfamiliar in multicultural and multilingual populations. As practitioners in teaching academic literacies in a Pre-University Program (PUP) as well as in a Bachelor of Education for Primary English Teachers Program (B.Ed. PET), the authors confirm that PUP socializes bilingual teacher candidates into academic literacies using a variety of formative/classroom assessment models that build up the skills of the students and prepares them for the demands of their academic work once they matriculate in the B.Ed. PET wherein the socialization process into academic literacies continues (Education and Training Quality Authority, 2016, p. 23). We have observed that the academic literacies acquired by PUP students stand in contrast to their peers who are direct-entry students. Direct entry students enter their first year of the bachelor's degree without having to go through the PUP because they have higher language proficiency. However, direct entry students report that they face challenges in their course work because, despite their language proficiency, they do not possess the social performative skills involved in academic literacies that their PUP peers acquired (Ebrahim et al. 2021). It is worth mentioning that the PUP has evolved from a gate-keeping function (which is akin to the goals of EAP programs that have high stakes exit exams) to a preparatory and socialization function (which is akin to the goals of academic bridge programs). EAP programs emphasize language proficiency, measure textual literacies, and the ability to perform with and upon texts that form the cognitive and processing aspect of EAPL (Anand & Ackley, 2021; Wingate 2015). High stakes exit exams in EAPs such as IELTS and TOEFL serve as gatekeepers and do not give a holistic picture of academic literacies because they assume cultural and social uniformity of the test subjects and ignore the multi-cultural nature of most EAPL student populations. As a result, variation in social or cultural capital among examinees may manifest in these instruments as proficiency, or lack thereof, in English. By contrast, bridge programs, like PUP, meet the needs of diverse students and have them participate in learning communities to emphasize the social and performative competencies pertaining to academic literacies in addition to easing the transition to college life, developing academic skills, and providing additional academic support (Arendale & Lee, 2018).

Bearing in mind the aforementioned considerations of assessment of academic literacies, our main aim in this chapter is to compare the two characteristic assessment practices at a national pedagogical institute. The chapter will compare the two assessment paradigms of summative and formative assessments as experienced by teacher candidates - first as students at the training institute and as trainee teachers during their practicum experience, and second as in-service teachers in the public school system. (The reader will note that we utilize the terms *formative assessments and classroom-based assessments* interchangeably in the chapter). We frame our comparison using Bronfenbrenner's (1999, 2005) bioecological model to describe the assessment continuum of formative and summative assessments, which ranges from microsystem to macrosystem, and is defined by systemic distance from the enactment of classroom instructional practices. We contend that proximal processes of formative assessments taking place in the microsystem of classroom instruction signify the gradual development of academic literacies over time. The main reason for choosing Bronfenbrenner's model is that, from the reflective stance of teacher trainers, we wanted to map assessments at different distances from the classroom assessment (see Table 1) and as observed in teacher candidates' practicum in addition to their experiences in public schools.

We conclude the chapter with recommendations of future directions for assessment of EAPL with a focus on oral/performative skills for bilingual and multilingual learners. The overemphasis on high-stakes tests that can undermine the validity of assessment tools will receive special attention. As noted from the vantage points of teacher training and teacher observation, language is but one facet of communication in academic literacies. Socio-pragmatic and interactional competencies are equally important measures of the development of academic literacies. We contend that traditional forms of assessment that do not conform to assessment of socially situated and interactional professional behaviours persist within the primary curricula of many 'English for Academic Purposes' programs.

THEORETICAL OVERVIEW OF SUMMATIVE AND FORMATIVE ASSESSMENTS, ENGLISH FOR ACADEMIC PURPOSES LITERACIES, AND BRONFENBRENNER'S BIOECOLOGICAL MODEL

In this section of the chapter, we comment on and provide an overview of the theories of assessment, the academic literacies models, and the bioecological model that we use to frame our discussion of the dual assessment systems (formative and summative) used at the Bahrain Teachers College.

Overview of Summative and Formative Assessments

In testing literature, two prototypes of assessment appear as *summative* and *formative* assessments. These are also known by other names depending on their purpose, uses and assessment contexts. For example, summative assessment, conducted at the end of an instructional cycle, is also known as norm-referenced, achievement testing or *assessment of learning*. Formative assessment, conducted either during or at the end of an instructional cycle, is also called criteria-referenced, *assessment for learning*, or simply classroom-based assessment. As such, the foundational assumptions underpinning summative and formative assessments diverge significantly. Another dichotomy in assessment is *external* and *internal* testing. While large-scale summative tests are administered by external bodies such as ministries of education, national or international bodies, classroom-based tests are internally administered by teachers. According to Fulcher (2010), externally mandated tests are directed by a group of people who generally "do not know a great deal about the local learning ecology [context], and probably don't even know the teachers and learners who will have to cope with the required testing regime" (p.2). Conversely, internally mandated formative assessments are part of classroom work related to "the needs of the teachers and learners working within a particular context and . . . are generally ecologically sensitive" (Fulcher, 2010, pp. 1–2).

On the one hand, classroom assessments of EAPL are directly tied to the curriculum content and activities, thereby making the curriculum ecologically sensitive (Popham, 2009). These classroom assessments, whether formal or informal, serve two primary purposes for teachers: first, to draw conclusions about students' language skills and knowledge, and second, to enhance ongoing instructional programs or adjust teaching methods accordingly (Popham, 2009). Aimed at improvement of teaching and learning, these assessments contribute to the enhancement of teaching strategies and learning outcomes and support the pursuit of higher achievement standards (Black & Wiliam, 1998). Most classroom-based assessments are continuous and consider each student's progress, including academic literacies like effort, motivation, and collaboration, aspects not typically outlined in the curriculum in an explicit manner. Notably, formative assessments emphasize the active involvement of students in their own assessment process, highlighting their responsibility in understanding and addressing their strengths and weaknesses to advance in their learning (Black & Wiliam, 1998). Therefore, *assessment for learning* often incorporates methods such as self-assessment and peer assessment, recognizing the pivotal role of students in their own progress.

Overview of English for Academic Purposes Literacies

Uneven development of literacy skills leads to challenges for a considerable number of incoming college students in meeting the literacy demands of their studies (Fox, 2004; Murray, 2018). These students face literacy difficulties and often turn to English for Academic Purposes (EAP) courses within their institutions. EAP courses underscore the link between language and learning in higher education (Murray, 2016; Lea & Street, 2006; Wingate, 2015). As mentioned earlier, traditionally, EAP was narrowly defined as proficiency in academic reading and writing and thereby considered literacy as a static set of generalizable skills transferable across contexts (Murray, 2016; Lea & Street, 2006; Wingate, 2015). However, a more inclusive perspective views EAP literacies as the socialization of all students (native and non-native alike) within their disciplinary communities, acknowledging the role of language within the culture of a discipline (Lea & Street, 1998, 2006; Murray, 2018).

This broader view, rooted in the New Literacies Studies approach (Lea & Street, 1998, 2006), emphasizes the social and cultural practices surrounding reading and writing, contrary to individual cognitive activities. It emphasizes "traditions of meaning-making" within disciplines (Murray, 2016, p. 55). Rex and McEachen

(1999) elaborate on these traditions, which extend to not only include concepts and vocabulary but also rhetorical structures and patterns of argumentation. Lea and Street (1998) have conceptualized academic literacies through three models: *the study skills model, the academic socialization model, and the academic literacies model.* The study skills model, often catering to non-native English speakers, focuses on remedial language teaching and emphasizes generic EAP and study skills but lacks engagement with subject content (Wingate, 2018). In contrast, the academic socialization model stresses communicative language teaching and assessment and integrates real-world language use situations encountered in academia (Bachman, 1990; Canale & Swain, 1980; Wingate, 2015). The academic literacies model, encompassing both prior models, places emphasis on disciplinary culture and meaning making while considering language embedded within a discipline (see Figure 1). These different models follow different assessment practices.

Assessment of EAP, particularly in the study skills model, has been reduced to language skills and procedural knowledge. It considers literacy as a cognitive skill, focuses on measuring surface level features of language forms in written and oral production, and stresses grammar and syntax. The study skills model assumes that students can seamlessly transfer their literacy skills from one context to another. This approach primarily involves constructing sentences and paragraphs, evaluated through multiple-choice questions, note-taking, and essays detached from context. Essays are typically assessed based on structural elements like topic sentences, temporal and logical markers, and transitions rather than coherent argumentation. However, these programs offer limited value to students due to their generic nature, lacking opportunities for engaging with subject-specific content essential for developing comprehensive skills akin to those encountered in the academic literacies model. The narrow emphasis on superficial language elements confines students within a limited scope, preventing them from accessing a broader, more intricate landscape of knowledge and meaning creation.

When the three key elements of academic literacies namely, linguistic (text internal), cognitive (text internal) and socio-performative (text external) aspects

Figure 1. Three domains of EAPL assessments
(Adapted from Anand & Ackley, 2021; Lea & Street, 1998, 2006)

are held up against the criteria of international high stakes standardized language tests, there are obvious discrepancies that arise (Anand & Ackley, 2021). Many countries, including the Arab Gulf states, have relied on international standardized language tests to measure the readiness of their students to enter higher education (see Morrow, 2017 for assessing academic literacy with IELTS, and Suleymanova & Hysaj, 2022 for undergraduate Emirati students' English assessment challenges, in the UAE). However, such examinations do not fully address the specific academic needs of students and the requirements of universities in the Gulf states (Morrow, 2017). While assessments for native speakers, like the GRE or SAT, seem to measure internal cognitive processing skills and literacy effectively, assessments tailored for non-native speakers, particularly in English proficiency tests like TOEFL or IELTS, appear to focus primarily on textual proficiency. As succinctly put by Bhatia (2017) the IELTS and TOEFL, the 'twin gatekeepers', test language as a body of knowledge and skills, not as a body of communication acts governed by academic and disciplinary conventions in a specialized discursive space. In EAPL, they fail to measure dialogic performativity.

The academic socialization model adopts a communicative approach to language teaching and evaluation, wherein communication skills are not only cultivated but also assessed as an integral aspect of the educational curriculum, promoting continuous personal and professional growth (Wingate, 2006). Unlike the traditional focus on mastering the four language skills, this model prioritizes the overall communicative abilities of learners (Bachman, 1990; Canale & Swain, 1980). Assessments within this framework concentrate on analyzing real-world language use scenarios encountered in academic or various linguistic contexts. Although these tests do not necessarily measure the disciplinary conventions in a specialized discursive space or the text-external socio-performative aspect, they do recognize language proficiency as a blend of linguistic and pragmatic knowledge. Prominent academic English proficiency tests like TOEFL, IELTS, and PET measure language aptitude by evaluating language knowledge, contextual abilities, sociocultural understanding, pragmatic knowledge, and the test taker's strategic competence (Bachman & Palmer, 2010; Chalhoub-Deville, 2003). These multifaceted competencies significantly influence a test taker's performance. For instance, in the integrated skills evaluation of TOEFL, examinees are prompted to comprehend a text through reading/listening and subsequently articulate their responses orally/written form. The academic socialization model is characterized by its emphasis on immersive and demanding literacy tasks. Integrated exams have emerged as vital instruments for evaluating English for Academic Purposes (EAP) proficiencies. Integrated exams aim to gauge the language capabilities of examinees in completing academic tasks that often require a blend of skills and reflect the potential of examinees to engage effectively in academic endeavours (Chapelle & Plakans, 2013) except for the performative aspect of academic literacies.

The current assessment methods in the academic literacies model predominantly involve reflective writing and peer evaluations across different genres and disciplines. In today's landscape of diverse academic fields, vocational paths, and rapid technological advancements, assessments within this model need to be adaptable (Parodi, 2010; Bhatia 2017, Hatakka et al., 2017). They must seamlessly transition across contexts while offering enough flexibility to accommodate various disciplinary discourses and genres. A notable limitation of this approach is its heavy reliance on writing as the predominant skill assessed, which overlooks the evaluation of other vital competencies.

In a review of academic literacy research, Li (2022) discovered a complex link between the growth of skills in academic reading and writing and the creation of subject-specific knowledge through investigative tasks. As discussed above, enhancing academic literacy involves more than just handling text—it includes engaging in purposeful, meaningful learning tasks. Activities like reading and writing are geared toward achieving genuine knowledge creation and fulfilling communication needs. Consequently, successful teaching of academic literacy combines language skill development with learning subject matter and integrating them into meaningful investigations within academic and social contexts. For instance, Jiajing (2007) advocates the practice of "future professional communication," (p. 98) emphasizing activities such as job interviews, and social interactions, within Chinese ESP programs. These perspectives on EAPL pedagogy emphasize integrating students into professional and academic discourse practices, a viewpoint supported by studies which view discursive genres as *enacted practices* rather than mere subjects of study (Bhatia, 2017; Patterson & Weideman, 2013). We note that although advances are made in academic and professional socialization through performative pedagogies, what seems to be missing is the equivalent models of assessments to support these pedagogical practices. One way to mitigate this issue could be the use of formative assessments in assessing the performativity of the academic socialization because of their inherent nature of being ecologically sensitive and performative in nature.

We now turn our attention to giving an overview of the ecology of classroom-based assessments to understand the influences of myriad individual and contextual factors on formative assessments. This understanding also illuminates how classroom-based assessment can be part of the academic socialization process and develop students' academic literacies over an extended period of time.

Overview of Bronfenbrenner's Bioecological Model

Though traditionally applied to contexts that involve the learning of children, over the past two decades there has been a rising interest in applying Bronfenbrenner's ecological theory to the development of adolescents and college-age students (Simpson, 2010; Anagurthi, 2017; Mayne, 2019). This is not just because of the fecundity of the model in spawning inquiry into human development for different age groups but also because of its explanatory potential for understanding the complex nature of that development across time.

To enable us to study human development across time, the Bioecological Theory comprises of four interconnected components forming the process-person-context-time (PPCT) model. Influenced by Vygotsky and Lewin, Bronfenbrenner proposed that a child's development isn't solely influenced by their immediate environment but also by the interconnections among the hierarchically organized systems within that environment. By systems, Bronfenbrenner (1979) meant a setting where people engage in interactions. This interaction, or the process component of the model, is reciprocal: the environment shapes a person, and the person, in turn, shapes the environment. An individual's characteristics could be both generative as well as disruptive. Generative forces such as curiosity, engaging in activities and willingness to defer gratification for long term goals contribute towards positive human development in stark contrast to disruptive forces such as impulsiveness, distractibility, and an inability to defer gratification, which have adverse effects on human development.

Context relates to the diverse settings or ecological environment that shape and modify proximal processes. Bronfenbrenner characterized the ecological environment as "a series of nested structures, likening it to a set of Russian dolls" (Bronfenbrenner, 1979, p. 3). Bronfenbrenner's conceptualization of the developmental environment comprises interconnected systems—microsystem, mesosystem, exosystem, macrosystem and chronosystem—forming distinct concentric circles. The interconnected systems incorporate the environments where individuals, like students and teachers, continually interact, and they include the physical, social, and economic aspects of those environments. The systems are intricately intertwined and delineating them brings into focus both immediate and more distant contexts. Time in this model is highlighted not only for its central position but also for its functional ties to both the environment and the evolving characteristics of an individual. Within these interconnected systems, sustained interpersonal engagements aimed at maximizing potential are termed as "proximal processes" (Bronfenbrenner & Ceci, 1994). These processes are characterized by "enduring, reciprocal, highly interactive exchanges between a developing organism and other elements within the environment" (Ceci, 2006, p. 173). The following description illustrates the primary proposition articulated by Bronfenbrenner and outlines the defining aspects of his model:

Proposition 1

Especially in its early phases, and to a great extent throughout the life course, human development takes place through processes of progressively more complex reciprocal interaction between an active, evolving biopsychological human organism and the persons, objects, and symbols in its immediate external environment. To be effective, the interaction must occur on a fairly regular basis over extended periods of time. Such enduring forms of interaction in the immediate environment are referred to as proximal processes (Bronfenbrenner, 1999, p. 5).

In the bioecological model, effective learners actively engage in interactions within their environment, consistently and for the long term – which means there are no short-cuts or accelerated processes when it comes to human development. Bronfenbrenner explicated the following features of the proximal processes:

1. For development to occur, the person must engage in an activity.
2. To be effective, the activity must take place "on a fairly regular basis, over an extended period of time." ....[T]o be developmentally effective, activities must take place long enough to become "increasingly more complex." Mere repetition does not work.
3. Developmentally effective proximal processes are not unidirectional; there must be initiation and response in both directions.
4. Proximal processes .... can also involve interaction with objects and symbols. Under these circumstances, for reciprocal interaction to occur, the objects and symbols in the immediate environment must be of a kind that invites attention, exploration, manipulation, elaboration, and imagination. (Bronfenbrenner, 1999, p.5).

As such, key to "proximal processes" are structured and scaffolded activities that are not mere replicas but activities that grow more complex with the passage of time.

In sum, to operationalize proximal processes, the classroom must be viewed as a unit of analysis and all the interactions derived from that unit need to be considered. In other words, the bioecological system provides a model that focuses on multiple levels of acquiring academic literacies simultaneously (i.e. student, teachers, classrooms, community, university life), and it also emphasizes the interaction between behavioural units (i.e. what happens during the assessment activities is affected by what occurs in the social life of the student and vice versa). The result is that the bioecological model would help teachers, students and administrators understand behaviour in context, and it also shows how these units of varying size and levels of complexity mutually influence each other. Hence, a congenial classroom atmosphere has the potential to enhance student learning, including peer and self-assessment.

Review of Studies That Integrate Second Language Learning With the Bioecological Model

Chong, Issac, and Mckinley (2023) point out that a growing number of studies have used the ecological systems theory and second language learning in relation to computer-assisted language learning, language policy, language teacher education, and second language classroom instruction, yet the body of research remains limited. Most of the studies that Chong et al. (2023) reviewed only partially apply the Ecological System Theory. Most studies do not capture its central tenets which include "interplay among (1) layers of contexts, and (2) contexts and people" (Chong et al., p. 336). So, while some studies focus only on a few levels of context (e.g., Song & Ma, 2023) rather than the holistic view of contexts, others (e.g. Hofstadler et al., 2021) study distinct levels of contexts excluding the people aspect of the PPCT model.

One significant study uses the ecological system theory to shed light on the acculturation into academic literacies of Arab Gulf female students in U.S. universities (Mayne, 2019). The study revealed that students with low English proficiency enrolled in ESL courses and that the courses were helpful for their academic literacy development. By contrast, students with high language proficiency did not have to take ESL courses but experienced frustration with the knowledge gaps in their academic literacy and, therefore, resorted to alternative channels. Though useful from a policy perspective, the study does not account for the role of formative assessment in relation to academic literacies.

In relation to L2 assessment, Huang, Juang and Yang (2021) blended different ecological theories such as Ecological Systems Theory, Complex Dynamic Systems Theory, and Activity Theory to study Chinese EFL teachers' technology-assisted formative assessment practices. The study yielded five types of benefits for formative assessment in domains related to the pedagogical, managerial, assessment, social, and developmental. A more recent study from the field of TESOL employs the ecological system to articulate a model for classroom-based assessment (Chong & Issac, 2023). The study argues for using formative assessments in the language classroom to develop the linguistic skills and proficiency of second language learners and maintains that the "ecological turn in TESOL" is long overdue especially given the limitations of training students to pass high-stakes tests.

Similarly, we contend that teaching, learning, and assessment of academic literacies can be reconceptualized as experiences distributed across agent, activity, and environment, contrary to the transmission-receiver model of learning associated with behaviorism, which simplifies the learning process by placing performance solely within the individual child or teacher. Bronfenbrenner's bioecological model sheds light on our notion, unveiling the intricate network of proximal, distal, and environmental influences that mold learners' everyday learning experiences and development. For instance, a teacher's ability to provide quality instruction improves with smaller class sizes, positively influencing academic language literacies.

Justifying the need and urgency to apply the ecological theory to L2 classroom-based assessment, Chong and Issac (2023) suggested its application: a) to capture the temporal dimension of classroom -based assessments as these happen on a moment-to-moment basis. This also helps in understanding how the learners and the classroom environment changes over time b) to understand various learner attributes and the use of formative assessment by learners in their own development c) to understand the interplay of learner variables and contextual variables i.e., how assessment is designed to cater to individual learners and how learners develop through involvement with classroom-based assessment.

The above discussion highlights various approaches in operationalizing Bronfenbrenner's ecological model. Taking all the aspects of process, person, context and time (PPCT) would require an extensive study and is beyond the scope and range of this chapter. Instead, this chapter focuses only on the two subsystems of the context i.e., microsystem and macrosystem. We consider the activities, roles, and interpersonal relations in a classroom to be part of formative assessments and, hence, firmly nested in the microsystem. It is within this immediate context of microsystem that proximal processes operate to produce sustainable development. The macrosystem can be correlated to the examination-oriented culture of a country (Chong & Isaacs, 2023), especially given that Bronfenbrenner considers the macrosystem as a "societal blueprint for a particular culture" and that it comprises "the overarching pattern of micro-, meso-, and excosystems characteristic of a given culture" (Bronfenbrenner, 1994, p. 40) Thus, an examination of the micro- and macrosystem can elucidate the broader trends in assessment practices in our context.

THE CONTEXT

Over the past two decades, Arab Gulf states have implemented several reforms in education to prepare their citizens for a post-oil economy that is knowledge-based, business- and technologically- oriented. English language policy reform has been a central component in the process. As Le Ha and Barnawi (2015) confirm "the desire to learn English [is] a national mission and [that] to internationalize their HE has been clearly articulated in Gulf countries' strategies, educational policy reforms and initiatives'' (p.4). Established in 2008, the Bahrain Teachers College constitutes an important part of Bahrain's National Education Reform Project to achieve its Economic Vision 2030. Its mandate is to prepare qualified teachers and educational leaders. Like its sister institute in Abu Dhabi, Emirates College for Advanced Education (ECAE), the BTC engaged in international partnerships and policy borrowing since it was modelled after the National Institute of Education (NIE) in Singapore. The teacher education programmes that the NIE designed for implementation emphasize "principles of holistic development of prospective teachers, purpose-driven programmes, theory-practice link, reflective communities of practice, partnerships, benchmarking beginning teacher standards, authentic and formative assessment and advancement of the teaching profession'' (World Data on Education, 2010/2011). The Bachelor of Education Program has four specializations for primary education: Grades 1-3 Teachers, and Grades 4-6 Teachers in English, or Arabic and Islamic Studies, or Math and Science. The annual intake of secondary school graduates is 300-400 students, which the Ministry of Education (MOE) decides. The students are placed into the four specializations after their first year in the B.Ed. program based on the results of a streaming exam, the MOE needs, and students' own preferences. Prior to matriculating in the B.Ed. program, students enrol in the Pre-University Program, previously known as the foundation year program. It is common for post-secondary institutions in the Gulf, including Bahrain, to place students in foundation programs. This is primarily because incoming students come from a school background where systemic challenges affect English language learning such as teachers with limited training, teacher-centred classes, emphasis on rote-memorization, minimal exposure to English in class, large class sizes, and traditional assessment methods (Malcom& Majed, 2013).

Regional colleges and universities in the Gulf have increasingly recognized the importance of early academic socialization into the discipline which goes beyond the study skills model of attaining language skills or proficiency. Some have addressed the issue through establishing discipline-specific foundation programs and others have incorporated components in the college curriculum like the ''first-year seminar in the major'' or ''the gateway course into the major'', a practice that is used internationally by universities who seek to increase student success and longevity (Hatakka et al., 2017). Although BTC admits Bahraini nationals only, these nationals reflect a mosaic of linguistic backgrounds. Most students speak Arabic as their home language, while others speak Urdu, Baluchi, Hindi, Tagalog or Persian. Having evolved from its function as gate-keeping program to weed out students who ''cannot cut it'', PUP is analogous to a bridge program that is intended to ease the transition from secondary school to college of these bilingual students as well as lay a foundation for the attainment of academic literacies.

Like PUP, the B.Ed. program in Primary English at the BTC has been through two revision cycles. The first took place in 2013-2014 based on the feedback of stakeholders such as MoE officials, School Principals, Senior Teachers, and BTC graduates. The second revision process is underway for 2024-2025. These revisions revolve around the following four needs: more content courses in the subject specialization, more focus on instructional practices for special needs students, more focus on formative assessment (Aldabbus et al., 2019, p. 9), and more focus on integrating theory with practice/professionalization. Reiterating the need for formative assessment, the BQA report (2016) recommended the development and implementation of "an overarching assessment policy to support the consistent monitoring of student achievement (Education and Training Quality Authority, 2016, p.14). The B.Ed. program continues to develop the academic literacies that the students acquire in the PUP. Our discussion in this chapter will focus on various assessments in the program specifically proximal processes, as suggested by Bronfenbrenner (1999, 2005), of formative assessments techniques such as oral presentations and group work which are considered to show the gradual development of these skills over time. One key achievement of BTC in this regard is the continuous development of digital literacies which will be explained in detail below.

Bronfenbrenner explains that proximal processes go beyond human interactions to extend to objects and symbols. He elaborates that the interaction with objects and symbols entails "attention, exploration, manipulation, elaboration, and imagination" (p.5). According to sociocultural theory digital tools are objects that mediate learners' learning and developmental processes. Since its inception BTC has used digital tools and technologies to contribute to the learning, development, and interactions of students. It has offered learning management systems such as Moodle and Google Classroom, and digital communication through email and texting. Faculty used digital tools for formative assessment such as Mentimeter, Kahoot and Plickers in the classrooms which are fully equipped with Smartboards and computers to enhance student learning and engagement (Elmahdi, AlHattami, & Fawzi, 2018). The BTC was primed for the transition to digital delivery of classes during the Covid-19 pandemic and there was no disruption to classes (Purinton, 2024). During that time, BTC shifted to using Blackboard as its main learning platform. Students were socialized into using digital collaboration tools through Blackboard Collaborate, Miro, Padlet, Canva, and Nearpod. In this way, digital tools created inclusion for all students thus contributing to ecological sustainability. BTC's leadership continues with its digital literacy initiatives post-Covid 19 and this includes the establishment of a digital empowerment committee wherein student volunteers give demonstrations for using digital tools that are relevant for teachers. With the emergence of AI tools, the leadership of the BTC has formed an AI committee to address student and faculty

AI awareness and training needs, and conversations are ongoing about rethinking assessment practices (Bahrain Teachers College, 2024).

MACROSYSTEM AND MICROSYSTEM ASSESSMENTS IN THE KINGDOM OF BAHRAIN

Like the BTC, the Educational Training Authority (BQA) was formed as part of the educational reform project in Bahrain. The BQA carries out objective reviews of all licenced educational and training institutions in the Kingdom as part of their quality assurance activities. Under the quality assurance activities, BQA's Directorate of National Examinations (DNE) conducts the National Examinations for grades 3, 6, 9 and 12 to map and evaluate the standards of performance of students, classes and schools. The DNE evaluates the learning progress against the national curriculum accredited by the Ministry of Education (Education and Training Quality Authority, 2020). The five main goals of the DNE are to assess students in the core subjects of Arabic, English, Mathematics and Science, to develop test specifications in line with international standards and the national curriculum, to develop valid and reliable tests, to make the results of national examination available to stakeholders such as schools and the Ministry of Education (The DNE code of Practice, 2016). These national examinations are also significant in measuring students' skills, competencies and knowledge to prepare students for the future knowledge economy. Furthermore, the Ministry of Education is also taking several initiatives to address the English language education policy in schools. Foremost among these is the benchmarking progress against other countries in the MENA region. Recently, the MOE has conducted training for, and administration of, the IELTS for the grade 12 students. Although Bahrain Teachers College doesn't have much involvement in developing assessment policies for schools, it does work closely with MOE to make sure that its programs align with the demands of MOE. The following interview extract of a senior leadership member shows that the pedagogical institute is preparing its students for both summative and formative assessments in public schools.

But we are very mindful of the fact that the Ministry is interested in using a proper range of assessments and we try to make sure that our own programs also have a good range of authentic assessments in them and that, you know, we're not overly reliant on focusing just on reading and writing and conventional examinations. (Personal communication, February 25, 2024)

However, the pre-service teachers and in-service graduates of BTC point out that one major issue with the national or centralized examinations is the oral skills which are a major part of formative assessments but are not formally tested. This brings in the negative washback (Cheng & Curtis, 2004; Messick, 1996) of the national exams because in the enacted curriculum, teachers and students alike would concentrate on what is being tested. To promote positive washback, Messick (1996) suggests minimizing threats to construct validity such as construct-under representation. He defines construct under-representation when "the assessment is deficient: the test is too narrow and fails to include important dimensions or facets of focal construct" (Messick, 1996, p. 244). Since the speaking skill is underrepresented in the national exams, teachers do not see the value of incorporating it in formal testing as one teacher participant in an interview suggested,

So, as I said, I think for now, especially for primary school students, speaking really shouldn't be the focus we need to build up the other skills. (Former BTC student, personal communication, February 26, 2024)

Similar views were voiced by other BTC graduates that are currently in-service teachers who cited challenges that range from logistical issues to the level of the students and their limited immersion in the language. In the next section of the chapter, we will self-critically examine the assessment practices promoted in our teacher training context through instructional practices and/or modeled assessment practices.

ALIGNMENT OF CLASSROOM-BASED ASSESSMENTS AND ENGLISH FOR ACADEMIC PURPOSES LITERACIES (EAPL)

The BTC is an exceptional provider of immersive training with a series of four practica, in each year of the Bachelor of Education program. As mentioned earlier, to enhance the academic literacies of L2 teacher-candidates, the college offers a year-long pre-university program (PUP as of AY 2021-22 after a curriculum revision). The program offers 4 courses in English: 2 in reading and writing, and 2 in oral communication; 3 courses in Arabic: 1 in applied skills, 1 in listening and speaking, and 1 in study skills; 1 course in math; and 1 in ICT.

The BTC recognizes the significant role of formative assessment in supporting students and building up their academic literacies. In 2021-2022, around 60 faculty members from a total of 106 participated in two professional development courses that focus on implementing formative assessment strategies in the classroom: ''Making Learning Visible'' and ''Making Thinking Visible'' (Harvard Graduate School of Education, 2022). The first course introduced strategies for making students participants in the documentation of their learning: (a) to help them focus on *process,* (b) to develop their self-awareness about how their learning about a topic or subject progresses over time, and (c) to render them into active participants in documenting evidence of learning to support accountability measures. The second course introduced thinking routines to use in the classroom to encourage students to engage with ideas and their peers as they discuss, grapple with, and develop their thinking about a topic or subject. Faculty have reported that student self-documentation of learning served as a type of formative assessment for students that helped them to reflect on their learning and identify points for improvement.

Although Bronfenbrenner didn't explicitly address proximal processes in the context of second or foreign language academic settings, the authors employ his model to illuminate the proximal processes of EAPL in the case of the BTC, specifically in relation to the formative assessment practices in different courses. Bronfenbrenner's proposition that human development occurs through intricate interactions between an individual and their immediate environment can be illustrated in our teacher training context. In the ecology of teaching and learning, the PUP aims to enhance EAPL and equip students with academic literacies necessary for university studies and the B.Ed. program builds on those skills to socialize students in their chosen discipline. Applying the bioecological model to understand proximal processes (see Figure 2) in this context involves regulating interactions among various elements: the student's behavior (form), the significance of the PUP for the trainee student-teachers, their classmates, the curriculum variability (content), and the students' progression into the Bachelor of Education (B.Ed.) program (direction).

In what follows, we use an ecological approach to discuss examples of formative assessments practices in some of our courses to argue that it has long-term value for developing PST's self-efficacy and learning outcomes in oral presentations and group work. At the same time, we propose that the ecological orientation sheds light on the divergence between the emphasis on the performative in formative assessment approaches practiced in the classroom and the summative assessment requirements at the institutional level (in the college and later in the curriculum in the schools).

We argue that students' developing the capacity for oral presentations is a fundamental part of their socialization into and attainment of academic literacies. Incoming students into the Pre-university Program have reported in focus group meetings that they find this skill to be the most challenging, and for which they have the least background/preparation (Ebrahim et al., 2021). This goes back to the school system that does not emphasize speaking skills as part of its overall assessment.

Figure 2 depicts the microsystem and macrosystem assessments as experienced by students at the BTC. Since formative assessments are part of the microsystem of classroom instructional practices and the external summative assessments are considered as part of macrosystem, we restrict our comparison of assessment practices to only these two systems.

18

Figure 2. Micro and macrosystem assessments in ecological model

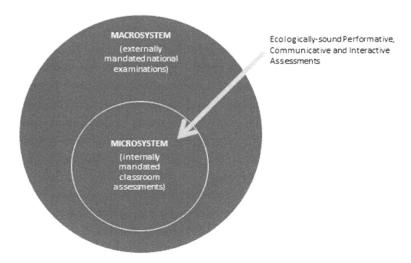

The bioecological theory advocates that strengthening human relationships within supportive environments can lead to more positive developmental outcomes (Smith, 2011). Similarly, we believe that enhancing mediation in classroom assessment can enhance the extent of learning and lead to positive outcomes. Mediation can encompass various elements, such as people, objects, or symbols. These mediational markers, according to Bronfenbrenner (1999), "can facilitate interaction between a human organism and its immediate external environment" (p. 5). In the context of the PUP, we see examples of these markers as learning outcomes (objects), peer support (individual), and academic register (symbol). We perceive that developing strategies that foster academic and social engagement is crucial to bolstering learning outcomes and future integration into the academic world. These systems interconnect in intricate ways but delineating them allows for a focused understanding that both immediate and more distant contexts and processes contribute to explaining the effects on teacher- trainees' academic and social integration. Within our classrooms, enduring patterns of proximal processes (referred to here as mediational markers) are evident in teacher-student, student-student interactions, skill acquisition, studying, group activities, and engaging in complex tasks.

In their B. Ed. Program teacher candidates learn about various assessment methods through their content and pedagogy courses. Predominant classroom-based assessments among these methods are collaborative learning, self- and peer-evaluations (see Table 1).

The proximal processes in the formative assessment methods grow in complexity over time (i.e. from PUP to 4th Year projects). These are structured and scaffolded in such a way that they are not mere replicas but activities that grow more complex with the passage of time. One such example of the complexity over time is the 'Oral Presentations' of our graduates. We demonstrate this with the help of the public speaking competence rubric developed by Schreiber, Paul and Shibley (2012). For example, the oral presentation project in PUP addresses discrete skills such as topic selection, organization of ideas, and clear communication through words and body language. In the poster project of the year 4 current trends, the standards expand to reflect the performative and interactive dimension of disciplinary practice and the emphasis is synthesizing and referencing, constructing solid arguments, and addressing a community of practice. So, we see a transformation from academic competence to professional performance.

In addition, teacher candidates also indirectly learn about assessment through the required assignments of the above courses, fostering an understanding of assessment primarily rooted in formative experiences. These assessments typically culminate in creative, group or individual projects highlighting pedagogical expertise rather than mere knowledge of pedagogy.

Within English content classes, preference is given to assessment formats that encourage differentiation and creativity, such as reader's theater performances, collaboration to create culturally relevant picture books that are often based on authentic or rewritten traditional folk tales collected from interviews with community elders, composing autobiographical essays employing visual life maps, devising character interviews for extensive reading, or crafting and presenting research on a current trend in EFL teaching in poster or gallery walk formats. Evident within these assessments is the aspect of social interactions. the performative, and externally visible interactions in academic literacies.

Table 1. Sample classroom-based assessments in different BTC courses

Courses	Assignments	Microsystem Formative Assessment
English Oral Communication (Foundation course)	Presentation on a Topic (individual and group)	Rubic Observation Group discussion
English Literacy (Year 2 course)	Dialogic Read Aloud Book Talk Microteaching	Oral presentation Peer assessment
Children's Literature (Year 3 course)	Read aloud videos creation Composition of culturally responsive picture book	Individual reflection Peer assessment Interviews
Current Trends (Year 4 course)	Oral poster presentation on a current trend or issue in teaching English	Individual reflection, Peer feedback, Rubric, Thinking routines

The goal of the teacher training institute is to excel in assessment practices by instructing prospective educators through three hands-on practicum courses integrated within the school system. These courses are strategically placed in the second, third, and fourth years of the program. In certain cases, supervisors utilize lesson planning templates that necessitate aspiring teachers to articulate an assessment strategy, outline performance benchmarks, and furnish checklists or rubrics before outlining the planned curriculum activities. In essence, the institute insists on establishing the assessment framework prior to implementing activities to ensure a structured approach that facilitates the measurement of targeted skills.

A former BTC student expresses her satisfaction with being thoroughly socialized into the formative assessment paradigm and how she further appreciated its value in informing her classroom instruction once she joined the schools. As she indicates:

I think overall why I did develop much more on formative assessment is because BTC was very sure to train me on how to question students and I think that is what benefited us the most throughout TP and the feedback that we got....Formative assessment in the classroom is an indication of what you're actually doing, how great of a job you're doing, and what kind of change do you need to apply in the classroom or even in different classrooms for different students. (BTC graduate, personal communication, February 27, 2024).

However, there is a tension that arises when we juxtapose the emphasis on formative assessment in the content knowledge, pedagogy, and practicum courses and the focus of the Language Testing and Assessment course that the teacher candidates take. In that course, teacher candidates learn mainly about summative assessment practices such as item writing for different skills, validity and reliability of tests and test item quality and discrimination. A similar misalignment is also noted in the enacted curriculum and summative assessments at the inter-school or national levels public school system. The emphasis is on manufacturing items that prioritize evaluating language proficiency over gauging language acquisition.

The tension that ensues from the two assessment paradigms is further confirmed by a study on the perceptions of Bahraini secondary school teachers of the impact of the National Examinations on their teaching. AlWadi (2020) points out that ''[t]eachers did not feel that the national examinations made their lessons more communicative but rather more skill-focused'' (p. 206). A significant finding from the study is that the national examinations have not proven to be effective in aiding teachers to enhance their pedagogy for teaching speaking skills. Essentially, there exist two conflicting perspectives on assessment at micro and macro levels as reflected in the BTC and the assessments encountered in Ministry of Education (MoE) schools. One aligns with the pedagogical content courses, advocating for comprehensive, formative, and performance-based assessments. The other perspective leans towards discrete item assessments of language proficiency, potentially stemming from the teacher training institute itself. Consequently, both trainee teachers and experienced educators find themselves navigating this dichotomy, grappling with their roles within these distinct assessment paradigms.

On one side, there is a desire on the part of teacher candidates to implement the formative and performance-driven assessments advocated in their training. Yet from another side, they feel compelled to equip learners for mandated language proficiency tests. As teacher trainees, BTC students become aware of the dichotomy between the two assessment paradigms, and as in-service teachers they are directly confronted with it so that they find themselves in a challenging position, trying to balance the stick between fulfilling curricular ideals and meeting the requirements of standardized proficiency tests.

Tensions Among Summative and Formative Assessment Practices

As discussed earlier, there are discrepancies between the standardized high stakes tests and teacher created classroom-based assessments in the higher education context. These are apparent in the summative and classroom-based assessment practices in the public school system as well. Even though our graduates are well-versed in the creation and use of formative assessment practices, the negative washback, i.e., the effects of testing on classroom teaching and learning, is visible in the assessment practices at the school level. When it comes to summative assessment, especially in grades 3 and 6, the stress is on mimicking the national exam patterns rather than the ecologically sound academic literacies.

There are differences between the enacted curriculum and the end-of-year summative assessments encountered in grades 1 to 6. Since speaking and communicative activities are not formally tested, there is a loss of communicative activities such as discussions, role play and pair or group speaking activities which require performativity in literacy skills. We have observed in our supervision of teacher trainees both face-to-face and online during Covid-19 (2020- 2022) that they engage in interactive and ecologically sound communicative and performative activities but the summative assessments at school-level exclude speaking and/or performative tasks in conformity with the tests supplied by the Directorate of Curricula for the midterm and the final examinations and in Grade 6, National Examinations. A comparison of the in-school Grade 4 and externally mandated Grade 6 examinations reveals that the test items are identical in task and question formation[1]

However, the exclusion of performative, interpretive and presentation skills is not in conformity with the prescribed textbook and de facto curriculum. Teachers are required by the Ministry of Education to include these activities in English in all lessons and they are penalized if they fail to do so (Education and Training Quality Authority, 2020, p. 25-26). Conversely, the BTC puts a high premium on the development of interactive and performative lessons for the teacher training in English language (see Table 1).

Furthermore, the textbooks currently used for the grade levels one to six, *Family and Friends*, Bahrain Edition, include phonics, pronunciation, speaking activities and oral presentations. Teachers follow the scope and sequence of each lesson as the designated and approved curriculum and assess these literacy skills formatively. The newly introduced National Geographic Textbooks, *Look*, for grades 1 and 4 as of the academic year 2023-24 will subsequently be extended to the other primary grades and are designed to further emphasize oral/performative skills and group work.

Based on insights gained from teacher training and observation, it is evident that the integration of innovative assessment methods and advances in digital literacies in the curriculum fall behind advancements in teaching and learning at the macrolevel (both at the local and national levels). Despite the recognized theoretical necessity for concurrent development, traditional assessment approaches that do not align with learner-centric language acquisition methods continue to prevail in primary education curricula (refer to both micro and distal assessments).

CONCLUSION AND FUTURE DIRECTIONS

We find that the classroom-based assessments in the microsystem are closer in concepts and tasks to the enacted curriculum observed in our situated context of BTC rather than the national examinations in the macrosystem for inter-school and national use. While the formative assessments provide tasks and topics that interest and motivate students, the summative assessments in the macrosystem rely on uninspiring and demotivating tasks distant from the performative and collaborative tasks of the enacted curriculum. An ecological view acknowledges the significance of context which includes social, material, temporal aspects of the interaction between learners and their environment. This is true in case of formative assessment tasks.

Reflecting upon the assessment cycles at the public-school level, it becomes evident that the macro and exco assessments are more interconnected with each other than with the central component-formative assessments at the microsystem. The microsystem, encompassing proximal assessments, is not merely detached from the curriculum as implemented in the classroom; it also seems to lack engagement with the positive pedagogical advancements driven by research. The overemphasis on high-stakes tests can undermine the validity of these assessment tools making them demotivating, uninspiring, and distant from the communicative experiences of the enacted curriculum in the enhancement of academic literacies of the bilingual learners. There seems to be less conclusive evidence which demonstrate that adopting high-stakes tests have raised the levels of language achievement in the foundation year programs (Morrow, 2017). We recommend that professional development of assessment literacy be expanded to administrative/ministerial personnel in local and regional assessment centres. We also propose that these personnel not only follow the research in pedagogy, but also become active partners in research process.

Returning to our opening premise, so well stated by Fulcher (2010), we confirm that internally mandated formative assessments related to the needs of teachers and learners are ecologically sensitive within a particular context. This premises can be extended to the two locations of assessments we have examined: microsystem, internal to BTC, and macrosystem, intra-school and inter-school at the national level.

That said, there seems to be a positive shift to include more formative assessment measures in the post-Covid-19 era with projects and oral presentations integrated with the recently updated assessment plan for all grade levels in government schools. Moreover, the MOE introduced in 2023 a new pilot for students in secondary schools to do the pre- and post- IELTS training test, which includes an oral component. It is likely that this new development will encourage teachers to place more emphasis on speaking and performance skills in the classroom. However, there remain challenges related to training teachers with necessary skills for on-the-spot assessment of speaking, as well as issues related to logistics for providing appropriate space and teacher-student ratio. Furthermore, there are also challenges of the advanced linguistic demands, equal weightage to four skills and the general communicative orientation of IELTS test that may not give valid and reliable decisions about the readiness of Arab students as suggested by Morrow (2017) in his study of assessing academic literacy through IELTS in the UAE. Alongside addressing these issues, we suggest using technology-driven formative assessment tools across all grade levels like the ones used by ETS or PET as well as cost-effective and appropriate ones that can be accessed from either a computer or mobile devices such as web-based applications like VoiceThread and Questionmark Perception, video-conference tools like Zoom and Google Hangouts, and technologies for assessment in virtual environments like Second Life to support oral skills' learning (Gutiérrez-Porlán et al, 2022; Levy & Gertler, 2015, Ngugen & Hegelheimer, 2021).

Researchers who have used an ecological view to study human development over time contend that to understand the functions of one level of the educational ecosystem, it is useful to look up and down one level as well as across time scales (Lemke, 2001; Gutierrez et al., 2017, Lee, 2017). Using an ecological framing, therefore, has not only enabled us to map formative assessment practices as a coherent whole rather than a collection of atomized strategies but also helped us emphasize how essential skills in academic literacies such as oral presentations and group work develop over time, and through multiple pathways. As observed from the vantage points of teacher training and teacher observation, it is noted that language is but one facet of communication in academic literacies and measuring socio-pragmatic and interactional competencies are equally important in the development of academic literacies. We note that traditional forms of assessment that do not conform to assessment of socially situated and interactional professional behaviours persist within primary curricula of many English for Academic Purposes programs.

REFERENCES

AlWadi, H. (2020). Bahrain's Secondary EFL Teacher' Belief of English Language National Examination: 'How it made teaching different?' *International Journal of Instruction. 13*: 1, 197-214. chrome-extension://efaidnbmnnnibpcajpcglclefindmkaj/ https://www.e-iji.net/dosyalar/iji_2020_1_13.pdf

Anagurthi, C. (2017). *Applying an ecological model to predict adolescent academic achievement.* [Doctoral thesis, Wayne State University]. https://digitalcommons. wayne.edu/oa_dissertations/1684

Anand, P., & Ackley, S. (2021). Assessment of 21 Century Skills & Academic Literacies: From Theory to Practice. Senior Editor: Paul Robertson, 119.

Arendale, D. R., & Lee, N. L. (2018). Bridge Programs. In R. F. Flippo & T. W. Bean (Eds.), *Handbook of College Reading and Study Strategy Research* (3rd ed., pp. 281–292). Routledge. doi:10.4324/9781315629810-20

Bachman, L. F. (1990). *Fundamental considerations in language testing.* Oxford University Press.

Bachman, L. F., & Palmer, A. S. (2010). *Language assessment in practice: Developing language assessments and justifying their use in the real world.* Oxford University Press.

Bahrain Teachers College [@btc]. (2024, February 21). *Artificial intelligence day as a* [Video]. Instagram. https://www.instagram.com/reel/C3m2ak1svWJ/?igsh= NjZiM2M3MzIxNA==

Bennett, R. E. (2011). Formative assessment: A critical review. *Assessment in Education: Principles, Policy & Practice, 18*(1), 5–25. doi:10.1080/096959 4X.2010.513678

Bhatia, V. (2017). *Critical genre analysis: Investigating interdiscursive performance in professional practice.* Routledge.

Bhatia, V., Anthony, L., & Noguchi, J. (2011). ESP in the 21st century: ESP theory and application today. *Proceedings of the JACET 50th Commemorative International Convention, Aug. 30-Sept.2,* (pp. 143-150). Seinan Gakuin University.

Black, P., & Wiliam, D. (1998). Assessment and classroom learning. *Assessment in Education: Principles, Policy & Practice, 5*(1), 7–74. doi:10.1080/0969595980050102

Bronfenbrenner, U. (1979). *The ecology of human development.* Harvard University Press. doi:10.4159/9780674028845

Bronfenbrenner, U. (1994). Ecological models of human development. *International encyclopedia of education, 3*(2), 37-43.

Bronfenbrenner, U. (1999). *Environments in developmental perspective: Theoretical and operational models.*

Bronfenbrenner, U. (2005). Making human beings human: Bioecological perspectives on human development. *Sage (Atlanta, Ga.).*

Bronfenbrenner, U., & Ceci, S. J. (1994). Nature-nurture reconceptualized in developmental perspective: A bioecological model. *Psychological Review, 101*(4), 568–586. doi:10.1037/0033-295X.101.4.568 PMID:7984707

Canale, M., & Swain, M. (1980). Theoretical bases of communicative approaches to second language teaching and testing. *Applied Linguistics, 1*(1), 1–47. doi:10.1093/applin/1.1.1

Ceci, S. J. (2006). Urie Bronfenbrenner (1917- 2005). *The American Psychologist, 61.* PMID:16478360

Chalhoub-Deville, M. (2003). Second language interaction: Current perspectives and future trends. *Language Testing, 20*(4), 369–383. doi:10.1191/0265532203lt264oa

Chapelle, C. A., & Plakans, L. (2013). Assessment and testing: Overview. In C. A. Chapelle (Ed.), *The encyclopedia of applied linguistics* (pp. 240–244). Blackwell/Wiley. doi:10.1002/9781405198431

Cheng, L., & Curtis, A. (2004). Washback or backwash: A review of the impact of testing on teaching and learning. In L. Cheng & Y. Watanabe (Eds.), *Washback in language testing: research contexts and methods* (pp. 3–17). Lawrence Erlbaum. doi:10.4324/9781410609731-9

Chong, S. W., & Isaacs, T. (2023). An Ecological Perspective on Classroom-Based Assessment. *TESOL Quarterly, 57*(4), 1558–1570. doi:10.1002/tesq.3201

Chong, S. W., Isaacs, T., & McKinley, J. (2023). Ecological systems theory and second language research. *Language Teaching*, *56*(3), 333–348. doi:10.1017/S0261444822000283

Ebrahim, P., Al-Moumni, M., Al-Hattami, A., & Ali, A. (2021). A study of student attrition in the foundation year program of a teachers' college. *International Journal of Lifelong Education*, *40*(3), 198–214. doi:10.1080/02601370.2021.1931973

Education & Training Quality Assurance. (2022). *Annual Reports*. Bahrain: BQA. https://www.bqa.gov.bh/En/Publications/Pages/AnnualReports.aspx

Education and Training Quality Authority. (2016). *Programmes-within-College Review Report: Bachelor of Education, Bahrain Teachers College*. Bahrain: BQA. https://www.bqa.gov.bh/En/Reports/UniReports/HigherEducationReport/BTC%20UOB%20edu%20en-after%20FA%20corrections%208Mar2017%20-%20V2.pdf

Education and Training Quality Authority. (2020). *Annual Report 2020: Education in a Changing World*. Bahrain: BQA. https://www.bqa.gov.bh/En/Publications/Pages/AnnualReports.aspx

Elmahdi, I., Al-Hattami, A., & Fawzi, H. (2018). Using technology for formative assessment to improve students' learning. *Turkish Online Journal of Educational Technology—TOJET, 17*(2), 182-188. https://www.learntechlib.org/p/189651/

Fox, J. D. (2004). Test decisions over time: Tracking validity. *Language Testing*, *21*(4), 437–465. doi:10.1191/0265532204lt292oa

Fulcher, G. (2010). *Practical language testing*. Routledge.

Gutiérrez, K. D., Cortes, K., Cortez, A., DiGiacomo, D., Higgs, J., Johnson, P., Ramón Lizárraga, J., Mendoza, E., Tien, J., & Vakil, S. (2017). Replacing representation with imagination: Finding ingenuity in everyday practices. *Review of Research in Education*, *41*(1), 30–60. doi:10.3102/0091732X16687523

Gutiérrez-Porlán, I., Prendes-Espinosa, P., & Sánchez-Vera, M. D. M. (2022). Digital technologies for the assessment of oral English skills. *Applied Sciences (Basel, Switzerland)*, *12*(22), 11635. doi:10.3390/app122211635

Hamp-Lyons, L. (2011). English for academic purposes. In *Handbook of research in second language teaching and learning* (pp. 89–105). Routledge.

Harvard University Graduate School of Education. (2022). *Project Zero*. Harvard. https://pz.harvard.edu/

Hattaka, M., Smaal, J., van der Merve, R. I., & Ainane, S. (2017). Addressing retention at an English-medium Engineering College: A case study of freshman students in the Middle East. In J.C. Quadrado, J, Bernardino, & J. Rocha (Eds), *Proceedings of SEFI 2017 annual conference* (pp. 903-910). European Society for Engineering Education SEFI.

Hofstadler, N., Babic, S., Lämmerer, A., Mercer, S., & Oberdorfer, P. (2021). The ecology of CLIL teachers in Austria – an ecological perspective on CLIL teachers' wellbeing. *Innovation in Language Learning and Teaching*, *15*(3), 218–232. doi:1 0.1080/17501229.2020.1739050

Huang, E., Jiang, L., & Yang, M. (2021). The affordances of a technology-aided formative assessment platform for the assessment and teaching of English as a foreign language: An ecological perspective. *Educational Technology Research and Development*, *69*(6), 3391–3412. doi:10.1007/s11423-021-10047-y

International Bureau of Education. (2011) Bahrain. *World Data of Education, 7th Edition, 2010/11*. UNESCO. https://www.ibe.unesco.org/

Jiajing, G. (2007 April). Designing an ESP course for Chinese students of business. *The Asian ESP Journal*, *3*(1), 97-106. https://www.asian-esp-journal.com/wp-content/uploads/2016/01/AESp-Volume-3-Issue-1-Apri-2007.pdf

Kirkpatrick, R., & Barnawi, O. Z. (2017). Introduction: English Language Education Policy in MENA. In R. Kirkpatrick (Ed.), *English language Education Policy in the Middle East and North African* (Vol. 13, pp. 1–8). Springer International Publishing. doi:10.1007/978-3-319-46778-8_1

Lea, M. R. (2017). Academic literacies in theory and practice. In B. V. Street & S. May (Eds.), *Literacies and language education: Encyclopedia of language and education* (pp. 147–158). Springer. doi:10.1007/978-3-319-02252-9_19

Lea, M. R., & Street, B. V. (1998). Student writing in higher education: An academic literacies approach. *Studies in Higher Education*, *23*(2), 157–172. doi:10.1080/03 075079812331380364

Lea, M. R., & Street, B. V. (2006). The" academic literacies" model: Theory and applications. *Theory into Practice*, *45*(4), 368–377. doi:10.1207/s15430421tip4504_11

Lee, C. D. (2017). Integrating Research on How People Learn and Learning Across Settings as a Window of Opportunity to Address Inequality in Educational Processes and Outcomes. *Review of Research in Education*, *41*(1), 88–111. doi:10.3102/0091732X16689046

Lemke, J. L. (2001). The Long and the Short of It: Comments on Multiple Timescale Studies of Human Activity. *Journal of the Learning Sciences*, *10*(1), 17–26. https://www.learntechlib.org/p/165494/. doi:10.1207/S15327809JLS10-1-2_3

Levy, T., & Gertler, H. (2015). Harnessing technology to assess oral communication in Business English. *Teaching English with Technology*, *15*(4), 52–59.

Li, D. (2022). A review of academic literacy research development: from 2002 to 2019. *Asian-Pacific Journal of Second and Foreign Language Education*, *7*(1), 1–22. doi:10.1186/s40862-022-00130-z

Malcolm, D., & Majed, M. (2013). Foundation-level Gulf Arab student response to self-access learning. *Studies in Self-Access Learning Journal*, *4*(4), 323–338. doi:10.37237/040408

Messick, S. (1996). Validity and washback in language testing. *Language Testing*, *13*(3), 241–256A. doi:10.1177/026553229601300302

Morrow, C. (2017). Assessing entry-level academic literacy with IELTS in the UAE. *Revisiting EFL assessment: Critical perspectives*, 151-169.

Murray, N. (2016). An academic literacies argument for decentralizing EAP provision. *ELT Journal*, *70*(4), 435–443. doi:10.1093/elt/ccw030

Murray, N. (2018). University gatekeeping tests: What are they really testing and what are the implications for EAP provision? *JACET Journal*, *62*, 15–27.

Parodi, G. (2010). Discourse genres, academic and professional discourses. In G. Parodi (Ed.), *Academic and professional discourse genres in Spanish* (pp. 7–16). John Benjamins. doi:10.1075/scl.40.05par

Patterson, R., & Weideman, A. (2013). The Refinement of a construct for tests of academic literacy. *Tydskrif vir Taalonderrig*, *47*(1), 125–151. doi:10.4314/jlt.v47i1.6

Pellegrino, J. W. (2002). Knowing what students know. *Issues in Science and Technology*, *19*(2), 48–52.

Phuong, N., & Hegelheimer, V. (2021). New Technologies in Second Language Spoken Assessment. In T. Haug, W. Mann, & U. Knoch (Eds.), *The Handbook of Language Assessment Across Modalities* (pp. 403–416). Academic., doi:10.1093/oso/9780190885052.003.0035

Popham, W. J. (2009). Assessment literacy for teachers: Faddish or fundamental? *Theory into Practice*, *48*(1), 4–11. doi:10.1080/00405840802577536

Purinton, T. (2024, March 2). *Ted Purinton Bio*. Google Sites. https://sites.google.com/view/tedpurinton/bio

Rex, L. A., & McEachen, D. (1999). If Anything Is Odd, Inappropriate, Confusing, or Boring, It's Probably Important":" The Emergence of Inclusive Academic Literacy through English Classroom Discussion Practices. *Research in the Teaching of English*, *34*(1), 65–129. doi:10.58680/rte19991685

Shepard, L. A., Penuel, W. R., & Pellegrino, J. W. (2018). Using learning and motivation theories to coherently link formative assessment, grading practices, and large-scale assessment. *Educational Measurement: Issues and Practice*, *37*(1), 21–34. doi:10.1111/emip.12189

Simpson, S. (2010). *Learning systems: An ecological perspective on advanced academic literacy practices of multilingual writers*. [Doctoral thesis, University of New Hampshire]. University of New Hampshire Scholars Repository. https://scholars.unh.edu/dissertation/530

Smith, L. (2011, January). Applying the bioecological theory of human development to learning. Enhancing student engagement in online learning. In *Proceedings of the 10th Teaching Matters Annual Conference* (pp. 1-8). Springer.

Song, Y., & Ma, Q. (2021). Affordances of a mobile learner-generated tool for pupils' English as a second language vocabulary learning: An ecological perspective. *British Journal of Educational Technology*, *52*(2), 858–878. doi:10.1111/bjet.13037

Suleymanova, S., & Hysaj, A. (2022, June). Undergraduate Emirati Students' Challenges of Language Barrier in Meeting Expectations of English Medium University in the UAE. In *International Conference on Human-Computer Interaction* (pp. 199-209). Cham: Springer International Publishing. 10.1007/978-3-031-05064-0_15

Wingate, U. (2015). *Academic literacy and student diversity: The case for inclusive practice*. Multilingual Matters. doi:10.21832/9781783093496

Wingate, U. (2018). Academic literacy across the curriculum: Towards a collaborative instructional approach. *Language Teaching*, *51*(3), 349–364. doi:10.1017/S0261444816000264

ADDITIONAL READINGS

Barnawi, O. (2018). *Neoliberalism and English Language Education Policies in the Arabian Gulf*. Routledge. doi:10.4324/9781315276717

Cheng, L., & Curtis, A. (2004). Washback or backwash: A review of the impact of testing on teaching and learning. *Washback in language testing*, 25-40.

Shelton, L. (2018). *The Bronfenbrenner primer: A guide to develecology*. Routledge.

Wingate, U. (2018). Academic literacy across the curriculum: Towards a collaborative instructional approach. *Language Teaching*, *51*(3), 349–364. doi:10.1017/S0261444816000264

Wyatt, M. (2023). English as a Medium of Instruction on the Arabian Peninsula: Shifting Perspectives, Developing Understandings. In English as a Medium of Instruction on the Arabian Peninsula (pp. 1-16). Routledge.

KEY TERMS AND DEFINITIONS

Enacted Curriculum: The teacher-provided learning activities that students experience in the classroom.

English for Academic Purposes (EAP): A specialized field in English language that helps students develop the skill and knowledge to use language in various academic contexts.

Formative/Classroom-Based Assessment: Assessment activities conducted by teachers and students to monitor and improve the quality of teaching and learning in classroom.

High-Stakes Testing: Tests with high importance or significant consequences attached to their outcomes. The results of these tests carry serious implications for people being assessed, such as academic promotion, graduation, or employment decisions.

Integrated Skills Tests: An integrated skill test incorporates several skills within one test. In academic English tests, students produce texts by summarizing, synthesizing, and presenting source ideas according to the stylistic conventions of a genre.

Proximal Processes: Complex reciprocal interactions in immediate environment or microsystem of students with people, objects and symbols over an extended period of time.

Summative Assessment: An assessment of learning that typically occurs at the end of a specific instructional period such as at the conclusion of a unit, semester or academic year to measure the overall knowledge, skills and understanding of students.

Washback: Washback is the intended and unintended effects of a high-stakes test on classroom teaching and learning. It can positively or negatively affect classroom practices which either promote or inhibit learning.

ENDNOTES

[1]   (Proposed Specifications for Preparing Test Items at the Intermediate Level (moe.gov.bh)

Chapter 2
Building a Reading Nation:
Insights Into School–Community Collaboration

Bonjovi H. Hajan
iD https://orcid.org/0000-0003-2911-5824
Tawi-Tawi College of Technology and Oceanography, Mindanao State University, Philippines

Wati Sheena M. Bulkia
Tawi-Tawi College of Technology and Oceanography, Mindanao State University, Philippines

Aljon L. Alpuerto
iD https://orcid.org/0009-0009-8148-4273
Tawi-Tawi College of Technology and Oceanography, Mindanao State University, Philippines

Clarissa Ayangco-Derramas
Tawi-Tawi College of Technology and Oceanography, Mindanao State University, Philippines

ABSTRACT

Reading literacy provides a gateway access to other more complex forms of literacies central for navigating the convolution of today's globalized, digital, and data-saturated world. Positioned within this view, this chapter offers a comprehensive literature review of school-community collaboration and literacy education to shed light on facilitators and barriers central to the partnering efforts in the development of reading literacy. Based on the thematic analysis of careful and exhaustive literature reviews, several interesting themes emerged that depict key facilitators and barriers of school-community collaboration in reading education. The chapter, drawing on the authors' critical reflections of the identified themes, charts the future directions of school-community collaboration in the reading education field, shaping the changing landscape of reading education practice, policy, and research.

DOI: 10.4018/979-8-3693-1777-8.ch002

INTRODUCTION

The world is changing, so is literacy. The ubiquity of modern technology today has metamorphosed our world into a globalized, digital and data-saturated space, transforming the way in which literacy is conceived and practiced. Because of the changing literacy demands of the complex world we live in, a plethora of new literacy-related concepts is now existent. Such concepts as 'new literacies' (Lankshear & Knobel, 2003), 'multiliteracies' (Cope & Kalantzis, 2000) and 'multimodality' (Kress & van Leeuwen, 2001) have become pervasive describing various forms of literacy skills necessary to navigate the networked, globalized world of today where multiple devices and media texts are ubiquitous for consumption and learning (Anani et al., 2021; Rowsell & Walsh, 2011). The National Council of Teachers of English (2019) describes these changing literacies as "interconnected, dynamic, and malleable" (para. 92), which include among others the ability to "(1) participate effectively and critically in a networked world, (2) explore and engage critically, thoughtfully, and across a wide variety of inclusive texts and tools/modalities, and (3) recognize and honor the multilingual literacy identities and culture experiences individuals bring to learning environments, and provide opportunities to promote, amplify, and encourage these differing variations of language" (para. 2).

Reflecting on this global literacy revolution, it can be argued that reading becomes a cornerstone serving as a rudiment for the development of more advanced literacy skills. Akyol (2012) describes reading as a meaning-making skill in which the reader actively negotiates meanings with the author through activating prior knowledge and making inferences. Hence, in a data-driven, networked world, reading skills are pivotal in allowing readers to comprehend the complex meanings of vast information, establishing a wealth of factual knowledge needed for a more advanced literacy and learning task. Along this line, Willingham (2006) draws on cognitive science research to elucidate the importance of significant knowledge acquisition in education with which reading as a skill serves as a gateway.

Those with a rich base of factual knowledge find it easier to learn more—the rich get richer. In addition, factual knowledge enhances cognitive processes like problem solving and reasoning. The richer the knowledge base, the more smoothly and effectively these cognitive processes—the very ones that teachers target—operate. So, the more knowledge students accumulate, the smarter they become (p. 30).

Such a claim reverberates the potency of reading as a skill highlighting its foundational role in further supporting the learners' literacy and learning development. However, despite its foremost importance in literacy education, reading remains as the most difficult language skill to master among learners globally. The World Bank

(2022) reports that "learning poverty has increased by a third in low- and middle-income countries, with an estimated 70% of 10-year-olds unable to understand a simple written text," (para. 1). In Australia, the Australian Curriculum, Assessment and Reporting Authority (2021) indicates that around 20% of Grade 9 students are at or below the national minimum standards, suggesting that students are likely to have difficulty comprehending texts at secondary school level. In the Philippines, 9 out of 10 children cannot read and comprehend texts well (The World Bank, 2022). An earlier report by the OECD (2019) shows a parallel result, showing the Philippines scored 340 in Reading in the 2018 Programme for International Student Assessment (PISA), all below the average of the OECD countries. The problems on students' poor reading skills have been further exacerbated by the COVID-19 pandemic as suggested by previous research (Dorn et al., 2020; Domingue, et al., 2022). These data clearly suggest a need for strategic redirection in literacy education practice, policy and research, ensuring that no one is left behind and that every country is groomed to be a reading nation.

Literacy development, just as learning development in general, is a concerted endeavor involving active participation from various concerned stakeholders. Epstein (2011) opines that because of their "overlapping spheres of influence" on children's learning and development, schools, homes, and communities need to establish greater collaboration to promote children's education. Collaborations are pivotal in strengthening, supporting, and even transforming individual partners, resulting in improved program quality, more efficient use of resources, and better alignment of goals and curricula (Harvard Family Research Project, 2010). In a similar vein, community engagements are a mandate to educational institutions because extension, apart from instruction and research, is one of the university core functions. In the Philippines, for example, all State Universities and Colleges (SUCs), as stipulated in The 1987 Constitution of the Republic of the Philippines (n.d.), are mandated to provide extension programs through various means (e.g. non-formal learning and out-of-school study programs) that cater to community needs. As such, Higher Education Institutions (HEIs), viewing community engagement as central to improving institutional performance, implement programs that are responsive to the needs of the community through field exposure of both teaching, staff, and students.

In the context of literacy education, collaborations are indispensable since early language and literacy begins at home and in the communities where children are exposed and is only reinforced at schools through formal education. Such a premise has then led to the existence of various collaborative literacy education practices. One such literacy education practice is through a school-community collaboration. Research shows that school-community collaboration is beneficial in promoting students' reading literacy (Cooper & Pace, 2004; Jones, 2018; Silbert & Bitso, 2015). Cabunilas et al. (2023), for instance, suggested that Community Learning Centers should be made functional and well-prepared for community teaching-learning to help improve students to become functionally literate. Their results specifically showed that 50% of the struggling readers who participated in the community-based reading program transformed into being instructional readers, reaffirming the affordances of school-community collaboration.

Notwithstanding the benefits of school-community collaboration on children's reading skills development, little is known about facilitating and inhibiting forces driving successful school-community collaboration in literacy education, particularly in reading, thus creating a knowledge gap in literacy education practice, policy, and research. This chapter draws on a thematic analysis of careful and comprehensive literature reviews of school-community collaboration and literacy education to provide an in-depth understanding of the facilitators and barriers in school-community collaboration in the reading education field. The chapter specifically discusses school-community collaboration in the context of reading education, shedding light on the various facilitators and barriers central to the development of children's reading literacy. By exploring key facilitators and barriers of school-community in reading education, the chapter maps out future directions for forging a successful school-community collaboration, thereby advancing a novel insight into literacy education practice, policy and research.

MAIN FOCUS OF THE CHAPTER

School-Community Collaboration

School-community collaboration is a broad concept with literature showing its different associated terms, such as school-community partnership (Valli et al., 2014) and community engagement (Hands, 2023; Sanders, 2003). Despite the differences in terminologies, their meanings, however, remain essentially coherent, all pertaining to the established collaborative efforts between the school and the community to accomplish a common goal. Hence, for the purpose of consistency and clarity, the term, "school-community collaboration," is used in this chapter.

School-community collaboration is founded on the fundamental theory of action stating that students can improve academic and personal life prospects if schools respond to a wide range of needs. This basically implies establishing a harmonious working relationship with the community and social service agencies to cater to the complex needs of learners, their families, and their entire community. Following this notion, a theory for educational collaboration called "overlapping spheres of influence" is given birth (Epstein, 2011, p. 466). According to this theory, schools, homes, and communities are the primary environments where children's education take place. Hence, optimal collaborations by those involved in the education of the students in these contexts can cultivate learning and development. The recognition that families and communities influence students' education is the heart of school-community collaboration practices. In establishing productive relationships with communities, schools consider the needs and beliefs of the families when planning engagement activities (Foster & Loven, 1992). When the local stakeholders in the community, including families, work harmoniously with the school personnel, a possibility for children to perform academically and develop positive outlook about school is limitless.

Forging partnerships with families and communities is an important way to promote and improve literacy (Jones, 2018; Silbert & Bitso, 2015). Schools that value the spirit of family support moralities are driven and committed in creating educational programs that are dutiful, responsive, and meaningful to the local needs of the learners, their families, and the community they live in. Schools should recognize their function in the community as building future productive and responsible citizens of the community as well as offering relevant support for the community's existing needs. Hence, schools should operate in conjunction with the community members, bridging the gap between the school and the community. When schools extend their support to the community for their needs, the relationship with the community becomes stronger. Schools can foster an empowered community with community-based programs, where students are emboldened to take ownership in acknowledging community needs, planning and delivering service-oriented programs to address those needs, and reflecting upon the social value of their initiatives in improving the community. Learning opportunities in academic areas such as reading and writing may be included in such projects. For instance, the pre-service teachers of a specific university may implement community-based reading programs, specifically for the adult non-readers in the community.

Given the usefulness of school-community collaboration in education, many schools and their districts have embraced school-community collaboration initiatives in different educational settings (Mayger & Hochbein, 2021; Sanders, 1999, 2001, 2018), including literacy education context (Cabunilas et al., 2023; Cooper & Pace, 2004; Jones, 2018; Silbert & Bitso, 2015). While it is true that school-community collaboration is never a substitute for "sound educational policies, adequate funding, or excellent teaching" (Sanders, 2003, p. 176), it can, however, be a powerful practice that goes a long way in the children's learning and development, allowing both teachers and community members to address the various needs of the children in the communities (Hands, 2005). School-community collaboration built on the active engagement of multiple stakeholders from across communities is a means to provide students with limitless opportunities to grow and develop holistically.

However, the successes and failures of school-community collaborations are dependent on several forces. Research shows that tangible elements such as resources, financial support, guidance, and school leadership are instrumental for effective collaboration (Sanders, 1999). Other less concrete factors such as constituents' mindsets and social contexts are also influential in driving school-community collaborative feats (Hands, 2023). While these external and internal forces are useful information, it seems that limited knowledge is known about key facilitators and barriers of school-community collaboration and how these can inform the reading education field. Considering the benefits of school-community collaboration in reading education (Cabunilas et al., 2023; Cooper & Pace, 2004; Jones, 2018; Silbert & Bitso, 2015), delving deeper into these key facilitators and barriers becomes increasingly essential. Hence, as surmised from the thorough thematic analysis of literature and studies collected on school-community collaboration and literacy education, the following present and discuss the different key facilitators and barriers, throwing significant light on reading education.

Facilitators of School-Community Collaboration

The thematic analysis of the comprehensive literature reviews reveals a multitude of interesting facilitators of school-community collaboration, which can be synthesized into seven principal themes: Negotiated and Mutually Beneficial Collaborations; Clear Communication of Shared Goals and Expectations; Collaborative School and Community Leadership Structures; Data-Driven Collaboration Implementation Schemes; Supportive Physical Infrastructures and Professional Development Activities; and Authentic and Empowering Literacy Pedagogies. These school-community collaboration facilitators are further discussed within this section of the chapter.

Negotiated and Mutually Beneficial Collaborations

A prevailing facilitator of school-community collaboration is creating a negotiated space that benefits both parties. This entails establishing collaborative groups of stakeholders to reach a shared goal based on common understanding of the needs of both parties (Epstein et al., 2018; FitzGerald & Quiñones, 2018). A clearly defined shared goal is crucial in establishing action planning and program monitoring which can later serve as a guide for school leaders to navigate partnership work and school policies (Benavides, 2002). Hence, it is important that through this process, schools are prepared to engage with diverse individuals coming from different perspectives and ways of working with others (Hands, 2023). Partnering efforts should reflect the needs of both parties, ensuring mutually beneficial collaborations. However, given the complex differences of stakeholders, school-community collaboration requires flexible negotiation and partnership terms built into the agreed collaboration (Hands, 2023). Flexibility is crucial in school-community collaboration to ensure relationships are relevant and workable. With flexibility, a structure is possible that is versatile enough to respond to the changing needs of both parties. However, flexibility does not mean being loose where "nobody knows quite what's happening, when it's happening, and how we are doing along the way" (Hands, 2023). In the context of school-community collaboration in reading education, it is important that stakeholders work closely to create shared resources that are crucial for students' acquisition of effective reading skills (Clary, 2008). These shared resources are negotiated based on flexible terms that are beneficial for both the school and the community where the reading programs are implemented. By allowing negotiation and flexibility, a sense of ownership on both ends may be developed, hence successes of collaborations in promoting reading literacy are likely to be anticipated.

Clear Communication of Shared Goals and Expectations

Communication is an integral component of successful school-community collaborations. Within the realm of school-community collaboration, communication means involving outlining expectations for partners (Anderson-Butcher et al., 2022). With clear communication, schools can communicate effectively what they can provide that aligns with the needs and interests of the potential collaborators (Hands, 2023). This communication, however, is not a one-way, one-shot activity. It needs to be open and consistent all throughout the collaboration process to ensure that on-going problems affecting both parties are properly identified, addressed, and avoided (Benavides, 2022). School leaders and community members should understand that collaborative efforts are always a work in progress. Open and consistent communication serves as a channel to repair any necessary problems that hinder progress and development. The importance of clear communication in school-community collaboration is especially paramount in contexts where there are financial resources involved. For example, school principals should maintain transparency in explaining financial allocations, clearly showing how solicited funds are spent and resources utilized (Benavides, 2022). Further, community leaders are likely to be more satisfied with school-community collaborations when direct relationship with the school leaders is established and line of communication is sustained (Badgett, 2016; Myende, 2018). Hence, clear communication of shared goals and expectations involving all stakeholders can facilitate successful school-community collaboration. This suggests that before any community-based reading programs can be implemented, the schools should clearly communicate the goals, objectives, and activities of the reading programs to the community members, especially the parents whose children are the target beneficiaries of the implemented programs. The communication should be a work in progress, ensuring that any issues and concerns surrounding the implementation of the reading programs are addressed promptly and used as inputs for further improving the programs.

Collaborative School and Community Leadership Structures

The school and community leadership structures are also important facilitating forces driving success for school-community collaborative initiatives. Anderson-Butcher et al. (2022) reported that buy-in and supportive leadership structures can positively influence the implementation of the Community Collaboration Model (CCM), a school-community collaboration model. The value of having collaborative leadership culture cannot be underestimated because schools and communities are operated and managed by leaders. Thus, if the leaders are open to collaborations, all initiatives of the teachers and other members in the community will not be put to waste. With collaborative school and community leadership structures, implementations of school-community collaboration programs will be supported and reinforced. For instance, school leaders encourage reading remediation after school hours or even during summer term (Cabunilas et al., 2023). In this connection, the availability of school leaders is equally important in school-community collaboration (Benavides, 2022). In addition, stakeholders' participation in school-community collaboration is influenced by their perceptions of the concepts of partnership (Cruzat et al., 2022). This means positive views about collaboration can result in active community engagements. School and community leaders should be among those who principally embrace positive outlook towards collaboration because their views are influential for their subordinates. Further, community's participation is also impacted by the school's practices involving them (Cruzat et al., 2022). Hence, favorable experiences that community members gain from school-community collaborations may enable them to commit in a more sustainable negotiated collaboration. With collaborative school and community leadership structures, the school and local officials may work collaboratively in producing enough funds (Clary, 2008), which is key to supporting the sustainability of the school-community collaboration programs. In the context of promoting reading literacy, school leaders, reading coordinators, and reading teachers must hold positive view about the supremacy of collaboration. As advocates of reading literacy, they should take the lead in creating partnering opportunities where the school and the community can forge strong collaborations for cultivating the love and reason for reading among children. Further, they should provide the necessary supports, especially technical assistance in reading instructions and reading materials, to ensure successful collaboration with the community members.

Data-Driven Collaboration Implementation Schemes

Successful school-community collaboration is built on data-driven implementation schemes. This means there is utilization of multiple forms of data to inform and guide implementation processes (Anderson-Butcher et al., 2016; Anderson-Butcher et al., 2018; Britt et al., 2022). Just as any educational program, school-community collaboration programs rely on rigid monitoring and evaluation as inputs for improvement. Formative assessments of school-community collaboration programs are necessary because they provide real-time data that can serve as instant fixes to the problems encountered before, during and after the course of the implementation of the school-community collaboration programs. The assessments should be generated from a wide range of data to ensure comprehensive understanding of the challenges and issues. It is important to underscore that practical problems can be resolved only when they are addressed with appropriate solutions, and appropriate solutions are but based on the accurate data that can pinpoint the problems at hand. Hence, using multiple data forms can strengthen problem-solution efforts in the implementation of school-community collaboration programs. Aside from formative assessments, the use of multiple data can also facilitate in the terminal or summative evaluation, that which assesses the impact of the implemented school-community collaboration programs. To ascertain whether a school-community collaboration program, for example, is impactful would necessitate looking at the different evidences and using such evidences as bases for affirming the impact. Hence, data-driven collaboration implementation schemes are indispensable to ensure monitoring, evaluation and sustainability of school-community collaboration programs. For reading programs, this means that monitoring and evaluation should not only be limited to the assessment of children's reading literacy, but also the appreciation of parents and other stakeholders of the implemented reading programs. This is aside from the multiple data collection necessary from the children in the programs to ensure reading literacy development. For instance, feedback from parents about how the reading programs have helped their children may be used as basis for improving the implementation of future reading programs.

Supportive Physical Infrastructures and Professional Development Activities

Physical infrastructures are learning spaces where partnering efforts occur, making school-community collaboration possible. The establishment of libraries to support literacy in schools with community involvement is one crucial feature of physical infrastructures (Joshi, 2017). Libraries that house a myriad of updated and relevant reading materials may serve as a powerful resource support for the development of students' literacy skills. Aside from physical libraries, conducive reading centers that are community-based are also of paramount importance, facilitating school-community collaboration in reading literacy development. Community reading centers that are functional and supportive of learning can serve to improve students' reading literacy (Cabunilas et al., 2023). These community-based reading centers are, however, worthless without the presence of committed and competent reading teachers. Hence, investment on continuous professional development for reading teachers and other relevant school-based professionals is essential (Anderson-Butcher et al. 2022; Anderson-Butcher et al., 2016). Due to the changing landscape of teaching and learning and the complex nature of community-based engagement, professional development can ensure that teachers are armed with culturally-responsive literacy pedagogies that tailor to the diverse needs of the students in the community (Darling-Hammond et al., 2005). In the case of lack of qualified reading teachers, the use of paraprofessionals or volunteers as tutors may be sought. Jones (2018) reported that with proper training, positive results of school-community collaboration programs on student learning may be achieved even with the use of paraprofessionals or volunteers as teachers. Therefore, both physical infrastructures and teacher professional development programs should be part of the school priorities in designing school-community collaboration programs, particularly in literacy development (International Reading Association, 2008).

Authentic and Empowering Literacy Pedagogies

Successful school-community collaboration programs in reading are marked with the use of authentic and empowering literacy pedagogies. Cooper and Pace (2004) outline how such pedagogies may be characterized. Authentic literacy pedagogies give emphasis on the relevance of reading, highlighting the cultivation of students' awareness on the importance of information and literature. More than ever, today's world is drenched with so much data. With the continuous rising of modern technology, data is everywhere. By cultivating awareness on the importance of information and literature, especially in the context of today's globalized, digital and data-driven world, students may find more reasons and meanings to engage in reading activities. Authentic literacy pedagogies also mean supporting students' multiple learning styles. Given the complex needs of readers as learners, reading teachers' instructional strategies should be differentiated catering to the diverse reading needs of the students. In addition, authentic literacy pedagogies foster reading and writing for a real-life purpose. This implies that school-community reading programs should provide students with opportunities to apply the skills in real-life situations. Hence, school-community reading programs may use simulations to help students see the real-world applications of the literacy skills being cultivated.

Meanwhile, empowering literacy pedagogies emphasize on the role of reading teachers to encourage students to make a personal contribution to less fortunate members of their community (Cooper & Pace, 2004). Such empowerment may be realized, for instance, by making advanced readers work in tandem with their peers who are struggling or poor readers. By so doing, more advanced students may not only get the chance to reinforce their reading skills but also develop a sense of ownership and responsibility of being "the little teachers". Additionally, the less advanced students may benefit significantly since they may feel less inhibited and pressured given that the instructions are from their peers.

Barriers of School-Community Collaboration

The thematic analysis of the relevant literatures and studies reveals paucity of research on barriers of school-community collaboration in the context of reading education. However, there are existing studies that reveal remarkable challenges of school-community collaboration in general that could shed light into reading education. Such challenges may be understood as Inhibiting Social Contexts of Collaboration, Mismatch of School and Community Expectations, Poor School Leadership Styles, Stakeholders' Poor Mindset of Collaboration, and Scarcity of Physical and Non-Physical Resources. Each of these themes of school-community barriers is further explained in this part of the chapter.

Inhibiting Social Contexts of Collaboration

One of the key barriers that negatively influences the school-community collaboration is the prevailing social contexts that inhibit collaboration. These inhibiting social contexts encompass a multitude of political and moral issues surrounding the school and the community. On the political level, several issues arise regarding school-community collaboration. One such issue is the presence of powerful entities that are trespassing the school property which can disturb the learning of the students (Abiodun-Oyebanji, 2019). This issue is also reported in a study of Hands (2023) where problems may occur when organizations are using school space after school hours. This is because questions about authority arise when school leaders are not in the campus after school hours and possible problems arise when classrooms are used. Similarly, a study by Lauwo and Mkulu (2021) shows that majority of the teachers reported that political interference is a key challenge hindering community from not involving to the fullest degree. Because politicians can have power in decelerating the community morale of participating, there is a tendency that they discourage parents from contributing to the school development. When this happens, they greatly affect the performance of the students, hence a failure to attain the quality of education. Nonetheless, even if governments manifest support for community engagement in education, some school policies can conflict with one another and impede collaboration (Hands, 2023). Furthermore, many schools are apprehensive of collaboration efforts, especially when they threaten to penetrate organizational planning and decision making (Shatkin & Gershberg, 2007; Sanders & Galindo, 2014). On the moral level, the school moral issues can result in decreased community support. Jordan (1998) noted that school culture may marginalize the role of the members of the community, hindering congenial school-community relations. The existence of such school moral culture depends mostly on the school administrators. For instance, the bad image of the school in the community threatens many parents in entrusting their children to attend schools. Communities may also lose interest in their schools due to bad moral habits, leaving the schools without much support; these may hinder good, school-community relations (Lauwo & Mkulu, 2021). This advises that the school and the community should agree on specific guidelines regarding the use of school campus for any community-based reading activities to avoid trespassing or disruption of classes. In addition, the school should lead initiatives involving the local government units to support its partnering efforts in reading literacy development. Further, schools that wish to extend reading services in the community should establish good reputation to gain the trust and support of the community that they vow to serve. By good reputation, the schools should ensure that they have the capacity to offer reading programs to be implemented by qualified experts in reading. By and large, parents need to feel that their children are taken care of by trusted and professional reading teachers.

Mismatch of School and Community Expectations

Apart from inhibiting social contexts, internal forces may also hamper partnering efforts. An interesting theme that emerged as an internal barrier in school-community collaboration is the mismatch of school and community expectations. Mismatch of school and community expectations occurs when there is a lack of clear communication and negotiation of shared goals that hamper mutual collaborating benefits (Neuphane & Dhakal, 2023). Collaborations are usually initiated based on a schools' agenda (Pushor, 2007), with goals that do not necessarily reflect the goals shared among community members (Hands, 2023). When the programs do not reflect the needs of the community, this results in a lack of awareness and understanding of the programs among the community members, hence a difficulty persuading them into the partnering efforts. Further, the mismatch may limit the provision of culturally relevant educational experiences to engage the students in their learning (Dei et al., 2000), perpetuating to break down communication and trust (Bryk & Schneider, 2002). In this case, open and consistent communication is key to addressing the prevailing mismatch of school-community expectations (Anderson-Butcher et al. 2022; Hands, 2023). Poor communication network with the community can result in the alienation of the community from the school, creating unhealthy school-community relations. Hence, it is imperative that schools clearly communicate their agenda and listen to the needs of the community, recognizing the views and expectations of community members that meet their personal, social, and educational welfare (Yunas, et al., 2021). School-community collaboration programs should be founded on both the needs of the school and the community. Furthermore, the mismatch of goals and expectations may prevail because of the existing differences in educators' and students' socioeconomic status or cultural experiences, creating a divide between the teachers and the community, whereby they work in isolation or, worst, in opposition to one another (Bryk & Schneider, 2002). It is therefore advisable for school administrator to carry along members of the community, especially the stakeholders in the regular operation of the school because effective communication between the school and the community could foster good school community relationship (Abiodun-Oyebanji, 2019). In partnering for promoting reading literacy, this suggests that schools should involve the community stakeholders in all phases of the reading program development, from its planning and design to its implementation and evaluation. The process for the reading program development should be participatory in that it enables the stakeholders to have a voice and develop a sense of ownership of the program. Hence, reading coordinators and reading teachers should invest in open communication and relationship building, fostering a harmonious working bond with the stakeholders.

Poor School Leadership Styles

School leaders as the managers of school activities play an important role in the successes and failures of school-community collaborations. The leadership styles of school leaders can influence the partnership efforts of the schools they manage (Lauwo & Mkulu, 2021). For example, a democratic leadership style strives to maintain good human relations with members of the community and consult them in the decision-making process in the school, creating a healthy community relation, whereas an autocratic leadership style does not respect the opinions of others and takes decisions solely without consulting others, endangering the school community relations. Muthoni (2015) shows that school leaders with poor leadership style do not establish a partnership with the community in the surroundings believing that community members are irrelevant to the schooling process. School leaders view that community members are illiterate or have poor educational profiles, thus engaging them in educational activities is a waste of time (Lauwo & Mkulu, 2021). Such vantage point opines that school leaders, reading coordinators, and reading teachers should develop the mindsets of not only as "leaders of learning" but also as "civic leaders of communities" (Cleveland, 2023), suggesting that the leadership roles of school administrators and reading advocates extend beyond the school settings. Along this line, an outward-looking perspective is indispensable, which sees community members as needing support rather than as providers of support (Auerbach, 2011; Keith, 1999). Hence, school leaders, reading coordinators, and reading teachers should employ participatory approach, creating opportunities for and promoting the active engagement of the school community in developing school reading priorities, setting reading targets, and participating in school-based reading activities (Yunas, et al., 2021).

Stakeholders' Poor Mindset of Collaboration

While the roles of school leaders are crucial in school-community collaboration, the roles of other stakeholders such as teachers and parents are also of prime importance. Hence, their mindset about collaboration plays a huge impact on the successes and failures of school-community collaboration efforts. Anderson-Butcher et al. (2022) showed that resistance to change, viewing the collaboration process as an "add-on", and a lack of buy-in, commitment, and interprofessional collaboration among school stakeholders is a key hindrance to successful school-community collaboration. It is important to understand that schools do not merely draw community resources into the school, but "open themselves to the community" (Schutz, 2006, p. 704). "Parents and community members contribute to school change and to children's learning" (Gold, et al., 2002, p. 10). Anaxagorou (2023) reports that, especially in urban schools, teachers express concerns about their professional autonomy being jeopardized by community involvement. Some teachers prefer to maintain a "professional" distance from parents and community stakeholders, raising concerns about dependence on parents as "suppliers" of pupils. To maintain their ability to carry out their core functions—effective teaching and learning, teachers may rationally feel the need to isolate themselves from "outsiders." This isolation provides a degree of professional autonomy that teachers value (Pearson & Moomaw, 2005), but that seriously constrains community. This poor mindset of collaboration positions teachers as outsiders in the community, hindering their willingness to engage in collaborative efforts. Another problem that relates to poor mindset is the parents' ignorance about the importance of school-community collaboration. Due to their ignorance, some parents do not know the value of collaboration, in which they only take their children to school and leave their responsibility to teachers. Inclusive involvement of the parents, teachers, and the government is vital for the holistic development of the students (Lauwo & Mkulu, 2021). For successful school-community collaboration in promoting reading literacy, this suggests that personal and professional developments for reading stakeholders highlighting growth mindset are necessary to change their perspectives about collaboration. Of all stakeholders, reading teachers must take the lead in understanding the influencing power of collaboration in fostering reading literacy skills among children. Professional development programs should be targeted to improve teacher collaboration literacy. Furthermore, parents who are partners of the teachers in the children's literacy journey should be calibrated to comprehend that their participation in supporting and enriching their children's reading literacy at home is irreplaceable. Hence, seminars for parents should include developing their mindset about the benefits of school-community collaboration in reading literacy development.

Scarcity of Physical and Non-Physical Resources

Resources are essential supports that can inhibit successes of school-community collaboration when not taken care of properly. These resources can be physical or non-physical. Physical resources include human and financial. Abiodun-Oyebanji (2019) indicated that, the purpose of school-community collaboration programs, however well-defined and inspiring, cannot be attained without necessary resources, especially the human resource. Resources should be well harnessed, harmoniously and efficiently used, as well as negotiated and managed effectively to attain the targeted objective of the program. In addition, teachers, students and other school staff need funds for their welfare. For instance, finances are necessary for building comfortable and convenient teacher and staff apartments. School-community relations may be obstructed where such welfare is not met. In general, financial resources can influence the various facets of education, including teacher and student welfare, building infrastructure, and community support (Abiodun-Oyebanji, 2019). Along this line, Prew (2012) asserted that the engagement of community members in partnering efforts relies on their economic levels. Some parents who are peasants and living in slums, for example, cannot afford to involve their children in community-based educational programs because they lack the money to support their children for schools. Hence, rather than prioritizing education, their primary focus shifts to livelihood (Lauwo & Mkulu, 2021). Apart from human and financial resources, other non-physical resources are also key barriers to school-community collaboration. These non-physical resources may include time constraints (Neupane & Dhakal, 2023; Sanders & Galindo, 2007; Ngobeni, 2022), disruption of daily school activities (Abiodun-Oyebanji, 2019; Neupane & Dhakal, 2023), and heavy teacher and staff workloads (Ngobeni, 2022; Zuckerman, 2020). All these non-physical resources when not taken into consideration can potentially hinder school-community partnerships. In the context of reading literacy development, schools should invest in both physical and non-physical resources to have successful community collaborations. There should be enough funds to institute community-based reading centers that can serve as useful spaces for developing and improving children's reading literacy. Contextualized reading materials should be in place as instructional resources to support reading development. Schedules allotted for regular reading activities should be specified and followed religiously to avoid disruption of other academic activities. The number of reading teachers or reading volunteers who are designated to implement community-based reading programs should be enough to avoid teacher burnout.

Future Directions of School-Community Collaboration in Reading Education

The facilitators and barriers of school-community collaboration discussed in this chapter offer several interesting insights into the reading education field, charting the future directions for reading education practice, policy, and research. How these facilitators and barriers inform practice, policy, and research in reading education are further explicated in the succeeding part of this chapter.

On Practice

As revealed from the literature review, successful collaborations are built on strongly negotiated goals and programs that foster partnering benefits. As such, strong communication serves as a central point that establishes and nurtures sustainable school-community relationships in reading education. Schools that institute community-based reading programs should establish working communication and coordination mechanisms that can result in building trust and confidence among the community members involved in promoting literacy. These communication and coordination mechanisms of community-based reading programs are not one-way, one-shot initiatives but are open, consistent activities that run throughout the collaboration efforts, ensuring that practical problems on both ends are addressed properly. In addition, on-going professional development programs should be in place for school leaders, reading teachers and reading assistants/volunteers to recalibrate their mindsets and skills of collaboration in reading education. School leaders as the top decision-makers of the school-community reading programs should understand that they are not only "leaders of learning" but "civic leaders of communities" (Cleveland, 2023). Hence, raising a nation of readers is a community-wide effort involving both the school and the community. Reading teachers should also understand that working in tandem with the community in improving children's reading literacy is not a compromise but rather a complement to their professional duties as educators. Reading teachers should then treat community members as partners in the design, implementation, and monitoring of reading programs for children in their community. Reading teachers and reading teacher assistants/volunteers should be trained pedagogically to implement research-based literacy instructions ((Darling-Hammond et al., 2005) that promote the love and reason for reading, value multiple learning styles, encourage reading and writing for an authentic purpose, and ultimately empower students to make a personal contribution to disadvantaged members of their community (Cooper & Pace, 2004). Moreover, there is a need to use data-driven implementation schemes for school-community reading programs. The use of multiple forms of data can guarantee that reading program implementation processes are based on sound decisions (Anderson-Butcher et al., 2016; Anderson-Butcher et al., 2018; Britt et al., 2022). Furthermore, schools should invest in the creation of community-based reading centers and provide enough financial allocations to support the successful operation of such centers.

On Policy

Policies are the guiding documents of any educational program. In the context of reading education, schools need to develop clear-cut policies on the planning, implementation, monitoring and evaluation of school-community reading programs. To ensure relevance and usefulness in meeting the school goals and objectives and the community needs, the policies on reading programs should be crafted on the basis of the national, regional, and local thrusts and priorities in reading education. Further, consultation should be conducted involving multiple stakeholders in the community, such as Local Government Units (LGUs), parents, students, and other community members. This is to ensure that the policies reflect the local needs of the community in which the reading programs are implemented. Such policy making strategies can ensure that the policies are mutually beneficial for both the school and the community in which the reading programs are instituted. Additionally, the policies should be comprehensive enough capturing all the essential elements for the school-community reading programs to work successfully. For example, the polices should stipulate funding allocations and relevant resources, such as the establishment of community-based reading centers, production and use of culturally relevant reading materials, and compensations and benefits of the reading teacher assistants/volunteers.

On Research

Future research into reading education should explore communication dynamics in school-community collaboration to understand key facilitators that contribute to successful partnerships in promoting reading literacy. It is important to underscore that school-community collaboration as a process in reading education involves a complex human relationship building, establishing a negotiated power with community members whose perspectives are diverse and, sometimes, conflicting. By exploring communication dynamics in school-community collaboration of reading programs, a communication model may be developed to guide the smooth implementation of school-community reading programs, where ideas are respected, differences are tolerated, and efforts are celebrated to achieve sustainable literacy education. In addition, research that delve into school leadership and teacher professional development are necessary to bring forth leadership and pedagogical frameworks that can guide school leaders and reading teachers in navigating the changing landscape of school-community collaborations in reading education. Specifically, in terms of school leadership, the studies may focus on understanding deeply the leadership structures of school leaders that are key to the management of school-community reading programs, throwing light on facilitating leadership styles for successful school-community collaboration in reading literacy development. As for teacher professional development, the research may focus on developing a competency-based framework for the efficient and effective implementation of school-community reading programs especially in linguistically and culturally diverse contexts. Such a teacher professional development framework can serve as a reference for reading teachers and reading teacher assistants/volunteers in meeting the negotiated expectations of both the school and the community. Lastly, future studies may consider looking at the possibility of designing data-driven monitoring and evaluation tools of school-community reading programs which are beneficial in the formative and summative assessments of the implemented school-community reading programs.

CONCLUSION

In conclusion, this chapter has provided a novel insight into the facilitators and barriers of school-community collaboration, shaping the landscape of reading education practice, policy, and research. The thematic analysis of the comprehensive literature reviews underlines several recurring patterns of key facilitators and barriers of school-community collaboration, highlighting negotiated and mutually beneficial collaborations are built on trust and confidence as a result of clear communication of shared goals and expectations. The chapter also emphasizes the influencing roles of collaborative school and community leadership styles complemented with supportive professional development activities and available physical and non-physical infrastructures. To ensure sustainable partnerships, the use of data-driven implementation schemes that inform decision making is vital, allowing for a quality and continuous improvement of the implemented school-community collaboration programs. In addition, authentic and empowering literacy pedagogies are especially pivotal in the feat of school-community reading programs.

Drawing on the identified facilitators and barriers of school-community collaboration, this chapter has contributed significantly to the improvement of practice, policy, and research in the reading education field. Given the multifaceted nature of school-community collaboration, the chapter explicates how communication, leadership, teacher professional development, and other relevant program supports such as funds and community-based reading centers play a central role in the collective effort of transforming children's reading literacy. Hence, by focusing on these facilitating and inhibiting forces in future reading education practice, policy, and research, the success for building a nation of readers through school-community partnerships is unprecedented. Truly, it takes a synergy of school-community collaboration guided by sound practice, clear guidelines and innovative research to build a reading nation that is thriving and flourishing in today's rapidly globalized, digital, and data-driven world.

REFERENCES

Abiodun-Oyebanji, O. J. (2019). Emerging issues in the school-community relations. In D. A. Adeyemo, D. A. Oluwole, & A. O. Busari (Eds.), *Counselling and contemporary social issues in multicultural settings*.

Akyol, H. (2012). *Türkçe ilk okuma yazma öğretimi*. Pegem Akademi.

Anani, G. E., Lamptey, H. K., & Frempong, C. O. (2021). Redefining literacy in a digital age: The role of instructors in promoting digital literacy. *Journal of English Language Teaching and Applied Linguistics*, *3*(8), 20–25. doi:10.32996/jeltal.2021.3.8.3

Anaxagorou, George. (2023). Teachers' and community stakeholders' perceptions about school-community relations in Cyprus. *International Journal about Parents in Education*, *1*. https://doi. doi:10.54195/ijpe.18249

Anderson-Butcher, D., Bates, S., Lawson, H. A., Childs, T. M., & Lachini, A. L. (2022). The community collaboration model for school improvement: A scoping review. *Education Sciences*, *12*(918), 1–20. doi:10.3390/educsci12120918

Anderson-Butcher, D., Lachini, A. L., Ball, A., Barke, S., & Martin, L. D. (2016). A university–school partnership to examine the adoption and implementation of the Ohio community collaboration model in one urban school district: A mixed-method case study. *Journal of Education for Students Placed at Risk*, *21*(3), 190–204. doi :10.1080/10824669.2016.1183429

Anderson-Butcher, D., Paluta, L., Sterling, K., & Anderson, C. (2018). Ensuring healthy youth development through community schools: A case study. *Children & Schools*, *40*(1), 7–16. doi:10.1093/cs/cdx026

Auerbach, S. (2011). Conceptualizing leadership for authentic partnerships: A continuum to inspire practice. In S. Auerbach (Ed.), *School leadership for authentic family and community partnerships: Research perspectives for transforming practice* (pp. 29–51). Routledge.

Australian Curriculum, Assessment and Reporting Authority. (2021, August 25). *NAPLAN 2021 summary results data: No major impacts on learning from COVID-19 evident - long-term trends positive* [Press release]. ACARA. https://www.acara. edu.au/docs/default-source/media-releases /20210813-naplan-results-med-rel.pdf

Badgett, K. (2016). School-business partnerships: Understanding business perspectives. *School Community Journal*, *26*(2), 83–105. https://files.eric.ed.gov/ fulltext/EJ1123994.pdf

Benavides, K. R. (2022). *Leading for sustainability in school- community partnerships*. [Thesis, ACU].

Britt, N., Bates, S., Anderson-Butcher, D., Edwards, R., Noteman, N., Bardy, C., DuMond, L., & Childs, T.M. (2022). University-assisted community schools as partners in neighborhood revitalization efforts. *Child. Sch.*

Bryk, A., & Schneider, B. (2002). *Trust in schools: A course resource for improvement*. Russell Sage.

Cabunilas, A. J. A., Gabutero, A. O., & Baluno, A. B. (2023). Enhanced implementation of community learning center based on the reading level of the learners of San Roque elementary school during pandemic. *AIDE Interdisciplinary Research Journal*, *4*, 51–62. doi:10.56648/aide-irj.v4i1.43

Clary, D. M. (2008). *Literacy learning communities in partnership*, 1-11.

Cleveland, B. (2023). A framework for building schools as community hubs: If it were simpler would it happen everywhere? In B. Cleveland, S. Backhouse, P. Chandler, I. McShane, J. M. Clinton, & C. Newton (Eds.), Schools as community hubs building 'more than a school' for community benefit (p. 11-28). Springer. doi:10.1007/978-981-19-9972-7_3

Cooper, L. Z., & Pace, J. (2004). Early literacy in a collaborative community service project. *Knowledge Quest*, *33*(2).

Cope, B., & Kalantzis, M. (2000). *Multiliteracies: Literacy learning and the design of social futures*. Routledge.

Cruzat, M., Cruzat, A. P., & Javillonar, M. G. (2022). The school and its stakeholders: Partners in building a strong school community. *International Journal of Multidisciplinary Research and Growth Evaluation*, *3*(4), 314–418.

Darling-Hammond, L., Holtzman, D. J., Gatlin, S. J., & Heilig, J. V. (2005). Does teacher preparation matter? Evidence about teacher certification, Teach for America, and teacher effectiveness. *Education Policy Analysis Archives*, *13*(42), 42. doi:10.14507/epaa.v13n42.2005

Dei, G. J., James, I. M., Karumanchery, L. L., James-Wilson, S., & Zine, J. (2000). *Removing the margins: The challenges & possibilities of inclusive schooling*. Canadian Scholars' Press.

Domingue, B. W., Dell, M., Lang, D., Silverman, R., Yeatman, J., & Hough, H. (2022). The effect of COVID on oral reading fluency during the 2020–2021 academic year. *AERA Open*, *8*. Advance online publication. doi:10.1177/23328584221120254

Dorn, E., Hancock, B., Sarakatsannis, J., & Viruleg, E. (2020, June 1). *COVID-19 and student learning in the United States: The hurt could last a lifetime*. Apucis. https://www.apucis.com/frontend-assets/porto/initial-reports/COVID-19- and-student-learning-in-the-United-StatesFINAL.pdf.pagespeed.ce.VHbS948yF4.pdf

Epstein, J. (2011). *School, family, and community partnerships: Preparing educators and improving schools* (2nd ed.). Routledge.

Epstein, J. L., Sanders, M. G., Sheldon, S. B., Simon, B. S., Salinas, K. C., Jansorn, N. R., & Williams, K. J. (2018). *School, family, and community partnerships: Your handbook for action* (4th ed.). Corwin Press.

FitzGerald, A. M., & Quiñones, S. (2018). Working in and with community: Leading for partnerships in a community school. *Leadership and Policy in Schools*, *18*(4), 511–532. doi:10.1080/15700763.2018.1453938

Foster, J. E., & Loven, R. G. (1992). The need and directions for parent involvement in the 90's: Undergraduate perspectives and expectations. *Action in Teacher Education*, *14*(3), 13–18. doi:10.1080/01626620.1992.10463127

Gold, E., Simon, E., & Brown, C. (2002). *Strong neighborhoods, strong schools: The indicators project on education organizing*. Cross City Campaign for Urban School Reform.

Hands, C. M. (2023). School-community collaboration: Insights from two decades of partnership development. In B. Cleveland, S. Backhouse, P. Chandler, I. McShane, J. M. Clinton, & C. Newton (Eds.), Schools as community hubs building 'more than a school' for community benefit (p. 11-28). Springer. doi:10.1007/978-981-19-9972-7_3

Harvard Family Research Project. (2010). *Partnerships for learning: Promising practices in integrating school and out-of-school time program supports*. HFRP. https://www.hfrp.org/publications-resources/browse-our-publications/partn

International Reading Association. (2008). Partnerships for improving literacy in urban schools. *The Reading Teacher*, *61*(8), 678–680.

Jones, C. (2018). SPARK early literacy: Testing the impact of a family–school–community partnership literacy intervention. *School Community Journal*, *28*(2).

Jordan, J. (1998). Constructing school partnerships with families and community groups. http://www.ncrel.or^sdrs/areas/issues/envrnmnt/farnnncmrn/pa400.htm. retrieved.

Joshi, P. (2017). *Collaboration to improve literacy: making learning sustainable in schools [Paper presentation]*. 42nd Association for Teacher Education in Europe (ATEE) *Annual Conference*, Brussels, Belgium.

Keith, N. Z. (1999). Whose community schools? New discourses, old patterns. *Theory into Practice*, *38*(4), 225–234. doi:10.1080/00405849909543858

Kress, G., & van Leeuwen, T. (2001). *Multimodal discourse: The modes and media of contemporary communication*. Bloomsbury.

Lankshear, C., & Knobel, M. (2003). *New literacies: Changing knowledge and classroom learning*. Open University Press.

Lauwo, H., & Gerold Mkulu, D. (2021). Challenges facing community involvement in ensuring quality education in public secondary schools in Meru district, Arusha Region-Tanzania. [IJELS]. *International Journal of English Literature and Social Sciences*, *6*(1), 074. https://journal-repository.theshillonga.com/index.php/ijels/article/view/3021. doi:10.22161/ijels.61.8

Mayger, L. K., & Hochbein, C. D. (2021). Growing connected: Relational trust and social capital in community schools. *Journal of Education for Students Placed at Risk*, *26*(3), 210–235. doi:10.1080/10824669.2020.1824676

Muthoni, K. C. (2015). *The impact of community involvement in public secondary schools management: A case of Machakos County, Kenya* [Masters Dissertation, Kenyatta University]. https://pdfs.semanticscholar.org/ffe8/0734efc2151ac327bb410a7c309b6ff7dbe9.pdf

Myende, P. E. (2018). Creating functional and sustainable school-community partnerships: Lessons from three South African cases. *Educational Management Administration & Leadership*, *47*(6), 1001–1019. doi:10.1177/1741143218781070

Neupane, K., & Dhakal, H. R. (2023). School-community partnership: A model of participatory governance for students' learning improvement. *ISAR Journal of Arts. Humanities and Social Sciences*, *1*(5), 1–9.

Ngobeni, S. T. (2022). Establishing and maintaining school-community partnerships: A challenge for school management teams. *International Journal of Leadership in Education*, 1–26. doi:10.1080/13603124.2022.2117414

OECD. (2019). *Programme for International Student Assessment (PISA) Results from PISA 2018*. OECD. https://www.oecd.org/pisa/publications/PISA2018_CN_PHL.pdf

Pearson, L. C., & Moomaw, W. (2005). The relationship between teacher autonomy and stress, work satisfaction, empowerment, and professionalism. *Educational Research Quarterly*, *29*(1), 38–54.

Prew, M. S. (2012). *Community involvement in school development: Modifying school improvement concepts to the needs of South African township schools*. SAGE Publishers.

Pushor, D. (2007). *Parent engagement: Creating a shared world*. In the Ontario Education Research Symposium [Symposium]. Toronto, Ontario, Canada.

Rowsell, J., & Walsh, M. (2011). Rethinking literacy education in new times: Multimodality, multiliteracies, & new literacies. *Brock Education*, *21*(1), 53–61. doi:10.26522/brocked.v21i1.236

Sanders, M. G. (1999). Schools' program and progress in the national network of partnership schools. *The Journal of Educational Research*, *92*(4), 220–232. doi:10.1080/00220679909597599

Sanders, M. G. (2001). The role of "community" in comprehensive school, family, and community programs. *The Elementary School Journal*, *102*(1), 19–34. doi:10.1086/499691

Sanders, M. G. (2003). Community involvement in schools: From concept to practice. *Education and Urban Society*, *35*(2), 161–180. doi:10.1177/0013124502239390

Sanders, M. G. (2018). Crossing boundaries: A qualitative exploration of relational leadership in three full-service community schools. *Teachers College Record*, *120*(4), 1–36. doi:10.1177/016146811812000403

Sanders, M. G., & Galindo, C. (2014). Communities, schools, and teachers. *Professional Development in Today's Schools*. https://llc.umbc.edu/wp-content/uploads/sites/15/2014/05/2014_Sanders-Galindo1.pdf

Schutz, A. (2006). Home is a prison in the global city: The tragic failure of school-based community engagement strategies. *Review of Educational Research*, *76*(4), 691–743. doi:10.3102/00346543076004691

Shatkin, G., & Gershberg, A. I. (2007). Empowering parents and building communities: The role of school-based councils in educational governance and accountability. *Urban Education*, *42*(6), 582–615. doi:10.1177/0042085907305044

Silbert, P. & Bitso, Constance (2015). Towards functional school libraries: supporting library assistants in under-resourced schools through a university-community-school partnership. *SA Jnl Libs & Info Sci*, *81*(1), 53-62. https://doi:. doi:10.7553/81-1-1553

The 1987 Constitution of the Republic of the Philippines – Article XIV (n.d.). *Education, science and technology, arts, culture and sports*. https://www.officialgazette.gov.ph/constitutions/the-1987-constitution-of-the-republic-of-the-philippines/the-1987-constitution-of-the-republic-of-the-philippines-article-xiv/

The National Council of Teachers of English. (2019). *Definition of literacy in a digital age*. NCTE. https://ncte.org/statement/nctes-definition-literacy-digital-age/

The World Bank. (2022). *70% of 10-year-olds now in learning poverty, unable to read and understand a simple text*. World Bank. https://www.worldbank.org/en/news/press-release/2022/06/23/70-of-10-year-olds-now-in-learning-poverty-unable-to-read-and-understand-a-simple-text

Valli, L., Stefanski, A., & Jacobson, R. (2014). *School-community partnerships: A typology for guiding systemic educational reform. Policy Brief.* College of Education. University of Maryland.

Willingham, D. T. (2006). The effectiveness of brief instruction in reading comprehension strategies. *American Educator*, (Winter), 39–45.

Yunas, M., Dad, R., Shakoor, A., & Wahid, F. (2021). Dimensions of school community relationship: Issues and concerns. *Psychology and Education*, *58*(4), 4587–4591. http://psychologyandeducation.net/pae/index.php/pae/article/view/5815/4990

Zuckerman, S. J. (2022). Beyond the school walls: Collective impact in micropolitan school- community partnerships. *Peabody Journal of Education*, *97*(1), 1–14. doi: 10.1080/0161956X.2022.2026724

Chapter 3
Civic Literacy and Engagement

M. Serhat Semercioglu
Gumushane University, Turkey

Melek Baba Öztürk
Faculty of Education, Ondokuz Mayis University, Turkey

ABSTRACT

This section elaborates on the definition, significance, and promotion strategies of civic literacy. The implementation of civic literacy within the context of life skills and social studies courses is extensively discussed, with a focus on the case of Turkey. Emphasizing the importance of integrating the life skills and social studies curriculum in fostering civic literacy, the challenges encountered in practice are also thoroughly examined. Furthermore, the discourse extends to the integration of civic literacy into technology, addressing both the challenges and advantages that citizens may encounter or experience. The role of civic literacy within widely-used social media applications, prevalent in today's technological era, is highlighted. Additionally, the technical application of civic literacy, exemplified by e-government initiatives, is scrutinized through various global instances. The concluding section reflects on the future of civic literacy and civic engagement.

INTRODUCTION

We are witnessing an era characterized by dizzying advancements in information, communication, and transportation technologies, which have fundamentally transformed communication and interaction networks. The developments we witness in this era trigger numerous individual, societal, and global changes, leading to significant consequences. The 21st century, considered the dawn of the digital age,

DOI: 10.4018/979-8-3693-1777-8.ch003

markedly differs from the previous century in terms of lifestyle, work patterns, and learning modalities and continues to evolve distinctively with each passing day (Beers, 2011; Voogt & Roblin, 2012). As a consequence of this differentiation, the requisites of both civilian life and professional spheres are evolving, necessitating individuals to acquire altered qualities. Our contemporary age now demands individuals to acquire new knowledge and skills that facilitate adaptation to the complex and rapidly changing nature of the 21st century and attain diverse literacies.

Voogt and Roblin (2012) define 21st-century skills as the adaptable cognitive and affective endowments enabling individuals to navigate the demands and dynamics of the current era, thereby contributing meaningfully to the flourishing of a knowledge society as informed and engaged citizens. In recognition of these skills' critical role in individual and societal success, states, driven by a vested interest in the educational, professional, and personal well-being of their citizens, have actively collaborated with diverse stakeholders, including civil society organizations, education experts, and business representatives. This collaborative effort has yielded a plethora of skill frameworks and standards outlining the essential qualities individuals require for success in the 21st century (Çiftçi, Sağlam, & Yayla, 2021).

A prominent outcome of the collaboration between the government of the United States and leading companies in the business and economic spheres, such as Apple and Microsoft, among others, under the initiative known as the "21st Century Learning Partnership," is the emergence of the "21st Century Learning Frameworks." This framework stands out as a cornerstone, delineating the knowledge, skills, expertise, and competencies requisite for students to thrive in civilian and professional domains (Gelen, 2017). Indeed, civil literacy, the subject of this section, constitutes one of the literacy types encapsulated within this framework, emerging under the overarching themes of the 21st century.

Civic literacy empowers individuals to cultivate a repertoire of knowledge, skills, understandings, attitudes, and behaviors pertaining to responsible citizenship. This enables their meaningful participation in the life of their communities, fostering social integration and contributing to societal progress within the legal and political frameworks (Kapusızoğlu, 2021). This genre of literacy is considered vital for the healthy functioning of democratic societies as it equips individuals with the knowledge and skills necessary to actively engage in civil and political processes both within their society and across others (Çakmak & Taşkıran, 2020). However, recent studies indicate a noticeable decline in civil and political participation, particularly among younger generations, and a tangible decrease in the level of civil literacy (Mulyono, Affandi, Suryadi & Darmawan, 2022; Hylton, 2015; Wilson, 2002). The decline in civil and political participation exacerbates individuals' distrust in democratic processes, thereby undermining societal tolerance. This situation is of significant concern for states and governments that embrace democratic forms of governance.

Consequently, democratic societies must implement preventive measures and incorporate efforts to enhance individuals' civil literacy. Thus, within the framework of this understanding, the present section initially focuses on defining the concept of civil literacy, its significance, and its components. Subsequently, emphasis is placed on the developmental trajectory of civil literacy and the developments influencing this process, accompanied by practical examples from Turkey and worldwide.

Civic Literacy: Definition and Importance

Many scholars have expressed their views on civic literacy, how it emerged, and its scope and components as a type of literacy that needs to be developed. For instance, according to McCabe and Kennedy (2014), civic literacy signifies an understanding that provides information about the history, constitution, and governmental structures of the United States. Cheng (1996), on the other hand, assumes that civic literacy is a combination of cultural, moral, political, and legal literacy, defining the concept in terms of behaviors, habits, norms, and knowledge associated with these domains (Yao, Cai & Qubibi, 2022). In the traditional sense, *civic literacy* can be defined as individuals possessing knowledge and awareness of citizenship-related issues and their rights and responsibilities as citizens. However, this expression reflects a shallow and contentious understanding of the nature of the concept. This is because civic literacy, fundamentally, is an approach that focuses on the importance of participation, requiring more than being an informed and responsible voter; it involves acquiring knowledge, knowing how to acquire knowledge, understanding the consequences of citizenship decisions, and actively participating in civil life.

Indeed, the "21st Century Learning Partnership" defines civic literacy as follows:

- Actively participating in civil life by understanding how to acquire knowledge and understand government processes,
- Applying the rights and responsibilities of citizenship in a broad context and perspective extending from local to global,
- Facilitating an understanding of the local and global impacts of civic decisions as a type of literacy (Battelle for Kids, 2019).

Civic literacy, which plays a key role in constructing democratic societies, encompasses information that assists individuals in actively and successfully participating in societal life (Flornes, 2017). This information entails more than being a responsible voter; it involves being effective in accessing and developing knowledge, understanding political issues and processes, knowing how to exercise one's rights as a citizen, and comprehending how to fulfill one's responsibilities (Nuryadi & Widiatmaka, 2023).

Civic literacy refers to a developmental process concerning the application of general literacy skills to the duties of citizenship and active community membership, at the heart of which individuals engage in the affairs of their society, creating fair and healthy environments, and making efforts toward sustainability (Wilson, 2002). According to Barber (1993), civic literacy is a fundamental skill that enables us to live in a civil society. This skill encompasses individuals' competence in participating in democratic societies, their ability to think critically and act through negotiation in a pluralistic world, and their willingness to empathetically engage with others in relationships despite conflicts of interest.

Having civic literacy contributes significantly to individuals both personally and educationally. The Urban Agenda (date unknown) outlines these contributions as follows:

1. Civic literacy provides individuals with an awareness of citizenship and societal issues.
2. It initiates a student communication and solidarity process that transcends racial, economic, regional, and religious differences.
3. It promotes curiosity about and participation in multicultural exchanges and global issues.
4. It creates an environment for democratic participation in multicultural settings.
5. It offers an interesting and enjoyable way to engage students in social studies classes.
6. It fosters discussion on norms and values even in a scientific/technological society.
7. It enhances students' conflict resolution and peer mediation skills.

In summary, civic literacy socially enhances individual welfare and contributes to a better and more democratic society (Yao, Cai & Qubibi, 2022). Civic literacy is closely related to political and legal literacy, particularly in terms of civic engagement (Yao, Cai & Qubibi, 2022). This is because civic literacy not only provides knowledge about political and legal matters but also encourages action in the usage and protection of rights (Kapusızoğlu, 2021). Therefore, it would be appropriate to review these concepts in order to better elucidate civic literacy.

As highlighted by Yao, Cai & Qubibi (2022), the most prominent concept emphasized in definitions of civic literacy is civic engagement. Civic engagement encompasses individuals' official and unofficial participation in political and civil institutions, including activities such as voluntary work, signature campaigns, voting, protesting against a company or organization, and attending a political rally (Akın, Çalışkan & Engin-Demir, 2016; Hylton, 2018; Spradley, 2021).

Civil engagement primarily pertains to serving the community and engaging in collective actions with other individuals in society. It is associated with active citizenship, encompassing all activities undertaken individually or collectively by individuals in this regard (Adler & Goggin, 2005). These activities may include solving societal issues, active membership in a group or association, regular voting, persuasion of others, contacting authorities, protesting against an individual, institution, or event, organizing and conducting email or written signature campaigns, boycotting, carrying stickers, badges, or placards, participating in campaigns, reading newspapers, group memberships, enabling others to voice their opinions, participating in community service projects, engaging in political processes, and working in volunteer organizations (Akın et al., 2016).

The purpose of civil engagement is to contribute to the development and sustainability of democracy, particularly in multicultural societies, by upholding ideals such as justice and equality (Einfeld & Collins, 2008). Additionally, civil engagement aims to foster the development of an inclusive society, thereby promoting the emergence of a more pluralistic structure in addressing public issues (İpat, 2015). According to Hylton (2018), being ready for participatory citizenship requires literacy in citizenship. Indeed, studies corroborate his view by demonstrating a dynamic, open-to-development, and mutually influential relationship between civic engagement and citizenship literacy (Galston, 2001; Spradley, 2021).

Another concept associated with civic literacy is political literacy. In its simplest form, political literacy refers to knowing political issues (Avcı & Geçit, 2022). Denver & Hands (1990) define political literacy as the knowledge individuals need to fulfill their roles as effective citizens of political processes and issues (Cassel & Lo, 1997). Bochel (2009), in his work titled "Political Literacy," characterizes political literacy as a behavioral phenomenon that involves not only possessing political knowledge, which enables individuals to recognize, identify, and analyze political institutions but also understanding and fulfilling political rights and responsibilities. Bochel's definition distinguishes itself from other definitions in the literature by emphasizing that political literacy requires not only knowledge but also the skills and values related to political issues and processes and the ability to translate them into action. Political literacy is not fundamentally a new concept or phenomenon. As Dağ and Koçer (2019) also noted, it is a form of literacy that builds upon the acquisition of literacy skills, requiring individuals to possess various specific abilities such as being knowledgeable about where and how political decisions are made, being involved, being familiar with different political ideas, developing a set of political values, and having the necessary skills and confidence to apply them.

Legal literacy is another concept emphasized in the literature concerning civic literacy. Legal literacy, also known as legal literacy, entails knowing legal rules, understanding legal concepts and processes, making inferences, and being able to implement legal rules. Legal literacy was initially conceived as a form of literacy relevant only to individuals educated in law. However, over time, with the recognition of the role of law in regulating social life, the concept has evolved, taking on a broader meaning that encompasses all individuals (Tokdemir & Beldağ, 2019). Being legally literate is essential for ensuring social justice and enabling people to live together in dignity (Changmai, 2020).

In conclusion, civic literacy is closely related to civic engagement, requiring individuals to acquire knowledge, skills, attitudes, and values related to citizenship, thus encompassing both political and legal literacy. This form of literacy is paramount, especially in developing countries such as Turkey, for the construction, strengthening, and sustainability of democracy. Indeed, the results of the "Democracy Index" study conducted by an international organization in its 2022 report confirm this notion. According to this report, Turkey ranks 103rd out of 167 countries in the democracy ranking. Furthermore, evaluations conducted in five different categories, namely "electoral process and pluralism, functioning of government, political participation, political culture, and civil liberties," reveal Turkey's lowest score of 2.06 in the civil liberties category. Following this category, Turkey received scores of 3.50 for the electoral process and pluralism, 5.00 for the functioning of the government, and 5.56 for political participation. The highest score, 5.63, belongs to the political culture category (Economist İntelligence Unit, 2023). These statistics highlight not only the state of democracy but also the state of civic literacy in Turkey.

Key Components of Civic Literacy

In contemporary society, it is imperative to cultivate individuals who possess an acute awareness of their environment, are adept at devising remedies for prevailing issues, and are well-versed in their rights and obligations as citizens. In the quest for active citizenship, individuals' requisite education and developmental processes are imparted through civic literacy. Reflecting on the historical trajectory of civic participation or literacy paradigms, the concept was initially confined to "voting" in the 1940s. However, following the post-World War II surge in prosperity in the Western world, it is discernible that these concepts underwent significant evolution in the early 2000s.

The concept of "civility within society," first coined by Locke in 1690, was not initially associated with democracy at the beginning of modern society. However, today, it is closely linked with democracy. In this context, societal civility is considered the most significant means of liberating society from authoritarian or military regimes and transitioning to democracy. Civil literacy supports individuals in exhibiting the distinct behaviors necessary for democratic living.

The concept of "civil" is commonly juxtaposed with "political knowledge" and traditionally connotes engagement in societal affairs (Dahlgren, 2013). Furthermore, civility encompasses a spectrum of community service endeavors, ranging from charitable donations to volunteering, aimed at aiding members of society (Arthur et al., 2017). The emergence of civil literacy is positioned as an impetus for civic engagement, encompassing elements of social participation and service alongside early political involvement (Arthur et al., 2017; Dahlgren, 2013; McLoughlin, 2023). Delivering civil education across all age groups is pivotal in nurturing the attitudes and competencies requisite for civil literacy and active citizenship (Hauge & Rowsell, 2020).

Civil literacy's foundation is formed by political knowledge, media literacy, volunteering, civic engagement, and voting. The focal point of all these phenomena is to ensure full public participation in democracy. First, there is a positive linear relationship between civil literacy and political knowledge (Eveland & Hively, 2009). Those more knowledgeable about politics engage in more intense civic participation than those less knowledgeable. Thus, there is also a positive linear relationship between political knowledge, civil literacy, and civic participation (Zúñiga & Diehl, 2019). Knowing where, when, and how to vote is possible with some basic political knowledge. Ultimately, all these phenomena are associated with the learning of civil literacy.

Assessing and Measuring Civic Literacy

There is a considerable lack of consensus on the best methods to measure the literacy of a scientific phenomenon. The debates have primarily occurred at a conceptual level, with these concepts being minimally or not empirically tested (Rundgren et al., 2010). At this juncture, there is a scarcity of studies that operationalize the criterion for civic literacy and assess civic literacy (McLoughlin, 2023). Upon reviewing the literature, the levels of civic literacy among children under 17 years of age in formal education settings were determined by examining the portfolio works they had prepared throughout the year. Teachers can use portfolios to "demonstrate the student's educational development over a specific period for defined learning objectives." By creating these portfolios, students demonstrate how they actively engage in the public policy process and share their suggestions with local, regional, and national authorities, which represents another form of civic participation (Bentahar & O'Brian, 2019; Brookhart & Nitko, 2008; Vontz et al., 2000).

In another study, the concept of civic literacy was measured using thought experiments with both adults and students. Thought experiments prompt students to contemplate enduring social issues using their knowledge and imagination. By encouraging students to draw connections between past experiences and contemporary issues, thought experiments underscore the significance of social studies (Zarnowski, 2009).

Apart from all these different measurement tools, the United States State's Center for Information and Research on Civic Learning and Engagement has developed a "civic literacy measurement tool" that it has used for many years. While there are still some disagreements about civic literacy, there is consensus within this measurement tool on measuring democratic processes and basic citizenship knowledge (Hylton, 2015). This scale also measures the ability to understand current policy issues and critically analyze them (Lyons et al., 2012).

Civic Literacy and Traditional Forms of Civic Participation in Society

In the 1990s, renewed interest in political socialization and, more broadly, civic engagement prompted researchers to examine the understanding of political realities. Many globally conducted studies have observed a notable need for more politically meaningful knowledge among citizens (Dudley & Gitelson, 2010). In this regard, civic literacy promotes the endorsement of democratic values and encourages participation in civil and political issues, such as voting and being informed about political parties. The more knowledge we have about the functioning of states, the greater the likelihood of supporting the fundamental values of democratic self-governance (Coley & Sum, 2012). Conversely, the absence of civic literacy knowledge leads to limited citizen participation, especially in fundamental areas such as voting and volunteering (Glaston, 2004).

At the core of civic literacy lie fundamental rights and freedoms such as social, political, and cultural rights, freedom of thought, freedom of speech, equality, and the ability to vote for the desired political party, enabling individuals to engage consciously in society and participate positively and effectively (Faiz, 2018). Voting is a cultural phenomenon. Many citizens encourage civic participation by exercising their right to vote. Cultural norms are more easily implemented when many people share the same values (Campbell, 2010). A citizen's political participation is not limited to voting alone. In addition, an informed voter actively engages in the governance of the state (Nar, 2021).

One of the significant forms of civic participation in civic literacy is volunteer work. Volunteering is a universal phenomenon encountered in various regions of the world, known by different names but prevalent everywhere. It can be performed by anyone, regardless of religion, language, race, gender, age, or geographical location, at any desired time and place (Arslan, 2018). Individuals engaged in volunteer activities contribute to projects benefiting their communities, thus fostering civic participation, and derive personal benefits in terms of professional development (Balaban & İnce, 2015).

The Development Process of Civic Literacy: When and How Should Training Be Provided?

When we acknowledge that civic literacy is fundamental to democracy, the question arises of when and how it should be instilled. The answer to this question is extremely valuable in terms of understanding the development process of civic literacy and developing effective practices. While researchers have developed various explanations and understandings regarding the definition and components of civic literacy, there is a consensus on one point: the necessity of early education. According to Fudge & Skipworth (2017), efforts and initiatives undertaken from the early stages of life are crucial for fostering civic literacy, which has significant implications for future political engagement and interaction processes. Therefore, if a child has not learned how the political process operates or how to engage in it, it is unlikely that they will be politically effective as adults. Therefore, it is essential to incorporate practices and initiatives that promote and enhance civic literacy in educational settings and daily life from an early age.

Spradley (2021) suggests that civic literacy is a form of education in classrooms, places of worship, social networks, organizations, and campaigns. While many individuals and institutions share responsibility for delivering this education, the most crucial ones are families and schools. According to Galston (2004), families and schools are fundamental agents of socialization in developing political knowledge and subsequent attitudes in children. Children can grasp the importance of voting by witnessing and listening to their parents' discussions about the electoral process, accompanying their families to the polls during elections, or participating in social responsibility projects, volunteer work, or community service projects with their families, thus understanding the significance of cooperation and solidarity, comprehending social issues better, and developing social sensitivities. Such examples provide children with knowledge about how the political system operates while laying the groundwork for understanding the importance of participation (Fudge & Skipworth, 2017). However, not every family may possess the awareness or competence to foster such awareness and development in their children. In such cases, schools seize the opportunity to fill this gap and assume the responsibility of enhancing children's civic literacy.

According to Wilson (2002), adopting an ecological perspective is highly beneficial and comprehensive in understanding the development process of adult civil literacy skills. An ecological perspective provides a fruitful pathway to comprehend the individuals, systems, and interactions that influence the development of civil literacy values. Figure 1. illustrates the developmental process of civil literacy in adults through the lens of this perspective.

From an ecological perspective, all aspects of human growth and development, including civil literacy, result from the interactions among individuals and the systems they are part of. Therefore, individuals who influence one's growth and development are equally responsible for developing civil literacy skills, among others. Discussions regarding civil literacy skills and values in informal learning environments with these influential individuals positively contribute to the developmental process of civil literacy (Wilson, 2002).

Civic Literacy Education in Schools: The Case of Turkey

Schools endeavor to instill knowledge, skills, and values related to citizenship in children who are future adults through structured lessons within a specific curriculum and extracurricular activities, social clubs, and student councils. Activities such as

Figure 1. An ecological view of civic literacy development in adults

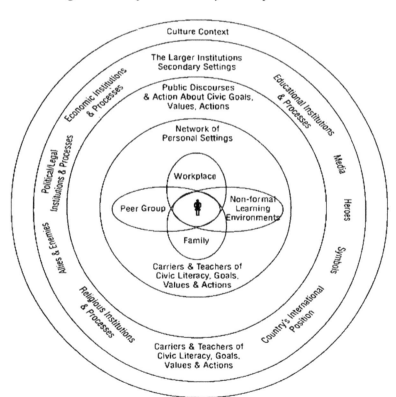

publishing newspapers, magazines, and yearbooks, organizing fairs and fundraising campaigns, and conducting election events and field trips are among the initiatives schools undertake to promote civic literacy. These efforts promote and enhance civic literacy by providing students with concrete, firsthand experiences. However, the fact that implementing these activities depends entirely on schools is detached from a standardized program and is associated with schools taking initiatives, which raises concerns about equal opportunities. From this perspective, lessons that provide a common framework for all students, especially courses such as Human Rights, Citizenship and Democracy, and Life Skills and Social Studies, play the most significant role in enhancing students' civic literacy. These courses stand out from others in their role in imparting citizenship knowledge, skills, and values.

The course on Human Rights, Citizenship, and Democracy emerged due to increasing interest in modern citizenship education and is entirely based on civic literacy. Through this course:

- Embracing humanitarian values,
- Discovering the privileges of being a child in terms of rights, freedoms, and responsibilities,
- Assuming responsibility for the use of rights and freedoms,
- Upholding justice and equality for the development of human rights and democratic culture,
- Participating in democratic decision-making processes based on cooperation and knowledge,
- Seeking consensus in solving issues related to coexistence,
- Supporting the protection and enhancement of rights and freedoms by adhering to rules,
- Embracing and acting by active citizenship,
- Assuming responsibility for the improvement and development of living conditions,
- Being aware of the contributions of the Republic and its values to developments in human rights, citizenship, and democracy aims to educate individuals who exhibit these characteristics (MEB, 2018).

The courses of "Life Skills" and "Social Studies," on the other hand, incorporate citizenship topics within distinct learning domains and achievements, differing from the course on Human Rights, Citizenship, and Democracy. Within the various dimensions of the curricula for these courses (competency frameworks, specific purposes, skills, and achievements), traces of civic literacy are discernible. Detailed relationships between civic literacy and curriculum programs are illustrated in Table 1 (MEB 2018b; MEB, 2018c).

As seen in Table 1, it is possible to observe various levels of civic literacy in the competency frameworks, specific purposes, skills, and achievements of the Life Knowledge and Social Studies curriculum programs. While the competency

Table 1. Dimensions related to civic literacy in the life skills and social studies curriculum

Associated Programme Dimension	Life Skills Curriculum (Primary School in Turkey)	Social Studies Curriculum (Primary School in Turkey)
Qualification Frameworks	Social and civic competences	
Special Purposes	• Acquires fundamental values of family and society. • Internalizes national, spiritual, and humane values into lived experiences. • Develops skills for social participation. • Demonstrates love for one's country and willingness to preserve its historical and cultural heritage.	• To be raised as citizens who love their country and nation, aware of their rights, utilizing them, fulfilling their responsibilities, and possessing a sense of national consciousness, • Understanding that legal rules are binding for everyone, and that all individuals and institutions are equal before the law, • Being able to utilize basic communication skills and the fundamental concepts and methods of social sciences to regulate social relations and resolve encountered problems, • Believing in the importance of participation and expressing opinions for the resolution of personal and societal issues, • Demonstrating sensitivity to issues concerning their country and the world.
Skill(s)	Decision-making, obeying rules, social participation	Critical thinking, legal literacy, decision making, self-control, political literacy, problem solving, social participation
Learning outcomes	• Participates in decision-making processes related to the class. • Engages in decision-making processes within the family. • Respects the ways of life and customs of people from different cultures living in our country. • Shows willingness to participate in social assistance and solidarity efforts at school. • Expresses desires and needs regarding school through democratic means. • Explains the governance structure of our country. • Explains the relationship between the development of the country and fulfilling one's own duties and responsibilities. • Participates in social responsibility projects aimed at addressing the problems of people from different cultures living in our country.	• Provides examples of the rights they possess as children. • Assumes responsibility for their words and actions in family and school life. • Suggests educational and social activities deemed necessary in school life. • Explains the relationship between the independence of their country and individual freedom.

frameworks are common for both educational programs, they aim to develop civic literacy by targeting social and citizenship-related competencies. Social competencies encompass personal, interpersonal, and intercultural skills, seeking individuals to engage in diverse work and societal environments effectively. On the other hand, citizenship competencies equip individuals with the knowledge of social and political concepts and structures, as well as the determination for democratic and active participation, enabling them to fully engage in civil life (MEB, 2018b; MEB, 2018c).

Civic Literacy Within the Context of Technological Advancements

In recent years, thanks to technological advancements, many individuals can perform numerous transactions they desire to accomplish as 'digital citizens' in digital environments. Especially with the global pandemic we have been experiencing, individuals have learned to fulfill their needs without leaving their homes, which has increased both the number of transactions conducted in digital environments and the significance of digital citizenship literacy (Ayaz, 2021). As a natural consequence of the increased pace of technology adoption and usage, the scope of technology's use in routine tasks will also broaden (Bekar & Sağlam, 2023). A study supports this phenomenon: Global internet usage was 3.48 billion people in 2017 and reached 5.6 billion people in 2023 (Ourworldindata, 2023).

The onset of the Covid-19 pandemic in 2019 brought about a significant social transformation, necessitating individuals of all ages to conduct their civic affairs in digital realms. Alongside civic transactions, the social necessity of family and friend gatherings has also transitioned to digital platforms (Buchholz et al., 2020). Before this period, principles for living in an interconnected digital world and practicing digital citizenship in secure, legal, and ethical manners had already been delineated in the United States. Some of these principles are enumerated below (Brooks-Young, 2016):

Empowered Learner (1b): Students construct social networks, customizing these networks to support learning environments and processes.

Digital Citizen (2b): Students engage in online social interactions or digital citizenship transactions using networked devices, exhibiting positive, safe, legal, and ethical behaviors.

Global Collaborator (7b): Students utilize collaborative technologies to work with others, including peers, experts, or community members, to examine problems and issues from multiple perspectives.

Technological advancements have facilitated the teaching of citizenship transactions, which are integral to civic literacy. Many digital platforms offer free training on this subject. Furthermore, through digital environments, individuals can learn about the norms and laws of their own society and the concepts of global citizenship (Prabhakar, 2022). Therefore, the expectations from a good citizen now extend beyond learning civil behaviors specific to one's own geography; it has become crucial to learn the requirements of global citizenship through digital platforms as well (Buchholz et al., 2020).

The Perspective of Different Generations Using Digital Media on Digital Citizenship

The awareness of citizens regarding civil engagement, rights, and digital technologies, as well as their direct capacity to utilize them, mainly influences the "intergenerational gap." This gap directly impacts the minimal adaptation to digital tools and the digital environment (Uğurlu, 2019). It can be argued that interruptions in citizenship affairs may be observed due to insufficient digital literacy among middle adulthood and older individuals.

Since the early 2000s, Prensky has significantly influenced various aspects of the digital world by introducing the metaphors "digital natives" and "digital immigrants. The generation that communicates through the internet, virtual games, and mobile devices, translating them into a digital language, is called 'digital natives.' In contrast, the older generation born before 1980, who find themselves alien to the world surrounded by digital technologies, is termed 'digital immigrants' (Prensky, 2001). Digital immigrants are described as attempting to learn the language of digital technologies while, due to their structures, also using this digital technology's language with an accent because of their past habits. For instance, the scenario where digital immigrants conceptualize printing and correcting a document instead of editing it directly on the screen as a manifestation of the 'digital immigrant accent' is noteworthy (Ayaz, 2021).

In recent years, digital natives have increasingly relied on digital environments for various aspects of their lives, including work and transactions. Moreover, social networks on digital platforms have become focal points for individuals to create social environments and for conducting educational, cultural, and artistic activities. In many countries, government institutions disseminate information to citizens through social networks (Ham et al., 2019). Particularly, government agencies aiming to reach digital natives enhance their presence on social media platforms to engage with citizens closely and ensure their participation. It is evident globally that many public institutions have both websites and social media accounts, serving as a bridge for communication with citizens (Yaşar & Altincik, 2018).

The increasing prevalence of digital media in recent years has led to digitizing citizenship procedures, thereby fostering awareness. It has been observed that individuals, particularly digital natives who actively engage with social media and were born into the era of digital technologies, seamlessly utilize digital platforms for citizenship transactions. Conversely, a prominent characteristic of digital immigrants is their reluctance to use e-government applications. Nevertheless, recent findings indicate that digital immigrants have increasingly utilized digital applications for entertainment, socializing, videos, and gaming. (Yurttadur & Süzen, 2016; Talay, 2018; Özbek & Karaarslan, 2020). However, it has been determined that digital immigrants have increasingly used digital applications for entertainment, socializing, video, and gaming purposes in recent years (Karabulut, 2015; Özbek & Karaarslan, 2020).

As a result of the metaphors of digital immigration or digital nativism, there is a reality emerging, particularly in recent years, where individuals spend more time on the internet and begin to identify themselves with the online platforms they use. This brings forth the concept of "digital citizenship" (Kerimoğlu & Keleşoğlu, 2023). Digital citizenship is a concept that enables citizens to understand the new skills, attitudes, and behaviors arising from social transformations and the development of social media. A qualified citizen must be able to adapt to the changing social order. In the context of citizenship reshaped by technology and the cultivation of future digital citizens, it should not be forgotten that the most significant digital resource lies within digital media tools (Kurt & Odabaşı, 2021). Individuals of all ages who use digital media now access more abundant and easily accessible information from social media innovations in societal, public, cultural, and political dimensions. Furthermore, it should be remembered that new media opportunities carry the potential to foster pluralism, participation, public space, digital citizenship, and digital activism, thereby contributing to the formation of a democratic society (Aydoğan Boschele, 2021).

The Case of Digital Citizenship in Turkey: E-Government (www.turkiye.gov.tr)

The necessity of coexistence prompts the state to generate realistic solutions and provide services to meet the needs and desires of its citizens. In line with this responsibility, the Republic of Turkey has introduced e-government (www. turkiye.gov.tr), an electronic platform designed to enable its citizens (users) to access government services swiftly (24/7), securely and seamlessly, as well as to access numerous educational contents free of charge (Yıldırım Kaptan, 2023). The e-government application, first emerging in the United States in the 1990s, was introduced as a project aimed at saving costs in public services during 1993-1998 (with a target of $108 billion in savings). Following the success observed in the United States, Turkey, like other countries, embarked on similar initiatives (Güler & Döventaş, 2009).

E-Government provides digital citizenship services and free software, design, career, and personal development training for adults through the platform. Furthermore, fundamental coding, essential artificial intelligence, safe internet usage, basic citizenship knowledge, global citizenship, and similar educational programs are also provided free of charge for children.

E-Government has strengthened the relationship between the government and its citizens. Long-standing bureaucratic challenges have been overcome, facilitating access to information and mitigating time wastage in governmental affairs. The philosophy behind E-Government, being communication-centric, has fostered interaction between the public and private spheres. Furthermore, the application has reinforced the values of digital citizenship, such as information access, increasing individual participation, and sharing, which are inherent to democracy. For instance, CIMER (Digital President Communication Center) is a significant project initiated in 2006 as an electronic public service tool through which individuals from all parts of Turkey can exercise their rights to petition and access information. CIMER, a rapid and efficient system through which citizens can easily convey any requests, complaints, or opinions regarding governance, is an indispensable necessity for the proliferation of democracy. Citizens wishing to make electronic applications can do so via "https://www.cimer.gov.tr/" or the e-government system.

Studies on the impact of e-government applications in Turkey suggest that citizens are generally satisfied with the services provided through e-government platforms. However, it has been observed that participants are only partially aware of all e-government services (Boyalı, 2023; Can, 2020; Duman & Aktel, 2021; Yılmaz, 2019). Despite the apparent effectiveness of digital citizenship initiatives in Turkey, the country ranks 53rd in the development index of e-government applications on a global scale. Similarly, in terms of citizen participation in digital citizenship initiatives, Turkey ranks 37th in the same survey (UN, 2018). To attain higher rankings in this development index, it is perceived that specific software and educational measures need to be implemented at the national level.

Other Country Examples in Digital Citizenship (E-Government)

With advancements in technology and telecommunications, numerous countries worldwide have integrated e-government applications into their administrative frameworks. In other words, technological developments enhance and transform the public services governmental entities offer citizens. Through e-government initiatives implemented by countries, citizens actively participate in governance processes (Bincan, 2020). One of the European Union's (EU) initial concrete steps in this domain was the adoption of the "e-Europe" 2002 Action Plan during the Feira Summit on June 19-20, 2000. Fifteen countries from Central and Eastern

Europe signed this action plan. One of the key provisions of this action plan was the "Electronic government: Access to public services electronically" (Information and Communication Technologies Department, 2024). Only Bulgaria and Romania had active e-government applications at the time of its signing. However, the "e-Europe" initiative is actively utilized in all EU member states today.

In the United States, government affairs among the 50 states are conducted through the "state portal." Many citizenship transactions are processed through these state portals. Furthermore, the "Access America" e-government application, which consolidates all public services online under one roof, has been used since 1993 (Paşaoğlu, 2017).

In Malaysia, the implementation of e-government occurred through the "Vision 2020" Project, enabling access to all online government agencies via the Central Government Portal and linking Malaysia's health services through the "Medical Subject Headings (MCSL)" (Ministry of Communication and Multimedia Malaysia, 2020).

In Japan, the Japanese government unveiled the e-Japan plan to the public on January 21, 2001. By the end of the 2003 fiscal year, Japan successfully eliminated paper-based transactions in all administrative affairs. Singapore established its e-government infrastructure in the late 1990s, consolidating all public services under one roof for citizens and businesses alike.

African countries must catch up in e-government applications due to difficulties accessing the internet and local telephone connections. Some e-government initiatives are underway in African countries. Following Ghana, Somalia has provided its citizens with web access. However, the country's inadequate infrastructure, like in other African nations, impedes the development of e-government initiatives.

Positive and Negative Aspects of Civic Engagement in the Digital World

In recent years, there has been extensive global discourse surrounding the impacts of technology on human rights and civil engagement. Technology, at the forefront of these discussions, is progressively digitizing every aspect of our lives, transforming all objects surrounding us into elements of a digital network. Advanced technologies such as artificial intelligence, machine learning, deep learning, and data analytics, serving as tools across various domains, from social policy to education, civil engagement to migration management, are facilitating the transition from the physical world to a more digitized reality (Niezen, 2020).

Digital tools can occasionally influence civic engagement both positively and negatively. When assessing the situation from a positive perspective, it is observed that many citizens can now conduct their transactions remotely thanks to the digital tools available today. The digital world is now considered a public domain. Regardless of their location, citizens can contribute to governance thanks to the internet, even if they reside in the remotest parts of a country. Many countries worldwide are considering moving elections to digital platforms, while efforts to transition to digital governance continue in some countries to develop planned economies.

In some countries today, the decision-making process in citizenship procedures can be prolonged due to the implementation of traditional methods, which aim to ensure the participation of as many individuals as possible and/or to await the opinions of committees or sub-commissions that may influence the decision-making process. This delay stems from the cumbersome structure inherent in traditional methods. However, this sluggishness is giving way to speed with the digitization of civic engagement. In this context, the adaptation of citizen engagement to digital transformation represents one of the positive impacts of the digital world on formal bureaucracy.

Similarly, attitudes of skepticism or distrust towards digitalization directly impact digitalized civil engagement. As the number of citizens exhibiting skepticism or distrust increases, the digital transformation process of civil engagement is adversely affected. At this juncture, the tendency of individuals to adhere to their habits and maintain traditional methods stands as a primary risk factor hindering digital development (Özen et al., 2021). Furthermore, due to digital media's manipulative and disinformation aspects, information within social media platforms can intentionally mislead individuals (Aydoğan Boschele, 2021). Moreover, in specific authoritarian regimes, criticisms of governmental actions made by citizens through digital media channels can lead to individuals being more easily subjected to legal investigations.

CONCLUSION

While it is evident that the civic literacy experiences and knowledge of any citizen residing in any country would encourage civic engagement, more is needed to know about the type of civic education and who it can encourage to participate. Considering the potential for young people to integrate their voices and actions as civic literates into their daily lives, it is essential to recognize the specific qualities of effective citizenship education programming and pedagogy. In conclusion, our aim in this section has been to provide a perspective on civic literacy. Especially in the new world order post-COVID-19 pandemic, intertwined with civic literacy, civic engagement, and democracy remain crucial. Furthermore, primarily upon literature review, more attention and effort should be directed towards children, young people, and socio-culturally disadvantaged citizens, the groups that should predominantly feature within the concept of civic literacy and deserve more attention and focus.

Civic literacy has the potential to eliminate societal marginalization, dissolve structural barriers within states, and empower marginalized citizens to effectively participate in governance by understanding their rights. Primarily, through educational endeavors conducted with a critical consciousness, civic engagement, democracy, rights and freedoms, and concepts of justice, we will attain a different dimension. While it is possible to observe increasing polarization among voters in various countries during recent months, it would not be far-fetched to suggest that civic literacy could mitigate this polarization.

In the future, promising endeavors concerning civic literacy are anticipated. For instance, pedagogical approaches aimed at refugees acquiring the essential information required by citizens of the host country as they endeavor to adapt, educational initiatives enabling marginalized youth to receive civic education, strategies aimed at bridging the civic participation gap, and efforts addressing the intergenerational digital knowledge gap's impact on civic literacy are foreseen. Moreover, it is believed that endeavors will increase to prevent escalating political polarization in countries.

At the same time, it is possible to assert that digital citizenship and e-government applications rapidly evolve worldwide, leading to the digitization of governmental affairs. Furthermore, utilizing these applications provides both governmental institutions and citizens with time and financial savings. However, when executing certain digital services, it may be necessary to strengthen databases and increase the number of existing servers to address system congestion and extended waiting times. Additionally, demonstrating how digital citizenship and e-government applications can be used more efficiently in the context of civic literacy education provided to citizens will facilitate transactional ease.

REFERENCES

Arslan, M. L. (2018). Sivil toplum kuruluşlarında gönüllülük: Sorunlar ve çözüm yolları. *İlke Politika Notları, 4*, 1-16. https://kurumsalyonetim.org/images/sivil-toplum-kuruluslarinda-gonulluluk-sorunlar-cozum-yollari-pdf-ilke-org-tr.pdf

Arthur, J., Harrison, T., Taylor-Collins, E., & Moller, F. (2017). *A habit of service: The factors that sustain service in young people (Report)*. Jubilee Centre for Character and Virtues, University of Birmingham.

Ayaz, H. (2021). Dijital Melezlerin Dijital Yurttaşlık Seviyelerinin Haber Yayılımı Bağlamında İncelenmesi. *Trt Akademi, 6*(12), 364-395. https://dergipark.org.tr/en/pub/trta/article/901959

Aydoğan Boschele, F. (2021). Dijital Tekolojilerin Vatandaşı ve Politikası. *Middle Black Sea Journal of Communication Studies, 6*(2), 58-63. https://dergipark.org.tr/tr/pub/mbsjcs/issue/67099/1009899

Balaban, A. Y., & İnce, İ. Ç. (2015). Gençlerin sivil toplum kuruluşlarındaki gönüllülük faaliyetleri ve gönüllülük algısı: türkiye eğitim gönüllüleri vakfı (tegv) örneği. *Dokuz Eylül University Journal of Faculty of Economics and Administrative Sciences, 30*(2), 149-169. https://dergipark.org.tr/en/pub/deuiibfd/issue/22713/242424

Beers, S. (2011). *21st century skills: Preparing students for their future*. U Maine. https: https://cosee.umaine.edu/files/coseeos/21st_century_skills.pdf

Bekar, S., & Sağlam, M. (2023). Siber âlem: Yeni medya ve dijital yurttaşlık. *Niğde Ömer Halisdemir Üniversitesi İletişim Fakültesi Akademik Dergisi, 2*(2), 133-144. https://dergipark.org.tr/en/pub/nohuifad/issue/81919/1374065

Bentahar, A., & O'Brien, J. (2019). Raising students' awareness of social justice through civic literacy. *Journal of social studies education research, 10*(1), 193-218. https://dergipark.org.tr/en/pub/jsser/issue/45447/570410

Bincan, S. (2020). E-Devlet Uygulamaları Üzerine Bir İnceleme: Polonya ve Slovakya Örneği. *ASSAM Uluslararası Hakemli Dergi, 7*(16), 41-57. https://dergipark.org.tr/en/pub/assam/issue/53879/626341

Boyalı, H. (2023). Türkiye'de Vatandaş Odaklı İdare: E- Devlet Ötesi Dijitalleşen Kamu. *Bucak İşletme Fakültesi Dergisi, 6*(2), 172–190. doi:10.38057/bifd.1325556

Brookhart, S., & Nitko, A. (2008). *Assessment and grading in classrooms*. Pearson Publishing.

Brooks Young, S. (2016). *ISTE Standarts for Young Students*. ISTE Publising.

Buchholz, B., DeHart, J., & Moorman, G. (2020). Digital citizenship during a global pandemic: Moving beyond digital literacy. *Journal of Adolescent & Adult Literacy, 64*(1), 11 17. doi: https://doi.org/ doi:10.1002/jaal.1076

Buchholz, B., DeHart, J., & Moorman, G. (2020). Digital citizenship during a global pandemic: Moving beyond digital literacy. *Journal of Adolescent & Adult Literacy, 64*(1), 11–17. doi:10.1002/jaal.1076 PMID:32834710

Campbell, D. E. (2010). *Why we vote*. Princeton University Press. doi:10.1515/9781400837618

Can, S., & Eke, E. (2020). E-Devlet Kullanıcılarının Bilgi ve Memnuniyet Düzeylerine Yönelik Bir Araştırma. *Dumlupınar Üniversitesi Sosyal Bilimler Dergisi (64)*, 19-37. https://dergipark.org.tr/tr/pub/dpusbe/issue/53850/621551

Coley, R. J., & Sum, A. (2012). *Fault Lines in Our Democracy: Civic Knowledge, Voting Behavior, and Civic Engagement in the United States*. Educational Testing Service.

Dahlgren, P. (2013). *The political web: Media, participation and alternative democracy*. Springer. doi:10.1057/9781137326386

Dudley, R. L., & Gitelson, A. R. (2010). Political Literacy, Civic Education, and Civic Engagement: A Return to Political Socialization? *Applied Developmental Science*, 6(4), 175–182. doi:10.1207/S1532480XADS0604_3

Duman, E., & Aktel, M. (2021). Türkiye'nin e-Devlet kapısı (Dijital Türkiye Portalı). *Süleyman Demirel Üniversitesi Hukuk Fakültesi Dergisi*, 11(2), 613–641. doi:10.52273/sduhfd..957529

Eschenfelder, K. R., Beachboard, J. C., McClure, C. R., & Wyman, S. K. (1997). Assesing U.S. Federal Goverment Websites. *Government Information Quarterly*, 14(2), 173–189. doi:10.1016/S0740-624X(97)90018-6

Eveland, W. P. Jr, & Hively, M. H. (2009). Political discussion frequency, network size, and "heterogeneity" of discussion as predictors of political knowledge and participation. *Journal of Communication*, 59(2), 205–224. doi:10.1111/j.1460-2466.2009.01412.x

Faiz, M. (2018). Chapter: Yurttaşlık Okuryazarlığı. (Teaching Social Studies in Primary School). Eğiten Kitap Publishing, Ankara.

Gelen, İ. (2017). P21-Program ve öğretimde 21. yüzyıl beceri çerçeveleri (ABD Uygulamaları). *Disiplinlerarası Eğitim Araştırmaları Dergisi*, 1(2), 15–29.

Gil de Zúñiga, H., & Diehl, T. (2019). News finds me perception and democracy: Effects on political knowledge, political interest, and voting. *New Media & Society*, 21(6), 1253–1271. doi:10.1177/1461444818817548

Güler, M., & Döventaş, E. (2009). Elektronik Devletten Mobil Devlete Geçişte Türkiye'de Yerel Yönetim Uygulamaları. *Hitit University Journal of Institute of Social Sciences, 1*(2), 25-48. https://dergipark.org.tr/en/pub/hititsosbil/issue/7708/100965

Ham, C. D., Lee, J., Hayes, J. L., & Bae, Y. H. (2019). Exploring Sharing Behaviors Across Social Media Platforms. *International Journal of Market Research*, 61(2), 157–177. doi:10.1177/1470785318782790

Hauge, C., & Rowsell, J. (2020). Child and youth engagement: Civic literacies and digital ecologies. *Discourse (Abingdon)*, *41*(5), 667–672. doi:10.1080/01596306. 2020.1769933

Hylton, M. E. (2015). Civic Engagement and Civic Literacy Among Social Work Students: Where Do We Stand? *Journal of Policy Practice*, *14*(3-4), 292–307. doi :10.1080/15588742.2015.1004396

Hylton, M. E. (2015). Civic engagement and civic literacy among social work students: Where do we stand? *Journal of Policy Practice*, *14*(3-4), 292–307. doi:1 0.1080/15588742.2015.1004396

Karabulut, B. (2015) Bilgi Toplumu Çağında Dijital Yerliler, Göçmenler ve Melezler, *Pamukkale Üniversitesi Sosyal Bilimler Enstitüsü Dergisi,* (21), 11-23. https:// dergipark.org.tr/en/pub/pausbed/issue/34743/384200

Kerímoğlu, C., & Keleşoğlu, S. (2023). Covid-19 Pandemisinde İnternet Kullanımı ve Dijital Yurttaşlık. [JFES]. *Ankara University Journal of Faculty of Educational Sciences*, *56*(2), 495–545. doi:10.30964/auebfd.1148787

Kurt, A. A. ve Odabaşı, F. (2021). Pandemi döneminde sınanan dijital vatandaşlık [Digital citizenship tested during the pandemic]. Anı Yayıncılık.

Lyons, J., Jaeger, W. P., & Wolak, J. (2012). The roots of citizens' knowledge of state politics. *State Politics & Policy Quarterly*, *13*(2), c, 183–202. doi:10.1177/1532440012464878

Mulyono, B., Affandi, I., Suryadi, K., & Darmawan, C. (2022). Online civic engagement: Fostering citizen engagement through social media. *Jurnal Civics: Media Kajian Kewarganegaraan*, *19*(1), 75–85. doi:10.21831/jc.v19i1.49723

Nar, M. Ş. (2021). Eğitim, İdeoloji, Demokrasi ile Oy Verme Davranışı Arasındaki İlişki: Türkiye Örneği. *Mecmua*, (12), 199-212. https://dergipark.org.tr/en/pub/ mecmua/issue/65116/990437

Niezen, R. (2020). *HumanRights: The technologies and politics of justice claims in practice*. Stanford University Press. doi:10.1515/9781503612648

Özen, Z., Körükmez, L., & Demirel, C. A. (2021). Dijital Çağda Sivil Toplum: İmkânlar ve Kısıtlılıklar. *İnsan hakları okulu raporu, 1.*

Paşaoğlu, D. (2017). Dünyada E-Devlet Uygulamaları. Güney, Y. ve Okur, M.R. (Ed.). Bilgi Toplumu Ve E-Devlet içinde (Ünite 4). Eskişehir: Anadolu Üniversitesi Yayınları.

Prabhakar, A. (2022). Digital citizenship for 21st century children. *Bhavaveena, 19*(6), 6476. https://www.researchgate.net/publication/361614925_Digital_Citizenship_For_21st_Century

Prensky, M. (2001). Digital natives, digital immigrants. *On the Horizon MCB University Press, 9*(5), 1-6. https://www.marcprensky.com/writing/Prensky%20-%20Digital%20Natives,%20Digital%20Immigrants%20-%20Part1.pdf

Rundgren, C.-J., Rundgren, S.-N. C., Tseng, Y.-H., Lin, P.-L., & Chang, C.-Y. (2010). Are you SLiM? Developing an instrument for civic scientific literacy measurement (SLiM) based on media coverage. *Public Understanding of Science (Bristol, England), 21*(6), 759–773. doi:10.1177/0963662510377562 PMID:23832159

Talay, Ö. (2018). *Mobil Ortam Reklamlarında Dijital Gözetim Algısı: Dijital Göçmenler ve Dijital Yerlilerin Karşılaştırılmalı Analizi*. Yüksek Lisans Tezi Akdeniz Üniversitesi Sosyal Bilimler Enstitüsü.

Tamer, M. G. (2010). Tarihsel süreçte sivil toplum. *Hacettepe Üniversitesi Edebiyat Fakültesi Dergisi, 27*(1), 89-105. https://dergipark.org.tr/en/download/article-file/615583

Uğurlu, H. Y. (2019). *Sivil Toplum çalışmalarına katılımı Motive Eden faktörler ve gönüllü üniversite öğrencileri arasında Bir araştırma* [Doctoral dissertation, Marmara University, Turkey].

United Nations (UN). (2018). *E-government survey: Gearing E-government to support transformation towards sustainable and resilient societies*. UN. https://publicadministration.un.org/egovkb/Portals/egovkb/Documents/un/2018-Survey/E-Government%20Survey%202018_FINAL%20for%20web.pdf

Vontz, T. S., Metcalf, K. K., & Patrick, J. J. (2000). *Project Citizen and the civic development of adolescent students in Indiana, Latvia, and Lithuania*. The ERIC Clearinghouse for Social Studies/Social Science Education.

William, A. (2004). Civic Education and Political Participation. Political Science Online. http://www.apsanet.org/imgtest/CivicEdPoliticalParticipation.pdf

Wilson, K. K. (2002). *Promoting civic literacy*. (ERIC Document Reproduction Service No. ED466924).

Yaşar, İ. H., & Altıncık, H. (2018). Türkiye Cumhuriyeti bakanliklarinin web sitelerinin halkla ilişkiler bağlamında değerlendirilmesi. *Dumlupinar University Journal of Social Sciences, 2*(55), 224-236. https://dergipark.org.tr/en/pub/dpusbe/issue/35683/333941

Yıldırım Kaptan, B. (2023). *Kamu Yönetimi Kuramlari ve E-Devlet Olgusu Arasında Bir İnceleme* [Doctoral dissertation].

Yılmaz, V. (2019). E-Devlet Uygulamasının güvenilirliği ve kullanım düzeyinin ölçülmesi: Bitlis ili örneği. *Assam Uluslararası Hakemli Dergi, 6(14),* 226-239. https://dergipark.org.tr/tr/pub/assam/issue/48907/577924

Yurttadur, M. ve Süzen, E. (2016). Türkiye'de Banka Müşterilerinin İnternet Bankacılığına Yaklaşımlarının İncelenmesi Üzerine Bir Uygulama, *Tüketici ve Tüketim Araştırmaları Dergisi, 8* (1), 93-120. http://hdl.handle.net/11363/1039

Zarnowski, M. (2009). The Thought Experiment: An Imaginative Way into Civic Literacy. *Social Studies*, *100*(2), 55–62. doi:10.3200/TSSS.100.2.55-62

Chapter 4
Early Literacy in Children With Hearing Loss

Hilal Atlar-Yildirim
https://orcid.org/0000-0001-7272-1462
Independent Researcher, Turkey

Yıldız Uzuner
Anadolu University, Turkey

ABSTRACT

Children realize that reading and writing have meaning in spoken and written language development. Over time, they use the sounds in their mother tongue and the letters in their native language alphabet. Early literacy is a combination of verbal language, phonological awareness, alphabetic knowledge, print awareness, concepts related to writing, and the development of scribbles/writings that reflect the child's discovery. In this context, the scope and importance of early literacy and the development of literacy in children with hearing loss are conveyed. Then, the characteristics of the literacy environment, the nature of the experiences, and the views of the family on literacy are presented with examples from the researchers' case studies. Furthermore, an action research example illustrates the role of educator-family collaboration in supporting the early literacy development of children with hearing loss. This chapter presents suggestions to families and teachers to support emergent literacy in daily routines.

INTRODUCTION

Children born in a literate culture are surrounded by many writings and readings used by adults that are significant to them. In this way, they notice the relationship

DOI: 10.4018/979-8-3693-1777-8.ch004

between literacy and the writings with written products around them in the early period. This development takes place in the child's home environment and inner circle. Adult-child interaction in daily routines allows children to observe adults' literate behavior and active participation. Children with hearing loss lack auditory inputs and cues essential for language development in their interactions with adults. For this reason, they may experience delays in listening, language, communication, and phonological awareness skills. But based on the characteristics of language environments, it is now known that they acquire language similarly to their hearing peers. One option for children with hearing loss to become well-literate in the later years of life is to enrich their early literacy experiences in the early period and support the interaction of parents with their children. Since the development of literacy skills in the early period affects the success of literacy and reading comprehension in the school period, parents of children with hearing loss should be aware of their roles in experiencing enriching interactions with their children.

Families and teachers are the adults; children interact within the early years. Therefore, it would not be wrong to say that the most important way to support a child with hearing loss in early language and literacy development is to support their families and teachers. Also, collaborating with educators and families is the cornerstone of early intervention. The most crucial thing is that the adults in the child's life learn how to work together for the child's benefit. So, it is essential to maintain teacher-family engagement and school-family cooperation during the preschool education period.

BACKGROUND

Early Literacy: What is The Scope and Why It is Important?

Children are active learners who try to make sense of the world around them to answer questions about the world (Ferreiro and Teberosky, 1983). They were born in a literate society and stepped into a written world (Justice and Sofka, 2010). Thus, children growing up with literacy experiences show typical literate behaviors. Although they do not start school as a reader who knows and applies the rules of literacy, it is known that many children learn how written language works and where it is used (Hall, 1987; Goodman, 1984). Clay's (1966) research with five-year-old children is the pioneer of research on early literacy (Constantine, 2004; Teale and Sulzby, 1986; Whitehurst and Lonigan, 1998; Williams, 2004). In research conducted in Auckland, New Zealand Clay (1966, as cited in Clay, 2015) observed the literate behaviors of five-year-old children until they reached the age of six. Observing the children every week in the classroom environment, Clay worked in collaboration with the mothers of the children to record their experiences at home. As a result of the research, it has been stated that children have literacy knowledge and acquire literate behaviors in the preschool period (Clay, 1966, cited in Clay, 2015, p. 11). Thus, the research carried out from the 1960s to the 1980s, as well as changing the thoughts and practices regarding how children begin to become literate, has brought with it more examination of the development of skills in the literacy process (Morrow, 2009).

Early literacy development forms the basis for children's literacy success in later years (Badian, 1995; Durkin, 1963; Ezell and Justice, 2000; Hart and Risley, 2003; Noble et al., 2006). Early language and literacy experiences are crucial for a child's reading comprehension skills. Without these experiences, children may struggle with comprehension even if they can read correctly. Ensuring equal access to quality early education for all children is important (Robertson, 2009; Schirmer, 2005; Vukelich and Christie, 2009). For this reason, developing skills such as oral language, phonological and print awareness, and conceptual knowledge about writing is critical for long-term success as a literate person.

EARLY LITERACY DEVELOPMENT IN CHILDREN WITH HEARING LOSS

Children with hearing loss may experience delays in listening skills, oral language, and phonological awareness development, depending on their disability (Kretstchmer, Kretschmer, and Truax, 1978). It is stated that these areas, which are expressed as sub-skills of early literacy, may cause children with hearing loss to progress slowly and differently from their peers in early literacy skills (Easterbrooks et al., 2008; Mayer and Trezek, 2015). However, it is mentioned that a child with hearing loss can develop literacy skills similar to hearing peers in a rich literacy environment, with qualified literacy experiences with those around him (Browns, 1979; Conway, 1985; Ewoldt, 1985; Truax, 1978; Uzuner, 1993). Moreover, in recent years, it has been stated that the oral language skills of children with hearing loss can be better supported and improved compared to previous years with the development of early diagnosis, device use, and cochlear implant technology (Wie et al., 2007).

Studies reveal that children's early literacy skills are related to their literacy experiences and literacy environments at home and school. They develop many skills, such as knowledge about writing, recognizing letters, pretending to read, trying to write, and relating games they play with reading and writing. Oral language skills and vocabulary are also supported (Constantine, 2004; Fein, 2000; Justice, 2006; Rowe, 2000). Early literacy experiences are influenced by culture, and studies reveal that families with similar socio-economic status may have different literacy experiences (Anderson-Yockel and Haynes, 1994; Brice Heath, 1983; Constantine, 2004).

Technological Changes and Trends in Promoting Early Literacy for Children with Hearing Loss

Through the provision of creative means to enhance language, literacy, and communication skills, digital tools have substantially contributed to the early literacy development of children with hearing loss. Studies have demonstrated the effectiveness of mobile applications as therapeutic instruments for speech, language, and literacy in children with auditory impairments, underscoring the need for family involvement. Research has shown how vital early intervention and specialized programs are for helping children with hearing loss to improve their language skills. Moreover, it has been demonstrated that parent mediation with digital technology tools—like tablets—supports young children's language and literacy development, highlighting the significance of appropriate and balanced use in the home and classroom contexts (Moeller, 2000; Soyoof, 2023). Also, preschoolers with cochlear implants may benefit from clinician-guided early literacy therapies that use interactive tablet technology to enhance their early literacy abilities (Brouwer et al., 2016).

Digital storybooks are the most important technological tools for supporting early literacy. With digital stories, children are exposed to verbally presented and imaged information simultaneously and perceive the structure as a whole (Sadoski and Palvio, 2013). In addition, multimedia tools allow the use of animations along with digital stories. Thus, digital stories positively affect children's understanding and telling of the story. It also supports vocabulary and phonological awareness (Ihmeideh, 2014; Roque et al., 2017). As with hearing children, digital storybooks are one of the materials used to support early literacy with technology development for children with hearing loss. Incorporating digital storybooks into interactive reading sessions has demonstrated encouraging outcomes in enhancing students' learning and engagement. According to research, children with hearing loss can greatly benefit from interactive reading using digital storybooks regarding language development and understanding. These interactive digital storybooks help children with hearing loss understand and participate with them by offering visual and auditory cues in addition to interactive features like highlighted text, sound effects, and animations. Individualized learning experiences are also made possible by using interactive reading with digital storybooks since children can repeat sections of the story and set the story's speed. Additionally, this interactive approach fosters communication skills and creates a good learning environment by encouraging active engagement and contact between the child and the caregiver or teacher. So, interactive reading using digital storybooks is a remarkable tool that helps children with hearing loss improve their language skills, comprehension, and overall educational experience by blending technology with literacy (Dirks and Wauters, 2018; Messier and Wood, 2015; Noble et al., 2020).

Over the last few years, there has been a notable increase in online early literacy programs, primarily due to the difficulties posed by the COVID-19 pandemic. Teachers should improve their digital literacy to use online educational methods (Sanchez-Cruzado et al., 2021). Scholars have examined the efficacy of virtual reading programs for five-year-old kids, emphasizing evidence-based approaches to early literacy instruction (Weiss et al., 2022). Research has also looked at how small-group early literacy treatments are implemented, emphasizing how crucial it is to improve implementation techniques to support preschoolers struggling with reading. Additionally, creative online exercises have been used to track children's narrative development, and educators have received training in analyzing data and implementing research-based strategies for teaching early reading (Piasta et al., 2022; Scott et al., 2022). Effective early literacy interventions have been found for children from linguistically varied backgrounds, focusing on phonological awareness, letter knowledge, and literacy engagement (Abreu et al., 2020).

Online early interventions designed for families of children with hearing loss can be broadly categorized under telepractice and teleintervention. These terms encompass a range of telehealth services, which facilitate remote support and guidance for these families. With these programs, families who cannot access qualified education specialists in their region, allows their children with hearing loss to participate in early education (King and Xu, 2021; McCarthy et al., 2020). Practices that support remote families and children with hearing loss support the family holistically as a system with family-centered approaches. With expert support that enriches the daily lives of families and children with hearing loss and improves the quality of parent-child interaction, it aims to develop families within their natural context. Special education teachers, speech and language therapists, audiologists, and psychologists are involved in these practices, and multidisciplinary teamwork is carried out. It is vital in technology-based practices to ensure that families can access early education where they live and prevent weather conditions, distance, illness, and so forth, from interrupting education. In addition to providing this access, another main objective of these interventions is to support children's listening and language skills by supporting the interaction strategies used by families, as in face-to-face education. Essential components of early literacy development are also enhanced, mainly by supporting language skills and facilitating accessibility to education. The practices called remote audiology services and remote health services, on the other hand, adopt these purposes and continue to provide information about the use of the devices and to maintain audiology follow-up by adjusting the device settings remotely. Practices can be conducted weekly, every two weeks, or once a month. The frequency of applications varies according to the specialists' programs and the families' needs. Recording the sessions allows the experts to follow up and the family to re-monitor the training. Two main challenges are encountered in the implementation process. These are technical problems and time planning. Technical issues are often problems with connection speed, the need for technical support for families, and the limited capabilities of standard video conferencing tools to conduct live, one-to-one training sessions. The second problem is that more time is needed for remote planning of practices compared to face-to-face education. Although online environments provide convenience in terms of scheduling joint time with the family for interventions, experts need more time to plan the intervention content (Blaiser et al., 2012; Chen and Liu, 2017; Gonzales et al., 2016; Hopkins et al., 2012; Lalios, 2012; Nickbakht et al., 2020; Yaribakht and Movallali, 2020).

The use of digital early literacy programs has grown significantly in recent years, particularly regarding children with hearing impairments. These initiatives assist children with hearing loss develop early literacy skills using interactive technology and digital platforms (Burnett and Merchant, 2013). Research revealed that children who participated in an early literacy digital program had a notable increase in vocabulary compared to those who did not. Also, digital early literacy programs effectively improved phonological awareness and reading comprehension skills. Moreover, children with hearing loss have been found to benefit from these programs in terms of increased motivation and engagement since the interactive digital platforms meet their sensory and learning needs (Lyons and Tredwell, 2015; Simpson et al., 2015). Early literacy programs greatly aid early literacy development for children with hearing loss in preschool-inclusive settings. These programs offer a welcoming and encouraging atmosphere where children with hearing loss can advance their literacy abilities alongside their peers (Friesen et al., 2014). Early literacy programs in inclusive environments assist children with hearing loss in developing critical pre-reading and pre-writing skills, such as phonemic awareness, letter recognition, vocabulary, and comprehension. These skills are developed through specialized instructional strategies and accommodations, such as visual aids, assistive technologies, and sign language interpretation (Yoshinago-Itano, 2017). They also foster a love for reading, providing opportunities for children with hearing loss to engage in experiences with their peers. Overall, early literacy programs in inclusive environments allow children with hearing loss to access various experiences that can holistically empower their motivation and developmental skills (Lyons and Tredwell, 2015).

Early Literacy Experiences and Mother-Child Interactions of a Child with Hearing Loss: A Case Study from Turkey

In Turkey, ICEM (Education and Research Center for Hearing Impaired Children) carries out systematically and scientifically based practices in the early education of children with hearing loss. ICEM also conducts research on children with hearing loss. However, research focusing on the early literacy development of children with hearing loss is still limited in Turkey (Atlar, 2022; Atlar and Uzuner, 2018; Dogan, 2018; Karasu, 2014; Gerek, Karasu and Girgin, 2018). There is so far only one study holistically examining the early literacy experiences of a child with hearing loss in Turkey. In this section, this study will be presented focusing on the following three research questions: 1) What are the characteristics of the literacy environment and nature of early literacy experiences in Kemal's inner circle? 2) What are the family literacy habits and views on literacy development? 3) What are the mother's views on the literacy development of her child with hearing loss? (Atlar and Uzuner, 2018).

Kemal and His Parents

The participants of the research were five-year-old Kemal and his parents. Kemal was diagnosed with severe (mean 97dB) hearing loss in his right ear and moderate (mean 74dB) hearing loss in his left ear during newborn screening. Kemal has been using hearing aids since he was three months old, and he had cochlear implant surgery for his right ear at the age of three. Children with hearing loss in Turkey can receive eight sessions of free training per month from special education teachers, starting from the early period, according to the report prepared in line with the evaluations of the Guidance and Research Centers (Decree Law N:573). During the research process, Kemal received special education from a special education center.

Kemal's mother was 34 years old at the time of the study and graduated university from the Department of Early Childhood Education. She has worked at a special education center for five years with mentally disabled children. She was not working in any job when the research data was collected. She is the family member who spent the entire day with Kemal. When the mother's reading habits were examined, it was determined that the mother read a book before bedtime on some days of the week. Kemal knows his mother's own reading time. It was also learned that the mother had difficulties learning to read and write and that her family supported literacy teaching at home. Kemal's father was 34 years old and graduated from the accounting department. He works as a driver and is not at home during the day. He learned to read and write in the first grade and did not experience any difficulties. There was no written or printed material belonging to the father in the home environment.

Characteristics of Kemal's Literacy Environment

Kemal's opportunities related to written language in his home environment were concentrated in Kemal's bedroom and kitchen. On the door of Kemal's room hangs a piece of paper with his name, created by combining small balls of colored and furry. There is a small desk and chair in the room. The child's crayons, pencil case, and toys are on the table. Kemal's name is written on the pencil case by his mother. There are also some written materials in the closet in his room. Below the photograph of Kemal with his teacher, it says "MY DEAR TEACHER" [CANIM ÖĞRETMENİM]. At the same time, a calendar was hung in his mother's closet. On the calendar, there is the logo and text of a foundation in Turkey with the text "Happy New Year" "[Mutlu Yıllar]" and the names of the days. Kemal encounters these writings every day.

There are reading and writing materials in the cabinet in Kemal's room. Kemal can reach this cabinet's books, notebooks, and paint materials. At the same time, several books belonging to his mother are also in it. Kemal states that he shares his library with his mother. He has 32 books and a magazine for children. These include stories, fairy tales, activities, picture words, and coloring books. Some of Kemal's books are individual products he and his teacher created together at the special education center. Some examples of these books are in the following image.

The rabbit book does not have a cover page. The teacher wrote, "Who?" [Kim?] and "Whose?" [Kimin?] questions at the top of the first page. The book has nine pages,

Figure 1. The products of Kemal and his special education teacher

and the number of pages is written in the upper left corner of each page. Below are descriptions of the pictures in written form. The book's second, seventh, and ninth pages have printed versions in English below the picture. The name of the other book that Kemal and his teacher wrote is Ali's Butterfly, and the teacher wrote the book's title in capital letters. In the lower right corner of the cover page, "Author:" and Kemal's name and surname are written. The book, consisting of six sheets and eight pages, was stapled together. The inner pages are on colored cardboard, with white pages with story illustrations and printed computer scripts. Each horizontally arranged page has the page number in the upper right corner. Kemal stated that he painted the pictures of the story himself. Kemal has a fairy tale book that he often reads with his mother. The cover page of this book has been broken, and it starts from the table of contents. There are also two board games in Kemal's room. The game's name is written in capital letters on the box, along with the matching game. The other board game is a game where predictions are made by giving clues about the physical characteristics of the people in the picture. The game's name is written on the box with a question mark.

The refrigerator is the focal point in the kitchen where the family's writings are displayed. The product's brand in capital letters is displayed on the refrigerator's top cover, along with a list of activities related to following the rules at home, Kemal's kindergarten menu, and a list of his friends. Kemal's products are usually exhibited in the lower part of the refrigerator.

In the kitchen, there is a recipe notebook that Kemal and his mother use together. The notebook's cover and the contact information page were torn. There

Figure 2. The writings and the drawings on the refrigerator

are calendars for the years 2000 and 2001. In addition, the numbers of months and days are written in English and Turkish. At the top of the inner pages of the recipe notebook, the month and day of the page are written in Turkish, English, German, and Russian. His mother wrote the titles of the recipes, sometimes in capital letters and sometimes in lowercase letters. In recipes, the names of the materials, their quantity, and short instructions are included. On the recipe notebook pages are scribbles of Kemal's three and four years old. While Kemal was preparing food with his mother, he looked at the notebook with his mother. His mother listened as he read the materials. He said that the scribbles on it belonged to him, and he explained what the recipe book was for.

Kemal also encountered writings in the special education center. For example, "PLEASE CLOSE THE DOOR" [LÜTFEN KAPIYI KAPATINIZ.] is written in the center of the door. Kemal asked his mother about this sentence, and later, he stated that this information was written on any door. The seasonal strip hanging on the wall on the right when you enter the classroom consists of pictures and texts glued to cardboard and prepared for four different seasons. Above the season strip are the names of the seasons, and above the class calendar are the terms of the years, months, and days. Before starting the lesson, Kemal and his teacher used the calendar and the seasonal chart to discuss the day and weather.

Figure 3. The recipe notebook in the kitchen

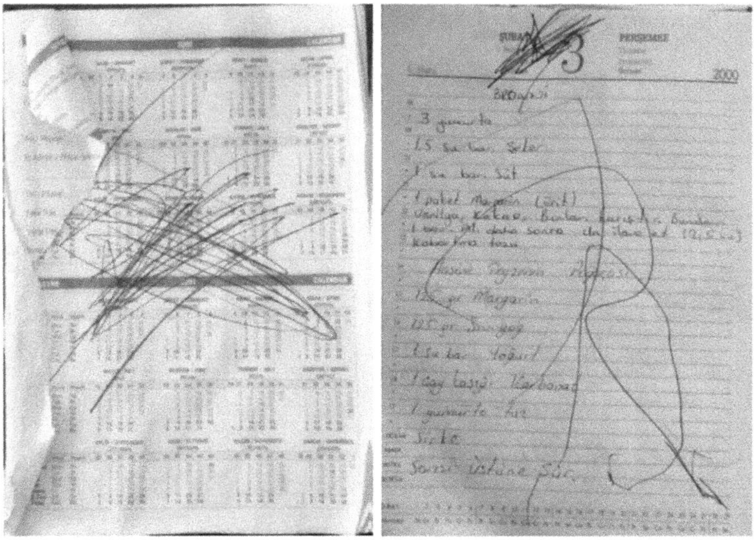

The writings that Kemal encounters in his inner circle are the articles in the market and in the store, where they frequently shopped, the writings on the restaurant menu, and the writings he encountered on the road.

There are two markets on the street. On the wall of the street, the letters "M," "B," "R," and "T" are written in capital letters. Kemal encounters these letters when he goes to the market with his mother. The name of the market is written in capital letters on the sign of one of the markets. Next to the market's name is the word "Shopping Center." A glass bread rack with two shelves is in front of the market. "BREAD IS INSIDE" [EKMEK İÇERİDE] is written on it in capital letters. Other writings that Kemal encountered in the market are the brands on the product packaging. At the same time, the logos and labels of the products are also included in Kemal's daily routine. The labels of some products in the market are larger texts written on the computer. On these labels, "DISCOUNT" [İNDİRİM], the product's brand, name, and price are written in capital letters. Two ice cream fridges are in front of the smaller market where Kemal and his mother shop. Brand inscriptions of the products are on the umbrella and ice cream cabinet.

When Kemal goes shopping with his mother, he encounters the writings in a clothing store. His mother stated that they always shopped at the same store for Kemal's clothes. On the store's ground floor, there is a signboard with the names of the floors and departments in capital letters. His mother and Kemal shared the writings on the sign by talking about which floor children's products are sold. Kemal also encounters the texts on the clothing labels and shares them with his mother.

Figure 4. The writings on the street and in the store

There is a restaurant where Kemal and his family always dine after shopping. The restaurant has a signboard with its name in capital letters. Inside the restaurant, signboards display images of the menus, their names, and pricing information. There is also a menu for the restaurant. The menu includes pictures, names, and price information of the food varieties on a red background on thick cardboard. There are also writings that Kemal often sees on the road and talks to his mother. For example, the advertising signboard at the bus stop includes the names of the advertised products and brand inscriptions. There is a second signboard at the bus stop with images and texts of public transport rules. Kemal and his mother look at the pictures together and discuss the writings. On the landscaping, followed by the bus, there are pictures and text shared by Kemal and his mother. It has a picture of Ataturk on both sides and his mother in the middle, and the words "A MOTHER CAN CHANGE THE WORLD" [BİR ANNE TÜM DÜNYAYI DEĞİŞTİREBİLİR.] in capital letters.

Kemal's Early Literacy Experiences and Early Literacy Development

Kemal's early literacy experiences have been observed as diversifying experiences with the adults around him. With all these experiences, a pattern has emerged. The pattern is shown in the figure.

The experiences in which children are provided with materials to experience literacy activities and various opportunities are used to draw the child's attention to writing are considered academic literacy experiences. Kemal's academic literacy experiences which will support the child's future literacy including reading and looking at books, reading and telling tales, nursery rhymes, and songs, making pictures and, drawings, and engaging in games (Dickinson and Caswell, 2007; Justice and Sofka, 2010; Morrow, 2009; Rhyner, 2009; Whitehurst and Lonigan, 2001).

Figure 5. The writings at the bus stop and on the road

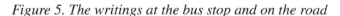

Figure 6. Kemal's early literacy experiences

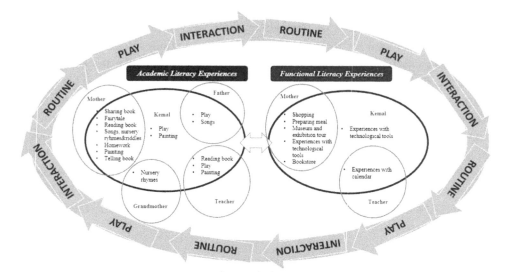

Kemal's experiences with books usually take the form of sharing pictures of a book with his mother, reading a book, and talking about the book with his mother. Word books, activity books, and story books are used in these experiences. Whatever the type of experiences with books, they occur based on dialogues. His mother states that they look at the word book so that Kemal can learn new words. Together, they talk about the names of objects, looking at the pictures in the book. Later, his mother asks Kemal to listen by saying an example sentence about using any object in the picture. He listens and shows the picture of the appropriate object. When he cannot show the proper object, his mother asks questions. For example, "This is how we spread jam on bread." she said, and Kemal tried to find the object. When Kemal could not find the sentence, she asked, "What do we put jam on the bread with?".

With the activity book, his mother shared the book's name and showed the writings she reads by following it. They keep interacting by talking about the pictures and instructions on each page. She explained they had previously studied the activity book used at school "for Kemal to become familiar." She also wanted him to guess the directions to "make Kemal's job a little more difficult." She shared songs with Kemal that he knew and showed suitable pictures on the page. For example, on a page with a snowman picture, she asked him, "Did you know the snowman song?". She waited, and Kemal started the song. When he broke into it, his mother completed it, and Kemal listened.

While looking at the pictures or reading the text of the storybooks, his mother reads the book's title and shows the text. She asks questions about the storybook's pages and confirms Kemal's answers. At the same time, by sharing the meanings of new words, she gives clues from the picture, and Kemal repeats the expression. Kemal's experiences of looking at books with his teacher are similarly based on interaction. Kemal's book-telling experiences started at preschool. Kemal prepared the tale of Pinocchio that he chose by telling his mother at home to tell his friends. His mother sometimes corrected his narrations and completed them at the end of the book.

Kemal's experiences with fairy tales were realized in two ways: his mother's reading and telling. Before bed, she read the tales he had chosen from his favorite fairy tale book. While reading the fairy tale, she asked him some questions, gave clues from the picture, and made explanations. In some evenings, his mother told Kemal fairy tales orally. Kemal's homework experiences are the homework prepared by his mother and the homework given by the school. His mother referred to this homework as "mother assignments." In these assignments, his mother prepared worksheets for him. They did them together with interaction.

In the games that Kemal played with his mother, it was observed that there was a memory game with pictures cut out of paper, a board game in which characters are guessed, and a game played with Legos. Sometimes Kemal and sometimes his mother started these games. His mother stated that Kemal sometimes plays games on the street with his father during the summer vacation, and they often play games on the phone together at home. It was seen that some of the games that he played with his teacher were related to the events in the story after the storybook they looked at together. In the games he played alone, Kemal used his toys, such as cars and animal figures. In the games he played alone, it was observed that he verbally explained his work and tried to set up a game.

When Kemal started preschool education, new songs were added to the children's songs he heard from his mother before. It was seen that there were songs in the "Family Communication Notebook" sent by the school during the summer vacation. There are also songs that he learned from cartoons. Kemal sang the songs with his mother, sometimes after the picture they shared while looking at the activity book and sometimes with the mother's guidance while examining the school file together. It was learned that Kemal and his father also listened to some songs by connecting to the video application on the phone. In addition, his mother stated that he learns a new song at school every Friday. His mother also asks Kemal about the riddles in the file. When Kemal cannot answer, his mother gives clues by asking questions. When there are words that the child does not know in the answers to the riddles, the mother shares the meaning of the word with explanations. For example, in the riddle "It comes with the rain, it takes everything away", Kemal answered "Lightning" and "Sun." His mother talked about "Flood". Kemal also sings nursery rhymes with his mother and grandmother. When he cannot say the rhymes correctly, his mother allows him to repeat them.

Kemal's painting experiences are alone, with his mother and teacher. But when he paints alone, he tells his mother these pictures. Kemal hung the pictures he made on the refrigerator and made additions to the pictures from time to time.

Sometimes, Kemal made drawings in the games he played with his mother. For example, he drew the figures they made in the Lego game. In the pictures Kemal made with his teacher, there are figures of a child with a flower in his hand, a house with a smoking chimney, grass, sun, and clouds.

Functional literacy is defined as capturing the meaning of daily life using reading and writing (Cobb, 1962). Kemal's functional literacy experiences include technological devices, labels, menus, bills, recipes, and signs. Kemal's experiences with technological devices are related to television, telephone and washing machine. Kemal usually watches cartoons on television. He selects the channel he wants, and he recognizes the channel logos. Additionally, he has started to recognize the names of television channels watched by him and his parents. While watching cartoons, he knows that the cartoon's name is displayed in the lower right corner of the screen and discusses these details with his mother. Kemal can also find the tales he wants

Figure 7. Kemal's paintings with some additions to them

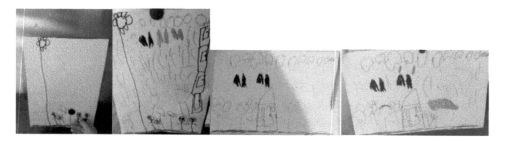

Figure 8. The figures from the game and Kemal's drawings

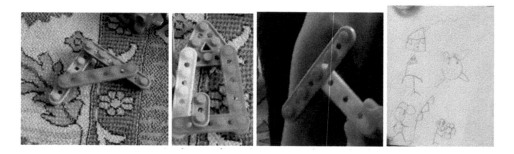

to listen to on the phone, recognizing the Wi-Fi symbol and the application logo to use the video program. When helping with housework, he observes the washing machine, mistaking the "CANCEL" text for "CLOSE."

Kemal's shopping experiences took place in a clothing store, market, and bookstore. Kemal examined the label in the clothing store himself and talked to his mother about the "age" and "price" parts. He found the products in the market by recognizing them from their packaging. When his mother bought a product of a brand they had not purchased before, she talked to Kemal about its writings. They also talked about the writings on the receipt after shopping. After shopping in a restaurant, they ordered by looking at the menu together. Kemal knows that the texts following to the pictures on the menu are the names of the foods.

Before each lesson, Kemal examines the calendar with his teacher at the special education center. They talked about the season and the weather using the seasonal strip. The teacher accepted Kemal's answers by asking what time of the month and year it was and writing it on the calendar. While Kemal was counting the days, she followed him by showing the writings on the calendar.

Kemal's mother stated that they usually make cakes and pastries. They made cakes together in one observation. His mother and Kemal looked at the recipe book and discussed the ingredients. His mother showed Kemal the materials she had read from the notebook. Kemal brought the missing materials from the closet himself. He recognized these materials from their packaging. While mixing the cake with the mixer, they talked about the numbers on the mixer and the concept of fast-slow.

His mother took Kemal on a tour of the memorial house on November 10, Ataturk's Day. During their tour, they read the signs and writings in the rooms together and shared information about Ataturk. Afterward, they sat in the garden cafeteria and listened to a concert where Ataturk's favorite songs were played. When they came home, his mother drew a picture of him to explain the concert concepts to Kemal. She told Kemal the names of musical instruments and the word orchestra.

Mother's Views on The Early Literacy Development of Kemal

The mother thinks there is literacy in the early experiences, which are reading books and looking at books and magazines together. She said, *"When we read a book or look at a magazine. It's more about reading and writing when we talk about the magazine's pictures. There may be texts. We have the activity book; we are talking in it, and he can guess the text under it."*. She also states that Kemal is more interested in reading than writing in the activities. His mother observes Kemal's early literacy skills. She explained, *"Sometimes he recognizes letters. I understand the child is now ready; the child gave me that message. Then I show the letters. For example,*

Figure 9. Drawings and written explanations about a concert

he knows A, E, and M". His mother states that Kemal is also interested in writing, expressing her thoughts as follows:

"...he has much interest in writing, especially on apartment doors. He asks, "Mom, what does it say here?" I explain, "Please close the door." ...even if something else is written on the other apartment doors, it says, "Please close the door?" "No," I correct it; I say what is written there. He also has an interest in the writings outside. He knows the letter M is the M of Migros (a grocery store chain in Turkey)."

His mother thinks that he will learn to read and write as he gets to know the letters and pretends to read. She thinks that hearing loss may make it difficult for him to pronounce sounds correctly. She thinks this problem will be solved by seeing the voice and letter he cannot produce by reading a book. During the family visit, the mother stated that she observed Kemal's literacy skills improving and thought he was progressing. In the interview, it was learned that the mother had concerns about Kemal being the last child to learn to read and write in the classroom. The mother described this situation as *"My worst nightmare. So, if he's the last person in the class to learn, I guess it would be a nightmare for me."*. She also mentioned that the reason for this fear is that people at school think that their child may have an intellectual disability.

Overall, The Results of This Case Study

Based on the results of this research, it can be stated that all these routine and non-routine experiences of Kemal, observed alone or with the adults, are in terms of frequency and quality compatible with the literacy experiences of hearing children in their daily routines. In addition, it has been revealed that children with hearing loss who have qualified literacy experiences in appropriate literacy environments exhibit literate behaviors similar to their hearing peers. As can be seen in Kemal's literate behaviors, interactive literacy experiences provided to him enabled him to develop early literacy skills like his hearing peers. Kemal's experiences affected his early literacy skills, with the nature of each experience and the roles of the participants. In addition, it would not be wrong to say that all literacy experiences have the nature of play in the eyes of the child.

COLLABORATION IN EARLY LITERACY DEVELOPMENT

Parents are the adults with whom the child shares their home and daily routines most. So, the literacy habits and culture of the parents affect literacy experiences (Brice Heath, 1983; Uzuner, 1983). The family system and its dynamics are integral to early literacy development (Bodrova and Leong, 2010; Brice Heath, 1983; Bronfenbrenner, 1979; Bruner, 1972). However, it is stated that hearing parents generally do not think that their children will be born with hearing loss. Therefore, parents' knowledge regarding the language and communication skills needs of a hearing loss child may be limited (Marscharch, Lang, and Albertini, 2002). In supporting the early literacy of children with hearing loss, it is necessary to improve families' interactions with their children. Therefore, ensuring teacher/specialist-family collaboration is essential to diversify and enrich early language and literacy experiences (Schirmer, 2005). Teachers can play a facilitating role in exploring opportunities to read and write with their children in the natural interactions of their daily routines. Families can be aware of literacy activities taking place at school. They can also receive suggestions on various experiences they can provide for their children at home. Understand that the skills children exhibit in preschool are the foundation of literacy and how they serve as a foundation for literacy in later years. Therefore, they can gain an up-to-date perspective on literacy development. They can move from collaborative to independent development regarding interaction strategies used in early language and literacy experiences. Thus, families will be able to develop their knowledge and skills in the context specific to their experiences with teacher/specialist/school support.

There are early literacy programs in various countries to strengthen family literacy and support children's early literacy development in collaboration with families. In some of these programs, families with children with hearing loss also participate. Storybooks are provided to families participating in the programs. This creates equal opportunities in literacy for disadvantaged children in the community. While supporting children's early literacy skills, families are also encouraged to enjoy their reading experiences (Allen, 2009; Becker, 2012; Moore and Wade, 2003; Needleman et al., 1991; Theriot et al., 2003; Sharif et al., 2002; Wade and Moore, 1993).

Early Literacy Teacher-Family Collaboration for Early Literacy Development of Children with Hearing Loss: An Action Research from Turkey

Early literacy programs or practices are one way to support early literacy development for children with hearing loss and their parents (van Steensel et al., 2011). Studies dealing with the relationships between early literacy skills and experiences reveal a significant relationship between the frequency of literacy experiences in the home environment, parents' perceptions of literacy, and the literacy strategies used by parents and verbal language skills of children with hearing loss. Researchers state that mothers have limitations in using strategies, and they can use strategies such as pointing directly at the picture, showing letters, and expanding the child's expressions. They add that parents should be supported in strategies such as asking open-ended questions and reorganizing (Desjardin et al., 2014; Desjardin et al., 2017). It is stated that children with hearing loss and their parents also participate in some early literacy programs. They considered together as participants in evaluating the programs, regardless of their individual differences. In addition, the information about the contents and implementation processes of the programs with this group is limited (Allen, 2010; Becker, 2012; Moore and Wade, 2003; Needleman et al., 1991; Theriot et al., 2003; Sharif et al., 2002).

Similarly, an interactive book reading program was developed for families of typically developing children in Turkey. Ergul, Dolunay Sarıca, and Akoglu (2016) state that their interactive book reading program (EKOP) effectively supports early literacy development. Researchers notified that EKOP can also be conducted with children with special needs and their parents.

In Turkey, a pilot study aiming to inform families with children with hearing loss about early literacy development and to support their literacy experiences has been carried out in recent years(Atlar, 2022). The study aims to examine the early literacy practices of three families with children with hearing loss between 0-6. At the same time, the aim is to solve the problems experienced by the families during the research process in cooperation with the teacher and to support the practices. This action research study collected data through video-recorded observations, semi-structured and unstructured face-to-face and online interviews, products, documents, and a research diary. In the first stage of the research, the general and individual needs of the families were determined. Thus, the general content of the support to be provided to families and the gains to be gained were determined. Accordingly, the common needs of the families include:

- Understanding the concept of early literacy and information about its scope,
- Knowledge about the characteristics of a rich literacy environment,
- Information on early literacy experiences and skills,
- Skills in selecting age-appropriate books for children and making simple adaptations,
- Knowledge and skills in interaction strategies for book-related activities,
- Awareness of the family's role in early literacy development.

Based on the common and individual needs of the families, the researchers prepared content consisting of six modules. These modules include video animations, video narratives, checklists, case studies, and storybooks sent to families online. At each step of the research, decisions were made by the credibility committee during the content preparation, implementation, and evaluation. In practice, three modules were presented as informative content. The concept of early literacy, the role and importance of the family in developing early literacy, the characteristics of a rich literacy home environment, literacy opportunities in the close environment, and how to diversify early literacy experiences were presented in three modules. Families watched video animations and narrations posted online and had a continuous one-to-one online interaction with the teacher-researcher. The teacher-researcher provided one-to-one feedback to the families throughout the modules. As families followed the content and communicated with the teacher-researcher, changes in the characteristics of the home environment and diversified literacy experiences. For example, the number of books in the home environment has increased, and the written environment has been enriched. Awareness of shared language opportunities related to signs, labels, etc., has developed. The images show examples of early literacy experiences that change with teacher-family interaction.

Figure 10. Melih and his mother's early literacy experiences

After watching the implementation videos, Melih's mother made some changes in her life through continuous interactions with the teacher-researcher. For example, he had routine reading hours with Melih. They prepared a shopping list together before shopping. Melih started making paintings and drawings; his mother put them on the refrigerator. Melih's mother stated that he learned information about early literacy after watching the informative videos. She said that her experiences changed as she interacted with the teacher-researcher and that she also enjoyed these experiences.

Although the frequency was low, Ozlem and her family's experiences included book reading. The mother made a reading routine after watching the videos and interacting with the teacher-researcher. After a while, her father also joined the reading routines. Ozlem's drawings and paintings were labeled with letters she knew and names she was familiar with. Ozlem's mother exhibited the child's products in various parts of the house.

Later, in addition to the writings Ozlem wrote on her paintings, there were also attempts to write with a purpose. Ozlem wrote "dangerous" on the oven. On the trash can in his father's office, he wrote "Garbage." In another experience, Ozlem prepared a shopping list.

His mother created a space for Mete to draw and doodle. The number of books in Mete's home increased rapidly. Routine reading experiences with both his mother and father were added. While shopping, his mother asked Mete to buy foods he recognized from the packaging. Together, they talked about the writing on the labels and packaging of the products. Similarly, they examined the writings on the signs of the shops they frequently saw on their way home.

On Father's Day, Mete's mother prepared an image with the words "Father's Day Souvenir" and photographs together with Mete. They took a photo in front of it by sticking it on the wall of the house and celebrated Father's Day. Mete's food preparation experiences also diversified. He and his mother prepared cakes, pastries,

Figure 11. Ozlem and her family's early literacy experiences

Figure 12. Ozlem's writings

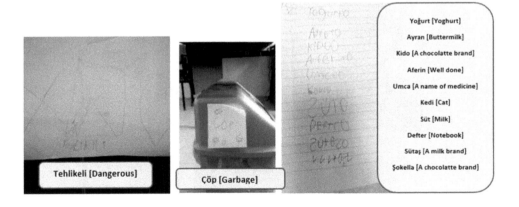

and cookies together by looking at recipes. Mete and his family started going on bookstore trips. When they returned from a bookstore, Mete tried to write his name on the first page of the new book. His mother prepared a songbook with songs Mete knew and shared the lyrics with Mete.

Figure 13. Mete and his family's early literacy experiences

Figure 14. Examples of Mete's early literacy experiences

In the fourth module of the implementation, early literacy skills were explained to families, and checklists were sent. Families evaluated their children's literacy skills by observing them. They also wrote examples of the skills they evaluated. Each family received one-to-one feedback. At the end of the module, case studies with literacy skills that develop at different ages were sent to the families. Families read the case examples and matched them with the appropriate early literacy skills. In the end-of-module evaluations, families were also given feedback on their responses to the case examples.

In the fifth module of the implementation, interactive reading experiences were supported. A printed booklet on interactive reading strategies was sent to families. In this booklet, traditional reading and interactive reading are explained, and the importance of interactive reading is emphasized. In addition, examples of simple adaptations they can make to books and supporting materials they can use when sharing a book with a child are given. In the online environment, strategies were posted with examples of videos of the researcher-teacher sharing books with the child. Families shared a video of themselves sharing the book with their children each week. Each family was given one-to-one feedback, and their strategies were explained. In the following week, new strategies were identified for them to develop. The mothers developed three strategies in the first phase by watching the videos: a) prepare for reading with the child and sit appropriately, b) hold the book appropriately, and c) tell and/or show the book's name.

At the end of the module, the mothers demonstrated improvement in the following strategies through continuous interaction with the teacher-researcher:

1. Checking if the child's hearing aid is functioning properly.
2. Drawing the child's attention to writing and discussing it.
3. Introducing and discussing books with the child.
4. Talking about the book's cover picture.
5. Asking questions related to the cover picture.
6. Reading to and/or showing the author's name to the child.
7. Following the child's interests and cues.
8. Asking open-ended questions.
9. Asking questions starting with WH- words (who, what, where, when, why).
10. Allowing the child time to think, formulate thoughts, and respond.

In the last module, informative expert videos were presented on various topics. Experts talked about language and literacy development in the early period, literacy development and difficulties that may be encountered during the school period, the role and importance of the family, and inclusion/integration practices. In their feedback, the families emphasized that the expert narratives were helpful. However, the expert videos alone would only be sufficient with the information conveyed from the research process's beginning and the teacher-researcher's supportive feedback.

After the implementation process, the support provided for the families was discontinued. During the monitoring and evaluation process, news was received from them. The mothers shared that their various and routine lives continued and that their reading routines continued. During the three months, they became independent with less and less interaction with the teacher-researcher. Mete's mother shared the changes in their lives with other mothers. She explained the importance of reading books and the development of early literacy to mothers who have children with hearing loss at the same age as their children. They decide to lend each other the storybooks they have at home.

The Results of This Action Research

As a result of the research, it was seen that families benefit from teacher-researcher collaboration to support the early literacy development of their children with hearing loss. Before the implementation, families' perspectives on literacy were more limited to reading and writing letters in primary school. The informative modules of the implementation process provided families with information about reading and writing development in the early period. It would not be wrong to say that changing families' experiences is not possible only through one-way information transfer. At this point, the constant interaction between the teacher-researcher and the mothers and the rapid feedback they received played a role in the changes in their experiences.

The common needs of the families were concepts related to early literacy, characteristics of the literacy environment, early literacy experiences, early literacy skills, and interactive book reading experiences. In addition to common needs, the feedback provided in the context of each family also met their individual needs. In remote support, mothers needed more or less technological support depending on their individual competencies. As families' knowledge and skills improved, they became more independent in their strategies to diversify experiences and interact with their children. One mother tried to transfer the knowledge and skills she had learned in practice to other mothers of children with hearing loss who were her child's peers. Thus, by lending storybooks from their homes to each other, the mothers created a small network, even if it needed to be more systematic. The mother who shared about early literacy took the first step in this community on her own. Therefore, the support provided by teachers and experts to families can help strengthen the family and create beneficial communities to support early literacy development.

SUGGESTIONS FOR PARENTS TO SUPPORT EARLY LITERACY DEVELOPMENT OF CHILDREN WITH HEARING LOSS

Early literacy skills have a strong relationship with experiences and the quality of parent-child interactions (Aram, Most and Mayafit, 2006; Desjardin et al., 2014; Desjardin et al., 2017). Parents' literacy habits and the language they direct to the child with hearing loss are crucial for literacy development. So, parents are a model for the child with hearing loss to observe literate behaviors and are also conversation partners in daily routines (Machado, 2012; Schirmer, 2005; Vygotsky, 1978). Based on this situation, it would be helpful to offer some suggestions for parents to support the literacy development of children with hearing loss.

1. The first step in supporting children's literacy development in the early years is to offer a rich literacy environment. A rich literacy environment is the whole of the literacy materials and experiences presented to the children and parents' literacy habits.

    ◦ It's important to have literacy materials in the child's room. Drawing papers, notebooks, prints, pencils, and crayons and a corner where they can use these materials will prepare them to practice reading and writing and to create products.

    ◦ Children's books are also important literacy materials. These books that are of interest to the child and suitable for developmental level should be chosen.

    ◦ On the other hand, books chosen and bought with the child give the child a meaningful experience and provide much more fun. You can keep children's books within their reach, and if possible, place the covers and title visible. Thus, the child can easily choose the book they want to read by recognizing the books by their covers over time.

    ◦ In addition to the literacy materials and opportunities, the literacy habits of parents and the child's inner circle are also a part of the richness of the literacy environment. Seeing adults reading books, newspapers, magazines, and other materials such as receipts, bills, and calendars and/ or using tablets, phones, and computers helps the child understand the meaning of reading and writing. You can allow your child to observe the situations in which you use reading and writing in your daily routine. For example, you can speak with your child about the calendar you use when planning a job or look at a bill together.

2. Follow the child's interest in all daily experiences and be an active listener.

○   After initiating the interaction, continue the conversation about the topic/situation/objects your child is interested in. When you establish a common interest with your child, you will support them in asking questions and expressing their thoughts, and you will see that they are willing to answer your questions. For example, you want to talk about the products you will buy while shopping together. Whereas product labels attract your child's attention. By allowing the child to guide this interaction, you can review the labels together and talk about them. In another example, you ask questions about the picture or text while reading a book together. At that time, your child is attracted to an animal he saw in the book. You can talk about this animal, ask questions about it, and then return to reading by reminding the characters of the book.

○   To be an active listener, consider your conversations. We wait while someone speaks to us, waiting for them to finish. Then it's our turn, and we start talking. You can also be a model for children to take turns in the conversation. Wait for him to finish speaking and take turns. You can also direct him to take turns.

3.   Reading with children is the most important experience that supports literacy development. Traditional reading is reading the book's text aloud by the adult without interrupting the child. This method of reading may cause the adult to lead the experience predominantly and the interaction opportunities to be missed. Research emphasizes that interactive reading experiences allow children to express their thoughts and expressions about words and pictures in books while reading. At the same time, the strategies adults use in interactive reading help support the child's oral and written language skills.

○   You can choose the book you want to read with your child together. Choosing the book will increase the enjoyment of the interaction for children.

○   You can accept when he wants to read the same book over and over again. Children have favorite books. Reading the same book over and over will facilitate the child to increase familiar words, understand the story structure more easily, make predictions, and focus on a different situation/language pattern in the same book that he should have paid more attention to in previous readings.

○   Before reading with your child, ensure the hearing aid is working. Before reading, choose a comfortable and noise-free place. Make sure to sit on the side of your child with the hearing aid.

○   You can talk to your child about the book's title, the author, and the picture on the cover. In this interaction, you can ask questions and make explanations. Following the text with your finger while reading the author and name of the book will also support print awareness.

- You may ask questions about the book. In addition to the questions your child can answer while asking these questions, you can vary your interaction with questions he can think about while answering, hear various question patterns, and sometimes model you in answering with your narration.

- Be sensitive and responsive to the child's answers. Please acknowledge and confirm the child's comments about an event/situation in the picture or text while reading and their answers to your questions.

- Be a model so that the child can reorganize their expressions. Children with hearing loss may have some difficulties developing various components of language. Although it varies according to the mother tongue, Errors in using suffixes and some grammatical syntax errors can be problematic. Naturally, these difficulties can also affect the other components of language, such as semantics and pragmatics. In this case, it is vital to be a model for the child by correcting the sentence he cannot express adequately.

- Enrich the language by making extensions. Your child's verbal expressions may include short answers concerning their language skills. You can respond by expanding the statement so that your child can repeat it with an appropriate syntax. Give your child the opportunity to repeat their expression when you present them in edits and expand upon them, but don't be persistent. Try twice so that it can repeat the edited or expanded expression. If you insist, the nature of the interaction will deteriorate, and your child's enjoyment will decrease.

- You can share the meanings of new words in the book. Ensure that the new words you will share for the first time are manageable. For example, if there are ten words in a book you think your child does not know, it will be sufficient to share the meaning of 3-4 new words important for understanding the story and that you use frequently.

- Read with your child daily. For example, you may have time to read every day after breakfast or before sleep.

4. Songs, lullabies, nursery rhymes, and riddles are experiences that support children's literacy development. Sing songs, lullabies, and nursery rhymes with your child. Play finger games. Ask riddles. Please encourage them to recognize rhymes in these interactions.

5. Use the literacy opportunities around. The signs of the stores, the signs on the roads you pass, the texts on the product labels and packaging, the texts on the

posters and tickets of the events such as cinema and theater, and the form of the brochure. You can talk about these writings with your child.

SUGGESTIONS FOR TEACHERS TO SUPPORT EARLY LITERACY DEVELOPMENT OF CHILDREN WITH HEARING LOSS

We will make a few suggestions to teachers on how to improve the quality of the classroom environment to promote literacy and, in turn, affect the home environment and families.

1. The first step in supporting children's literacy development in the early years is to offer a rich literacy environment.
   ◦ Enrich the written environment in the classroom. Children need to encounter writing in the classroom throughout the day. You can put labels with the children's names on the cabinets and objects that they own. You can name the areas where toys and other materials are kept. In this way, children will benefit from the written environment when looking for things that belong to them or that they will use.
   ◦ Create reading and seating areas in classrooms that children can access independently. Place interesting books appropriate to children's developmental level on the bookshelf in the reading area. Placing the books to make the cover pages visible will give children clues.
   ◦ Present the children's drawings and scribbles, their first written products, in the classroom. This will also show how much you value the children's work.
   ◦ Use calendars, activity charts, and written and picture corners in the classroom.
2. Children affected by disability and/or disadvantaged in terms of socio-economic status may have limited experience with language in the home environment. One crucial component of literacy development is encouraging vocabulary growth in the classroom.
   ◦ Read books with the children, share books, and talk about the pictures in the books.
   ◦ When sharing books, ask children questions about the pictures. Please encourage them to make predictions about events and people, to make cause-and-effect connections, and to imagine. Let them ask questions, too. Make them realize that the text on the book's pages is related to the pictures.

- ◦ Give them a chance to choose books that they read together or books they can "pretend" to read.
- ◦ Talk about the books you have shared with the children and have discussions about the book.
- ◦ Identify tools to assess children's language and literacy skills. These can be scales, checklists, and observation records. Make use of a variety of measurement tools.

3.   As in all areas of child development, it is important to cooperate with the family to support literacy development.

- ◦ Emphasize that you are on the same team with families. Collect information about the family's daily routine. This will help you to realize what kind of experiences children have at home and how you can enrich them together.
- ◦ Creating a family-school communication notebook can be helpful for sustainable interaction. You can ask families to write down what they do at home. You can also add what is done at school. This way, communication will continue even when immediate verbal interaction is impossible.
- ◦ Talk and write about what is good, giving supportive and encouraging feedback to the family.
- ◦ Inform families about the ways to use literacy in their daily routines. Tell the family, for instance, that literacy-promoting activities include making a list for grocery shopping, preparing food by looking at a recipe together, parents having their reading hours, and using the writings on household appliances while using them. These are literate behaviors.
- ◦ Inform families that it is essential to read with their children and that it should become routine. For this routine, you can suggest reading a book before bedtime.
- ◦ You can support families by recording videos of their reading experiences with their children at home and creating individual storybooks together.
- ◦ You can hold regular meetings with families to inform them about literacy development and learn about their needs.

CONCLUSION

Early literacy experiences are one way children become well-literate later in life (Dickinson and Caswell, 2007; Justice and Sofka, 2010; Morrow, 2009; Rhyner, 2009; Whitehurst and Lonigan, 2001). Children with hearing loss may experience difficulties in language and communication skills due to their disabilities. However, regardless of the communication modality used, it reveals that children participate in literacy experiences in the home environment in the early period; they like to read a book over and over again, and the interactions are important (Ewoldt, 1990; Henderson, 1976; Lutz, 2013; Maxwell, 1984; Swanwick and Watson, 2007; Uzuner, 1993; Williams, 1994).

Parents need support regarding interactions with their children. It is important to support parents with skills such as expanding their children's expressions through literacy activities and making explanations to them. Also, they need support having conversations with the child about the events in the books instead of focusing on the word itself and providing (scaffolding) appropriate support when necessary (Bergeron, 2013; Swanwick and Watson, 2007; Vygotsky, 1978). Therefore, early literacy programs that strengthen parents will improve children's language and literacy development with hearing loss. Furthermore, educational programs related to early literacy can positively affect the professional development of teachers.

FUTURE RESEARCH DIRECTIONS

The primary headings include extensive information to provide a perspective for future research as well as discussions regarding the research. Based on this information, research suggestions can be made.

- Research can be conducted to examine the early literacy experiences and skills of hearing-impaired children in different cultures.
- Also, research on developing, implementing, and evaluating early literacy programs that support the families of children with hearing loss is crucial.
- From the perspective of inclusive education, early literacy practices that include children with hearing loss can be carried out in the school environment.
- In-service training programs can be developed for the professional development of special educators working with children with hearing loss.
- In addition, there is still a need for systematic review studies on early literacy in children with hearing loss.

REFERENCES

Abreu, P. M., Fricke, S., & Wealer, C. (2020). Effects of an early literacy intervention for linguistically diverse children: A quasi-experimental study. *Frontiers in Psychology, 11*, 569854.

Allen, N. (2009). Making a difference – Better beginnings family literacy program. *The Australian Library Journal*, *58*(4), 369–376. doi:10.1080/00049670.2009.10 735925

Anderson-Yockel, J., & Haynes, O. W. (1994). Joint book-reading strategies in working-class african american and white mother-toddler dyads. *Journal of Speech and Hearing Research*, *37*(3), 583–593. doi:10.1044/jshr.3703.583 PMID:8084190

Aram, D., Most, T., & Mayafit, H. (2006). Contributions of mother-child storybook telling and joint writing to literacy development in kindergartners with hearing loss. *Language, Speech, and Hearing Services in Schools*, *37*(3), 209–223. doi:10.1044/0161-1461(2006/023) PMID:16837444

Atlar, H., & Uzuner, Y. (2018). Okul oncesi donemdeki isitme kayıplı bir cocugun gelisen okuryazarlık yasantılarının incelenmesi [Examining the emergent literacy experiences of a preschool child with hearing loss]. *Journal of Qualitative Research in Education*, *6*(1), 54–89. doi:10.14689/issn.2148-2624.1.6c1s3m

Becker, K. (2012). 24 hours in the children's section: An observational study at the public library. *Early Childhood Education Journal*, *40*(2), 107–114. doi:10.1007/s10643-011-0499-0

Bergeron, J. P. (2013). *Effectiveness of parent training on shared reading practices in families with children who are deaf and hard of hearing*, [Phd Dissertation, Atlanta Georgia State University, USA].

Better Beginnings report: Making a difference: the evaluation of the better beginnings birth to three family literacy program 14 years (2017). Australia: School of Education Early Childhood Research Group Edith Cowan University. https://www.better-beginnings.com.au/research/research-about-better-beginnings/making-difference

Blaiser, K. M., Edwards, M., Behl, D., & Munoz, K. F. (2012). Telepractice services at sound beginnings at Utah State University. *The Volta Review*, *112*(3), 365–372.

Bodrova, E., & Leong, J. D. (2010). *Zihnin araçları erken çocukluk eğitiminde Vygotsky yaklaşımı* (T. Güler, F. Şahin, A. Yılmaz, & E. Kalkan, Eds.). Anı Publishing.

Bookstart report: An evaluation of the bookstart corner programme parents' survey. (2014). UK: BookTrust/ActionPoint Marketing Solutions. https://www.buchstart.at/data/bookstart-corner-evaluation.pdf

Brice Heath, S. (1983). *Ways with words language, life and work in communities and classrooms*. Cambridge University Press. doi:10.1017/CBO9780511841057

Bronfenbrenner, U. (1979). *The ecology of human development: experiments by nature and design.* Cambridge University Press. doi:10.4159/9780674028845

Brouwer, K., Downing, H., Westhoff, S., Wait, R., Entwisle, L. K., Messersmith, J. J., & Hanson, E. K. (2017). Effects of clinician-guided emergent literacy intervention using interactive tablet technology for preschool children with cochlear implants. *Communication Disorders Quarterly, 38*(4), 195–205.

Browns, F. (1979). Beginning reading instruction with hearing-impaired children. *The Volta Review*, 100–108.

Bruner, J. (1972). Child's play. J. Bruner (Ed.),(2006), In search of pedagogy volume I: The selected works of Jerome S. Bruner içinde (s. 162-166). Oxon: Routledge.

Burnett, C., & Merchant, G. (2013). Learning, literacies and new technologies: The current context and future possibilities. The Sage handbook of early childhood literacy, 2, 575-586.

Chen, P. H., & Liu, T. W. (2017). A pilot study of telepractice for teaching listening and spoken language to Mandarin-speaking children with congenital hearing loss. *Deafness & Education International, 19*(3-4), 134–143.

Clay, M. M. (1975). *What did I write? beginning writing behaviour.* Heinemann Educational Books.

Clay, M. M. (2015). *Becoming literate the construcition of inner control.* The Mary Clay Literacy Trust.

Constantine, J. L. (2004). *Relationships among early lexical and literacy skills and language-literacy environments at home and school.* [Phd Dissertation, A.B.D: South Florida Collage of Education].

Conway, D. (1985). Children recreating writing: A preliminary look at the purposes of free-choice writing of hearing impaired kindergarteners. *The Volta Review, 87*, 91–107.

Decree Law No 573, MoNe [Ministry of National Education]. (1997). Decree law on special education no. 573, Official Gazette dated 06.06.1997 and numbered 23011.

Desjardin, J. L., Doll, E. R., Stika, C. J., Eisenberg, L. S., Johnson, K. C., Hammus Gangully, D. M., Colson, B. G., & Henning, S. C. (2014). Parental support for language development during joint book reading for young children with hearing loss. *Communication Disorders Quarterly, 35*(3), 167–181. doi:10.1177/1525740113518062 PMID:25309136

Desjardin, J. L., Stika, C. J., Eisenberg, L. S., Johnson, K. C., Hammus Gangully, D. M., Henning, S. C., & Colson, B. G. (2017). A longitudinal investigation of the home literacy environment and shared book reading in young children with hearing loss. *Ear and Hearing*, *38*(4), 441–454. doi:10.1097/AUD.0000000000000414 PMID:28234669

Dickinson, D. K., & Caswell, L. (2007). Building support for language and early literacy in preschool classrooms through in-service professional development: Effects of the literacy environment enrichment program. *Early Childhood Research Quarterly*, *22*(2), 243–260. doi:10.1016/j.ecresq.2007.03.001

Dirks, E., & Wauters, L. (2018). It takes two to read: Interactive reading with young deaf and hard-of-hearing children. *Journal of Deaf Studies and Deaf Education*, *23*(3), 261–270.

Dogan, S. (2018). *Bir ogretmenin okul oncesi donemdeki isitme kayıplı bir cocukla kitap okuma uygulamalarinin incelenmesi.* [Md Dissertation. Eskisehir: Anadolu University].

Dyson, H. A. (2005). Children out of bounds: the power of case studies in expanding visions of literacy development. J. Flood, S.B. Heath ve D. Lapp (Eds.), Handbook of research on teaching literacy through the communicative and visual arts içinde (s.167-180). New Jersey: Lawrance Erlbalum Associates Publishers.

Easterbrooks, R. S., Lederberg, R. A., Miller, M. E., Bergeron, P. J., & Connor McDonald, C. (2008). Emergent literacy skills during early childhood in children with hearing loss: Strengths and weaknesses. *The Volta Review*, *108*(2), 91–114. doi:10.17955/tvr.108.2.608

Eliot, S. (2016). National bookstart week england evaluation 2016. UK: BookTrust. https://www.booktrust.org.uk/globalassets/resources/research/national-bookstart-week-2016-report-final.pdf

Ergul, C., Akoglu, G., Dolunay Sarıca, A., & Karaman, G. (2016). *Etkilesimli kitap okuma programı (EKOP).* Egiten Kitap.

Erturk Mustul, E., Turan, Z., & Uzuner, Y. (2016). İsitme kayıplı cocugu olan bir annenin etkilesim davranıslarının aile egitimi baglamında incelenmesi [Investigation of interaction behaviors of a mother with a child with hearing loss in the context of family education]. *Ankara Universitesi Egitim Bilimleri Fakultesi Ozel Egitim Dergisi*, *17*(1), 1–22. doi:10.1501/Ozlegt_0000000236

Ewoldt, C. (1985). A descriptive study of the developing literacy of young hearing impaired children. *The Volta Review*, *87*, 109–125.

Fein, G. G., Ardila-Rey, A. E., & Groth, L. A. (2000). The narrative connection: Stories and literacy. In K. A. Roskos & J. F. Christie (Eds.), *Play and literacy in early childhood research from multiple perspectives* (pp. 27–44). Lawrance Erlbaum Associates.

Ferreiro, E., & Teberosky, A. (1983). *Literacy before schooling*. Heinemann Publishing.

Friesen, A., Butera, G., Kang, J., Horn, E., Lieber, J., & Palmer, S. (2014). Collaboration and consultation in preschool to promote early literacy for children: Lessons learned from the CSS curriculum. *Journal of Educational & Psychological Consultation*, *24*(2), 149–164.

Fung, P. C., Chow, B. W. Y., & McBride-Chang, C. (2005). The impact of a dialogic reading program on deaf and hard-of-hearing kindergarten and early primary school–aged students in Hong Kong. *Journal of Deaf Studies and Deaf Education*, *10*(1), 82–95. doi:10.1093/deafed/eni005 PMID:15585750

Gerek, A., Karasu, H. P., & Girgin, U. (2018). İsitme kayipli bir cocugun okul oncesi donemde okumaya hazirlik becerilerinin paylasilan okuma etkinligi ile desteklenme surecinin incelenmesi. *Akdeniz Egitim Araştırmaları Dergisi*, *12*(25), 203–229.

Girgin, U. (1999). *Eskisehir ili ilkokul 4. ve 5. sınıf isitme engelli ogrencilerinin okumayi ogrenme durumlarının cozumleme ve anlama duzeylerine gore degerlendirilmesi*. Anadolu University.

Girgin, U. (2003). İsitme engelli cocuklar icin erken donem okuma yazma egitimi. In U. Tufekcioglu (Ed.), *İsitme, konusma ve gorme sorunları olan cocukların egitimi* (pp. 139–163). Anadolu University Publishing.

Gonzales, A., Zappler AuD, A., Coco AuD, L., & Julie, C. (2016). The future of healthcare delivery: IPE/IPP audiology and nursing student/faculty collaboration to deliver hearing aids to vulnerable adults via telehealth. *Journal of Nursing & Interprofessional Leadership in Quality & Safety*, *1*(1), 1–11.

Goodman, Y. (1984). The development of initial literacy. In H. Goelman, A. Oberg, & F. Smith (Eds.), *Awakening to literacy* (pp. 102–109). Heinemann.

Hall, N. (1987). The emergence of literacy. (1.Ed.). Portsmouth: Heinemann Publishing.

Hannon, P., Morgan, A., & Nutbron, C. (2006). Parents' experiences of a family literacy programme. *Journal of Early Childhood Research*, *4*(1), 19–44. doi:10.1177/1476718X06059788

Henderson, M. J. (1976). Learning to read: A case study of a deaf child. *American Annals of the Deaf*, *121*(5), 502–506. PMID:983909

Hines, M., & Brooks, G. (2005). *Sheffield babies love books: an evaluation of the sheffield bookstart Project*. The University of Sheffield.

Holdaway, D. (1979). *The foundations of literacy*. Ashton.

Hopkins, K., Keefe, B., & Bruno, A. (2012). Telepractice: Creating a statewide network of support in rural maine. *The Volta Review*, *112*(3), 409–416.

Ihmeideh, F. M. (2014). The effect of electronic books on enhancing emergent literacy skills of pre-school children. *Computers & Education*, *79*, 40–48.

Jordan, G. E., Snow, C. E., & Porche, M. V. (2000). Project EASE: The effect of a family literacy project on kindergarten students' early literacy skills. *Reading Research Quarterly*, *35*(4), 524–546. doi:10.1598/RRQ.35.4.5

Justice, M. L. (2006). Emergent literacy: Development, domains and intervention approaches. In L. M. Justice (Ed.), *Clinical approaches to emergent literacy intervention* (pp. 3–27). Plural Publishing Inc.

Justice, M. L., & Sofka, E. A. (2010). *Engaging children with print building early literacy skills through quality read-alouds*. The Guilford Press.

Karasu, P. H. (2014). İsitme engelli cocuklara okul oncesi donemde uygulanan okuma yazmaya hazirlik grup etkinlikleri. *Egitim ve Bilim.*, *39*(174), 297–312. doi:10.15390/EB.2014.2602

King, A., & Xu, Y. (2021). Caregiver coaching for language facilitation in early intervention for children with hearing loss. *Early Child Development and Care*, *191*(10), 1507–1525.

Kretschmer, R. R., Kretschmer, W. L., & Truax, R. T. (1978). *Language development and intervention with the hearing impaired*. University Park Press.

Lalios, A. P. (2012). ConnectHear teleintervention program. *The Volta Review*, *112*(3), 357–364.

Lutz, L. (2013). *Early reading development in young deaf children supportive family context*. [Md Dissertation, University of Virginia: USA].

Lyons, C. D., & Tredwell, C. T. (2015). Steps to implementing technology in inclusive early childhood programs. *Computers in the Schools*, *32*(2), 152–166.

Machado, J. M. (2012). Early chilhood experiences in language arts: early literacy (10. Ed.). USA: Wadsworth.

Marschark, M., Lang, H. G., & Albertini, J. A. (2002). Reading, writing and literacy. In M. Marschark, G. L. Harry, & J. A. Albertini (Eds.), *Educating deaf students. From research to practice* (pp. 157–186). Oxford University Press.

Maxwell, M. (1984). A deaf child's natural development of literacy. *Sign Language Studies*, *44*(1), 191–224. doi:10.1353/sls.1984.0001

Mayer, C., & Trezek, B. J. (2015). *Early literacy development in deaf children.* Oxford University Press. doi:10.1093/acprof:oso/9780199965694.001.0001

McCarthy, M., Leigh, G., & Arthur-Kelly, M. (2020). Children's hearing and speech centre telepractice programs. *The Volta Review*, *112*(3), 429–433.

Mendelshon, A. L., Mogilner, L. N., Preyer, B. P., Forman, J. A., Weinstein, S. C., Broderick, M., Cheng, K. J., Magloire, T., Moore, T., & Napier, C. (2001). The impact of a clinic-based literacy intervention on language development in inner-city preschool children. *American Academy of Pediatrics*, *107*(1), 130–134. PMID:11134446

Messier, J., & Wood, C. (2015). Facilitating vocabulary acquisition of children with cochlear implants using electronic storybooks. *Journal of Deaf Studies and Deaf Education*, *20*(4), 356–373.

Moeller, M. P. (2000). Early intervention and language development in children who are deaf and hard of hearing. *Pediatrics*, *106*(3). Advance online publication. https://doi.org/10.1542/peds.106.3.e43

Moore, M., & Wade, B. (2003). Bookstart: A qualitative evaluation. *Educational Review*, *55*(1), 1, 3–13. doi:10.1080/00131910303250

Morrow, M. L. (2009). Literacy development in the early years. (6.Ed.). U.S.A: Pearson.

Needlman, R., Fried, L. E., Morley, D. S., Taylor, S., & Zuckerman, B. (1991). Clinic-based intervention to promote literacy: A pilot study. *American Journal of Diseases of Children*, *145*(8), 881–884. doi:10.1001/archpedi.1991.02160080059021 PMID:1858725

NELP. (2008). *National early literacy panel report.* USA: National Institute for Literacy. https://lincs.ed.gov/publications/pdf/NELPReport09.pdf

Nickbakht, M., Meyer, C., Scarinci, N., & Beswick, R. (2020). Exploring factors influencing the use of an eHealth intervention for families of children with hearing loss: An application of the COM-B model. *Disability and Health Journal, 13*(4), 1–8.

Noble, C., Cameron-Faulkner, T., Jessop, A., Coates, A., Sawyer, H., Taylor-Ims, R., & Rowland, C. F. (2020). The impact of interactive shared book reading on children's language skills: A randomized controlled trial. *Journal of Speech, Language, and Hearing Research: JSLHR, 63*(6), 1878–1897.

Pharness, G., & Weinstein, L. (2004). Community literacy: from home to work and back. In J. Flood, S. B. Heath, & D. Lapp (Eds.), *Handbook of research on teaching literacy through the communicative and visual arts* (pp. 386–393). Routledge.

Piasta, S. B., Logan, J. A., Zettler-Greeley, C. M., Bailet, L. L., Lewis, K., & Thomas, L. J. (2023). Small-group, emergent literacy intervention under two implementation models: Intent-to-treat and dosage effects for preschoolers at risk for reading difficulties. *Journal of Learning Disabilities, 56*(3), 225–240.

Primavera, J. (2000). Enhancing family competence through literacy activities. *Journal of Prevention & Intervention in the Community, 20*(1-2), 85–101. doi:10.1300/J005v20n01_07

Rhyner, P. M. (2009). *Emergent literacy and language development*. The Guilford Press.

Rix, J., Perry, J., Durry, R., Messer, D. & Hancock, R. (2015). The family experience of bookstart corner an evaluation of bookstart corner. *The Open University Bookstart*, 1-43.

Roque, V. J., Teodoro, L. A., Cunanan, B. M., & Evangelista, M. T. (2017, June). Using animated e-storybooks to develop Filipino vocabulary and story comprehension among preschool children. In *De La Salle University Congress*.

Rottenberg, J. C., & Searfoss, W. L. (1992). Becoming literate in a preschool class: Literacy development of hearing impaired children. *Journal of Reading Behavior, 24*(4), 463–479. doi:10.1080/10862969209547791

Rowe, D. W. (2000). Bringing books to life: The role of book-related dramatic play in young children's literacy learning. In K. A. Roskos & J. F. Christie (Eds.), *Play and literacy in early childhood research from multiple perspectives* (pp. 3–45). Lawrance Erlbaum Associates Inc.

Ruiz, T. N. (1995). A young deaf child learns to write: Implications for literacy development. *The Reading Teacher, 49*(3), 206–217.

Sadoski, M., & Paivio, A. (2013). *Imagery and text: A dual coding theory of reading and writing*. Routledge.

Sánchez-Cruzado, C., Santiago Campión, R., & Sánchez-Compaña, M. T. (2021). Teacher digital literacy: The indisputable challenge after COVID-19. *Sustainability*, *13*(4), 1858.

Sandvik, M. J., Daal, V., & Ader, J. H. (2014). Emergent literacy:preschool teachers' beliefs and practices. *Journal of Early Childhood Literacy*, *14*(1), 28–52. doi:10.1177/1468798413478026

Schirmer, R. B. (2005). Language and literacy development in children who are deaf. (2.Ed.) MA: Allyn and Bacon.

Scott, A., & Gillon, G. (2022). The evolution of an innovative online task to monitor children's oral narrative development. *Frontiers in Psychology*, *13*, 903124. https://doi.org/10.3389/fpsyg.2022.903124

Sharif, I., Rieber, S., Ozuah, P. O., & Reiber, S. (2002). Exposure to reach out and read and vocabulary outcomes in inner city preschoolers. *Journal of the National Medical Association*, *94*(3), 171. https://www.ncbi.nlm.nih.gov/pmc/articles/PMC2594107/pdf/jnma00320-0069.pdf PMID:11918387

Simpson, A., El-Refaie, A., Stephenson, C., Chen, Y. P. P., Deng, D., Erickson, S., Tay, D., Morris, M. E., Doube, W., & Caelli, T. (2015). Computer-based rehabilitation for developing speech and language in hearing-impaired children: A systematic review. *Deafness & Education International*, *17*(2), 111–119. https://doi.org/10.1179/1557069X14Y.0000000046

Snow, C. E., Burns, M. S., & Griffin, P. (1998). *Preventing reading difficulties in young children*. National Academy Press.

Soyoof, A., Reynolds, B. L., Neumann, M., Scull, J., Tour, E., & McLay, K. (2024). The impact of parent mediation on young children's home digital literacy practices and learning: A narrative review. *Journal of Computer Assisted Learning*, *40*(1), 65–88.

Sulzby, E., & Teale, W. H. (1987). *Young children's storybook reading: Longitudinal study of parent-child interaction and children's independent functioning*. Spencer Foundation, The University of Michigan.

Swanwick, R., & Watson, L. (2005). Literacy in the homes of young deaf children: Common and distinct features of spoken language and sign bilingual environments. *Journal of Early Childhood Literacy*, *5*(1), 53–78. doi:10.1177/1468798405050594

Teale, W. H., & Sulzby, E. (1986). Introduction: Emergent literacy as a perspective for examining how young children become writers and readers. In W. H. Teale & E. Sulzby (Eds.), *Emergent literacy* (pp. vii–xxii). Ablex Publishing.

Theriot, J. A., Franco, S. M., Sisson, B. A., Metcalf, S. C., Kennedy, M. A., & Bada, H. S. (2003). The impact of early literacy guidance on language skills of 3-year-olds. *Clinical Pediatrics*, *42*(2), 165–172. doi:10.1177/000992280304200211 PMID:12659391

Truax, R. R. (1978). Reading and language. In R. R. Kretschmer, L. W. Kretschmer, & R. R. Truax (Eds.), *Language development and intervention with the hearing impaired* (pp. 279–309). University Park Press.

Tufekcioglu, U. (2007). Cocuklarda isitme kaybının etkileri. U. Tufekcioglu (Ed.), İsitme konusma, gorme sorunu olan cocukların egitimi icinde (pp.1-45). Eskisehir: Anadolu University Publishing.

Turan, Z. KucukOncu D., Cankuvvet, N. & Yolal, Y. (2012). Koklear implant ve isitme cihazı kullanan isitme kayıplı cocukların dil ve dinleme becerilerinin degerlendirilmesi [Evaluation of language and listening skills of the children with hearing loss who use cochlear implants and hearing aids]. *Gulhane Tip Dergisi*, *4*, 142-150. https://cms.gulhanemedj.org/Uploads/Article_33377/GMJ-54-142-En.pdf

Turan, Z., Koca, A., & Uzuner, Y. (2019). İsitme kayıplı cocugu olan bir annenin aile egitimi surecinin incelenmesi. *Ankara Universitesi Egitim Bilimleri Fakultesi Ozel Egitim Dergisi*, *20*(1), 93–117. doi:10.21565/ozelegitimdergisi.417177

Uzuner, Y. (1993). *An investigation of a hearing mother's reading aloud efforts to her preschool age hearing and hearing impaired children before bedtime.* [Phd Dissertation. A.B.D: Cincinnati University].

van Steensel, R., McElvany, N., Kurvers, J., & Herppich, S. (2011). How effective are family literacy programs? results of a meta-analysis. *Review of Educational Research*, *81*(1), 69–96. doi:10.3102/0034654310388819

Vygotsky, L. S. (1978). *Mind in society the development of higher psychological processes*. Harvard University Press.

Wade, B., & Moore, M. (1993). *Bookstart in Birmingham: a description and evaluation of an exploratory British project to encourage sharing books with babies.* Book Trust.

Waldbart, A., Meyers, B., & Meyers, J. (2006). Invitations to families in an early literacy support program. *The Reading Teacher*, *59*(8), 774–785. doi:10.1598/RT.59.8.5

Weiss, Y., Yeatman, J. D., Ender, S., Gijbels, L., Loop, H., Mizrahi, J. C., Woo, B. Y., & Kuhl, P. K. (2022). Can an online reading camp teach 5-year-old children to read? *Frontiers in Human Neuroscience*, *16*, 52.

Whitehurst, G. J., & Lonigan, C. J. (1998). Child development and emergent literacy. *Child Development*, *69*(3), 848–872. doi:10.1111/j.1467-8624.1998.tb06247.x PMID:9680688

Wie, O. B., Falkenberg, O. T., & Tomblin, B. (2007). Children with a cochlear implant: Characteristics and determinants of speech recognition, speech recognition growth rate, and speech production. *International Journal of Audiology*, *46*(5), 232–243. doi:10.1080/14992020601182891 PMID:17487671

Williams, C. (2004). Emergent literacy of deaf children. *Journal of Deaf Studies and Deaf Education*, *9*(4), 352–365. doi:10.1093/deafed/enh045 PMID:15314011

Yaribakht, M., & Movallali, G. (2020). The effects of an early family-centered tele-intervention on the preverbal and listening skills of deaf children under tow years old. *Iranian Rehabilitation Journal*, *18*(2), 117–124.

Yoshinaga-Itano, C., Sedey, A. L., Wiggin, M., & Chung, W. (2017). Early hearing detection and vocabulary of children with hearing loss. *Pediatrics*, *140*(2).

Chapter 5
Early Literacy in the Digital Age:
Parental Roles Reimagined

Al Ryanne Gabonada Gatcho
ⓘD https://orcid.org/0000-0001-6825-2296
Hunan Institute of Science and Technology, China

Xin Geng Mao
Hunan Institute of Science and Technology, China

Fu Ting
Hunan Institute of Science and Technology, China

ABSTRACT

This chapter examines digital technology's impact on early literacy and parental roles. Traditional involvement, like reading and storytelling, now extends to overseeing digital content and using literacy tools. The authors analyze this shift, highlighting the dual role of parents as facilitators in blending digital and traditional literacy. This conceptual analysis underscores the need for parents to navigate digital platforms effectively, ensuring a balance between digital and traditional practices. Challenges include enhancing parental digital literacy for enriched learning experiences. The authors advocate for a collaborative approach among educators, parents, and policymakers to adapt to technological advancements in literacy education, pointing towards the evolving nature of parental guidance in a tech-rich educational environment. This work adds insight into the dynamic parental role in fostering early literacy amidst digital growth.

DOI: 10.4018/979-8-3693-1777-8.ch005

INTRODUCTION

In this digital epoch, the early literacy landscape emerges not only as an academic concern but as a crucible of societal evolution (Flewitt et al., 2015). This early stage of learning, once firmly rooted in the tactile world of printed texts and linear narratives, now grapples with the pervasive and often enigmatic influence of digital technology. The infiltration of this technology into the foundational layers of reading and writing has precipitated a significant shift in the pedagogical terrain. Early literacy, traditionally encapsulated within the pages of books and the spoken word, now finds itself inextricably interwoven with the pixels and interactive interfaces of digital media (Kucircova, 2017). This transition extends beyond a mere change in mediums. It represents a profound transformation in the very conduit through which young minds encounter and engage with language (Fauzi, 2020).

As the 21st century progresses, the implications of the digital revolution on literacy development are becoming increasingly intricate. This era, defined by swift technological progress and the omnipresence of smart devices, fundamentally challenges traditional literacy paradigms (Lestari et al., 2020). Today's children are active agents in a multimedia-saturated environment, not just passive absorbers of text (Xanthopoulou & Papagiannidis, 2012). Not only does this digital landscape offer a rich array of learning opportunities, but it also brings unique challenges in cultivating young learners' emerging literacy skills (Billington, 2016; Poveda, 2019). The fusion of conventional literacy with digital proficiency demands a rethinking of existing educational strategies and the roles of educators and parents. Effective navigation in this blended realm requires more than just teaching the mechanics of reading and writing; it involves fostering a comprehensive literacy that encompasses the varied and dynamic methods of communication and information exchange in the digital age.

Given the context of this digitally-dominated landscape, the imperative to redefine parental roles is paramount. As custodians of early education, parents are called upon to navigate and mediate the multifaceted dimensions of literacy, which now encompass digital acumen alongside traditional reading (Marsh et al., 2017). This shift is not merely adjunctive but fundamental. This ensures that children not only develop balanced literacy competences but also engage with the digital sphere with discernment and astuteness (Head, 2020). As the contours of literacy expand beyond conventional bounds, parental engagement must similarly evolve, adapting to these novel educational exigencies with alacrity and foresight.

In this concept analysis, we endeavor to accomplish several key objectives within the scope of redefining parental roles in early literacy amid the digital age. Firstly, we aim to articulate a comprehensive understanding of what constitutes parental involvement in early literacy in this new digital context. This involves dissecting the traditional paradigms and juxtaposing them against the contemporary digital landscape. Secondly, our analysis seeks to identify and elucidate the nuanced attributes that now characterize effective parental engagement in children's literacy development in a digital milieu. An additional objective is to explore the impacts, both potential and actualized, of this evolved parental role on children's literacy outcomes. This will encompass an examination of the challenges and opportunities presented by digital media in shaping these roles. Lastly, we offer insights and practical strategies for parents and educators, facilitating an adaptive and proactive approach to nurturing early literacy in a world increasingly dominated by digital influences. Through these objectives, our chapter strives to contribute a substantive and pragmatic discourse to the field of literacy education, addressing the exigencies of the 21st century's digital landscape.

Traditional Views of Parental Roles in Early Literacy

In the annals of early literacy development, the role of parents has been historically essential, often regarded as the primary architects of their children's initial foray into the world of words and meanings (Castro et al., 2015; Saracho, 2019). This traditional perspective positioned parents as the initial educators, a role imbued with the responsibility of igniting the spark of literacy in the nascent stages of a child's life. Their influence in these formative years laid the foundational stones of language acquisition, comprehension, and the overall relationship a child would develop with reading and writing (Nutbrown et al., 2017; Saracho, 2019).

Traditionally, parental involvement in early literacy hinged on direct, tangible methods (Cairney & Munsey, 1995; Howat, 2006; Machen et al., 2005). This included reading bedtime stories, introducing alphabet books, engaging in oral storytelling, and providing access to a range of print materials such as children's books and educational games. These activities, cherished as familial rituals, were pivotal in acquainting young minds with the rhythm and structure of language. Over time, the resources at parents' disposal evolved, particularly with the advent of public libraries (Aabo & Audson, 2012; Bracken & Fischel, 2008) and the proliferation of children's literature (Hourihan, 2005; Hunt, 2006; Nodelman, 2008). Additionally, the increasing recognition of early literacy's importance in child development research led to more structured approaches, with parents being guided on effective strategies to foster reading and writing skills (Burns et al., 1999; Jeynes, 2010). However, despite these developments, the essence of parental roles remained centered around direct engagement and the provision of reading materials, underscoring the timeless value of shared reading experiences (Sheridan et al., 2011).

This historical perspective of parental roles in early literacy, characterized by direct engagement and the provision of traditional resources, sets a critical backdrop against which the impact of the digital age can be understood. As we pivot to a more technologically integrated era, it becomes imperative to examine how these traditional roles are being reshaped. The advent of digital technology in the realm of literacy not only introduces new tools and platforms but also signifies a paradigm shift in how parents participate in and guide their children's literacy journey (Billington, 2016). This transition to the digital age, while retaining some foundational aspects of traditional practices, promises a complex, yet enriching landscape for early literacy development.

Digital Transformation Vis-a-vis Parental Involvement in Early Literacy

The arrival of the digital age brought with it sweeping changes across many fields, with early literacy experiencing some of the most significant transformations (Ahmad et al., 2021; Johnson, 2015). As an array of digital tools started to become integral to education, they profoundly influenced the landscape of early literacy. This influence necessitated a fresh look at how parents contribute to developing literacy skills in their children, moving beyond traditional practices to embrace new roles in a digitally-enriched environment (Berkowitz et al., 2021; Connell, et al., Hammer et al., 2021; Koch, 2018).

Far from the past focus on physical books and oral storytelling, the digital age introduces a plethora of interactive learning methods (Fatonah, 2020). E-books, educational apps, and various online platforms have broadened the avenues available for engaging young learners. In this technologically enriched landscape, parents find themselves adopting roles beyond traditional reading guides; they are now curators and companions in a digitally diverse educational journey, selecting suitable content and exploring alongside their children (Sung & Chiu, 2022; Troseth et al., 2020; Vezzoli et al., 2020). Simultaneously, an essential aspect of modern parenting is emerging as the mediation of digital content (Brito & Dias, 2020; Durak & Kaygin, 2020; Gozum & Kandir, 2021; Sciacca et al., 2022). Ensuring that children's encounters with technology are both beneficial and age-appropriate has become a key responsibility. Moreover, the ease of access to educational resources and learning communities in the digital realm has empowered parents from various backgrounds (Dias & Victor, 2022; Hammer et al., 2021). This newfound accessibility provides tools and information that were once challenging to obtain, leveling the educational playing field and diversifying the learning experiences available to children.

Overall, the influence of the digital age on how parents support early literacy is both profound and far-reaching. Gone are the days when parental involvement was limited to traditional reading and storytelling. Now, it encompasses guiding digital literacy, mediating the content children interact with, and adeptly using a range of advanced digital tools (Fatonah, 2020; Johnson, 2015). This evolution mirrors the larger shifts in our technological landscape and signals a deeper change in our understanding and approach to literacy in young children. As the digital era continues to unfold, parental roles are dynamically evolving, balancing between time-honored practices and the innovative demands of tech-infused education.

Parental Involvement in Early Digital Literacy Research

Early digital literacy presents a field abundant in both innovation and exploration. The growing emphasis on digital literacy signifies a pivotal shift in educational priorities, recognizing the essential role that technology plays in the early stages of children's learning (Kaye, 2016; Palaiologou, 2016; Schriever, 2018; Undheim, 2022. This body of research, expanding rapidly, seeks to unravel the complexities of how parents can most effectively support their children's literacy in an increasingly digital world.

Recent studies shed light on the multifaceted nature of parental involvement in early digital literacy (Connell et al., 2015; George & Odgers, 2015; Laranjeiro et al., 2018; Patrikakou, 2016). Findings consistently underscore the positive impacts of engaged and informed parental guidance, linking it to enhanced literacy skills, better comprehension, and more positive attitudes towards reading in digital formats among children. However, these studies also bring to light evolving challenges. These include the need for parents to keep pace with technological advancements (McDaniel, 2019; McDaniel & Radesky, 2018), the importance of discerning high-quality digital content (Kildare & Middlemiss, 2017, Thompson at al., 2015), and the balancing act between screen time and traditional reading (Hiniker et al., 2016; McDaniel, 2019; Novianti & Garzia, 2020).

Researchers have also highlighted the critical role of parental digital literacy, noting that parents' own skills and attitudes towards digital media significantly influence their effectiveness in supporting their children (Mulya et al., 2023; Velez et al., 2017). Despite the wealth of insights, the current research landscape is not without its gaps and areas of contention. Some studies point to a lack of comprehensive understanding of the long-term impacts of digital literacy practices (Boonk et al., 2018), while others call for more diverse and inclusive research that accounts for varying socio-economic backgrounds (Benner et al., 2016) and access to technology (Hall & Bierman, 2015). Additionally, the rapidly evolving nature of digital media means that research findings can quickly become outdated, posing a challenge for both parents and educators seeking to stay informed (Ahmad, 2015).

The insights gleaned from contemporary research are invaluable, particularly when viewed through the lens of this concept analysis paper. By examining the current state of parental involvement in early digital literacy, this research not only enriches our understanding but also lays a foundation for the analytical exploration in our study. It acts as a guiding light in our pursuit to redefine and contextualize parental roles in the digital era. As we chart our course through the evolving landscape of digital literacy, these research findings and discussions become instrumental. They inform the development of strategies, policies, and practices tailored to effectively nurture and support the literacy development of the emerging generation of digital natives.

ANALYTICAL APPROACH

In the quest to unravel the complexities of redefining parental roles in early literacy within the digital age, our analysis employs the structured methodology developed by Walker and Avant (2011). Renowned for its rigor and clarity, Walker and Avant's method provides a systematic approach to concept analysis, ensuring a thorough and comprehensive exploration of the concept in question. The methodology encompasses eight critical steps:

The selection of Walker and Avant's method as the analytical framework for this chpater is underpinned by its structured and comprehensive approach, which is particularly conducive to the nuanced exploration required in redefining parental roles in early literacy in the digital age. This method's systematic nature allows for an in-depth examination of the concept, ensuring that every aspect is thoroughly explored and articulated. Its emphasis on identifying defining attributes, antecedents, and consequences aligns consistently with the objective of this paper, which seeks to not only redefine parental roles but also to understand the broader implications of this shift within a digital context. Furthermore, the inclusion of model and borderline cases in Walker and Avant's framework offers a robust means to delineate the concept clearly, a critical factor when dealing with the complex interplay of digital technology and early literacy. In essence, this method provides a balanced blend of rigor and flexibility, necessary for dissecting and recontextualizing a traditional concept like parental roles in the evolving landscape of digital literacy.

CONCEPT ANALYSIS

Defining Key Concepts: Parental Roles and Early Literacy in the Digital Age

In the context of this concept analysis, 'Parental Roles' in early literacy encompass a spectrum of responsibilities and activities that parents undertake to foster their children's reading and writing skills. Historically, this role was primarily centered

Table 1. Walker and Avant's concept analysis methods

Step	Description
Selecting a Concept	Identification of the concept to be analyzed, in this case, 'parental roles in early literacy in the digital age'.
Determining the Aims or Purposes of the Analysis	Clarifying the goals of the concept analysis, specifically focusing on understanding and redefining the concept within the current digital context.
Identifying All Uses of the Concept	An extensive review of literature to gather various instances and applications of the concept, providing a broader understanding of its scope and significance.
Determining the Defining Attributes	Identifying the essential characteristics that appear repeatedly in relation to the concept, forming the core of the concept's definition.
Identifying Model Cases	Examples that embody all the identified attributes of the concept, providing clear and definitive illustrations of the concept in its purest form.
Identifying Borderline, Related, Contrary, Invented, and Illegitimate Cases	Examination of cases that are not clear-cut examples of the concept, helping to further clarify and delineate the concept's boundaries.
Identifying Antecedents and Consequences	Identifying the events or incidents that need to occur before the concept can happen (antecedents) and the events that happen as a result of the concept (consequences).
Defining Empirical Referents	Determining how the concept can be measured or tested in the real world, which helps in operationalizing the concept for research or practical application.

around direct interactions such as reading aloud, storytelling, and providing access to books, fundamentally positioning parents as the primary facilitators of their children's initial encounters with language and text (Damber, 2015). In contemporary times, however, these roles have expanded and adapted in response to the digital age (Collins & Halverson, 2018). Parents now also act as guides and mediators in their children's engagement with digital literacy tools, such as e-books, educational apps, and online learning platforms. This modern understanding of parental roles in early literacy reflects a dynamic balance between traditional, hands-on involvement and the navigation of the digital literacy landscape.

'Early Literacy', within the scope of this paper, refers to the foundational skills and understandings about reading and writing that children develop from birth to the beginning of formal education. It is a critical period where children learn the basics of language, including phonemic awareness, vocabulary, and narrative skills, typically through traditional mediums like books and oral storytelling (Snow, 2017). In the digital age, the concept of early literacy has evolved to incorporate digital competencies. It now includes children's interactions with digital text, their comprehension of multimedia content, and their ability to navigate and interpret information from various digital sources. This expanded definition acknowledges that literacy in the 21st century is not just about reading and writing in the traditional sense but also involves a set of skills and knowledge necessary to effectively engage with digital media.

Digital Influence on Parental Roles: Key Attributes Redefined

One of the key attributes of the redefined parental role in early literacy is the role of parents as facilitators of digital learning experiences (Connell et al., 2015; George & Odgers, 2015; Laranjeiro et al., 2018; Patrikakou, 2016). This encompasses more than just providing access to digital tools and resources; it involves actively engaging with children in these environments. Parents today are expected to co-explore digital platforms with their children, assist in interactive learning apps, and encourage digital problem-solving skills. This role shifts the focus from passive observation to active participation and guidance in the digital learning process.

Another critical attribute is the integration of digital literacy skills. In the modern era, parents are not only responsible for introducing traditional reading and writing skills but also for guiding their children in navigating the digital world (Fatonah, 2020; Johnson, 2015). This involves teaching them how to access and comprehend information from digital sources, discerning the credibility of online content, and understanding the nuances of digital communication. It is a role that blends the basics of alphabetic and phonemic awareness with the complexities of digital navigation and comprehension.

The third attribute is the balanced integration of traditional and digital literacy methods (Berkowitz et al., 2021; Connell, et al., Hammer et al., 2021; Koch, 2018). This aspect recognizes the value of harmonizing the conventional approach of reading physical books with the interactive nature of digital literacy tools. Parents who embrace this attribute, ensure their children benefit from the tangible feel and focused attention of traditional reading while also engaging with the dynamic and interactive learning experiences that digital platforms offer. This balanced approach fosters a comprehensive literacy environment, accommodating both time-honored reading practices and the innovative demands of the digital era.

The fourth and equally important attribute revolves around the concept of parental mediation in digital consumption (Sung & Chiu, 2022; Troseth et al., 2020; Vezzoli et al., 2020). In this era, where children are exposed to an overwhelming array of digital content, parents are required to be gatekeepers and mentors. They need to manage screen time, ensure age-appropriate content, and facilitate meaningful digital interactions. This role is crucial in balancing the benefits of digital literacy tools with the potential risks associated with excessive or inappropriate digital exposure.

To visually illustrate the redefined parental roles in early literacy amid the digital age, let us look at the FIBI Engagement Model. This conceptual framework brings to light the nuanced interplay between four pivotal attributes: Facilitation of Digital

Figure 1. Gatcho, Mao, and Ting's FIBI parental engagement model: Redefined roles of parents in early literacy in the digital age

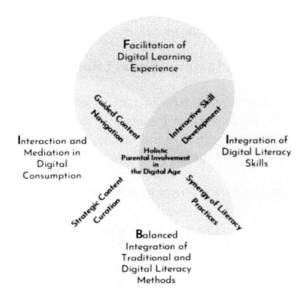

Learning Experience, Integration of Digital Literacy Skills, Balanced Integration of Traditional and Digital Literacy Methods, and Interaction and Mediation in Digital Consumption. The model's intersecting circles reveal where these roles overlap and enrich one another, highlighting the multifaceted nature of modern parental engagement in literacy.

In the FIBI Engagement Model, the core concept of 'Holistic Parental Involvement in the Digital Age' is posited to potentially illustrate the intersections among key attributes. At the intersection of Facilitation and Integration, it is conceivable that parents may engage with their children in co-developing literacy skills using digital tools. The overlap of Integration and Balanced Methods might hint at a blending of traditional and digital literacy practices. Similarly, the connection between Balanced Methods and Interaction could imply a strategic role for parents in diversifying literacy inputs, while the juncture of Interaction and Facilitation may emphasize guiding and mediating digital literacy experiences. Collectively, these interconnections suggest a dynamic and comprehensive view of parental roles, underlining the potential need for adaptability, active participation, and thoughtful mediation in nurturing a holistic literacy environment for children in the digital world. It is important to note, however, that the points of convergence described here are not the only instances of interconnection within the model. Other intersections are likely to exist, contributing further to the comprehensive nature of this model. These additional interconnections, although not explicitly detailed here, are crucial in understanding the full scope and depth of parental involvement in the digital age, providing a more nuanced and multidimensional perspective of the model.

Illustrative Cases: Navigating Digital Literacy in Parental Roles

To imagine the redefined parental roles in early literacy within the digital age, let us consider the following hypothetical scenarios. These cases are constructed to demonstrate how different aspects of digital influence might manifest in real-world parenting situations, reflecting the key attributes identified in our concept analysis.

Guided Exploration: Mark's Proactive Role in Digital Learning

In our first case, we explore a father's dedicated role as a facilitator in his children's digital learning journey. Mark recognizes that the digital world is an integral part of modern education and is committed to ensuring that his children benefit from it in a structured and meaningful way. He has developed a routine that allocates specific times for his children to explore educational websites, a strategy that brings both regularity and importance to their digital learning experiences.

Mark's approach is characterized by active participation rather than passive supervision. During these digital learning sessions, he sits alongside his children, engaging with the content they are exploring. This involvement allows him to directly gauge the quality and appropriateness of the educational material. He ensures that the websites and apps they use are not only engaging but also align with their learning levels and curriculum needs. This hands-on method enables Mark to provide immediate assistance and clarification, thereby enhancing the learning process. Additionally, Mark uses these sessions as opportunities to teach his children about more than just academic subjects. He recognizes the importance of internet safety and the responsible use of digital media. Through practical examples and guided exploration, he educates them on how to navigate the digital world securely, discern reliable from unreliable information, and understand the implications of their digital footprint. These lessons are crucial in preparing his children to be savvy and responsible digital citizens.

Mark's active role in these digital learning experiences fosters a collaborative environment. His children not only learn from the digital content but also from their interactions with him. This collaborative approach nurtures a positive attitude towards learning and technology, helping his children see the digital world as a resourceful and safe space for knowledge and growth.

Through the lens of Mark's case, we witness how a parent's role as a facilitator of digital learning experiences can profoundly impact a child's educational journey. His proactive and involved approach exemplifies the evolving nature of parental roles in the digital age, highlighting the importance of guiding and participating in children's digital learning activities.

Interactive Storytelling: John's Digital Engagement in Literacy

In our second case, we delve deeper into John's approach to integrating digital literacy skills in his son Alex's early education. John, cognizant of the burgeoning role that technology plays in modern learning, has embraced storytelling apps as a key tool in Alex's language development. This decision marks a significant shift from the conventional bedtime story routine, infusing it with the interactivity and engagement that digital platforms offer.

John's methodology is meticulous and thoughtful. He does not randomly select apps; instead, he spends time researching and choosing those with narratives that are not only age-appropriate but also intellectually and emotionally stimulating for Alex. This careful curation ensures that the digital content aligns with Alex's current developmental needs and interests, making the learning experience both enjoyable and effective. However, John's involvement goes far beyond just providing the right tools. He actively immerses himself in the storytelling sessions, making them interactive and dynamic. As the app narrates stories, John pauses at key moments to discuss the plot with Alex. He asks open-ended questions, prompting Alex to think about the characters' motivations, the storyline's progression, and the underlying themes. This dialogue transforms the experience from passive listening to an active learning process. It not only aids in developing Alex's language comprehension but also fosters critical thinking skills and emotional intelligence.

John also uses these sessions to highlight the nuances of language and storytelling. He points out new vocabulary, explains complex sentences, and discusses the moral or lesson of the story. This approach ensures that the digital storytelling experience is as rich and educational as traditional reading, if not more. Furthermore, John's participation in these digital literacy activities strengthens the bond between him and Alex. They share moments of laughter, curiosity, and learning, creating memories that extend beyond the realm of literacy development.

Through John's case, we see a vivid example of how the integration of digital literacy skills in parental roles can enrich and enhance the traditional aspects of early literacy. His approach demonstrates how technology, when used thoughtfully and interactively, can be a powerful tool in nurturing a child's love for stories and learning.

Blending Worlds: Linda's Hybrid Approach to Literacy

Linda's strategy in fostering her daughter Maya's literacy development exemplifies the third attribute of blending traditional and digital literacy methods. Her approach is a thoughtful integration of the classic and the contemporary, recognizing the unique benefits of each medium in the context of early literacy.

Linda appreciates the timeless value of traditional books – the tactile experience of turning pages, the visual appeal of illustrations, and the personal interaction during reading sessions. These moments with physical books are not just about reading; they are cherished bonding experiences that also instill a love for literature in Maya. Linda chooses books that are not only age-appropriate but also rich in storytelling and imagery, sparking Maya's imagination and curiosity.

Simultaneously, Linda embraces the advantages of digital technology in literacy. She introduces e-books as a complementary tool and not as a replacement for physical books. These digital books come with interactive features like animated illustrations, read-along audio, and interactive games that enhance comprehension and engagement. Linda carefully selects e-books that align with the themes or subjects of their physical book counterparts. For example, if Maya is reading a physical book about space, Linda might choose an e-book that delves deeper into specific aspects of astronomy or space exploration, making the learning experience more comprehensive and interactive.

This hybrid approach ensures that Maya's literacy experience is multifaceted. It combines the depth and focus of traditional reading with the interactivity and engagement of digital platforms. By moving seamlessly between physical books and e-books, Linda provides Maya with a rich, varied literacy diet that is well-suited for the digital age. It is a strategy that recognizes the value of each medium and uses them in concert to create a well-rounded literacy experience.

Linda's case is a testament to the evolving nature of parental roles in literacy development. Her balanced approach of integrating traditional reading with digital exploration exemplifies the effective combination of these two worlds, offering a comprehensive and enriching literacy environment for Maya.

Curating Digital Tools: Sally's Approach to Literacy Enhancement

Sally's approach to her daughter Rina's early literacy development exemplifies the vital role of parental mediation in digital consumption. Sally takes an active and discerning role in curating the digital tools that Rina uses. Her method is meticulous and thoughtful, reflecting a deep commitment to ensuring that Rina's engagement with digital media is both beneficial and appropriate for her age and learning stage. Her strategy involves a careful selection of educational apps. She looks for applications that are not only visually appealing and engaging but also rich in educational value. Her focus is particularly on apps that enhance phonemic awareness and early reading skills, fundamental building blocks in literacy. This careful curation process means Sally often spends time researching and evaluating different apps, reading reviews from other parents and educators, and even trying them out herself before introducing them to Rina.

However, Sally's involvement does not end with the selection of digital tools. She actively monitors Rina's interaction with these apps. This ongoing evaluation is not merely about screen time but about the quality of engagement and learning. Sally observes how Rina interacts with the app, the progress she makes, and how effectively the app reinforces and expands her literacy skills. This continuous assessment helps Sally in making informed decisions about whether to continue using an app, try different approaches, or introduce new applications that align with Rina's evolving needs and interests.

Moreover, Sally's role extends to moderating the balance between digital and traditional literacy experiences. She ensures that Rina's exposure to screens is balanced with hands-on activities like reading physical books, writing, and drawing. This balance is crucial in developing a well-rounded literacy foundation.

Through Sally's case, we see the embodiment of the modern parent's role in mediating digital consumption. Her proactive approach in selecting, evaluating, and balancing digital literacy tools demonstrates the crucial role of parents in navigating the plethora of digital resources available. Sally's involvement ensures that Rina's digital literacy journey is not only engaging and educational but also tailored to her individual development, exemplifying effective parental mediation in the digital age.

Clarifying the Concept: Borderline, Related, and Contrary Cases

When redefining complex concepts like parental roles in early literacy in the digital age, it is pivotal to explore a range of scenarios. Borderline cases demonstrate where the concept is present but not fully actualized, helping to define its nuanced edges. Related cases, while sharing similarities, are fundamentally different, distinguishing the primary concept from adjacent ideas. Contrary cases, being the direct opposite, offer a stark contrast, clarifying what the concept is not. Examining these varied case types provides a comprehensive understanding (Walker & Avant, 2011), essential for a thorough redefinition of the concept.

Borderline Case: Theo's Passive Digital Approach

Consider the scenario of Theo, a parent who recognizes the significance of digital literacy in his child's education but demonstrates minimal involvement. Theo ensures that his child has access to various educational apps, perceiving them as beneficial tools for learning. However, his involvement typically ends there. He does not actively participate in or guide his child's engagement with these digital resources. For instance, while his child uses an app to learn new vocabulary, Theo is not present to discuss the content, ask questions, or provide additional support. This lack of active engagement is particularly evident during the evenings, when Theo prefers to let the app serve as a substitute for his involvement in the learning process.

Theo's approach represents a borderline case in the context of redefined parental roles in digital literacy. While he understands and appreciates the importance of digital tools in his child's literacy development, he falls short of fully embracing these tools as integral components of a comprehensive literacy strategy. His stance is one of passive approval rather than active participation. This approach partially aligns with the redefined concept, acknowledging the value of digital literacy but lacking in proactive, engaged facilitation and guidance. Theo's case exemplifies the threshold where acknowledgment of digital importance exists but is not complemented by active and involved parenting in the digital literacy process.

Related Case: Lance's Hesitation Towards Digital Integration

Lance's approach to his son's literacy development provides a related case that differs distinctly from the redefined concept of parental roles in the digital age. Lance is a dedicated father, deeply committed to his son's traditional literacy development. He spends time reading physical books to him, enthusiastically bringing stories to life and engaging in rich discussions about the characters and plots. This nightly ritual has been a cornerstone of their bonding and educational journey.

However, Lance's involvement noticeably diminishes when it comes to digital literacy activities. Despite having access to various educational websites and e-book platforms, he rarely encourages his son to use them and does not participate in these digital learning experiences. His hesitancy towards digital platforms stems from a belief that traditional books offer a more authentic and focused learning experience. This reluctance to embrace digital tools represents a gap in Lance's approach to literacy. He excels in fostering a love for reading through traditional means but overlooks the expanding scope of literacy in the digital era.

Lance's case is related to the concept of parental roles in early literacy but does not fully align with the redefined model that incorporates digital literacy. His strong focus on traditional literacy is commendable, yet his limited engagement with digital platforms highlights a crucial aspect of the evolving parental role that he has yet to embrace. This scenario illustrates the need for a balance between traditional and digital literacy approaches in modern parenting.

Contrary Case: Bella's Traditionalist Stance

In a stark contrast to the redefined concept of parental roles in early literacy, Bella's approach serves as a contrary case. As a mother, she firmly adheres to traditional literacy methods, exclusively using physical books for her daughter's reading and learning activities. Bella's belief is deeply rooted in the idea that traditional books are the only valid and effective tools for literacy development. She views storytime as an irreplaceable ritual, involving turning the pages of a book and exploring its physical content.

Bella consciously avoids incorporating any form of digital media into her daughter's literacy journey. She is skeptical of the educational value of digital platforms and e-books, concerned about screen time and the sensory experience that digital devices offer. This decision to exclude digital tools is based on her belief that the best method to develop her daughter's literacy skill is similar to how she was taught.

Her stance places her in direct opposition to the evolving landscape of early literacy, which increasingly recognizes the importance of integrating digital literacy alongside traditional methods. By dismissing the potential benefits and educational opportunities that digital media can offer, Bella's approach contradicts the redefined concept of parental roles. This includes actively engaging with digital tools and guiding children in navigating the digital world as part of their literacy development. Bella's case vividly illustrates a perspective that overlooks the significant role digital literacy plays in modern education and child development.

CHANGING DYNAMICS IN THE DIGITAL AGE

Technological Influences on Parental Roles in Early Literacy

The digital age has ushered in transformative changes in early literacy, significantly altering the traditional landscape of parental involvement (Ahmad et al., 2021; Johnson, 2015). One notable influence is the advent of interactive e-books and storytelling apps, which have expanded the dimensions of reading beyond the physical page (Fatonah, 2020). These tools offer multimedia features such as animations, sound effects, and interactive games that not only capture children's attention but also enhance comprehension and engagement (Berkowitz et al., 2021; Connell et al., 2015). Parents are increasingly incorporating these technologies into reading routines, transitioning from solely being story readers to facilitators of a multi-sensory learning experience, as exemplified by the hybrid approach of combining traditional books with digital media (Hammer et al., 2021; Koch, 2018).

Another significant technological influence is the rise of educational platforms and apps designed specifically for young learners. These platforms often include activities that build foundational skills such as phonemic awareness, vocabulary, and narrative understanding. The role of parents has evolved in this context as well; they are now curators of digital content, selecting appropriate and effective apps, and co-navigators in their children's digital learning journey (Fatonah, 2020; Johnson, 2015). This shift highlights a move towards a more involved and participatory role for parents, requiring them to be more proactive and knowledgeable about the digital tools and resources available (George & Odgers, 2015; Laranjeiro et al., 2018; Patrikakou, 2016).

Overall, the influence of technology on parental roles in early literacy is profound and far-reaching. It has not only introduced new tools and methods for literacy development but has also necessitated a rethinking of the parental role. The traditional image of parents reading a book to their child still holds value but now exists alongside a broader spectrum of digital engagement. This expansion reflects a deeper integration of technology in everyday life and signifies a broader cultural shift in how literacy skills are developed and nurtured. Parents, in this digital landscape, are required to be both guides and partners in their children's literacy journey, adapting to the changing dynamics brought about by technological advancements.

Challenges and Opportunities

Digital platforms, although brimming with educational potential, come with their own set of challenges that parents must navigate. The issue of screen time is a major concern, with its potential to impact young children's health and developmental processes (Kaye, 2016). Excessive use of screens, especially among the very young, is often linked to disruptions in sleep, shorter attention spans, and reduced physical activity. Another pressing challenge for parents is the daunting task of filtering through a vast array of digital content (Poveda, 2019). With a blend of both enriching and distracting materials available online, finding age-appropriate and genuinely educational content can be overwhelming. Furthermore, as children increasingly engage with digital platforms, concerns over data privacy and security have become more pronounced (Billington, 2016; Poveda, 2019; Marsh et al., 2017). These challenges highlight the need for careful consideration and proactive management of children's interactions with digital media (Kaye, 2016; Palaiologou, 2016; Schriever, 2018; Undheim, 2022).

While digital platforms pose certain challenges, they simultaneously offer substantial opportunities for enhancing early literacy, including the potential for closer collaboration between parents and teachers. These platforms provide access to a diverse and interactive array of educational content, which can accommodate various learning styles and needs, making literacy development more inclusive and tailored (George & Odgers, 2015). They are particularly effective in engaging reluctant readers through interactive e-books, educational apps, and online story platforms. Crucially, digital tools enable a stronger partnership between parents and educators, allowing seamless integration and reinforcement of classroom learning at home. Additionally, they broaden children's perspectives by connecting them to global stories and educational materials, fostering cultural awareness and a sense of global community (Connell et al., 2015; George & Odgers, 2015; Laranjeiro et al., 2018; Patrikakou, 2016). This multifaceted approach not only enriches the literacy experience but also cultivates a more comprehensive understanding of the world.

The key to harnessing the potential of digital platforms in early literacy lies in finding a balance between these challenges and opportunities (Connell et al., 2015; Patrikakou, 2016). On one hand, digital platforms pose concerns such as managing screen time to safeguard young children's health and development, filtering through an overwhelming mix of content to find valuable educational material, and addressing issues of data privacy and security. These challenges necessitate careful consideration and proactive involvement from parents to ensure children's interactions with digital media are safe and beneficial. On the other hand, these platforms open doors to vast, diverse, and interactive educational content that can greatly enhance literacy, catering to different learning needs and styles. They offer unique opportunities for engaging reluctant readers and facilitate stronger collaboration between parents and educators, creating a cohesive learning experience that extends beyond the classroom (George & Odgers, 2015). Moreover, the global reach of digital platforms enriches children's learning experiences, broadening their cultural perspectives and connecting them to a wider community. Thus, while the challenges require mindful navigation, the opportunities, when harnessed effectively, can significantly enrich the landscape of early literacy, making it more inclusive, engaging, and expansive.

EMPIRICAL REFERENTS

Measurable Outcomes

The evolution of parental roles in early literacy, particularly with the integration of digital tools, can be observed in various tangible ways. One clear indicator is the nature of parent-child interactions during learning activities (Connell et al., 2015;

George & Odgers, 2015; Laranjeiro et al., 2018; Patrikakou, 2016). Traditional roles often involved parents reading books to children or helping them with homework, which can now be complemented or enhanced by digital interactions (Berkowitz et al., 2021; Connell, et al., Hammer et al., 2021; Koch, 2018). For example, parents may now be seen engaging with their children through educational apps, discussing digital content, or co-navigating online learning platforms. Another observable change is the shift in the types of resources parents use for their children's literacy development (Fatonah, 2020; Johnson, 2015). The inclusion of digital tools such as e-books, educational websites, and language learning apps alongside traditional books marks a significant alteration in parental approaches to literacy support.

Measuring the impact of these changes in parental roles on children's literacy development involves a combination of qualitative and quantitative approaches (Johnson, 2015). Surveys and interviews with parents and educators can provide insights into how parental involvement has shifted with the advent of digital tools. These qualitative methods can explore parents' perceptions of their roles, the challenges they face, and the strategies they find most effective. Quantitatively, researchers can assess literacy outcomes in children through standardized tests or assessments that measure reading comprehension, vocabulary, and other key literacy skills. Comparisons can be made between children who experience varied levels of digital interaction facilitated by parents and those with more traditional literacy exposures. Additionally, tracking usage patterns of digital tools and correlating them with literacy outcomes can offer concrete data on the effectiveness of these new parental approaches in real-world settings.

IMPLICATIONS FOR LITERACY EDUCATION

The fusion of digital and traditional literacy methods represents a critical pedagogical shift (Billington, 2016; Poveda, 2019). Traditional teaching methodologies are now thoughtfully interspersed with digital innovations. This shift, more than just following technological trends, enriches the educational experience with interactive elements that resonate with today's learners (Marsh et al., 2017). Educators find value in integrating tools like interactive e-books and educational apps alongside time-honored teaching practices, a blend that is strategic to keep literacy education in pace with digital competencies required in contemporary society (Kaye, 2016).

A pivotal aspect of enhancing literacy education extends beyond merely incorporating digital literacy into curricula. It necessitates a deliberate focus on bolstering parental involvement in early literacy (Palaiologou, 2016). The formulation of policies that actively support educational programs for parents, particularly in digital literacy, enables parents to become effective partners in their children's learning (Schriever, 2018). This approach should advocate for regular updates of digital resources and promote collaborative platforms between parents and teachers, bridging the gap between classroom learning and home education (Connell et al., 2015). Moreover, policy frameworks should aim to establish robust communication channels between schools and families, facilitating updates on academic progress and encouraging parental engagement in early literacy programs (George & Odgers, 2015; Laranjeiro et al., 2018). Acknowledging the diversity of family backgrounds is crucial, ensuring equitable access to these resources irrespective of socio-economic status, thus promoting a more equitable educational landscape (Patrikakou, 2016). Implementing these policies is instrumental in creating a literacy education framework that is comprehensive, inclusive, and responsive to the evolving demands of the digital era.

FUTURE DIRECTIONS

In the evolving interplay between early literacy and digital technology, further research is crucial to understand the changing dynamics of parental roles (Boonk et al., 2018; Durak & Kaygin, 2020; Hall & Bierman, 2015). Key areas for investigation include the impact of digital literacy tools on parent-child interactions and learning outcomes. Research is needed to assess how different digital platforms influence parents' ability to support their children's literacy development and how these interactions shape children's cognitive and emotional growth. Another vital area is exploring strategies that enable parents from diverse backgrounds to effectively utilize digital tools, ensuring equitable access and addressing the digital divide. Additionally, studies on the effectiveness of parental training programs in digital literacy, and their impact on children's literacy skills, are essential. This research will not only deepen our academic understanding but also guide practical applications in literacy education, helping to shape policies and practices that support parents in their evolving roles in the digital age.

Further, current technological trends are significantly reshaping parental roles. The proliferation of interactive learning apps, augmented reality (AR) storybooks, and voice-assisted devices has created new avenues for engaging children in literacy activities (Flewitt et al., 2015; Kervin, 2016; Neumann & Neumann, 2017). These technologies not only enhance the reading experience but also provide parents with innovative tools to engage with their children. For instance, AR storybooks bring stories to life, offering a multisensory reading experience that can captivate both parents and children. Similarly, voice-assisted devices like smart speakers are introducing new interactive ways for families to engage with storytelling and literacy games, making reading a more dynamic family activity.

Looking ahead, we can anticipate further advancements in technology that will continue to transform parental roles in literacy education. Emerging technologies like artificial intelligence (AI) and machine learning could lead to more personalized learning experiences, adapting content to suit individual children's reading levels and interests. Virtual reality (VR) might offer immersive reading environments, creating interactive and engaging worlds that encourage a deeper connection to literature. These technological advancements could redefine the way parents support their children's literacy, offering more tailored and immersive experiences. As these technologies become more integrated into everyday life, parental roles could evolve from facilitators of reading to guides in a broader, more interactive literary world.

The prospect of these advancements underscores the importance of preparing for a future where parental roles in literacy are continually evolving. This preparation involves not just keeping abreast of technological trends but also understanding how to integrate these tools effectively into children's literacy development. Educators and policymakers need to consider strategies for training parents in these new technologies, ensuring they can guide their children through these advanced literacy experiences. Schools and educational institutions will play a crucial role in bridging the gap between emerging technologies and practical literacy applications, providing resources and support to help parents navigate this ever-changing landscape.

CONCLUSION

This analysis, guided by Walker and Avant's framework, has illuminated the evolving nature of parental roles in early literacy within the digital age. Key findings underscore the significant shift from traditional literacy practices to a more dynamic, technology-integrated approach. We have identified critical attributes such as the integration of digital literacy skills, facilitation of digital learning experiences, and mediation in digital consumption. Additionally, the role of parents has expanded to include active engagement with digital tools, a balance of traditional and digital literacy methods, and collaboration with educators. These shifts highlight the need for a more inclusive, multifaceted approach to literacy education, one that embraces the challenges and opportunities presented by digital platforms.

Utilizing Walker and Avant's method provided a structured approach to dissect and understand the complex concept of parental involvement in digital age literacy. It allowed for a comprehensive exploration of attributes, antecedents, and consequences, leading to a more nuanced understanding of the concept. In conclusion, the redefinition of parental roles in early literacy is not just a response to technological advancements but a necessary adaptation to a digitally-enriched educational landscape. This evolution calls for ongoing research, updated educational policies, and proactive strategies to ensure parents are equipped to effectively guide their children's literacy journey. Embracing these changes is crucial for preparing young learners to navigate an increasingly digital world, ensuring they acquire not only the foundational skills of reading and writing but also the critical ability to interact with digital media.

REFERENCES

Aabø, S., & Audunson, R. (2012). Use of library space and the library as place. *Library & Information Science Research*, *34*(2), 138–149. doi:10.1016/j.lisr.2011.06.002

Ahmad, F. K. (2015). Use of assistive technology in inclusive education: Making room for diverse learning needs. *Transcience*, *6*(2), 62–77.

Ahmad, Z., Soroya, M. S., Tariq, M., & Chaudhry, M. S. (2021). An empirical analysis of parental involvement in leisure reading development of the children. *Library Philosophy and Practice*, *5012*, 1–20.

Benner, A. D., Boyle, A. E., & Sadler, S. (2016). Parental involvement and adolescents' educational success: The roles of prior achievement and socioeconomic status. *Journal of Youth and Adolescence*, *45*(6), 1053–1064. doi:10.1007/s10964-016-0431-4 PMID:26847424

Berkowitz, R., Astor, R. A., Pineda, D., DePedro, K. T., Weiss, E. L., & Benbenishty, R. (2021). Parental involvement and perceptions of school climate in California. *Urban Education*, *56*(3), 393–423. doi:10.1177/0042085916685764

Billington, C. (2016). *How digital technology can support early language and literacy outcomes in early years settings: A review of the literature*. National Literacy Trust.

Boonk, L., Gijselaers, H. J., Ritzen, H., & Brand-Gruwel, S. (2018). A review of the relationship between parental involvement indicators and academic achievement. *Educational Research Review*, *24*, 10–30. doi:10.1016/j.edurev.2018.02.001

Bracken, S. S., & Fischel, J. E. (2008). Family reading behavior and early literacy skills in preschool children from low-income backgrounds. *Early Education and Development*, *19*(1), 45–67. doi:10.1080/10409280701838835

Cairney, T. H., & Munsie, L. (1995). Parent participation in literacy learning. *The Reading Teacher*, *48*(5), 392–403.

Castro, M., Expósito-Casas, E., López-Martín, E., Lizasoain, L., Navarro-Asencio, E., & Gaviria, J. L. (2015). Parental involvement on student academic achievement: A meta-analysis. *Educational Research Review*, *14*, 33–46. doi:10.1016/j.edurev.2015.01.002

Collins, A., & Halverson, R. (2018). *Rethinking education in the age of technology: The digital revolution and schooling in America*. Teachers College Press.

Connell, S. L., Lauricella, A. R., & Wartella, E. (2015). Parental co-use of media technology with their young children in the USA. *Journal of Children and Media*, *9*(1), 5–21. doi:10.1080/17482798.2015.997440

Damber, U. (2015). Read-alouds in preschool–A matter of discipline? *Journal of Early Childhood Literacy*, *15*(2), 256–280. doi:10.1177/1468798414522823

Dias, L., & Victor, A. (2022). Teaching and learning with mobile devices in the 21st century digital world: Benefits and challenges. *European Journal of Multidisciplinary Studies*, *7*(1), 26–34.

Durak, A., & Kaygin, H. (2020). Parental mediation of young children's internet use: Adaptation of parental mediation scale and review of parental mediation based on the demographic variables and digital data security awareness. *Education and Information Technologies*, *25*(3), 2275–2296. doi:10.1007/s10639-019-10079-1

Fatonah, N. (2020). Parental involvement in early childhood literacy development. *In International Conference on Early Childhood Education and Parenting 2019 (ECEP 2019)* (pp. 193-198). Atlantis Press. 10.2991/assehr.k.200808.038

Fauzi, A., Ridwan, T., & Sholihah, P. (2020, March). Digital Literacy as a Media to Introduce Technology for Elementary School Children. *In International Conference on Elementary Education* (Vol. 2, No. 1, pp. 1507-1518).

Flewitt, R., Messer, D., & Kucirkova, N. (2015). New directions for early literacy in a digital age: The iPad. *Journal of Early Childhood Literacy*, *15*(3), 289–310. doi:10.1177/1468798414533560

George, M. J., & Odgers, C. L. (2015). Seven fears and the science of how mobile technologies may be influencing adolescents in the digital age. *Perspectives on Psychological Science*, *10*(6), 832–851. doi:10.1177/1745691615596788 PMID:26581738

Gözüm, A. İ. C., & Kandır, A. (2021). Digital games pre-schoolers play: Parental mediation and examination of educational content. *Education and Information Technologies*, *26*(3), 3293–3326. doi:10.1007/s10639-020-10382-2

Hall, C. M., & Bierman, K. L. (2015). Technology-assisted interventions for parents of young children: Emerging practices, current research, and future directions. *Early Childhood Research Quarterly*, *33*, 21–32. doi:10.1016/j.ecresq.2015.05.003 PMID:27773964

Hammer, M., Scheiter, K., & Stürmer, K. (2021). New technology, new role of parents: How parents' beliefs and behavior affect students' digital media self-efficacy. *Computers in Human Behavior*, *116*, 106642. doi:10.1016/j.chb.2020.106642

Head, E. (2020). Digital technologies and parental involvement in education: The experiences of mothers of primary school-aged children. *British Journal of Sociology of Education*, *41*(5), 593–607. doi:10.1080/01425692.2020.1776594

Hiniker, A., Schoenebeck, S. Y., & Kientz, J. A. (2016, February). Not at the dinner table: Parents' and children's perspectives on family technology rules. In *Proceedings of the 19th ACM conference on computer-supported cooperative work & social computing* (pp. 1376-1389).

Hourihan, M. (2005). *Deconstructing the hero: Literary theory and children's literature*. Routledge. doi:10.4324/9780203974100

Howat, H. (2006). Maximizing family involvement in early literacy. *Contemporary Issues in Communication Science and Disorders*, *33*(Fall), 93–100. doi:10.1044/cicsd_33_F_93

Hunt, P. (Ed.). (2006). *Understanding children's literature*. Routledge. doi:10.4324/9780203968963

Jeynes, W. (2010). *Parental involvement and academic success*. Routledge. doi:10.4324/9780203843444

Johnson, L. (2015). Rethinking parental involvement: A critical review of the literature. *Urban Education Research & Policy Annuals, 3*(1).

Kaye, L. (Ed.). (2016). *Young children in a digital age: Supporting learning and development with technology in early years*. Routledge. doi:10.4324/9781315752709

Kervin, L. (2016). Powerful and playful literacy learning with digital technologies. *Australian Journal of Language and Literacy*, *39*(1), 64–73. doi:10.1007/BF03651907

Kildare, C. A., & Middlemiss, W. (2017). Impact of parents mobile device use on parent-child interaction: A literature review. *Computers in Human Behavior*, *75*, 579–593. doi:10.1016/j.chb.2017.06.003

Koch, L. A. (2018). *Parent Involvement in Early Childhood Education and Its Impact on the Development of Early Language and Literacy Skills: An Exploration of One Head Start Program's Parent Involvement Model*. Drexel University. doi:10.17918/ D84D49

Kucirkova, N. (2017). New literacies and new media: The changing face of early literacy. In *The Routledge international handbook of early literacy education* (pp. 40–54). Routledge. doi:10.4324/9781315766027-5

Laranjeiro, D., Antunes, M. J., & Santos, P. (2018). Tablets in kindergarten for learning and parental involvement. In *EDULEARN18 Proceedings* (pp. 5089-5096). IATED. 10.21125/edulearn.2018.1245

Lestari, H., Siskandar, R., & Rahmawati, I. (2020, March). Digital Literacy Skills of Teachers in Elementary School in The Revolution 4.0. *In International Conference on Elementary Education* (Vol. 2, No. 1, pp. 302-311). IATED.

Machen, S. M., Wilson, J. D., & Notar, C. E. (2005). Parental involvement in the classroom. *Journal of Instructional Psychology*, *32*(1), 13–17.

Marsh, J., Hannon, P., Lewis, M., & Ritchie, L. (2017). Young children's initiation into family literacy practices in the digital age. *Journal of Early Childhood Research*, *15*(1), 47–60. doi:10.1177/1476718X15582095

McDaniel, B. T. (2019). Parent distraction with phones, reasons for use, and impacts on parenting and child outcomes: A review of the emerging research. *Human Behavior and Emerging Technologies*, *1*(2), 72–80. doi:10.1002/hbe2.139

McDaniel, B. T., & Radesky, J. S. (2018). Technoference: Longitudinal associations between parent technology use, parenting stress, and child behavior problems. *Pediatric Research*, *84*(2), 210–218. doi:10.1038/s41390-018-0052-6 PMID:29895837

Mulya, Y. H., Putra, Z. H., & Hermita, N. (2023). The Correlation between Parents' Digital Literacy Knowledge and Parents' Perception of Digital Literacy Knowledge of Elementary School Students. AL-ISHLAH. *Jurnal Pendidikan*, *15*(2), 1965–1978.

Neumann, M. M., & Neumann, D. L. (2017). The use of touch-screen tablets at home and pre-school to foster emergent literacy. *Journal of Early Childhood Literacy*, *17*(2), 203–220. doi:10.1177/1468798415619773

Nodelman, P. (2008). *The hidden adult: Defining children's literature*. JHU Press. doi:10.56021/9780801889790

Novianti, R., & Garzia, M. (2020). Parental engagement in children's online learning during covid-19 pandemic. *Journal of Teaching and Learning in Elementary Education (Jtlee)*, *3*(2), 117–131. doi:10.33578/jtlee.v3i2.7845

Nutbrown, C., Clough, P., Levy, R., Little, S., Bishop, J., Lamb, T., & Yamada-Rice, D. (2017). Families' roles in children's literacy in the UK throughout the 20th century. *Journal of Early Childhood Literacy*, *17*(4), 551–569. doi:10.1177/1468798416645385

Palaiologou, I. (2016). Children under five and digital technologies: Implications for early years pedagogy. *European Early Childhood Education Research Journal*, *24*(1), 5–24. doi:10.1080/1350293X.2014.929876

Patrikakou, E. N. (2016). Parent Involvement, Technology, and Media: Now What? *School Community Journal*, *26*(2), 9–24.

Poveda, D. (2019). Researching digital literacy practices in early childhood: Challenges, complexities and imperatives. In *The Routledge handbook of digital literacies in early childhood* (pp. 45–63). Routledge. doi:10.4324/9780203730638-4

Saracho, O. N. (2019). Literacy in the twenty-first century: children, families and policy. In Research in Young Children's Literacy and Language Development (pp. 332-345).

Schriever, V. (2018). Digital technology in kindergarten: Challenges and opportunities. Handbook of research on mobile devices and smart gadgets in K-12 education, 57-76.

Sciacca, B., Laffan, D. A., Norman, J. O. H., & Milosevic, T. (2022). Parental mediation in pandemic: Predictors and relationship with children's digital skills and time spent online in Ireland. *Computers in Human Behavior*, *127*, 107081. doi:10.1016/j.chb.2021.107081 PMID:34720386

Sheridan, S. M., Knoche, L. L., Kupzyk, K. A., Edwards, C. P., & Marvin, C. A. (2011). A randomized trial examining the effects of parent engagement on early language and literacy: The Getting Ready intervention. *Journal of School Psychology*, *49*(3), 361–383. doi:10.1016/j.jsp.2011.03.001 PMID:21640249

Snow, C. E. (2017). Early literacy development and instruction: An overview. The Routledge international handbook of early literacy education, 5-13.

Sung, Y. Y. C., & Chiu, D. K. (2022). E-book or print book: Parents' current view in Hong Kong. *Library Hi Tech*, *40*(5), 1289–1304. doi:10.1108/LHT-09-2020-0230

Thompson, B. C., Mazer, J. P., & Flood Grady, E. (2015). The changing nature of parent–teacher communication: Mode selection in the smartphone era. *Communication Education*, *64*(2), 187–207. doi:10.1080/03634523.2015.1014382

Troseth, G. L., Strouse, G. A., Flores, I., Stuckelman, Z. D., & Johnson, C. R. (2020). An enhanced eBook facilitates parent–child talk during shared reading by families of low socioeconomic status. *Early Childhood Research Quarterly*, *50*, 45–58. doi:10.1016/j.ecresq.2019.02.009

Undheim, M. (2022). Children and teachers engaging together with digital technology in early childhood education and care institutions: A literature review. *European Early Childhood Education Research Journal*, *30*(3), 472–489. doi:10.1080/1350 293X.2021.1971730

Vélez, A. P., Olivencia, J. J. L., & Zuazua, I. I. (2017). The role of adults in children digital literacy. *Procedia: Social and Behavioral Sciences*, *237*, 887–892. doi:10.1016/j.sbspro.2017.02.124

Vezzoli, Y., Kalantari, S., Kucirkova, N., & Vasalou, A. (2020, April). Exploring the design space for parent-child reading. *In Proceedings of the 2020 CHI Conference on Human Factors in Computing Systems* (pp. 1-12). 10.1145/3313831.3376696

Walker, L. O., & Avant, K. C. (2011). *Strategies for Theory Construction in Nursing* (5th ed.). Prentice Hall.

Xanthopoulou, D., & Papagiannidis, S. (2012). Play online, work better? Examining the spillover of active learning and transformational leadership. *Technological Forecasting and Social Change*, *79*(7), 1328–1339. doi:10.1016/j.techfore.2012.03.006

Chapter 6

Empowering Communities Through Literacy:
Policy Insights From Indonesia's AKRAB Literacy Initiative

Jeremiah Paul Giron Manuel
🆔 https://orcid.org/0000-0001-6597-1295
Sekolah Pelita Harapan Kemang Village, Indonesia

ABSTRACT

This policy brief explores the implementation of Aksara Agar Berdaya (AKRAB) in Indonesia. AKRAB seeks to eradicate adult illiteracy in the country believing that literacy creates power for the families and the communities. This paper critically examines the AKRAB program's objectives as well as its implementation challenges and offers a proposal based on the materials visited and analyzed for its enhancement. Drawing on the program's comprehensive analysis, AKRAB 2.0 is proposed, presenting an enhanced version of the program with modifications related to the resolutions deemed to be helpful towards the examined challenges. This brief serves as an insightful resource for policymakers, stakeholders, and interested agents seeking a well-rounded understanding of AKRAB and the action items that it needs for its better implementation.

INTRODUCTION

Literacy possesses multiplier effects on one's full stewardship as a citizen, whatever profession one holds (The Jakarta Post, 2020). People bearing high proficiencies of

DOI: 10.4018/979-8-3693-1777-8.ch006

literacies enjoy comfortable and privileged lives regardless of their settings. With this in mind, it is unsurprising to see communities, even countries, organize numerous programs to eradicate illiteracy or improve a collective literacy level. In Indonesia, the adult literacy rate improved to 96% after a year of having a 90.51% rate (Ycharts, 2020). The country's Education and Culture Ministry's Early Childhood, Basic and Secondary Education Director General, Jumeri, commended the national efforts espoused in lowering illiteracy rates among adults. Despite such efforts, however, the literacy rates have dropped to worrying figures among the schooling age. For instance, the most recent PISA results present Indonesia's reading levels as below the standards of the Organization for Economic Cooperation and Development (OECD) (2023). Therefore, the School Literacy Movement (SLM) is devised to foster a culture of reading among communities and, in the same way, raise the literacy levels of its constituents. SLM advocates for Indonesian schools to allocate a 15-minute reading time for its populace to get a book and engage in reading. Laksono and Retnaningdyah (2018) explored the country's literacy infrastructures on SLM implementation. They discovered that while the local schools displayed enthusiasm for implementing literacy programs, access to books and the system were below standards. Kartikasari and Nursayana (2022) probed a set of literature related to SLM. They found the same concern: pointing out that books were still scarce in the schools, and the students needed more material that could pique their interest. While studies suggest that basic education reading programs were lacking in productivity, adult literacy programs served the nation with impressive implementation, leading to the recent numbers of literate Indonesians. Nonetheless, these adult literacy programs are confronted with challenges. Aksara Agar Berdaya (AKRAB) is one of these initiatives that encourages thousands to improve their literacy proficiencies. AKRAB proves helpful to the reading adults but has yet to come into its perfect form. Moreover, while the program has abundant resources pertaining to its decade-long implementation, recent explorations on AKRAB have slowed production, with limited analysis from non-Indonesian perspectives. This paper intends to contribute to the diminishing body of literature on AKRAB's role in Indonesia's pursuit for adult literacy.

The AKRAB program was conceived to improve adult literacy nationwide (Hanemann, 2015). The phrase "Aksara Agar Berdaya" was coined as an allusion to UNESCO's program, "Literacy Initiative for Empowerment (LIFE)," assuming a similar stance through its meaning, "Literacy Creates Power." The program organized three age brackets for instructions, which were (1) youth, with ages from 15 to 24; (2) adults, with ages from 25 to 59; and (3) older ones, whose ages are 60 and beyond. Emphasis on poor women and marginalized groups was given a premium in the program, which led to the development of women empowerment groups. With the United Nations Sustainable Development Goals (SDG) on poverty eradication and quality education mandates, the country seeks to subdue the remaining 2.07% or 3,387,035 illiterate adult Indonesians and convert them into literate and productive citizens of the country (Kristanto, 2020). There is no wonder why practitioners and researchers keep developing frameworks and programs to help advance the cause of the AKRAB initiative (Rinawati, 2020; Mualo, 2020; Amaria & Hafidz, 2021).

This policy brief explores the AKRAB initiative in Indonesia, its implementation towards its goal, and how it dictates the general atmosphere of the country's literacy level. This paper critically analyzes the program administration across diverse languages, tribes, religions, and socioeconomic statuses. By examining the challenges, difficulties, inconsistencies, and disparities in the program, action items towards the improved version of AKRAB will be proposed, hence propelling a more effective and efficient implementation of the program. The proposed actionable items would be foundational to a stronger system, addressing the diverse learner needs and meeting AKRAB's ultimate aim to eradicate the remaining illiterate populace across the country. Moreover, this paper will contribute to the resources of adult litreacy which researchers could explore in future research.

THE AKSARA AGAR BERGAYA (AKRAB) MOVEMENT

It was in 2006 when the Indonesian government started a militant movement against illiteracy. Aksara Agar Berdaya (AKRAB) served as its inter-ministries program, involving five (5) departments in mapping, planning, training, and even implementation. While AKRAB is a government-contingent program, it is decentralized, which allows various partners to be involved. The program lies in the institutionalizing of Community Learning Centers (CLC) and its tripartite drive towards (1) acceleration of literacy, (2) multiple and entrepreneurship literacy, and (3) fostering a culture of reading (UNESCO, 2016). Through these CLCs, adult Indonesians participated to be a part of a program that ensured the improvement of their literacy. Tutors joined to lead these CLCs, which offered a variety of programs tailored to the literacy and even economic needs of the volunteering participants. Ten participants per tutor were organized and trained in three methods: participatory approach, which involved life skills in the instructional delivery; mother tongue-based approach, initial instructions utilizing the mother tongue, then a mixed with a Bahasa Indonesia as the term progressed, and transliteration approach, the utilization of Arabic and Quran characters in its formative sessions. This participation from these organizations presupposed the presence of non-government groups in its operation, having the religious communities be involved in its CLCs. The role of the community in the proliferation of literacy among adults shows a good stance as AKRAB sought its people to secure the success of its implementation. The system

Figure 1 AKRAB's community learning center tripartite framework

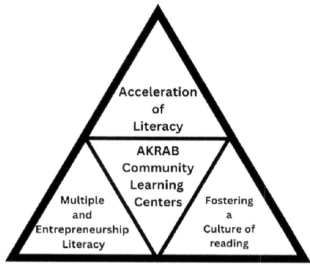

capitalized on one's familiarity with the *Aksara* or the alphabet, leading to the attainment of UNESCO's goals with LIFE. With the national agenda of making Indonesia just, prosperous, and democratic, educational agencies emphasized literacy and its role in their livelihood and market (Ministry of Education of Indonesia, 2010). Its implementation focused on the solid development of functional literacy, entrepreneurship literacy, family literacy, literacy for extraordinary communities based on folk tales, and local cultural literacy. AKRAB also included collaborating between formal and non-formal educational agencies to advance its cause in the country. The *Belai Belajar Bersama* (Center for Learning Together) stood through collaborations between these agencies. Pribudhiana (2013) presents the experiences of students, heads, and tutors in Community Learning Centers, which are believed to have successfully implemented the AKRAB system regarding functional literacy but failed to address economic literacy demands. Moreover, the students who completed the AKRAB program needed to convert their learning to economic advancements, and their failure hurt the calling of the locals to be fully interested in the program. The entrepreneurial side of the program displayed a deficient curriculum, which led to weaker productions for the economic portion of AKRAB. Similarly, while there is an assumption of integration of technology utilization within the program, the scarcity of materials relative to its role in AKRAB is a handicap. Explorations in this concern could help the program strengthen its arm in this issue.

Studies concerning the implementation of CLC include a variety of designs, especially in its seminal days. Arbarini et al. (2015) elaborate on the complexity of AKRAB's operation and find its systematic presentation linked with people and the social patterns around them. Necessary core integrations: reading, writing, calculating, and articulation were organized and implemented within the program. Local wisdom, a folk belief among the locals in Jember, East Java, is also utilized as a complementing material in teaching functional literacy among the locals (Laksono et al., 2018). Accordingly, findings reveal that local wisdom triggers the reception of learning among the students. The locals' preference to place value on folk wisdom implicates the value that locals place on community beliefs and values. Rasyad et al. (2020) share the competencies of the learning facilitators whose production is contingent on their perceived self-esteem. The value of their perceived self-worth is based on their level of education, experience in teaching, and the specific training they have taken for the task. Arbarini et al. (2017) emphasize the strength of the CLCs and their use of participatory learning, engaging adult students to perform in non-formal classes. The use of environmental media is also capitalized among the CLCs, which helps the program to be efficient in its agenda. The underlying commonality among the studies explored about adult education in Indonesia seems to wander around community involvement. Moreover, the prevalence of adult education centers in the big cities of Indonesia, Jakarta, Semarang, and Bandung, have helped the people observe a rapid acceleration of literacy expansion (Star, 2022). The collaboration of the agencies in the country has categorized learning into formal, informal, and non-formal, which has caused a boost in community engagement and literacy advancement among the cities. Fahkruddin (2019) opens a case study in Pati and recognizes the presence of superior non-formal schooling. The strength of the program lies in more than just urban locations alone. While the cities possess better learning infrastructure, this provides hope for those in rural areas to acquire the same level of CLCs, a superior one. He shares the vital role of the community in Pati, which translated to influencing the schools in their literacy provision, hence creating economic applause for the region. Fahkruddin also implicates the school's role in communicating the country's agenda on adult education, articulating a need for the institutions to provide alternatives for those who come differently, look away from how schooling usually works, and fail its institutional demands.

The Indonesian drive for this noble endeavor parallels the programs of its neighboring Southeast Asian countries. Singapore implemented the 1,000 Reading Fathers program, which demanded fathers' presence in their children's reading development. While 1,000 Reading Fathers has the younger generation as its capital output, the fathers must present themselves as literacy partners of their children. The program indirectly impacted the adult population of Singapore and enhanced the literacy levels, case in point, the fathers of the country (Rusydiyah et al., 2023). Malaysia also visualized a community of readers after a decade of implementing a program, the National Reading Decade (NDK) (Samsuddin et al., 2021). Following the national maxim of "*Bangsa Membaca Bangsa Berjaya*" (a prosperous nation is a reading nation), its national library agency endorsed a communal development of the nation, including the adult population. Similarly, the Philippines launched a program to develop adult literacy through the Alternative Learning System (ALS). Baccal & Ormilla (2021) confidently conclude that the implementation of ALS in the Philippines, with all its supporting linkages and support from government and non-government organizations, has produced satisfactory delivery. ALS calls the private stakeholders with government-operated schools to collaborate towards their goal of schooling out-of-school-youth learners and even adults. These three international literacy programs come as AKRAB's fellow runners in the race of enhancing their respective countries' adult literacy levels. While explicit differences may be observed in some of their tenets, a common idea among their programs on adult literacy development is evident in its specifications on community considerations. AKRAB spells its ways differently as it has a more liquefied system, emphasizing the diversity both of its trainers and its students. Moreover, each program has called the schools and its respective communities for program implementation.

AKRAB is responsible for the recent rise in adult literacy rates (ages 15-59). The strong mandate of the government to eradicate illiteracy among adults is motivated by its desire to make Indonesia a place for good citizenry, with prosperity and privileged living within its setting. Yulaelawati (2015) connects AKRAB with UNESCO's LIFE, which aims to empower people and their lives. This seems consistent with the mandate of the UN SDGs and the upliftment of socioeconomic states on a global scale. With AKRAB's platform in action, Moretti (2016) confidently states its capacity to contribute to the nation's progress, mainly since the program includes innovative forms of literacy such as entrepreneurial literacy, local cultural art literacy, folk literacy, family literacy, and even literacy for peace. . In a similar vein, Hanemann (2015) reports on the impact of AKRAB from 2008 to 2012. The author cited that out of more than 4 million population as registered in the the National Statistics Bureau of the country, 3 million of them were awarded certificates of completion. This finding buttresses the author's presentation of the country's literacy movement with a positive remark, highlighting how the culturally-contingent activities lead to its successful campaign. Calling the communities to collaborate with the program seems to have made a positive impact to the general progress of the AKRAB . While it has not achieved its ultimate agenda of completely eradicating adult illiteracy in the country, Indonesia joins hands with the world as it seeks to provide quality education to its own people and help them build comfortable and enjoyable lives, one that poverty does not know of.

CHALLENGES IN THE IMPLEMENTATION OF AKRAB

AKRAB's implementation in Indonesia has led the country to a higher populace capable of literacy-based tasks. Nevertheless, the efforts towards painting the entire country with an excellent literacy rate seems to be challenging as several factors hamper its campaign.

Primary in these challenges is its geographical setting (Hanemann, 2015). Considering the distribution and placement of thousands of its islands within southeast Asia, reaching the last frontiers of the setting remains difficult. The attitude of the older population, aged 45 years old and above, also worsens the difficulty as the motivation to be literate is so low that the program needs to be addressed (Windisch, 2015). The assumed reason for this indifference towards literacy is the misconceptions about the necessity of literacy in their personal lives, considering that most of the unreached population comes from extremely remote areas in the country and has detached but collective means of survival. As long as the motivation is low, AKRAB organizers will always find it hard to persuade people of a different opinion regarding its positive economic use. Local communities would be implicated in better implementation efficiency and effectiveness of CLCs concerning the geographical issue.

Another factor that halts the efforts of Indonesia to totally eradicate adult illiteracy is the difficulty of the natives in communicating using the national language, Bahasa Indonesia (Yulaelawati, 2012). The country has thousands of islands and the formation of varieties of dialects affects the existence of a national language for unified learning. This problem has far-reaching consequences, considering that AKRAB has implications to other spheres such as economy, livelihood, and even digital literacy. This is corroborated by Windisch (2015) who argues that the difficulty stems from one's limited exposure due to the existence of various mother tongues in the participants' respective regions. The difference of the dialects to the national language is large enough to confound communications and even common conversations among locals (Sari, et al., 2018). Rinawati (2021) opines that deliberate immersion to the national language is low due to the preference of the natives in utilizing their own regional dialects in various contexts, including in their use of technology, hence exacerbating the problem in AKRAB's implementation. This highlights implications on the environmental language of the Indonesians in growing years and its functional detachment from the national language. The school's focus on the strength of the national language in the local curriculum implies a stronger demand to help its locals to develop a better proficiency with it. Moreover, communal utilization of Bahasa Indonesia seems to measure a disengaged use towards economic value that locals outside the central regions do not find important for their own livelihood.

AKRAB completers falling back to illiteracy is another concern raised in its implementation (Windisch, 2015). Nur and Abdullah (2022) consider literacy as strongly linked to community empowerment and the latter reinforces the level of presence of the former in a community. With the completers living in a community whose dominant culture neglects the necessity of literacy, they are in danger of reversing their learnings in AKRAB. Especially in the outer regions of Indonesia where civilization is yet to contribute, the ethnic groups do not find outer practices valuable in their lives. Hence, participants coming from these regions have high tendencies to simply forget their literacy, especially on its communal and economic significance, due to the lack of reinforcement from their own local setting.

Yulaelawati (2012) and Windisch (2015) share their observation relative to the varying proficiency levels of the tutors in AKRAB centers. Apparently, their findings show that the populace that came with the gigantic geography of the country led to non-standard proficiencies of the tutors themselves. With this at the front of the learning centers, it is not wrong to assume that the levels of productivity are also varying. Those whose centers hail proficient tutors would be capable of delivering adults with better literacy while those whose centers are led with tutors of lesser proficiency, the outputs are hardly the same. Similarly, the learning centers across Indonesia do not possess standardized infrastructures (Windisch, 2015). While various institutions volunteer services to assist in the accomplishment of the national mandate of illiteracy eradication, this variety also contributes to the capability of each volunteer organization, which presumably do not come in the same levels of resources. Organizations whose placements are in urban areas, even those with better funding and manpower, could establish optimized service to AKRAB. This impacts the production of literate adults via the program, as learning settings contribute to this production as well. This problem leads to unequal distribution of optimized AKRAB services to the natives, hence ultimately producing imbalanced and less-than-standard tutorials to those whose centers do not possess the same resources. While Hanneman (2015) attests to the standardization of the tutors as well as that of the curriculum and community learning centers, studies indicate that accrediting organizations must have varying tolerance and evaluation leading to this issue (Yulaelawati, 2012; Windisch, 2015).

Lastly, studies show that while the program is nationally mandated and supported, local agencies do not possess similar enthusiasm (Yulaelawati, 2012; Windisch, 2015). The levels of production do not come in similar numbers, relative to its target completing participants. Understandably, Indonesians give priority to other national concerns such as biodiversity, economics, natural resources, energy subsidies, and national literacy, albeit relatively considering the tapping of non-government entities in AKRAB's implementation.

These challenges that beset the implementation of AKRAB demand definitive action items to ensure that the program attains its vision, that is, total eradication of illiteracy in the country. By addressing these challenges, the literacy program can achieve its ultimate goal relative to illiteracy, thus empowering its people to live comfortably.

RECOMMENDED ACTION ITEMS

Drawing from the challenges presented in this paper, AKRAB 2.0 is hereby proposed for a comprehensive resolution of its difficulties and challenges, transforming the literacy growth and development in the country. AKRAB 2.0 envisions community learning centers with more standardized levels in terms of tutors, and study centers. This modified version will capitalize on seamless and strengthened partnerships between home, school, and the community. A firmer accreditation of these factors shall be implemented to maintain compliance with the standards aligned to the development of effective adult literacy, hence a step towards the original goal of the program. In this regard, the government may establish linkages with external accrediting organizations to seek for funds that can be allotted for the accredited centers and tutors to increase their motivation, hence the drive to maintain standards. Moreover, quota-based recognition of regions implementing the programs may also be integrated within AKRAB 2.0.

Regarding the concern about its enormous land mass and its implications to the indifference of those who are near the outskirts of the cities and developments, AKRAB 2.0 can be useful by mapping the population and funding the communities that can grow people with hearts for literacy. Information about the benefits of literacy can be optimized by organizing community-based seminars or family-based information sessions to ensure the maximal participation of every family in each setting. Deliberate visualizations and implementations of the program are necessitated in these activities, thereby contributing favorably to the improvement of AKRAB. With several studies affirming the significant role of communities in influencing positive change in the program implementation (Arbarini, et al., 2015; Arbarini, et al., 2017; Star, 2022), the geographical concern can-not be of a serious problem. The focus of having competent CLCs regionally is to address the other prevailing threats that this concern raises.

The challenge of reverting back to illiteracy due to low immersion of the natives in the community can be addressed by utilizing technological innovations in the areas that have low literacy presentations and functions. By utilizing voluntary stances of non-government organizations in the country, devices can be slowly integrated in the governance of communities. Such technological integration should demand constant practice, taking appropriate actions for literacy. Additionally, the regional governments can integrate these technological innovations to the livelihood of the locals which will necessitate them to reinforce their industries with literacy. By doing so, technology immersion shall be high which will implicate a high demand of literacy for the locals to perform better. A top-to-bottom implementation of this proposal shall demand the regional governments to prioritize AKRAB 2.0 and start funding its operation. While the democratic foundation may deter a standardized funding of the proposed program, a priority on funding the activity may be given emphasis in the mandate. Similarly, schools can complement technological advancement since the institutions can integrate digital literacy in classes. This is especially beneficial in the post-Covid context when the country has already started issuing devices in schools. Communities can be influenced with the academic tech infusion and can grow its use locally. Ultimately, this will pull the locals to make its use normative in their everyday lives.

Likewise, the issue raised on the low level of a centralized language deterring the progress of AKRAB can be addressed by technology immersion. Placing Bahasa Indonesia as a controlling language of the devices utilized in the community, the locals will have stronger exposure to the language, hence a higher level of Indonesian language proficiency. The demand to centralize language will be high among the locals because of livelihood concerns which will lead them to utilize Bahasa Indonesia on a common goal. The *Belai Belajar Bersama* could benefit a lot from this as a more common tongue would unite the students, tutors, CLCs, and even the content to a more focused system towards functional literacy, and ultimately economic development. The utilization of a standardized language in the system can further address the concerns about the varying levels of the tutors (Yulaelawati, 2012; Windisch, 2015). Hanneman's (2015) attestation of the efforts to standardize the levels of the tutors would also be given credit and it would require easier efforts from the administrators of the program to help attain AKRAB's goal. The concern raised by Rasyad et al. (2020) on the self-esteem of the tutors as a contributing factor to their efficiency will be addressed in the standardization system, too.

The goal of AKRAB 2.0 is intently to eradicate illiteracy in the country. With the challenges given resolutions, the slow drag of its original implementation will come at a faster pace towards its vision.

POLICY IMPLICATIONS

The challenges examined in the implementation of AKRAB bear valuable insights that imply policy necessities vis-a-vis education and beyond. The following are

Figure 2 AKRAB 2.0 policy implications

significant implications implied in the proposed AKRAB 2.0, allowing the attainment of the program in a more efficient and effective manner.

1. Centralization of Language - AKRAB 2.0 proposes the wider utilization of Bahasa Indonesia as an actual national language, on top of its proclamation in history. While the language is primarily utilized in more developed settings, the proposal intends to widen its actual use beyond the cities. This implies the lowering of usage levels of regional dialects in community programs, encouraging the locals to be immersed more in the national language. This can be started with families strengthening the utilization of Bahasa Indonesia in their own families. Capitalizing its usage at home would strengthen one's proficiency with the language leading to its broader communal use, hence a demand for the Indonesian diverse communities to follow the course. Moreover, Bahasa Indonesia may also be given a premium in the national schools allowing its utilization in different disciplines. The propagation of the language use in the academic walls will strengthen proficiency levels among its pupils, enabling the community to normalize its use in a broader sense. In a similar vein, it will have an effect on the homes of the students leading to a use of the national language beyond the classrooms. This will ease the CLCs in its propagation of literacy development regardless of the locality of the operation since Bahasa Indonesia will not be deemed as a foreign language by its students and tutors.
2. Stronger Integration of Technology in Governance and Implementation - The proposal capitalizes on the utility of technological devices which implies the

resolution for the challenges mentioned in AKRAB implementation such as the difficulty of reaching people, low proficiency in Bahasa Indonesia, non-standardized tutors and centers, and the unequal funding among regions. Ensuring the integration of these devices beyond leisure use will widen the reach of the resolutions offered in this media. Moreover, considering the widening usage of these devices all over the archipelago, with exceptions to places such as Papua and other similar regions, this move will demand the locals to pursue digital literacy especially if their livelihood in their respective markets demands them to do so. Implications on the areas of the home, school, and local communities cannot be discounted as activities may be organized based on digitized information. For instance, the home and the school could collaborate through digital means and create a community-wide collaborative program towards functional and economic literacy. This also demands the first policy implication to be implemented which concerns a wider utilization of Bahasa Indonesia among the CLCs across the archipelago.

3. Funding on Adult Education - This enhanced version of AKRAB seeks to go beyond the current numbers from seeking assistance from NGOs and religious organizations to making a direct appeal to the national government for direct funding. Utilization of the funds can be directed to recognition activities, or management and distribution of resources, all in the name of AKRAB 2.0. Moreover, funding non-formal education in the local communities could also aid the program in making the locals aware of the benefits of being functionally literate. This could translate to giving the previous implications of the visualized program, at home and in school, priority in organizing budgets. Families could consider the necessity of running along the technological vista of the country, and the high premium of centralizing Bahasa Indonesia at the comfort of their homes regardless of their regional location and dialect.

While AKRAB 2.0 keeps the program sustainable in community levels, the national government can place emphasis on the school and home partnership to help the alleviation of its challenges, and perhaps, attain its ultimate aim of completely painting the country with literacy. The centralization of Bahasa Indonesia in the CLCs can be augmented by the school which will demand the stakeholders for its normative utilization. Moreover, the technological integrations that schools will consider will require the community to fill its role of sharing with the upbringing of the students, hence the need for technology use to go beyond the school walls. Finally, funding has an implication not just in the government budgets but also in the family expenses and community considerations, especially that schools require stakeholders in their operation.

FUTURE DIRECTIONS

With the implementation of the offered resolutions of AKRAB 2.0, Indonesia can rest knowing that illiteracy is soon to be completely eradicated in its islands. Illiteracy rates among adults will keep decreasing in the future. The challenges that the original program encountered will turn to strengths, allowing the CLCs to strengthen its programs. Bahasa Indonesia will gain prominence and a more unified Indonesia might be observed through communal conversations and language utilization in the digital space. People from Papua to the Western end of the country will not have difficulties understanding each other through the national language. Moreover, better technological infrastructure will be installed across the country with considerations on the digital literacy levels of its people. Family, school, and community concerns may be addressed through the utilization of technological devices implicating the proficient levels in its use, and the norming of Bahasa Indonesia as a casual means for communication. All these will demand a priority in funding the program as it assures a better country in its implementation. Policymakers can consider the program, including the funding, curriculum and implementation, from a top-to-bottom system since it already requires the collaboration of a variety of government agencies and non-government organizations. Practitioners could anticipate continuous technological developments and their normalized societal utilizations, putting the seemingly endless innovation to its CLC programs. Researchers could explore the challenges presented in this paper and offer alternatives from different perspectives and settings, most especially that Southeast Asian countries have similar intentions in their adult literacy programs. Moreover, the continuing development of technology and its integration to literacy education could be probed further, including an examination for possible materials for adult literacy.

CONCLUSION

The AKRAB program holds a promising future for the Indonesian people. This proposed policy brief highlights its dominant objectives, key components, and vision. While current studies show a number of prevailing challenges of the AKRAB program, this paper has provided feasible communal resolutions for better efficiency of the program. Implications on giving premium on school and community programs in conversational language, and technological utilization will demand the local homes to boost literacy advancement. Ultimately, implementing the resolutions of AKRAB 2.0 will offer the country opportunities to develop a higher level of literacy among its people, thus fostering a much more emphasized cultural heritage and an empowered society in terms of socioeconomic stances.

REFERENCES

Amaria, K. H., & Hafidz, N. (2021). Upaya pemberdayaan masyarakat oleh rumah kreatif wadas kelir melalui penguatan literasi. *Jurnal AKRAB*, *12*(2), 12–19. doi:10.51495/jurnalakrab.v12i2.405

Arbarini, M., Jutmini, S., Djoyoatmojo, S., & Sutarno, S. (2015). Implementation of functional literacy education by participatory learning as effort of lifelong learning. In *Proceeding of the International Conference on Teacher Training and Education, 2*(1), 734-745. https://jurnal.uns.ac.id/ictte/article/view/7630 accessed March 10, 2024.

Arbarini, M., Jutmini, S., Joyoatmojo, S., Jutmini, S., & Joyoatmojo, S. (2017). Participatory learning model on adults literacy education of rural communities. *International Journal of Education, Psychology and Counseling, 2*(6), 153-164. http://www.ijepc.com/PDF/IJEPC-2017-06-12-09.pdf

Baccal, V. S., & Ormilla, R. C. G. (2021). The implementation of alternative learning system in public schools in Isabela, Philippines. *EDUCATUM Journal of Social Sciences*, *7*(1), 19–29. doi:10.37134/ejoss.vol7.1.3.2021

Fakhruddin, I. S. (2019). The impact of non-formal education in community development: A case study in pati, indonesia. *International Journal of Innovation. Creativity and Change*, *5*(5), 339–352.

Hanemann, U. (2015). *The evolution and impact of literacy campaigns and programmes, 2000-2014.* Hamburg [Germany]: Unesco, Institute for Lifelong Learning, 2015. https://redined.educacion.gob.es/xmlui/bitstream/handle/11162/118504/234154e.pdf?sequence=1&isAllowed=y

Kristanto, N. (2020). Model penyelenggaraan program pendidikan keaksaraan dasar melalui pelibatan pemerintah kampung dan tokoh agama. *Jurnal Akrab*, *11*(2), 1–9. doi:10.51495/jurnalakrab.v11i02.335

Laksono, B. A., & Wahyuni, S. (2018). An investigation of local wisdom to support adult literacy program. *PEOPLE: International Journal of Social Sciences*, *4*(2), 1320–1336. doi:10.20319/pijss.2018.42.13201336

Laksono, K., & Retnaningdyah, P. (2018). Literacy infrastructure, access to books, and the implementation of the school literacy movement in primary schools in Indonesia. In IOP Conference Series: Materials Science and Engineering (Vol. 296, No. 1, p. 012045). IOP Publishing. doi:10.1088/1757-899X/296/1/012045

Ministry of Education of Indonesia. (2010). *Country Paper: Status and Major Challenges of Literacy in Indonesia. United Nations Educational, Scientific, and Cultural Organization.* UNESDOC. https://unesdoc.unesco.org/ark:/48223/pf0000191512 accessed February 29, 2024.

Moretti, G. A. S. (2016). Youth and adult literacy and education: a good practice analysis (No. 56). International Policy Centre for Inclusive Growth. *Econ Papers.* https://econpapers.repec.org/RePEc:ipc:pbrief:56

Mualo, Y. (2020). Pembelajaran keaksaraan dasar berbasis kearifan lokal sebagai upaya pemberantasan buta aksara. *Jurnal AKRAB, 11*(2), 62–79. doi:10.51495/jurnalakrab.v11i02.354

Nur, A., & Abdullah, M. S. (2022). Barru literacy community as the alternative literacy movement: A study on cultivating reading literacy toward society in Barru Regency, South Sulawesi Province. *Salus Cultura: Jurnal Pembangunan Manusia Dan Kebudayaan, 2*(1), 11–25. doi:10.55480/saluscultura.v2i1.41

Organization for Economic Cooperation and Development (OECD). (2023). *PISA 2022 Results: Factsheets.* OECD. https://www.oecd.org/publication/pisa-2022-results/country-notes/indonesia-c2e1ae0e/

Pribudhiana, R. (2013). *Case Study of Post-Literacy Program in Indonesia.* Scholar Works. https://scholarworks.umass.edu/cie_capstones/78/

Rasyad, A., Wiyono, B. B., & Rahma, R. A. (2020). An analysis of workshop program implementation and competency improvement for adult education facilitators in Indonesia. *Int. J. Innov, 10*(10), 15. https://www.researchgate.net/profile/Bambang-Wiyono-2/publication/345038849_An_Analysis_of_Workshop_Program_Implementation_and_Competency_Improvement_for_Adult_Education_Facilitators_in_Indonesia/links/5f9cd4ff299bf1b53e546aa8/An-Analysis-of-Workshop-Program-Implementation-and-Competency-Improvement-for-Adult-Education-Facilitators-in-Indonesia.pdf

Rinawati, N. K. A. (2020). Meningkatkan motivasi belajar dengan bermain kartu pada program keaksaraan dasar. *Jurnal Akrab, 11*(2), 52–61. doi:10.51495/jurnalakrab.v11i02.352

Rusydiyah, E. F. (2023). Literacy policy in southeast Asia: A comparative study between Singapore, Malaysia, and Indonesia. *Center for Educational Policy Studies Journal, 13*(2), 79–96. doi:10.26529/cepsj.1214

Samsuddin, S. F., Shaffril, H. A. M., Mohamed, N. A., & Bolong, J. (2021). Into the unknown: Do people in low literacy rate areas practise digital reading? *Malaysian Journal of Library and Information Science*, 26(2), 23–36. doi:10.22452/mjlis. vol26no2.2

Sari, B. T., van de Vijver, F. J., Chasiotis, A., & Bender, M. (2019). Contextualized bilingualism among adolescents from four different ethnic groups in Indonesia. *The International Journal of Bilingualism*, 23(6), 1469–1482. doi:10.1177/1367006918803678

Star, J. (2022). *Application of Adult Education in Indonesia*. Kompasiana. https://www.kompasiana.com/bintangjayezvara/6399130408a8b552e75f4d42/penerapan-pendidikan-orang-dewasa-adult-education-dalam-pendidikan-di-indonesia

The Jakarta Post. (2020). HAI 2020: Indonesia's literacy programs show great success. *The Jakarta Post*. https://www.thejakartapost.com/adv/2020/09/07/hai-2020-indonesias-literacy-programs-show-great-success.html

UNESCO Institute of Learning. (February 26, 2016). *AKRAB! Literacy Creates Power, Indonesia*. UNESCO. https://uil.unesco.org/case-study/effective-practices-database-litbase-0/akrab-literacy-creates-power-indonesia#:~:text=Aksara%20Agar%20Berdaya%20(AKRAB!),local%20languages%20and%20Bahasa%20Indonesia

Windisch, H. C. (2015). *Adults with low literacy and numeracy skills: A literature review on policy intervention*. doi:10.1787/19939019

Ychart. (2020). *Indonesia Adult Literacy Rate (I:IALRUY)*. y Charts. https://ycharts.com/indicators/indonesia_adult_literacy_rate#:~:text=Indonesia%20Adult%20Literacy%20Rate%20is%20at%2096.00%25%2C%20compared,higher%20than%20the%20long%20term%20average%20of%2090.51%25.

Yulaelawati, E. (2016). *AKRAB! Literacy Creates Power, Indonesia*. UNESCO. https://uil.unesco.org/case-study/effective-practices-database-litbase-0/akrab-literacy-creates-power-indonesia

Chapter 7

From Consultation to Implementation:
Reflective Pathways in Designing Technology–Mediated Community Literacy Programs

Al Ryanne Gabonada Gatcho
(iD) https://orcid.org/0000-0001-6825-2296
Hunan Institute of Science and Technology, China

ABSTRACT

Exploring the intersection of technology and community literacy, this reflection chronicles the design and implementation of technology-mediated community literacy (TMCL) programs. It scrutinizes the symbiosis of digital tools and literacy enhancement, addressing challenges like the digital divide and educator resistance. Successes, challenges, and insights from two principal TMCL programs—one for children during COVID-19 and another for adult literacy—are analyzed. Emphasizing core principles such as community engagement and continuous improvement, the chapter outlines future TMCL trajectories influenced by technological advancements and educational policy shifts. Personal reflections offer a vision for TMCL's impact on community literacy.

INTRODUCTION

In the ever-evolving domain of literacy education, one encounters a myriad of technological integrations, a phenomenon profoundly inspired by Hawkins' (1991)

DOI: 10.4018/979-8-3693-1777-8.ch007

exposition of Technology-Mediated Communities for Learning. In this discourse, 'Technology-Mediated Community Literacy' (TMCL) is utilized as a key term, referring to programs that seamlessly blend technology into the framework of community literacy. These initiatives, which might also be characterized as technology-based or technology-enabled, stand apart in their approach — they act as facilitators, creating a harmonious integration of digital tools with community-focused literacy efforts (Menon et al., 2017; Vasquez, 2007). The adoption of 'technology-mediated' as a term in this chapter is a deliberate choice, underscoring the pivotal role of technology in sculpting and enhancing the educational narratives within community literacy endeavors.

The pertinence of TMCL programs is markedly discernible in confronting the multifaceted educational challenges of the current era, as well as in capitalizing on emergent opportunities (Barrat-Pugh et al., 2022; Cook, 2016; Garcia & Hasson, 2004). These initiatives adeptly address imperative pedagogical objectives, particularly inclusivity and engagement, thereby ameliorating the pervasive disparities in literacy across varied educational milieus (Didiharyono & Qur'ani, 2019). In an age where digital integration is indelibly interwoven into the societal fabric, the cultivation of digital literacy is as integral as conventional literacy skills (McKee & Blair, 2007; Wason-Ellam, 2004). The congruence of TMCL with these contemporary educational imperatives elevates it to a prominent position in the vanguard of innovative literacy education methodologies.

In this chapter, I endeavor to elucidate the multifarious elements involved in the design and implementation of TMCL programs. My primary objective is to thoroughly examine the nuanced interplay between technology and community literacy, dissecting how digital tools can be strategically employed to bolster and transform conventional literacy paradigms (Burnett et al., 2006; Kellner, 2004; Mills, 2010). Central to my exploration is an analysis of the implementation processes, from the genesis of program ideas rooted in community needs to the practical realities and challenges faced in their execution. By delving into these aspects, I aim to furnish a comprehensive understanding of TMCL programs, infused with insights garnered from my professional experiences. This inquiry is intended to contribute significantly to the academic discourse on literacy education, providing valuable perspectives and practical strategies for educators, policymakers, and community advocates navigating the ever-evolving landscape of digital literacy. Further, this chapter's contribution to the realm of community literacy and technology integration is both significant and timely. It delves into the nuances of TMCL program design, highlighting the considerable impact and transformative potential of these initiatives in literacy education. By offering an in-depth analysis of well-structured TMCL programs, the chapter not only enriches the academic dialogue but also serves as a pivotal resource for practitioners and policymakers. The insights provided herein are instrumental in shaping effective literacy strategies, thereby reinforcing the integration of technology as a cornerstone of modern educational practice (Nazirjonovich, 2021).

Prior to my academic engagement at a university in China, my professional path in literacy was multifaceted, shaped not only by research endeavors during my PhD in Reading Education but also significantly enriched by numerous consultancy roles. Even as I transitioned to an academic role in China, I continued to extend my consultancy services remotely, maintaining active involvement with literacy initiatives in the Philippines. This enduring commitment illustrates the flexibility and global scope of my professional practice, allowing me to contribute meaningfully across borders.

Post-completion of my doctorate, a proliferation of consultancy opportunities emerged, enabling me to collaborate extensively with diverse literacy programs, both in educational institutions and initiatives led by the Department of Education in the Philippines. My consultancy work, particularly in TMCL, gained momentum during and after the COVID-19 pandemic. This period underscored the imperative for digital integration in education, as traditional learning paradigms faced unprecedented disruptions. My involvement ranged from formulating digital literacy curricula to advising on the deployment of technology in bridging educational gaps exacerbated by the pandemic. The shift towards TMCL during this era was not merely a contingency response but a strategic adaptation to the evolving educational landscape, where digital proficiency became as essential as conventional literacy skills. This phase of my career was crucial in refining my expertise in TMCL, wherein I navigated the complexities of integrating technology with literacy education to create inclusive, resilient, and adaptive learning environments. These experiences have been pivotal in shaping my comprehensive perspective on TMCL, underscoring its significance in contemporary literacy education and its potential in addressing the dynamic challenges of a post-pandemic world.

During my consultancy stint, I witnessed firsthand the transformative power of technology in reshaping community literacy landscapes. One particularly enlightening experience was my involvement in a project that aimed to integrate digital tools into rural literacy programs in the Philippines. The initial skepticism from the local educators, accustomed to traditional teaching methods, gradually gave way to enthusiasm as they observed the palpable impact of these tools on student engagement and learning outcomes. This project not only reinforced my belief in the efficacy of TMCL programs but also highlighted the critical role of technology in democratizing education, especially in under-resourced areas.

These experiences have profoundly informed my perspective on TMCL, fostering a conviction that technology is not just an adjunct but a pivotal element in literacy education. I have come to view TMCL as a bridge connecting the present and future of literacy, where technology acts as a catalyst for innovation and inclusivity. This perspective is underpinned by the understanding that in our rapidly digitizing world, literacy extends beyond traditional reading and writing to encompass digital fluency, a skill indispensable for navigating contemporary life (Jamil & Almunawar, 2021; Murray & Perez, 2014). My work in various settings has solidified my viewpoint that well-designed TMCL programs are essential in equipping communities with the literacy skills needed for the 21st century.

BACKGROUND AND THEORETICAL FRAMEWORK

TMCL programs, represent a confluence of digital tools and traditional literacy approaches, designed to enrich community-based learning. These programs aim to enhance literacy by embedding technology into educational frameworks, thereby addressing diverse community needs. They encompass a dual focus: fostering foundational literacy skills and promoting digital fluency, essential in today's technologically driven landscape. TMCL initiatives thus serve not only to bridge literacy gaps but also to cultivate critical digital competencies within community settings (Bers, 2010).

The genesis of TMCL programs can be traced back to the advent of the digital revolution. Initially, the integration of technology in literacy programs was rudimentary, primarily focused on supplementing traditional teaching methods with basic digital tools (Cook, 2016). However, as technological advancements accelerated, so did the evolution of these programs. The emergence of the internet, multimedia resources, and interactive platforms transformed the once peripheral role of technology in literacy education into a central, dynamic force (Barratt-Pugh, 2022; Wickham & Carbone, 2018).

Over time, TMCL programs have undergone significant metamorphosis, mirroring the rapid progression of digital innovations and the shifting paradigms of literacy. The early 21st century witnessed a marked shift towards more holistic and integrated approaches, where digital tools were no longer mere adjuncts but integral components of literacy education (Ullah & Anwar, 2021). This shift was driven by the growing recognition of digital literacy as a fundamental skill, alongside traditional reading and writing. As digital technologies became more pervasive, TMCL programs evolved to encompass a broader spectrum of skills, including critical thinking, digital communication, and information processing (Nelson & Braafladt, 2012; Shrestha & Krolak, 2015). This evolution reflects an ongoing response to the changing literacy needs of diverse populations in a world increasingly mediated by technology.

Scholarly discourse surrounding TMCL programs reveals a multifaceted impact on literacy development. Research has consistently underscored the efficacy of TMCL in enhancing digital literacy skills regardless of learners' backgrounds (Detlor et al., 2022; Lev-On, et al., 2021; Statti & Torres, 2020). Further, studies highlight that when learners interact with digital content, their engagement levels increase, leading to improved reading comprehension and writing skills (Lin, 2023; Ullah & Anwar, 2021). This is attributed to the multimodal nature of digital tools which cater to various learning styles, making literacy acquisition more accessible and appealing (Sindoni & Moschini, 2021). However, literature on TMCL programs illuminates both their transformative potential and the challenges they face. A critical issue is the digital divide, which risks deepening educational inequalities. Despite TMCL's capacity to make literacy education more inclusive, disparities in technological access and digital literacy skills remain significant hurdles (Didiharyono & Qur'ani, 2019). Furthermore, the effectiveness of these programs depends heavily on educators' ability to integrate technology into literacy instruction, necessitating continuous professional development. Studies emphasize that without equitable access to digital tools and robust educator support, the implementation of TMCL initiatives can be compromised, particularly in under-resourced settings such as rural communities (Barratt-Pugh et al., 2022; Bers, 2010; Cook, 2016; Menon et al., 2017). This body of research advocates for balanced strategies that not only harness the benefits of TMCL but also address these critical challenges to ensure its successful and equitable deployment.

In understanding the theoretical frameworks that underpin TMCL programs, several key models and theories are instrumental: the RAT Model, SAMR, TPACK Framework, Digital Bloom's Taxonomy, and Connectivism. Each of these offers unique insights into the integration of technology in literacy education.

The RAT (Replacement, Amplification, Transformation) Model (Hughes et al., 2006) provides a lens to evaluate how technology is utilized in educational settings. It categorizes technology use into three levels: replacing traditional methods with minimal functional change, amplifying the effectiveness of teaching practices, and transforming learning experiences in innovative ways. In TMCL programs, this model helps assess whether technology is merely substituting traditional methods or genuinely enhancing and reshaping literacy education. SAMR (Substitution, Augmentation, Modification, Redefinition) is a hierarchical model that similarly examines the impact of technology in teaching (Puentedura, 2013). It ranges from basic substitution, where technology acts as a direct tool substitute, to redefinition, where technology allows for new, previously inconceivable educational tasks. TMCL programs often strive towards the higher levels of this model, seeking not just to integrate technology but to redefine literacy learning. On the other hand, TPACK (Technological Pedagogical Content Knowledge) Framework (Koehler & Mishra, 2006) emphasizes the intersection of technology, pedagogy, and content knowledge. Effective TMCL programs require educators to operate at this intersection, integrating technology in ways that are pedagogically sound and content-appropriate. Digital

Bloom's Taxonomy (Goranova, 2019) extends Bloom's well-known taxonomy of educational objectives to the digital age, incorporating digital skills like creating, evaluating, and analyzing with digital tools. This is particularly relevant in TMCL, as it underscores the need to develop higher-order thinking skills through technology. Finally, Connectivism, as a learning theory for the digital age, posits that learning occurs through networks and connections across digital platforms (Duke et al., 2013; Jung, 2019). In TMCL programs, this theory supports the idea of learning as a distributed process, facilitated by technology, where the community and digital networks play a vital role in knowledge construction and sharing. These frameworks collectively form the theoretical bedrock of TMCL programs, guiding how technology is integrated to enrich literacy education in a digitally connected world.

Building on the foundation of digital literacy theories, TMCL programs also deeply integrate community engagement theories, notably Asset-Based Community Development (ABCD) and Social Capital theory. ABCD theory (McKnight & Russell, 2018) shifts the focus to leveraging inherent community strengths and resources, aligning perfectly with TMCL's aim to utilize local assets for literacy development. This approach ensures that programs are not only tailored to community needs but also reinforce existing capabilities. Complementing this, Social Capital theory (Putnam, 2001) underscores the importance of building robust community networks. It highlights how trust, mutual understanding, and shared values within communities can significantly enhance the effectiveness of TMCL programs, facilitating a collaborative and supportive learning environment.

Further enriching this framework are the Community of Practice (CoP) theory and the Public Participation model. CoP theory (Wenger, 2000) posits that learning is a communal activity, thriving on shared experiences and collaborative practices. This resonates with TMCL's ethos, where community members collectively engage in literacy practices, creating a dynamic learning space. The Public Participation model (Quick & Bryson, 2022) reinforces this by advocating for active community involvement in all stages of TMCL program development. It emphasizes the need for transparent and inclusive decision-making processes, ensuring that the programs are not only informed by but also owned by the community. This inclusive approach is critical for the sustainability and relevance of TMCL initiatives, empowering communities to shape their literacy landscapes.

In TMCL program design and implementation, the seamless fusion of digital literacy theories and community engagement models is essential. Theories like the RAT Model, SAMR, TPACK Framework, Digital Bloom's Taxonomy, and Connectivism shape the technological aspects of these programs. They guide the strategic use of digital tools to not only supplement traditional literacy methods but to transform learning experiences. Concurrently, community engagement theories such as Asset-Based Community Development, Social Capital Theory, Community of Practice Theory, and the Public Participation Model inform the collaborative and inclusive nature of TMCL programs. These models emphasize leveraging community strengths and fostering interactive, participatory learning environments. By integrating these diverse theoretical insights, TMCL programs are effectively tailored to meet both the digital and communal needs of learners, creating a comprehensive and impactful approach to literacy education.

PERSONAL JOURNEY INTO TMCL

My professional journey into TMCL programs began with a foundational career in literacy program development, a path that has been both enriching and enlightening. As a consultant, I have had the privilege of guiding and shaping various literacy initiatives, a role that evolved significantly alongside my academic pursuits, particularly during my PhD studies. This period marked a transition, deepening my engagement with the intricacies of literacy education and leading me towards the innovative intersection of technology and community-based learning. My experiences, spanning diverse educational settings and a range of literacy projects, gradually steered me towards TMCL. This was a natural progression, fueled by a growing recognition of the pivotal role technology plays in modern education and my growing interest in harnessing its potential to enhance traditional literacy approaches within community settings (Burnett et al., 2006; Kellner, 2004; Mills, 2010).

In the early stages of my consultancy, I engaged with a spectrum of literacy programs, each offering a distinct perspective on the challenges and opportunities within the field. My initial projects were primarily rooted in traditional literacy approaches, focusing on fundamental reading and writing skills. During these formative years, my role often involved curriculum development and teacher training, aiming to enhance instructional techniques and learning outcomes.

The nascent integration of technology in these early programs was cautious yet optimistic. I recall my first encounter with a project that tentatively incorporated digital tools into its curriculum. My role in this initiative was to assist in the seamless incorporation of technology in a manner that complemented, rather than overshadowed, the core literacy objectives (Nazirjonovich, 2021). This experience was revelatory; it provided my first glimpse into the potential of technology as a catalyst in literacy education. The initial successes of these modest integrations were encouraging. However, they also highlighted a range of challenges, from technological accessibility to the need for adequate teacher training in digital tools. These early experiences laid the groundwork for my evolving perspective on TMCL, shaping my understanding of how technology could be harnessed to not only support but significantly enhance community literacy efforts (Wickham & Carbone, 2018).

As my involvement in literacy program development deepened, so did my comprehension of the multifaceted nature of TMCL programs. Initially, my perception of technology's role in literacy was primarily as an ancillary tool, a supplementary element to traditional teaching methods. However, with increased exposure to diverse educational contexts and the evolving needs of learners, my understanding began to shift (Barratt-Pugh, 2022; Wickham & Carbone, 2018). I observed the profound impact that well-integrated technology could have, not just in enhancing literacy skills, but in transforming the entire learning experience.

This evolution in my understanding was marked by a series of projects that increasingly focused on the integration of digital tools into literacy curricula. I began to see technology as a fundamental component in literacy education – a means to engage learners more deeply, to make education more accessible, and to open up new avenues for interaction and exploration (Sindoni & Moschini, 2021). My approach evolved from one of cautious integration to actively seeking ways to innovate and enrich literacy programs through technology. This progression in my perspective was also influenced by the growing body of research in TMCL, which reinforced the idea that technology, when used thoughtfully and creatively, could significantly elevate the efficacy of literacy programs (Lin, 2023; Ullah & Anwar, 2021). This newfound understanding underscored the need for a holistic approach, where technology, pedagogy, and community needs are seamlessly interwoven to create impactful and sustainable literacy initiatives.

During the peak of the COVID-19 pandemic, a period marked by unprecedented educational challenges, my consultancy services extended to various school divisions and regional offices of the Department of Education in the Philippines. This era was pivotal, giving rise to two significant TMCL programs that profoundly influenced my understanding and approach to community literacy.

The first program was aimed at children, involving schools and local communities in a collaborative effort to sustain literacy development amid the pandemic. My role was to assist in designing a TMCL curriculum that could be effectively delivered in a remote learning environment. This initiative required not only the integration of technology for online instruction but also the involvement of community members to support children's learning at home. The challenges were manifold, from ensuring equitable access to digital tools to training teachers and parents in their effective use. Despite these hurdles, the program achieved remarkable success, evidenced by sustained student engagement and measurable improvements in literacy skills. This project underscored the importance of community involvement and adaptability in TMCL programs, especially in crisis situations. The second significant project was an adult literacy program initiated by my former university as part of their outreach initiatives. This program was designed to empower adults with literacy skills that could translate into livelihood opportunities, particularly crucial during the economic downturn caused by the pandemic. My contribution involved the development of a curriculum that integrated digital literacy with vocational skills, delivered through a blend of online and community-based workshops. The challenge lay in making the program accessible to adults with varying levels of digital proficiency and in ensuring the practical applicability of the skills taught. The outcome was gratifying, as the program not only improved literacy levels but also equipped participants with skills to generate income, thereby making a tangible impact on their lives. These two projects were instrumental in shaping my perspective on the potential and scope of TMCL, highlighting its role in addressing diverse literacy needs across different age groups and community settings.

The challenges I faced in my stint as a consultant for TMCL programs offered valuable lessons and professional growth. The first was the digital divide, a prevalent issue in many communities with limited access to technology (Fang et al., 2019; Van Dijk, 2017). Addressing this required innovative strategies, such as mobilizing local resources and creating low-tech educational alternatives. This challenge underscored the importance of adaptability in TMCL development, ensuring accessibility for all learners (Nedungadi et al., 2018). Another significant hurdle was the initial resistance to technological integration in traditional literacy settings (Howard & Mozejko, 2015; Pangrazio & Sefton-Green, 2020; Warschauer, 2006). Overcoming this necessitated not only patience but also effective training and support mechanisms for educators and community members, highlighting the need for a supportive transition towards digital literacy. Further challenges included maintaining the relevance and engagement of TMCL programs (Invernizzi et al., 2021). In several instances, designing content that resonated with diverse community groups proved complex, requiring a deep understanding of local contexts and needs (Schmidt & Lazar, 2019). This called for a nuanced approach in curriculum development, blending technological tools with culturally relevant content. Lastly, evaluating the impact of TMCL programs posed its own set of challenges. Developing effective assessment tools to measure both literacy gains and digital competency was crucial, yet often intricate, demanding a balance between quantitative and qualitative metrics. These challenges collectively informed and refined my approach to TMCL program development, emphasizing the need for flexibility, cultural sensitivity, and comprehensive evaluation methods (Caretelli, 2009; Roche, 2017).

It is crucial to note that while I have only shared insights from just two projects, they represent only a fraction of the diverse initiatives I have been involved in. These examples, though limited in number, are rich in lessons and should not be overlooked. They have profoundly shaped my understanding of effective TMCL program design, showcasing the transformative potential of technology in literacy education and the importance of overcoming challenges such as the digital divide and resistance to technological integration. These experiences highlighted the critical need for adaptability, community involvement, and a nuanced understanding of the learners' context as foundational elements of TMCL program design. It is these insights that inform the design principles I advocate for—principles that prioritize the seamless integration of technology, pedagogy, and community engagement to foster meaningful and sustainable literacy advancements. This understanding not only reaffirms my commitment to leveraging technology in literacy programs but also transitions smoothly into the discussion of specific design principles that have emerged from my journey, guiding the development of TMCL initiatives to meet the evolving needs of communities and the educational landscape.

DESIGN PRINCIPLES OF TMCL PROGRAMS

In TMCL programs, the role of well-defined design principles cannot be overstated. These principles act as the foundational pillars that guide the development, execution, and evaluation of TMCL initiatives. They are crucial in ensuring that the integration of technology into literacy programs is not only effective but also aligns with the educational goals and needs of the community (Durrant & Green, 2000; Eady, 2015). In TMCL programs, design principles serve multiple purposes: they provide a roadmap for creating engaging and relevant content, ensure that technology is used as a powerful enabler rather than a mere accessory, and facilitate the alignment of program objectives with the diverse learning styles and needs of participants (Beetham & Sharpe, 2019; Dalton, 2017; D'Ignacio & Bhargava, 2016; Grabill, 2001; Long, 2008). Essentially, these principles are the bedrock upon which successful and impactful TMCL programs are built, ensuring that they deliver on their promise of enhancing literacy through the strategic use of technology within community settings.

Community engagement emerges as a cornerstone in the design and implementation of TMCL programs, underpinning their success from conception through to execution and evaluation. This principle acknowledges that for literacy initiatives to be effective, they must be deeply embedded within the fabric of the community they aim to serve, aligning with local values, cultures, and needs. The process of engaging the community begins with active consultation, where the voices and perspectives of community members, including educators, parents, local leaders, and learners, directly shape the program's objectives and content. Such a participatory approach not only ensures the cultural relevance of TMCL programs but also addresses specific community challenges and opportunities, fostering a program evolution that resonates with community input through strategies like collaborative workshops, focus group discussions, and regular feedback mechanisms (Durrant & Green, 2000; Long, 2008). This deep-rooted engagement cultivates a sense of ownership among community members, significantly enhancing motivation and participation while making the learning environment more inclusive. It extends literacy initiatives beyond traditional educational settings, integrating practical and relevant digital tools, and reflecting community insights in the program, thus enhancing its relevance and effectiveness for impactful literacy outcomes (Eady, 2015; D'Ignacio & Bhargava, 2016). By weaving the community's fabric into every aspect of TMCL programs, this comprehensive involvement not only tailors these initiatives to meet specific educational needs but also lays a foundation for ongoing social and economic development. Consequently, TMCL programs become collaborative, resilient, and dynamically responsive learning experiences, capable of leveraging technology for a broader impact and ensuring they remain relevant within the ever-evolving educational landscape.

The second critical principle in TMCL program design is the judicious selection of digital tools, a decision pivotal to the success and efficacy of these programs. Choosing the right digital tools involves careful consideration of several key criteria, foremost of which are accessibility and user-friendliness. The tools must be accessible to all participants, considering factors such as availability, affordability, and ease of use, to ensure no learner is left behind due to technological barriers (Dalton, 2017). User-friendliness is equally crucial, as tools that are intuitive and easy to navigate foster greater engagement and learning efficacy, particularly for participants who may be less familiar with digital technology (Durrant & Green, 2000). In addition to accessibility and usability, the alignment of digital tools with educational objectives is essential (Eady, 2015; Long, 2008). The selected technologies should complement and enhance the literacy goals of the program, whether it's through interactive e-books for reading proficiency, writing platforms for composition skills, or multimedia resources for comprehensive literacy. The integration of these tools should also support varied learning styles, catering to visual, auditory, and kinesthetic learners. When chosen and utilized effectively, digital tools have the potential to transform traditional literacy education, making it more engaging, interactive, and adaptable to individual learner needs. In TMCL programs, the strategic selection of digital tools is not just about incorporating technology into the curriculum; it is about enhancing and revolutionizing the way literacy is taught and learned in community settings.

The third principle crucial to TMCL programs is the effective development of curriculum, a process that requires meticulous planning to ensure the seamless integration of technology with literacy goals. Effective curriculum development in TMCL begins with a clear understanding of the literacy objectives, which should be closely aligned with the technological tools and resources being utilized (Grabill, 2001). This alignment ensures that technology is not an afterthought but an integral part of the learning journey, facilitating the achievement of specific literacy outcomes. Developing an effective TMCL curriculum involves crafting learning experiences that are not only engaging but also reflective of the community's needs and contexts (Beetham & Sharpe, 2019; Eady, 2015). This means incorporating local stories, examples, and experiences into the curriculum, thereby making it more relatable and relevant for the learners. The curriculum should be flexible enough to adapt to varying levels of digital literacy among participants, allowing for differentiated learning paths tailored to individual capabilities and progress. Moreover, the TMCL curriculum should be designed to encourage active participation and interaction, leveraging the interactive capabilities of digital tools to foster a more dynamic learning environment (D'Ignacio & Bhargava, 2016; Long, 2008). This could include the use of online forums for discussions, digital storytelling tools for creative expression, and interactive quizzes for literacy assessments. The key is to create a curriculum that not only imparts literacy skills but also engages learners in a meaningful and culturally resonant way, harnessing the power of technology to enrich the overall educational experience.

Recognizing the importance of feedback and flexibility serves as the fourth key principle in the realm of TMCL program design. The ongoing collection and incorporation of feedback from participants and stakeholders are essential in shaping and fine-tuning these programs (Eady, 2015; Dalton, 2017; D'Ignacio & Bhargava, 2016). Employing tools such as surveys, focus groups, and regular review sessions, TMCL initiatives can gather critical insights into their effectiveness, the appropriateness of digital tools, and the levels of learner engagement. This constant stream of feedback ensures that the program remains relevant and responsive to the community's evolving needs and preferences, allowing for timely adjustments and enhancements (Beetham & Sharpe, 2019). To provide further insight into this phase, excerpts of feedback received from the community highlight the substantial impact of TMCL programs. One educator noted, "*The feedback mechanism has been pivotal. It has allowed us to tailor the program more closely to our learners' needs, making learning more accessible and engaging for everyone involved.*" Another comment from a parent in the community underscored the value of this approach: "*Seeing our suggestions and concerns addressed has not only improved the program but also strengthened our trust and investment in these literacy initiatives.*" These reflections from the stakeholders illustrate the significance of feedback in continuously refining the programs, ensuring they effectively meet the community's literacy needs while fostering a collaborative and supportive learning environment.

Simultaneously, flexibility in both the design and implementation of TMCL programs is paramount. This principle involves adapting to changing technological trends, educational needs, and feedback from the community. Such flexibility might entail updating digital tools, revising curriculum content, or modifying teaching methodologies to better align with the community's current requirements (Long, 2008). Flexibility also equips TMCL programs to address unexpected challenges, ensuring they can pivot and evolve as necessary. By prioritizing this principle of feedback and flexibility, TMCL programs can sustain their dynamism and efficacy, continually adapting to serve their communities effectively (Beetham & Sharpe, 2019; D'Ignacio & Bhargava, 2016).

The final principle in TMCL program design is continuous evaluation and improvement, a process critical for maintaining the efficacy and relevance of these initiatives. Regular assessment of TMCL programs is fundamental to understanding their impact and effectiveness. This involves not just evaluating learner outcomes in terms of literacy skills but also assessing the integration and utility of digital tools, the effectiveness of teaching methodologies, and the program's overall alignment with community needs (Beetham & Sharpe, 2019; Dalton, 2017; Grabill, 2001). Such assessments can be conducted through various methods, including learner feedback, performance metrics, and program analytics. This continuous evaluation serves as a foundation for ongoing improvement, allowing program designers and facilitators to identify areas for enhancement and make necessary adjustments. It is crucial that these evaluations are not seen as one-time events but as integral, ongoing components of the program lifecycle (Long, 2008). This iterative process ensures that TMCL programs remain dynamic and responsive to changing educational landscapes and technological advancements. By committing to continuous evaluation and improvement, TMCL programs can evolve and adapt over time, consistently meeting and exceeding their objectives while remaining attuned to the needs of the communities they serve (Beetham & Sharpe, 2019).

I present a flowchart that distills the TMCL program design process into its fundamental stages, reflecting the principles I have established through experience. It begins with Community Engagement, crucial for grounding the program in the community's cultural and educational landscape. The Digital Tool Selection stage draws from my work on choosing accessible and pedagogically aligned tools. This is followed by Curriculum Development, where these tools are woven into engaging content, a step informed by my curriculum design experience. The process is designed to be iterative, incorporating Feedback and Flexibility, embodying the adaptability that my experience has shown to be essential. The cycle concludes with Continuous Evaluation and Improvement, ensuring the program's relevance and efficacy. This flowchart serves as a personal blueprint, guiding the methodical application of these interconnected stages in TMCL initiatives, providing a clear visual guide from conception to execution.

The principles outlined and visualized in the flowchart converge to establish a unified approach to TMCL program design. This cohesive strategy ensures that from the foundational community engagement to the selection of digital tools, curriculum development, and the integration of feedback, each element is interlinked, reinforcing the others. Together, they create a robust framework that enhances the

Figure 1. Design principles of technology-mediated community literacy (TMCL) programs

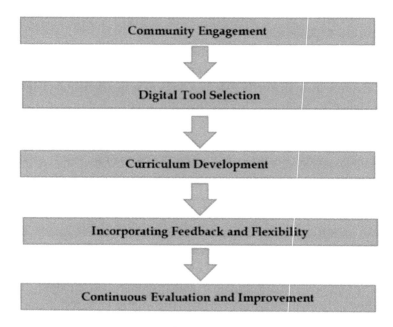

effectiveness of TMCL programs, ensuring that they are responsive to community needs and adaptable to the ever-evolving digital landscape (Durrant & Green, 2000; Eady, 2015). The collective impact of these principles is significant, as they form the backbone of TMCL initiatives that are not only theoretically sound but also practically successful and impactful.

SUCCESSES, CHALLENGES, AND PRACTICAL INSIGHTS

In this section, I revisit the cases previously mentioned in this chapter, now including additional examples from my diverse experiences in TMCL program design. These cases are critical for a comprehensive understanding of TMCL implementation. They illuminate the multifaceted nature of TMCL programs, showcasing not only the successes and challenges encountered but also the practical insights gained (Durrant & Green, 2000; Eady, 2015). Through this deeper analysis, these cases will provide a richer understanding of the factors contributing to success in TMCL programs and the strategies for navigating the challenges that arise.

The first case, a child-focused literacy initiative during the COVID-19 pandemic, exemplifies a success story in TMCL implementation. This program was designed to sustain literacy development amid the challenges of remote learning. My role involved creating a TMCL curriculum that effectively utilized technology for online instruction while engaging community members to support home-based learning. The key strategies included equitable access to digital tools and training educators and parents for effective technology use. The program achieved significant success, marked by sustained student engagement and measurable improvements in literacy skills. The critical success factors in this case were the adaptability of the program, robust community involvement, and the development of an engaging and accessible curriculum (Invernizzi et al., 2021; Schmidt & Lazar, 2019). In this program, several challenges were encountered. The foremost hurdle was tackling the digital divide, as equitable access to digital tools was a significant issue, especially in under-resourced areas (Fang et al., 2019; Van Dijk, 2017). Another challenge was the resistance to technological integration from educators and parents, who were accustomed to traditional teaching methods (Howard & Mozejko, 2015; Pangrazio & Sefton-Green, 2020; Warschauer, 2006). This required not only technical training but also sensitization to the benefits of digital literacy. The program's success, despite these hurdles, was a testament to the effectiveness of the strategies implemented, but these challenges underscored the complexities of TMCL implementation in crisis situations.

The second case involved an adult literacy program at my former university in the Philippines. The program was designed to empower adults with literacy skills that could lead to livelihood opportunities, a critical initiative during the pandemic-induced economic downturn. My role encompassed developing a curriculum integrating digital literacy with vocational training, delivered through a mix of online and community-based methods. The program's success was notable, with participants showing significant improvements in literacy and practical skills application. Key success factors included the tailored curriculum catering to varying digital proficiencies and the practical applicability of the skills taught, reflecting a deep understanding of adult learning needs and economic realities. This approach aligns with the strategies recommended by Nedungadi et al. (2018) for creating adaptable educational programs and addresses the digital divide (Fang et al., 2019; Van Dijk, 2017). There were hurdles that I needed to surmount in my encounter with this program. Catering to adults with diverse digital proficiency levels was a significant hurdle, requiring the curriculum to be both accessible and adaptable. Additionally, ensuring the practical applicability of the skills taught was crucial, as the program aimed to translate literacy skills into real economic opportunities. These challenges highlighted the need for a nuanced understanding of adult education, particularly in integrating digital literacy with vocational training in a way that was both engaging and relevant to the participants' real-life needs. The methodologies for overcoming resistance to technological integration, (Howard & Mozejko 2015; Pangrazio &

Sefton-Green, 2020; Warschauer, 2006), provided a foundational framework for addressing these challenges effectively.

TMCL programs utilize technology not just for content delivery but as a key element in fostering engaging and interactive learning for various age groups (Barratt-Pugh, 2022). Through digital platforms for e-reading, online storytelling, and vocational training modules, these programs meet diverse literacy needs while promoting digital fluency. The application of educational analytics for program fine-tuning further illustrates the critical role of technology in enhancing literacy education, demonstrating its effectiveness in improving accessibility, engagement, and program adaptability, thereby supporting literacy development and digital skill acquisition.

In addition to the primary case studies, my experiences include several other TMCL projects, each offering unique insights. One such mini-case involved a digital literacy program in a barangay in the Philippines, targeting out-of-school youths and unemployed residents. This project required adapting TMCL strategies to cater to a community with limited access to technology. The challenge of engaging volunteers, like local teachers, and tailoring the content to local needs was significant, yet the program achieved success through strong community collaboration and resourcefulness. These efforts align with the importance of community engagement and adaptability in TMCL programs, especially in crisis situations (Wickham & Carbone, 2018; Barratt-Pugh, 2022).

Another example was a weekend reading program for children in a rural community, where parents were actively involved as tutors. The program emphasized creating a supportive, technology-fused literacy environment at home. While the initiative successfully fostered parent-child engagement, it also faced challenges in maintaining consistent participation and balancing the educational content with diverse literacy levels of both parents and children. These additional cases underscored the importance of understanding and adapting to specific community contexts, both in terms of challenges and strategies for success (Invernizzi et al., 2021; Schmidt & Lazar, 2019).

Reflecting on these TMCL case studies, the overarching lessons learned are multifarious. Successes were often rooted in strong community engagement and the adaptability of program design to meet specific local needs. Recurring challenges included technological barriers, varying levels of digital literacy, and maintaining consistent community involvement. These experiences have profoundly informed my approach to TMCL, emphasizing the need for flexibility, cultural sensitivity, and resourcefulness. They highlight that successful TMCL programs require not just technological solutions, but a deep understanding of and responsiveness to the community's unique educational landscape (Fang et al., 2019; Van Dijk, 2017; Nedungadi et al., 2018).

The practical insights gained from my TMCL consultancy experiences are invaluable, particularly for those designing and implementing similar programs. Key insights include the importance of deeply understanding and integrating into the community context, the necessity of flexible and adaptable program design, and the critical role of balancing technological solutions with hands-on, culturally sensitive approaches. These insights also emphasize the importance of continuous learning and evolution in program design to meet changing community needs and technological advancements, offering a roadmap for others in the field of TMCL (Howard & Mozejko, 2015; Pangrazio & Sefton-Green, 2020; Warschauer, 2006).

LIMITATIONS

Following my reflections on the successes, challenges, and practical insights gleaned from the implementation of TMCL programs, I recognize the importance of addressing the limitations of my work. This chapter, rooted in my experiences, does not encapsulate the entirety of the challenges faced nor does it cover all potential solutions within the realm of TMCL. I am aware that factors such as geographic, socio-economic, and rapid technological changes impose significant constraints on the access to and effectiveness of these programs. Moreover, the dynamic nature of technology and education means that some aspects discussed may quickly become outdated. Acknowledging these limitations not only grounds my reflections in reality but also paves the way for the recommendations I propose. It is within these recommendations that I seek to address the gaps identified, offering pathways for further research and the continual adaptation of TMCL programs to better meet the evolving needs of our communities.

FUTURE DIRECTIONS AND RECOMMENDATIONS

Looking towards the future TMCL programs, it is evident that emerging trends in technology and education will play a pivotal role in shaping their evolution. We are likely to see advancements in digital tools that could transform content delivery methods, making TMCL programs more accessible and interactive. Changes in educational policies might further embrace and support digital literacy initiatives, potentially leading to a wider acceptance and integration of TMCL in mainstream education. Additionally, new approaches to community engagement, possibly influenced by evolving communication technologies, could offer more inclusive and effective ways to involve diverse community groups. These trends are expected to not only enhance the accessibility and quality of TMCL programs but also broaden their impact on communities, potentially making them a more integral part of the educational landscape (Nazirjonovich, 2021; Jamil & Almunawar, 2021).

For practitioners and educators in the field of TMCL, it is crucial to embrace continuous learning and adapt to emerging technologies. Staying updated with technological advancements ensures that TMCL programs remain relevant and engaging. Engaging diverse communities effectively requires understanding their unique needs and cultural contexts. Integrating TMCL into existing literacy initiatives can also enhance their reach and effectiveness. Emphasize the importance of ongoing professional development and collaboration among educators, practitioners, and community stakeholders to foster a supportive network for TMCL programs. This is vital for ensuring that TMCL initiatives are not only theoretically sound but also practically successful and impactful (Durrant & Green, 2000; Eady, 2015).

To policymakers focused on enhancing educational landscapes, it is important to consider measures that can facilitate the growth and effectiveness of TMCL programs. I recommend developing funding strategies that specifically support TMCL initiatives, ensuring they have the resources necessary to thrive. Policymakers should also consider creating regulatory frameworks that encourage and prioritize digital literacy, making it a key component of educational standards. Additionally, fostering partnerships between educational institutions and technology providers can lead to innovative solutions and improved access to digital tools for TMCL programs. These policy measures can play a crucial role in expanding and strengthening the impact of TMCL initiatives, as emphasized by the integration of technology as a cornerstone of modern educational practice (Nazirjonovich, 2021).

FINAL REFLECTIONS

As I reflect on my experiences as a TMCL consultant, my journey has been marked by a series of enlightening encounters and learnings. Each project, whether it focused on children's literacy or adult education, has significantly contributed to my understanding and methodology in TMCL. Key learnings from these experiences include the critical importance of addressing and navigating technological challenges, the effectiveness of engaging communities, and the profound impact these programs can have. These moments of insight have not only refined my approach to TMCL but also deepened my appreciation for its transformative potential in various educational contexts (Fang et al., 2019; Van Dijk, 2017).

My personal insights, gleaned from diverse TMCL consultancy experiences, carry profound implications for the future of TMCL programs. These experiences underscore the necessity of continual learning and adaptation in the rapidly evolving field of technology-mediated education. The insights I've gained highlight the need for future TMCL designs to be dynamic, responsive to technological advancements, and deeply rooted in the specific needs of communities (Nedungadi et al., 2018). Emphasizing these aspects can significantly enhance the effectiveness and relevance of TMCL programs in the years ahead.

Within the intricate weave of my endeavors in TMCL programs, the constructed visual representation embodies the depth and subtlety of my strategic approach. At the top, 'Integrated Learning' reflects my commitment to creating educational experiences where technology and pedagogy are in harmony, enhancing the learner's journey. 'Community Engagement' and 'Digital Fluency,' foundational to my practice, represent the dual pillars of my approach: fostering a participatory environment and equipping individuals with the skills to navigate the digital landscape confidently (Howard & Mozejko, 2015; Pangrazio & Sefton-Green, 2020). At the center lies 'Reflective Growth,' emblematic of my introspective journey. This central element is a personal testament to the iterative process of development and learning that underpins my work. It is through this lens of reflection that I assess the impact of my programs, ensuring they remain responsive to the evolving needs of learners and communities. This representation not only illustrates my methodology but also my philosophy that effective TMCL programs are built on a bedrock of community collaboration, digital competence, and a commitment to continuous improvement (Warschauer, 2006).

As I reflect on the evolving landscape of community literacy in the digital age, my thoughts coalesce around a vision where TMCL programs stand as pivotal conduits of empowerment and inclusion. These programs, I believe, will continue to bridge the

Figure 2. The construct of TMCL program design: A reflective framework

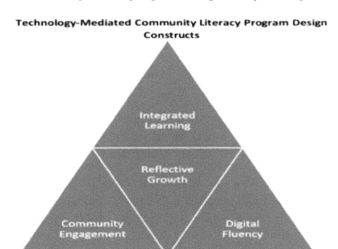

gaps in literacy by harnessing the ever-expanding potential of digital tools, shaping a future where every individual has the opportunity to engage, learn, and grow within their communities. The horizon for TMCL is one of endless possibilities, promising a transformative impact on community literacy that resonates with the needs and aspirations of our digitally interconnected world.

REFERENCES

Barratt-Pugh, C., Hill, S., Johnson, N. F., Barblett, L., & Parker, A. (2022). Designing and implementing a family literacy program through smartphones: How does recruitment method influence uptake and attrition? *Early Childhood Education Journal*, 1–12. Advance online publication. doi:10.1007/s10643-022-01433-z PMID:36597553

Beetham, H., & Sharpe, R. (Eds.). (2019). *Rethinking pedagogy for a digital age: Principles and practices of design*. Routledge. doi:10.4324/9781351252805

Bers, M. U. (2010). Beyond computer literacy: Supporting youth's positive development through technology. *New Directions for Youth Development*, *2010*(128), 13–23. doi:10.1002/yd.371 PMID:21240949

Burnett, C., Dickinson, P., Myers, J., & Merchant, G. (2006). Digital connections: Transforming literacy in the primary school. *Cambridge Journal of Education*, *36*(1), 11–29. doi:10.1080/03057640500491120

Cartelli, A. (2009). Frameworks for digital literacy and digital competence assessment. In *Proceedings of the 8th European Conference on e-Learning* (pp. 116-123). IEEE.

Cook, S. (2016). *Integrating Technology in Early Literacy: A Snapshot of Community Innovation in Family Engagement*. New America.

D'Ignazio, C., & Bhargava, R. (2016). *DataBasic: Design principles, tools and activities for data literacy learners*.

Dalton, E. M. (2017). Beyond universal design for learning: Guiding principles to reduce barriers to digital & media literacy competence. *The Journal of Media Literacy Education*, *9*(2), 17–29. doi:10.23860/JMLE-2019-09-02-02

Detlor, B., Julien, H., La Rose, T., & Serenko, A. (2022). Community-led digital literacy training: Toward a conceptual framework. *Journal of the Association for Information Science and Technology*, *73*(10), 1387–1400. doi:10.1002/asi.24639

Didiharyono, D., & Qur'ani, B. (2019). Increasing community knowledge through the literacy movement. To Maega. *Jurnal Pengabdian Masyarakat*, *2*(1), 17–24. doi:10.35914/tomaega.v2i1.235

Duke, B., Harper, G., & Johnston, M. (2013). Connectivism as a digital age learning theory. *The International HETL Review*, *2013*(Special Issue), 4–13.

Durrant, C., & Green, B. (2000). Literacy and the new technologies in school education: Meeting the l(IT)eracy challenge? *Australian Journal of Language and Literacy*, *23*(2), 89–108.

Eady, M. J. (2015). Eleven design-based principles to facilitate the adoption of internet technologies in Indigenous communities. *International Journal of Social Media and Interactive Learning Environments*, *3*(4), 267–289. doi:10.1504/IJSMILE.2015.074010

Fang, M. L., Canham, S. L., Battersby, L., Sixsmith, J., Wada, M., & Sixsmith, A. (2019). Exploring privilege in the digital divide: Implications for theory, policy, and practice. *The Gerontologist*, *59*(1), e1–e15. PMID:29750241

Garcia, D. C., & Hasson, D. J. (2004). Implementing family literacy programs for linguistically and culturally diverse populations: Key elements to consider. *School Community Journal*, *14*(1), 113–137.

Goranova, E. (2019). Creation of electronic learning objects for the high cognitive levels of Bloom's digital taxonomy. *KNOWLEDGE-International Journal*, *31*(2), 585–590. doi:10.35120/kij3102585g

Grabill, J. T. (2001). *Community literacy programs and the politics of change.* SUNY Press.

Hawkins, J. (1991). Technology-mediated communities for learning: Designs and consequences. *The Annals of the American Academy of Political and Social Science*, *514*(1), 159–174. doi:10.1177/0002716291514001013

Howard, S. K., & Mozejko, A. (2015). Teachers: technology, change, and resistance. In M. Henderson & G. Romeo (Eds.), Teaching and Digital Technologies: Big Issues and Critical Questions (pp. 307-317). Cambridge University Press. https://www.researchgate.net/publication/292971267_Teachers_technology_change_and_resistance

Hughes, J., Thomas, R., & Scharber, C. (2006, March). Assessing technology integration: The RAT–replacement, amplification, and transformation-framework. *In Society for Information Technology & Teacher Education International Conference* (pp. 1616-1620). Association for the Advancement of Computing in Education (AACE).

Invernizzi, M., Rosemary, C., Juel, C., & Richards, H. C. (2021). At-risk readers and community volunteers: A 3-year perspective. In *Components of Effective Reading Intervention* (pp. 277–300). Routledge. doi:10.4324/9781315046365-6

Jamil, M. I. M., & Almunawar, M. N. (2021). Importance of digital literacy and hindrance brought about by digital divide. In *Encyclopedia of Information Science and Technology* (5th ed., pp. 1683–1698). IGI Global. doi:10.4018/978-1-7998-3479-3.ch116

Jung, I. (2019). Connectivism and networked learning. In Open and distance education theory revisited: Implications for the digital era (pp. 47-55). Springer. doi:10.1007/978-981-13-7740-2_6

Kellner, D. (2004). Technological transformation, multiple literacies, and the re-visioning of education. *E-Learning and Digital Media*, *1*(1), 9–37. doi:10.2304/elea.2004.1.1.8

Koehler, M., & Mishra, P. (2009). What is technological pedagogical content knowledge (TPACK)? *Contemporary Issues in Technology & Teacher Education*, *9*(1), 60–70.

Lev-On, A., Steinfeld, N., Abu-Kishk, H., & Pearl Naim, S. (2021). The long-term effects of digital literacy programs for disadvantaged populations: Analyzing participants' perceptions. *Journal of Information. Communication and Ethics in Society*, *19*(1), 146–162. doi:10.1108/JICES-02-2020-0019

Lin, Y.-T. (2023). Learning performances towards the BookRoll e-book system for flipped classrooms in software engineering education. *Journal of Educational Technology & Society*, *26*(3), 190–202. https://www.jstor.org/stable/48734330

Long, E. (2008). *Community literacy and the rhetoric of local publics*. Parlor Press LLC.

McKee, H., & Blair, K. (2007). Older adults and community-based technological literacy programs: Barriers & benefits to learning. *Community Literacy Journal*, *1*(2), 2. https://www.semanticscholar.org. doi:10.25148/CLJ.1.2.009516

McKnight, J. L., & Russell, C. (2018). *The four essential elements of an asset-based community development process: What Is Distinctive about Asset-Based Community Process*. Nurture Development.

Menon, R., Nedungadi, P., & Raman, R. (2017). Technology enabled teacher training for low-literate, remote and rural multi-grade education centers. 2017 *International Conference on Advances in Computing, Communications and Informatics (ICACCI)*, (pp. 1594-1599). Semantic Scholar. https://www.semanticscholar.org

Mills, K. A. (2010). A review of the "digital turn" in the new literacy studies. *Review of Educational Research*, *80*(2), 246–271. doi:10.3102/0034654310364401

Murray, M. C., & Pérez, J. (2014). Unraveling the digital literacy paradox: How higher education fails at the fourth literacy. *Issues in Informing Science and Information Technology*, *11*, 85. doi:10.28945/1982

Nazirjonovich, K. Z. (2021). The use of modern educational technologies in the organization of physical education is a guarantee to increase the effectiveness of education. *ACADEMICIA: An International Multidisciplinary Research Journal*, *11*(10), 477–480.

Nedungadi, P. P., Menon, R., Gutjahr, G., Erickson, L., & Raman, R. (2018). Towards an inclusive digital literacy framework for digital India. *Education + Training*, *60*(6), 516–528. doi:10.1108/ET-03-2018-0061

Nelson, J., & Braafladt, K. (2012). *Technology and literacy: 21st century library programming for children and teens*. American Library Association.

Pangrazio, L., & Sefton-Green, J. (2020). The social utility of 'data literacy.'. *Learning, Media and Technology*, *45*(2), 208–220. doi:10.1080/17439884.2020.1707223

Puentedura, R. (2013). SAMR: Moving from enhancement to transformation. Hippasus. http://www.hippasus.com/rrpweblog/archives/2013/05/29/SAMREnhancementToTransformation.pdf

Putnam, R. (2001). Social capital: Measurement and consequences. *Canadian Journal of Policy Research*, *2*(1), 41–51.

Quick, K. S., & Bryson, J. M. (2022). Public participation. In *Handbook on Theories of Governance* (pp. 158–168). Edward Elgar Publishing. doi:10.4337/9781800371972.00022

Roche, T. B. (2017). Assessing the role of digital literacy in English for Academic Purposes university pathway programs. *Journal of Academic Language and Learning*, *11*(1), A71–A87.

Schmidt, P. R., & Lazar, A. M. (Eds.). (2019). *Practicing what we teach: How culturally responsive literacy classrooms make a difference*. Teachers College Press.

Shrestha, S., & Krolak, L. (2015). The potential of community libraries in supporting literate environments and sustaining literacy skills. *International Review of Education*, *61*(3), 399–418. https://eric.ed.gov/?id=EJ1071442. doi:10.1007/s11159-014-9462-9

Sindoni, M. G., & Moschini, I. (Eds.). (2021). *Multimodal literacies across digital learning contexts*. Routledge. doi:10.4324/9781003134244

Statti, A., & Torres, K. M. (2020). Digital literacy: The need for technology integration and its impact on learning and engagement in community school environments. *Peabody Journal of Education*, *95*(1), 90–100. https://eric.ed.gov/?id=EJ1247203. doi:10.1080/0161956X.2019.1702426

Ullah, A., & Anwar, S. (2020). The effective use of information technology and interactive activities to improve learner engagement. *Education Sciences*, *10*(12), 349. doi:10.3390/educsci10120349

Van Dijk, J. A. (2017). Digital divide: Impact of access. The International Encyclopedia of Media Effects, 1-11.

VÁSquez, O. A. (2007). Technology out of school: What schools can learn from community-based technology. *Teachers College Record*, *109*(14), 182–206. doi:10.1177/016146810710901410

Warschauer, M. (2006). Literacy and technology: Bridging the divide. *Cyberlines*, *2*, 163–174.

Wason-Ellam, L., Ward, A., Fey, C., King, A.-L., Gilchrist, B., & Townsend, L. (2004). Community literacy: Commodifying children's spaces. *Language and Literature*, *6*(1). doi:10.20360/G2MS4H

Wenger, E. (2000). Communities of practice and social learning systems. *Organization*, *7*(2), 225–246. doi:10.1177/135050840072002

Wickham, C. A., & Carbone, E. T. (2018). "Just Say It Like It Is!" Use of a Community-Based Participatory Approach to Develop a Technology-Driven Food Literacy Program for Adolescents. *International Quarterly of Community Health Education*, *38*(2), 83–97. doi:10.1177/0272684X17749572 PMID:29283040

Chapter 8
Literacy, Resilience, and Financial Well-Being in Higher Education Students

Patrícia Dias
ISAG, European Business School and Research Center in Business Science and Tourism (CICET-FCVC), Porto, Portugal

Ana Pinto Borges
(iD) https://orcid.org/0000-0002-4942-079X
ISAG, European Business School and Research Center in Business Science and Tourism (CICET-FCVC), Porto, Portugal & Center for Research in Organizations, Markets and Industrial Management (COMEGI), Porto, Portugal

Elvira Vieira
(iD) https://orcid.org/0000-0002-9296-3896
ISAG, European Business School and Research Center in Business Science and Tourism (CICET-FCVC), Porto, Portugal & IPVC-Polytechnic Institute of Viana do Castelo and Applied Management Research Unit (UNIAG), Instituto Politécnico de Bragança, Portugal

ABSTRACT

The authors assessed the determinants of the overall financial literacy indicator of higher education students in Portugal and the relationship between the financial literacy indicator and the indicators of resilience and financial well-being. Based on a non-parametric quantitative analysis, the authors used a sample of 469 higher education students. They observed that students present globally more satisfactory indicators compared to the Portuguese population and are influenced by demographic factors such as age, gender, level of education, and income. The results are far from reasonable, especially in the dimension related to knowledge. As also statistically confirmed, there exists a positive and significant relationship between the financial literacy indicator and the indicators of resilience and financial well-being. Therefore, this study adopts a novel approach that intends to link these indicators with higher education students, as there is still a lack of research that addresses the concept of digital financial literacy within this context.

DOI: 10.4018/979-8-3693-1777-8.ch008

INTRODUCTION

As with the 2008 financial crisis and the 2010 recession, the pandemic caused by the SARS-CoV-2 virus also led to a worsening of economic conditions worldwide. These successive and recurring economic restrictions bring to the fore the need for and importance of making appropriate, informed, and conscious financial decisions. This relevance is even greater when we consider the ease with which the digital world provides financial products and services.

Portugal has very low levels of financial literacy. Portugal was the second-least financially literate nation in the European Union in 2023, according to a poll conducted by the European Commission (2023). Additionally, the Organisation for Economic Cooperation and Development (OECD) found that Portugal's inhabitants' level of financial literacy barely improved between 2020 and 2023 in its most recent study, which was released in 2023 (OECD, 2023). In this study, the Portuguese were able to correctly answer 63% of the questions asked about financial knowledge, attitudes and behaviours, increasing just one percentage point compared to the 2020 study (OECD, 2020; 2023). Despite this small improvement, Portugal has above average results in financial attitudes and behaviour, but remains below average in terms of financial knowledge (OECD, 2023).

A low level of financial literacy remains a significant concern in Portugal, as evidenced by various studies and indicators (Banco de Portugal et al., 2021; Mesquita et al., 2021; OECD, 2020; 2023). Even with initiatives to increase financial literacy, a lot of people still find it difficult to comprehend basic financial concepts, manage their money effectively, and make informed decisions about investing, saving, and paying off debt. This lack of financial literacy jeopardises not just the financial security of the individual but also the stability and expansion of the economy as a whole. Furthermore, given the critical transitional stage that students in higher education experience, which is marked by an increase in financial obligations and decision-making, it is imperative that financial literacy be addressed among this population. These students are especially vulnerable since they frequently lack the information and skills needed to deal with the challenges of personal finance. Improving higher education students' financial literacy is vital because it gives them the information and resources they need to make prudent financial choices, form healthy financial habits at a young age, and eventually promote long-term financial well-being. University students' financial literacy levels can be studied and addressed by policymakers, educators, and stakeholders to equip the upcoming generation with the financial skills necessary to succeed in an increasingly complex financial environment. Decision-making will influence not only the present, but also the future, so it is crucial to recognize the relevance of financial literacy in university students as an essential factor for the future macroeconomic stability.

In this sense, the main purpose of this study is to calculate the overall indicator of financial literacy of higher education students in Portugal by determining the indicators of attitude, behaviour, and financial knowledge. Additionally, we intend to analyse their determinants, as well as assess the relationship between the financial literacy indicator and the indicators of resilience and financial well-being. This research is unique because it aims to simultaneously determine these three indicators in higher education students, assuming the importance of these agents as decision makers for the future of the Portuguese economy. The reasoning behind selecting these indicators is that the characteristics of attitude, behaviour and knowledge form the foundation of the most widely accepted definition of financial literacy. According to the same perspective, the OECD (2013) defines financial literacy as the set of information and abilities that empowers a person to make confident and successful financial decisions, hence promoting the growth of both individual and societal financial well-being.

This chapter encompasses 5 chapters. Chapter 1 introduces and motivates the topic. Chapter 2 presents the literature review and defines the study hypotheses. Chapter 3 describes the methodology and sample. The results and discussion are presented below (chapter 4) and the conclusions are described in the last chapter (chapter 5).

LITERATURE REVIEW

Financial Literacy Concept

Among the earliest definition of financial literacy is its understanding as solely related to the money use and management, proposed by Noctor, Stoney and Stradling (1992). A few years later, Schagen and Lines (1996) further elaborated on the concept with de definition that the financial literacy: "encompasses the abilities to understand key concepts related to capital management, to understand the workings of financial institutions, services, and systems, to analyses, and to control one's finances responsibly" (Schagen & Lines, 1996, p. 91). In the following decade, Kempson, Collard and Moore (2006) designed a model to assess an individual's financial capability, in which they compare financial literacy areas with knowledge, attitude, and behaviour. For the authors, an individual's financial capability is increased by the interrelationship of the three elements, with the behaviour being considered the most important.

Various definitions continue to emerge from different institutions and authors, however, it appears that some central ideas are common (Kadoya & Khan, 2020). Concretley, financial literacy definition grounding on the three domains, namely knowledge, attitude, and behaviour, is still today the most consensual and recurrent definition in various international studies. The OECD (2013, p. 144) bases its definition on these three domains of financial literacy and defines it as "the knowledge and understanding of financial concepts and risks, the skills, motivation, and confidence to apply this knowledge and understanding to make effective decisions in financial contexts, to improve the financial well-being of individuals and society, and to enable participation in economic life". This definition is corroborated by authors such as Messy and Monticone (2016), Sayinzoga, Bulte and Lensink (2016) and Rai, Dua and Yadav (2019). Kempson, Collard & Moore (2005) presented a matrix of two entries which relates the three elements of financial literacy with budget, comfort, products, planning and information (see Table 1).

In addition to establishing a clear and comprehensive definition of financial literacy, it is crucial to highlight the importance of actively promoting this literacy. The promotion of financial literacy serves as a vital tool for consumer protection, aiming to provide individuals with access to credible and relevant information to make advantageous financial decisions. This is crucial as low literacy levels can result in detrimental financial choices, impacting both present circumstances and future prospects (Tavares & Almeida, 2020). However, the significance of financial literacy extends beyond individual outcomes, influencing societal and economic performance at the national level. Financial decisions play a pivotal role in shaping the economic landscape of a country and should thus be a matter of global concern (Banco de Portugal, Comissão de Mercado de Valores Mobiliários, & Autoridade de Supervisão de Seguros e Fundos de Pensões, 2011; Borg, 2017; Trunk & Dermol, 2015). In Portugal, the emphasis on promoting financial literacy is underscored by the imperative to prevent economic crises, particularly given the economy's high indebtedness and low savings rates (Banco de Portugal et al., 2011).

Table 1. Financial literacy mastery matrix

Element	Budget	Comfort	Products	Planning	Information
Knowledge	Understanding the need for, and how to balance the family budget	Understanding of the control of the financial situation	Choice and selection of products	Understanding future planning	Getting information and support
Attitude	Motivation and confidence in balancing the budget	The motivation and confidence to keep the financial control	Motivation and confidence in the products you select	Motivation and confidence in planning for the future	The motivation and confidence to get information and help
Behaviour	Balancing the budget in practice	Keeping control in practice	Choosing products in practice	Planning the future in practice	Keeping informed in practice

Source: Adapted from Kempson, Collard and Moore (2005) and Tavares and Almeida (2020).

Furthermore, the contemporary digital era introduces a new dimension to financial literacy: digital financial literacy. In today's world, proficiency in digital technologies is essential, as financial products and services are predominantly accessed through digital platforms (Azeez & Akhtar, 2021). Morgan, Huang, and Trinh (2019) propose conceptualizing digital financial literacy based on four core dimensions: knowledge of digital financial products and services, awareness of digital financial risks, digital risk management, and understanding consumer rights and return procedures. Azeez and Akhtar (2021, p. 9) define digital financial literacy as "the appropriate awareness of digital financial risks, the best use of knowledge of digital financial products, and risk control." This evolving concept underscores the necessity for individuals to not only possess traditional financial literacy skills but also to adapt to the digital landscape to make informed financial decisions effectively.

Measuring Financial Literacy

Measuring financial literacy has become increasingly important in today's society, as it plays a pivotal role in enabling individuals to make informed and conscious economic and financial decisions (Mitchell & Lusardi, 2011). While efforts to measure financial literacy have been ongoing since the beginning of the millennium, the lack of a consensus model poses challenges for accurately comparing financial literacy levels across nations. Researchers have developed various approaches, often utilizing questionnaires designed to assess individuals' understanding of key financial concepts such as interest rates, inflation, and risk diversification (Ouachani, Belhassine, & Kammoun, 2021).

However, the complexity of financial literacy measurement necessitates careful consideration of the questionnaire's design to ensure reliability and validity. To mitigate subjectivity and address issues of temporality, scholars advocate for the use of simple, concise questions that focus on the knowledge essential for everyday financial decision-making (Lavoura, 2017; Lusardi & Mitchell, 2014). By adopting this approach, researchers can obtain more accurate assessments of financial literacy levels while minimizing biases introduced by overly complex or time-bound questions. Additionally, the emphasis on everyday financial knowledge ensures that the measurement captures practical skills relevant to individuals' financial well-being in real-world contexts.

Furthermore, integrating diverse perspectives from researchers across disciplines can enrich the development of financial literacy measurement tools. Collaborative efforts allow for a comprehensive understanding of the multifaceted nature of financial literacy and facilitate the identification of culturally relevant indicators. By incorporating insights from various scholars, policymakers can refine measurement methodologies and tailor interventions to address specific challenges faced by different populations. Ultimately, advancing the measurement of financial literacy contributes to the development of targeted interventions and policies aimed at enhancing individuals' financial well-being and promoting economic stability on a global scale.

Financial Literacy in Portugal

The 2008 financial crisis demonstrated that the financial literacy level was globally low. Based on this evidence, most governments have publicly recognized the importance of financial literacy as a pillar in promoting the efficiency and stability of the financial system.

Based on this finding and as happened in other countries, Portugal started to take special care with Financial Literacy and, in 2008, designed a National Survey on the Financial Literacy of the Population, which only took place in 2010. The preparation of this survey complied to the best practices established by the International Network on Financial Education (INFE), a network supported by the OECD and made up of experts, public authorities, and financial regulators who have worked hard to define and spread guidelines on financial literacy promotion. Although the results obtained have been globally positive, asymmetries were revealed at the level of financial literacy of the respondents, with population segments with lower income and with a lower level of education showing a greater lack of financial knowledge (Banco de Portugal et al., 2011). Henriques (2010) profiled the population groups with the highest literacy level: between 25 and 44 years; male; married or living with a partner; qualified; in the labour market; high incomes; who know/have some financial products and services; and who consider that they have more knowledge and financial information.

Aware of the relevance of monitoring the financial literacy evolution and simultaneously assessing the effectiveness of the initiatives developed by the National Financial Training Plan (NFTP), the 2nd Financial Literacy Survey was conducted in 2015 (Banco de Portugal et al., 2016). The data from this second survey continued to reveal gaps in financial knowledge, but also greater prudence in family planning attitudes and behaviour. The groups with the best results were: respondents with higher education, with a gross monthly income of more than 1000€, with more than two types of financial products, and with regular savings habits (Banco de Portugal, et al., 2016).

In 2020, the 3rd Financial Literacy Survey was conducted. As in 2015, the study was a component of the global financial literacy comparison project organised by the INFE of the OECD. This organisation established a series of inquiries deemed necessary (core questions) for the assessment and comparison of attitudes, behaviours, and financial literacy on a global scale. The results obtained are in line with those of 2010 and 2015, revealing the need to strengthen the population's financial knowledge but highlighting greater proactivity in the application of the savings (Banco de Portugal, et al.,2021). Table 2 analysis reveals that the global financial literacy indicator has a negative fluctuation in results, primarily as a result of a decline in the knowledge indicator.

Following the OECD guidelines, the financial resilience and financial well-being indicators were also presented at Banco de Portugal et al (2021) report. The financial resilience indicator aims to assess, on a scale of 0 to 100, an individual's ability to react to predictable financial stocks, such as retirement, or unpredictable ones, such as unemployment. The data collected allowed to quantify this indicator with 60 points and to conclude that "it increases with the level of education and household income" (Banco de Portugal et al., 2021, p. 87). The population groups with the best results were: men, aged between 25 and 54, with higher education, workers, and with a gross monthly income of more than 2500€. This understanding of financial resilience sheds light on how different demographic factors intersect with financial preparedness, influencing individuals' abilities to navigate economic challenges effectively.

Similarly, the measurement of financial well-being is conducted through a scale ranging from 0 to 100, and in 2020, Portugal obtained a score of 45 points. The population groups with the best results were: males, aged 16-24, with higher education, students, and with a gross monthly income above 2500 € (Banco de Portugal et al., 2021). These findings highlight the intricate relationship between financial well-being and various demographic characteristics. By identifying demographic groups with higher levels of financial well-being, policymakers can target interventions to support those who may be more vulnerable to financial instability. Additionally, understanding the factors that contribute to financial well-being, such as education and income, enables the development of tailored strategies to enhance overall financial

Table 2. Financial literacy indicators, 2015 and 2020, Median (normalized on a scale of 0 to 100)

Indicator	2015	2020
Financial attitude	58,3	58,3
Financial behaviour	77,8	66,7
Financial knowledge	71,4	57,1
Global financial literacy	68,3	61,7

Source: Adapted from the Banco de Portugal et al (2021, p.80).

resilience at both individual and societal levels. Therefore, the presentation of these indicators not only provides insights into the current state of financial well-being in Portugal but also informs future policy decisions aimed at promoting financial inclusion and stability.

More recently, in 2023, Portugal was ranked 13th globally in the financial literacy indicator (OECD, 2023). Portugal scored 63 points out of 100, which equals the average score of OECD countries and surpasses the average of participating countries, which stands at 60 points. This result represents a slight decrease of 1 point compared to the score obtained in 2020 (62 points). Notably, Portugal excelled in the category of attitudes, securing the seventh position globally, thereby surpassing the average of the countries analyzed. In terms of financial behavior, Portugal ranked 11th globally, also achieving an above-average score. Remarkably, 97% of respondents indicated that they do not resort to borrowing money when faced with specific income inadequacy issues, while 87% stated that they consistently pay bills on time. However, Portugal showed room for improvement in the financial knowledge category, where it ranked 21st globally, falling below the average of the countries evaluated. Among the countries assessed, Germany claimed the top position with 76 points, followed by Thailand and Hong Kong (China) tied at 71 points. Conversely, countries with the lowest rankings include Yemen (42 points), Cambodia (49 points), and Paraguay (50 points).

Financial Literacy Level in Higher Education

Various studies focused on assessing university students' financial literacy have consistently revealed low levels of financial knowledge and, consequently, a deficiency in financial literacy (Santos, 2015; Vieira, 2018; Sarabando et al., 2023). According to Jorgensen and Savla (2010), students in higher education often lack the essential knowledge required to navigate adult life with financial stability. However, the authors noted that there is scientific evidence indicating an improvement in financial knowledge as students' progress through their academic careers, demonstrating more appropriate attitudes, knowledge, and behaviors over time. Dias (2017) identified income, gender, age, and parental education as key determinants of college students' financial literacy levels. Similarly, Pires (2014) found statistical evidence supporting the influence of income, age, and gender on the financial literacy level of college students. Furthermore, Carvalho (2019, p. 58) observed significant relationships between the level of financial literacy and factors such as the area of study, age, and employment status among students. This suggests that various socio-economic factors play a crucial role in shaping students' financial literacy.

Sarabando et al. (2023) conducted a study among Portuguese students entering the polytechnic higher education system, revealing concerning gaps in financial literacy.

In their study, more than two-thirds of the sample were unaware of Euribor and Spread, while approximately one-third did not grasp the consequences of inflation. Moreover, 16.9% lacked understanding of term deposits, and derivative products and savings certificates were perceived as similar in terms of risk. Interestingly, students who initially opted for business-related courses exhibited slightly higher financial literacy levels, albeit still falling below expectations. Ultimately, the prevalence of low financial literacy among university students stems from a fundamental lack of understanding of financial concepts and phenomena, both broadly and deeply (Rainho, Santos, Sousa, & Tavares, 2017, p. 301).

Determinants of Financial Literacy

Determinants of financial literacy are an important area of research that aims to pinpoint the variables affecting people's proficiency and understanding of finance. These factors, which include a variety of contextual, individual, and socioeconomic traits, are important in determining how well-a person manages their finances.

Age is consensually considered the main influencer of the level of financial literacy (Borg, 2017; Luksander, Beres, Huzdik, & Nemeth, 2014; Monticone, 2010; Mouna & Anis, 2017; Pires, 2014; Smyczek & Matysiewicz, 2015; Walstad, Rebeck, & MacDonald, 2010). Several authors pointed out that individuals, during their lifetime, have to make financial decisions, such as borrowing or choosing an investment, which by inference increase literacy. Walstad et al. (2010) defined the influence of age in a U-inverted profile, which represents that individuals accumulate knowledge until age 40-60, and then it depreciates.

Although age is widely recognised as a determinant of financial literacy, some studies do not corroborate its significant influence (Carvalhom 2019; Monte et al, 2018; Wood & Doyle 2002). In this sense, we intend to understand whether age affects the level of literacy, and the following hypothesis was defined: *H1: Age influences the level of financial literacy.*

Regarding gender, several authors argue that males systematically show greater financial literacy, compared to females (Carvalho, 2019; Dias, 2017; Luksander et al., 2014; Lusardi, 2019; Monticone, 2010; Pires, 2014; Smyczek & Matysiewicz, 2015; Walstad et al., 2010; Wood & Doyle, 2002). However, this result is not consensual since Mandell and Klein (2009) and Monte et al. (2018) found no empirical evidence of the same effect. In this scope, we define the following hypothesis: *H2: Gender explains the level of financial literacy.*

In relation to education level, Lusardi (2019), Monticone (2010), Walstad et al. (2010), and Wood and Doyle (2002) concluded that the higher an education level, the higher their financial literacy level; this is because there is an easier grasp of concepts and a lower cost of learning. Interestingly, some investigations did not find statistical proof of the link between education and financial literacy (Hallahan, Faff, & McKenzie, 2004; Monte et al., 2018). In order to evaluate the influence on the level of education with literacy, the following hypothesis was defined: *H3: The level of education influences the level of financial literacy.*

Employment status is also a factor considered when trying to assess the determinants of financial literacy. As Carvalho (2019), Monticone (2010), and Pires (2014) have shown that employed people have higher financial literacy when compared to unemployed individuals or students. According to Bilal and Zulfiqar (2016) working woman has a greater level of financial knowledge, especially when working in the education sector. The following hypothesis evaluates the relationship between the level of employability and financial literacy: *H4: Employment status has a positive influence on the level of financial literacy.*

In relation to income, several studies proving that families with higher incomes have greater financial knowledge (Dias, 2017; Luksander et al., 2014; Monticone, 2010; Mouna & Anis, 2017; Pires, 2014; Smyczek & Matysiewicz, 2015; Wood & Doyle, 2002). In contrast, Mandell and Klein (2009) and Türkmen and Kılıç (2022) inferred that income is not a determinant of financial literacy. Once again, there is no consensus in the literature, and in this sense, income was included as a variable to be studied in the following hypothesis: *H5: Income is positively related to literacy level.*

Financial Literacy and Financial Resilience and Well-Being

Fostering financial education is a relevant mechanism to increase financial literacy that in turn helps the population to be more resilient in times of crisis and external chocks (Erdem & Rojahn, 2022). The results obtained by Erdem and Rojahn (2022) indicate that financial resilience was found to increase with financial literacy. Additionally, financial literacy has a positive contribution to the financial resilience, as it reduces risks, such as taking on too much debt (Klapper & Lusardi, 2020). Klapper and Lusardi (2020) highlight the need of increasing the financial literacy among the population in order to protect consumers. "Governments and businesses should take note of the emerging literature on these topics, as financial inclusion becomes a bigger part of the development policy agenda and as digital financial products proliferate" (Klapper & Lusardi, 2020, p. 610).

According to the OECD (2020) individual financial resilience can be assessed by a set of six elements:

- Keep control of money by monitoring the financial situation and avoiding debt;
- Think about expenses, namely about the need and the ability to meet them;
- To have funds available to cover expenses in case of loss of income;

- To have faced financial stress situations, namely situations in which expenses were higher than income;
- Plan personal finances, maintaining regular savings habits;
- Sensitivity to identify and avoid fraud.

In this context, we intend to evaluate if *H6: Individuals with a higher level of financial literacy have greater financial resilience.*

According to Banco de Portugal et al. (2021, p. 93) "Financial literacy contributes to the proper management of personal finances and the making of prudent financial decisions, namely, in terms of saving and indebtedness. Thus, individuals with higher levels of financial literacy are also expected to have higher levels of financial resilience and financial well-being" Furthermore, for the OECD, financial well-being is considered the ultimate goal of financial literacy and occurs when an individual can meet their current and future obligations. When this happens, people feel confident about the future and have greater freedom to make choices, thus increasing their quality of life (Consumer Financial Protection Bureau, 2015). Following the findings of Bilal and Zulfiqar (2016) both, financial literacy, and financial attitude directly, significantly, and positively affected the financial well-being of working women. In the Philippas and Avdoulas (2020) work, financial well-being among Greek university students is accessed. The authors confirmed that the financially literate students are more prepared to lead with unexpected financial shock and are more prone to achieve financial well-being. Thus, financial knowledge is crucial for making appropriate financial choices and therefore essential to financial well-being (Philippas & Avdoulas, 2020). In this context, we define the following hypothesis: *H7: A high level of financial literacy leads to greater financial well-being.*

The conceptual model is presented at Figure 1.

METHOD AND SAMPLE

Method

The study is based on a quantitative perspective, through "the analysis of observable facts and phenomena and the measurement/evaluation of behavioural and/or socio-affective variables that can be measured in comparison and/or related in the course of the empirical research" (Coutinho, 2014, p. 24). This perspective considers that data can be quantifiable and analysed using statistical methods. For that, we design a survey that was adapted from studies, like Banco de Portugal et al. (2011), OECD (2016, 2020), Consumer Financial Protection Bureau Consumer Financial Protection Bureau (2015), and Potrich, Vieira and Mendes-Da-Silva (2016), and was composed

Figure 1. Conceptual model
Source: Own elaboration.

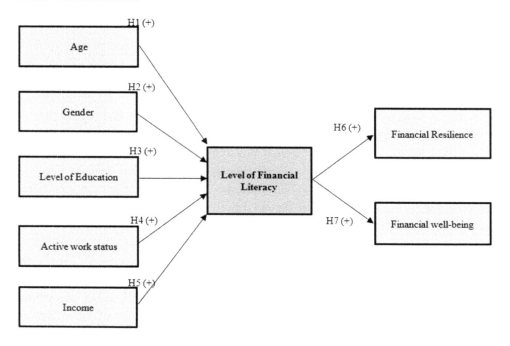

of 23 questions organized as follows: characterization of the interviewee; financial attitude indicator; financial behaviour indicator; financial knowledge indicator; financial well-being indicator.

Additionally, the values present in the questions measuring financial knowledge were also changed so as not to allow students to access the correct answer through searches, since the online distribution does not guarantee the answer without consulting the survey.

The survey, before being distributed, was subject to a pre-test of 30 students, to flag inaccuracies and assess the difficulties detected in their responses. The sample response study was used to calculate the various indicators and then subject to statistical treatment, using the software IBM SPSS statistics . After determining the indicators, a descriptive analysis of the data will be performed to characterize the sample and a statistical inference analysis, using nonparametric techniques, to carry out the study of the research hypotheses.

Sample

The survey was made available through Google Forms and disseminated in several higher education institutions between January 18 and February 2, 2022, through which 469 valid responses were obtained. The target of this research is the higher education students in Portugal. According to the Direção-Geral de Estatísticas da Educação e Ciência (2021) in the academic year 2020/2011 411.995 students were enrolled in higher education (191.144 men and 220.851 women). Although ideally a random sample would be desired, the nonprobability convenience sampling method was used. However, the sample is significant with a confidence interval of 95% and a margin of error of 5%.

RESULTS AND DISCUSSION

The sample description can be seen in Table 3. The sample consists mainly of students aged between 18 and 23 years (49%), female (56%), studying in the north of Portugal (68%), attending a bachelor's degree course (59%), working students (62%), whose gross monthly household income is between 706 and 1.410€ (40%). Most of those surveyed saw their income drop due to the pandemic (62%). Most of the respondents have not participated in any financial education program, either those promoted by the National Financial Education Plan (79%) or by the various banking institutions (82%).

Financial Literacy Indicator

As explained above, the general indicator of financial literacy is obtained by summing up the indicators of attitude, behaviour, and financial knowledge.

Financial Attitude Indicator

To assess the respondents' financial attitudes towards money and saving, they were asked to rate some statements according to the following scale: strongly disagree (1 point), disagree (2 points), neither agree nor disagree (3 points), agree (4 points) and strongly agree (5 points). The average weighting of the classification of the statements resulted in the financial attitude indicator, which for the sample under analysis, stands at 4,37 points. The result obtained is significantly higher than that obtained by the OECD (2020), in which the financial attitude indicator in Portugal stood at 3,2 points. This results are in line with those presented by the OECD (2023) where Portugal displayed an indicator of financial attitudes similar to that of the doctors in the group's countries. All statements under analysis obtained, on average, a position of the agreement of the respondents showing a high awareness of the importance of expenditure planning and saving.

Table 3. Sample description (%)

Variable		Collected sample
Age (years old)	18 to 23	49%
	24 to 29	33%
	30 to 35	8%
	36 to 41	5%
	≥42	5%
Gender	Female	56%
	Male	44%
Region of the institution attended by the student	North	68%
	Centre	16%
	Lisbon and Vale do Tejo	12%
	Alentejo	0%
	Algarve	4%
The level of education of the student is attending	Higher Technical Professional Course	6%
	Bachelor's degree	59%
	Master's degree	33%
	PhD	2%
Employment status	Working Student	62%
	Student	38%
Gross monthly household income	No income	7%
	Up to 705€	16%
	Between 706€ and 1.410€	40%
	Between 1.411€ and 2.499€	22%
	More than 2.500€	15%
Drop in income due to pandemic	Yes	62%
	No	38%
Participation in a PNFF initiative	Yes	1%
	No	79%
	Don't know	20%
Participation in a banking institution initiative	Yes	2%
	No	83%
	Don't know	16%

Source: Own elaboration

Considering the analysis of financial attitudes by socio-demographic subgroups, it is observed that the groups that show less favourable results are men, respondents under 23 years old, those attending a higher technical professional course, working students, and whose households have a gross monthly income below 705€ (see Table 5). Statistically, there was a very weak positive correlation between age and financial

Table 4. Average rating given to the statements of the financial attitude indicator

Statements	Average
It is important to have control over monthly expenditure	4,58
It is important to set financial goals for the future	4,39
It is important to save every month	4,31
The way I manage my money today will affect my future	4,35
It is important to work out a monthly budget	4,35
When using credit solutions, it is important to compare different offers	4,24
It is important to be cautious when accessing digital financial products and services	4,38
It is important to know the consumer's rights and duties in situations of financial risk	4,38
It is important to have control over monthly expenditure	4,58
Financial attitude indicator	4,37

Source: Own elaboration

attitude and between income and the same indicator, for a significance level of 10%. These results show that the indicator of main determinants of the financial attitude in higher education students are in line with those of the Portuguese population (Banco de Portugal et al., 2021; OECD, 2020, 2023).

Financial Behaviour Indicator

To assess respondents' behaviours about managing personal finances, they were asked to rate 12 statements according to a 5-point Likert scale of agreement. In general, individuals demonstrated less adjusted financial behaviours when compared to the attitudes shown. An example of this is their disagreement with the statements "I have savings of more than three times my monthly income" and "I use programs to avoid financial risk situations".

There was also an unbiased position, where the agreement was expected, to the statements:

- "I compare prices before making a purchase";
- "I set long-term financial goals";
- "I am cautious in accessing and managing digital financial products and services";
- "I pay my bills promptly";
- "I pay my bills without delay";
- "I control my expenses".

Table 5. Socio-economic characteristics of respondents and tests on the financial attitude indicator (average relative value)

Socio-economic characteristics		Mean value	Test	*P-value*	Correlation coefficient
Age	18 to 23	4,31	*Kruskal-Wallis Spearman*	0,007 *** 0,050 *	- 0,15
	24 to 29	4,43			
	30 to 35	4,34			
	36 to 41	4,50			
	≥42	4,51			
Gender	Female	4,38	*Mann-Whitney*	0,575	-
	Male	4,36			
Level of education attended	Higher Technical Professional Course	4,24	*Kruskal-Wallis*	0,167	-
	BSc	4,36			
	MSc	4,42			
	PhD	4,42			
Employment situation	Working Student	4,36	*Mann-Whitney*	0,365	-
	Student	4,39			
Gross monthly household income	No income	4,37	*Kruskal-Wallis Spearman*	0,000 *** 0,050 *	- 0,24
	Up to 705€	4,14			
	Between 706€ and 1.410€	4,38			
	Between 1.411€ and 2.499€	4,45			
	Over 2.500€	4,47			

Source: Own elaboration. Note: Significance level of * p-value < 0,10; *** p-value < 0,01.

The results are in line with those recently obtained by the OECD. According to OECD results (2023), Portugal distinguished itself in this category, coming in 11th place, also with an above average score (66 out of 100 compared to the OECD average of 62), with 97% of interviewees indicating that they do not borrow money when faced with a specific problem of insufficient income and with 87% stating that they pay their bills on time.

Next, table 7 presents the financial behaviours by socio-demographic subgroups. The groups that show the least favourable results are men, respondents under 23 years old, those attending university, working students, and whose households have a gross monthly income below 705€.

Statistical tests allowed us to validate the influence of age, level of education, and income on the financial behaviour indicator. A weak positive correlation was found for age and income at a 5% significance level. Similarly, to what was found

Table 6. Average rating given to the statements of the financial behaviour indicator

Statements	Average
I am concerned about managing my money efficiently	4,22
I control my expenses	3,96
I set long-term financial goals	3,89
I pay my bills promptly	3,95
I have savings of more than three times my monthly income	2,75
I compare prices before making a purchase	3,68
I am cautious about accessing and managing digital financial products and services	3,91
I use programs to avoid financial risk situations	2,92
Regularly	4,18
I use a credit card when I don't have enough money to cover my expenses	2,24*
I use more than 10% of my monthly income to pay for credit	2,02*
I buy on impulse	2,61*
Financial behaviour indicator	4,37

Source: Own elaboration. Note: * Inversely attributed score.

in the attitude indicator, the determinants of the behaviour indicator are the same as in the general population (Banco de Portugal et al., 2021; OECD, 2020; 2023).

Financial Knowledge Indicator

The respondents were asked seven questions about financial knowledge, which assesses not only knowledge about financial numeracy, but also knowledge about understanding of what inflation and interest are, or about the relationship between return and risk in an investment (see Table 8). The average number of correct answers was 5, higher than the 4 answers obtained in 2020 in Portugal (OECD, 2020). Approximately 18% of respondents answered all the questions correctly, a positive result considering the 10% achieved by the Portuguese population in the 3rd Financial Literacy Survey of the Portuguese Population (Banco de Portugal et al., 2021). Additionally, in the 2023 results, Portugal came in 21st place and below the average of the OECD countries evaluated (OECD, 2023), so in this sample the results were clearly positive, going opposite the average for the Portuguese population.

The table 9 show the financial knowledge by socio-demographic subgroups. The results highlight that The average number of correct answers is higher among men, respondents between 30 and 35 years old, those who are studying for a Ph.D., working students, and whose households have a monthly income of up to 705€. Statistical tests confirmed the influence of all factors on the indicator of financial

Table 7. Socio-economic characteristics of respondents and tests on the financial behaviour indicator (average relative value)

Socio-economic characteristics		Mean value	Test	P-value	Correlation coefficient
Age	18 to 23	5,34	*Kruskal-Wallis Spearman*	0,000 *** 0,040 **	- 0,20
	24 to 29	6,00			
	30 to 35	6,08			
	36 to 41	6,07			
	≥42	6,68			
Gender	Female	5,73	*Mann-Whitney*	0,778	-
	Male	5,71			
Level of education attended	Higher Technical Professional Course	5,90	*Kruskal-Wallis*	0,049 **	-
	BSc	5,56			
	MSc	5,90			
	PhD	6,94			
Employment situation	Working Student	5,65	*Mann-Whitney*	0,320	-
	Student	5,83			
Gross monthly household income	No income	5,41	*Kruskal-Wallis Spearman*	0,000 *** 0,040 **	- 0,25
	Up to 705€	4,50			
	Between 706€ and 1.410€	5,80			
	Between 1.411€ and 2.499€	6,28			
	Over 2.500€	6,07			

Source: Own elaboration. Note: Significance level of ** p-value < 0,05; *** p-value < 0,01.

knowledge, except for age. A very weak negative correlation was found for income at a significance level of 10%.

Overall Financial Literacy Indicator

The average of the global indicator of financial literacy is 14,93 and the respondents had a better performance in the indicator of financial attitude. Compared with the results of the Portuguese population, students in higher education show overall more satisfactory results. The same is true when compared to the OECD average. The average overall financial literacy indicator of the Portuguese population is 13,10 and for the OECD it is 13,00 (OECD, 2020). Considering, the overall indicator of financial literacy by socio-demographic subgroups (see Table 10), it is evidence that the groups showing the least favourable results are women, respondents under 23

Table 8. Percentage of correct answers to questions on financial knowledge

Questions	%
Assume that the 2 brothers have to wait one year to receive their share of the 2,000€. If the inflation rate is 2%, in a year they will be able to buy: *Less than they could buy today*	57%
If you lend a friend 100€ and he pays you back the EUR 100 the next day, how much interest did he pay? *0*	98%
Suppose you place 200€ in a term deposit with an annual interest rate of 2%. How much will you have in your account after one year? *204*	76%
And at the end of 5 years? *More than 220 euros*	37%
Please rate this as true or false: High inflation means the cost of living drops rapidly. *False*	68%
Please rate this as true or false: An investment with a high return usually has a low risk associated with it. *False*	80%
Please rate this as true or false: Generally, if we buy a diversified set of stocks we increase the risk of investing in the capital markets. *False*	69%
The average number of correct answers	5

Source: Own elaboration.

years of age, those attending a higher technical professional course, students, and those whose households have a gross monthly income of less than 705€. Statistically, it was possible to confirm the influence of all factors on the level of financial literacy, except employment status. A very weak positive correlation was found between the level of financial literacy, age, and income at a significance level.

In relation to the defined hypotheses, it can be assumed that:

H1 – *"Age influences the level of financial literacy"* - the positive influence was verified (Borg, 2017; Dias, 2017; Luksander et al., 2014; Monticone, 2010; Mouna & Anis, 2017; Pires, 2014; Smyczek & Matysiewicz, 2015; Walstad et al., 2010).

H2 – *"Gender explains the level of financial literacy"* - it was validated that male individuals present more satisfactory results (Carvalho, 2019; Dias, 2017; Luksander et al., 2014; Lusardi, 2019; Monticone, 2010; Pires, 2014; Smyczek & Matysiewicz, 2015; Walstad et al., 2010; Wood & Doyle, 2002).

H3 – *"The level of education influences the level of financial literacy"* was verified (Lusardi, 2019; Monticone, 2010; Walstad et al., 2010; Wood & Doyle, 2002).

H5 – *"Income is positively related to literacy level"* - a positive correlation was found (Banco de Portugal et al., 2011, 2016, 2021).

H4 – *"Employment status has a positive influence on the literacy level"* is rejected.

Table 9. Socio-economic characteristics of respondents and tests on the financial knowledge indicator (average relative value)

Socio-economic characteristics		Mean value	Test	P-value	Correlation coefficient
Age	18 to 23	4,87	*Kruskal-Wallis*	0,265	-
	24 to 29	4,74			
	30 to 35	5,19			
	36 to 41	4,48			
	≥42	5,17			
Gender	Female	4,56	*Mann-Whitney*	0,000 ***	-
	Male	5,21			
Level of education attended	Higher Technical Professional Course	4,14	*Kruskal-Wallis*	0,016 **	-
	BSc	4,91			
	MSc	4,81			
	PhD	6,00			
Employment situation	Working Student	4,98	*Mann-Whitney*	0,039 **	-
	Student	4,63			
Gross monthly household income	No income	5,31	*Kruskal-Wallis Spearman*	0,000 *** 0,050 *	- -0,04
	Up to 705€	5,68			
	Between 706€ and 1.410€	4,28			
	Between 1.411€ and 2.499€	4,85			
	Over 2.500€	5,25			

Source: Own elaboration. Note: Significance level of: * p-value < 0,10; ** p-value < 0,05; *** p-value < 0,01.

Financial Resilience Indicator

In scope of financial resilience indicator, it was measured based on 5 areas: money control, weighing expenses, time to cover expenses, financial stress, and concern, and planning personal finances. Through the Table 11, it is observed that the worst results were in the time to cover expenses, where only 22% have savings to cover expenses for 3 months, and in the financial stress and concern, where just 43% of respondents do not bother that money will not last forever. These results are alarming since experts argue that all individuals should have a working capital corresponding at least to the value of 3 months of expenses, since only in this way can they cope with periods of prolonged absence of income (Leary, 2017; Pitsker & Cross, 2016; Scott, Williams, Gilliam, & Sybrowsky, 2013).

Table 10. Socio-economic characteristics of respondents and tests to the overall indicator of financial literacy (average relative value)

Socio-economic characteristics		Mean value	Test	*P-value*	Correlation coefficient
Age	18 to 23	14,52	*Kruskal-Wallis Spearman*	0,001*** 0,040**	- 0,18
	24 to 29	15,16			
	30 to 35	15,61			
	36 to 41	15,04			
	≥42	16,36			
Gender	Female	14,67	*Mann-Whitney*	0,014**	-
	Male	15,28			
Level of education attended	Higher Technical Professional Course	14,28	*Kruskal-Wallis*	0,010**	-
	BSc	14,83			
	MSc	15,13			
	PhD	17,36			
Employment situation	Working Student	14,98	*Mann-Whitney*	0,545	-
	Student	14,86			
Gross monthly household income	No income	15,09	*Kruskal-Wallis Spearman*	0,000*** 0,040**	- 0,19
	Up to 705€	14,32			
	Between 706€ and 1.410€	14,45			
	Between 1.411€ and 2.499€	15,58			
	Over 2.500€	15,80			

Source: Own elaboration. Note: Significance level of ** p-value < 0,05; *** p-value < 0,01.

The table 12 presents the relationship between the socio-economic characteristics of respondents and the financial resilience indicator. It is showed that the groups with the least favourable results are men with 23 years, those attending a technical and professional higher education course, working students, and those whose households have a monthly income of up to 705€.

It was possible to confirm the age and income influence on the indicator of financial resilience. A very poor positive correlation was found for age and income, with a significance level of 10% and 5%, respectively.

Table 11. Areas of financial resilience

Areas	Statements	%
Money Control	Does not use credit to cover expenses	64%
	Controls personal expenses	71%
Expenses weighting	Does not make impulse purchases	54%
	Pays bills on time	71%
Time covering expenses	Saves 3 times the monthly income	22%
Stress and financial concern	Concerns about the efficient management of money	91%
	Concerns that money does not last forever	43%
	Feels that financially it just keeps on going	51%
Personal Finance Planning	Have made savings in the last year	89%
	Recognizes the importance of long-term financial goals	90%

Source: Own elaboration.

Financial Well-Being Indicator

Similarly to the previous indicator, on the financial well-being indicator, the respondents show lower results. Contributing to this low performance is the response to statements such as:

- "I am guaranteed a financial future" where on average respondents answered somewhat;
- "I worry that my money will not last forever" where on average respondents responded somewhat;
- "Finances control my life" where on average, respondents answered sometimes.

The Table 14 presents the relationship between the socio-economic characteristics of respondents and the financial well-being indicator. It is observed that the groups that present less favourable results are women, respondents aged between 36 and 41 years old, attending a technical higher education course, who are working students, and whose households have a monthly income of up to 705€. Statistically, the influence of all socioeconomic factors on the financial well-being indicator was confirmed, except for gender and employment status. A very weak positive correlation was found for age and a weak positive correlation for income, for a significance level of 10% and 5% respectively.

Table 12. Socio-economic characteristics of respondents and tests on the financial resilience indicator (average relative value)

Socio-economic characteristics		Mean value	Test	P-value	Correlation coefficient
Age	18 to 23	6,14	Kruskal-Wallis Spearman	0,003*** 0,050*	- 0,17
	24 to 29	6,76			
	30 to 35	6,94			
	36 to 41	7,04			
	≥42	6,61			
Gender	Female	6,50	Mann-Whitney	0,721	-
	Male	6,45			
Level of education attended	Higher Technical Professional Course	6,31	Kruskal-Wallis	0,180	-
	BSc	6,36			
	MSc	6,67			
	PhD	7,50			
Employment situation	Working Student	6,47	Mann-Whitney	0,917	-
	Student	6,49			
Gross monthly household income	No income	5,66	Kruskal-Wallis Spearman	0,000*** 0,040**	- 0,37
	Up to 705€	4,86			
	Between 706€ and 1.410€	6,71			
	Between 1.411€ and 2.499€	7,07			
	Over 2.500€	7,03			

Source: Own elaboration. Note: Significance level of: * p-value < 0,10; ** p-value < 0,05; *** p-value < 0,01.

Table 13. Average rating given to the statements of the financial well-being indicator

Statements	Average
Could cope with an unexpected expense	2,55
I have a secure financial future	3,02
The way I manage my money enables me to enjoy life	2,74
I have money left over at the end of the month	2,58
Because of my financial situation, I feel I will never get the things I want in life	3,49 *
I feel that financially I am just managing myself	3,46 *
I worry that my money will not last forever	3,10 *
Giving a gift for a wedding, birthday or another occasion would damage my finances for the month	3,46 *
Finances control my life	3,29 *
I am in arrears	3,97 *

Source: Own elaboration. Note: * Inversely assigned score.

The Relationship Between Financial Literacy, Financial Resilience, and Financial Well-Being

The results of the study show, as expected, that the higher an individual's financial literacy, the higher his/her level of resilience and financial well-being. This relationship was statistically corroborated, finding a moderate positive correlation between financial literacy level and resilience and a weak positive relationship between literacy level and an individual's financial well-being at a 5% significance level.

Thus, we can conclude that "*H6 - Individuals with a higher level of financial literacy have greater financial resilience*" and "*H7 - A high level of financial literacy leads to greater financial well-being*" are verified, confirming the findings highlighted in existing literature (Bilal & Zulfiqar, 2016; Erdem & Rojahn, 2022; Klapper & Lusardi, 2020; Philippas & Avdoulas, 2020). This relationship was also

Table 14. Socio-economic characteristics of respondents and tests on the financial well-being indicator (average relative value)

Socio-economic characteristics		Mean value	Test	P-value	Correlation coefficient
Age	18 to 23	23,30	*Kruskal-Wallis Spearman*	0,030** 0,050*	- 0,11
	24 to 29	24,80			
	30 to 35	24,19			
	36 to 41	23,26			
	≥42	23,48			
Gender	Female	23,84	*Mann-Whitney*	0,925	-
	Male	23,92			
Level of education attended	Higher Technical Professional Course	23,41	*Kruskal-Wallis*	0,047**	-
	BSc	23,71			
	MSc	23,98			
	PhD	29,50			
Employment situation	Working Student	23,54	*Mann-Whitney*	0,325	-
	Student	24,42			
Gross monthly household income	No income	20,25	*Kruskal-Wallis Spearman*	0,000*** 0,040**	- 0,43
	Up to 705€	19,14			
	Between 706€ and 1.410€	24,28			
	Between 1.411€ and 2.499€	25,64			
	Over 2.500€	26,74			

Source: Own elaboration. Note: Significance level of: * p-value < 0,10; ** p-value < 0,05; *** p-value < 0,01.

confirmed in the study of the Portuguese population, thus proving the importance of financial literacy (Banco de Portugal et al., 2021).

CONCLUSION

The incessant economic crises and the sophistication of financial products and services bring to the spotlight the need to financially educate the Portuguese population, and in particular university students. This research aimed at measuring the overall financial literacy indicator of higher education students in Portugal by determining the indicators of attitude, behaviour, and financial knowledge. We also analysed their determinants and assess the interplay of the financial literacy indicator and the indicators of resilience and financial well-being.

Our results revealed that university students have globally satisfactory indicators of attitude, behaviour, knowledge, and financial literacy, when compared with the Portuguese population and the OECD average but are below the reasonable.

In the overall indicator of financial literacy, the groups that scored highest were men, respondents aged over 42 years, those attending Ph.D. studies, working students, and those whose households with a gross monthly income of more than 2500 €. The existence of relationships between this indicator and age, gender, level of education, and income was statistically proven.

As far as the financial resilience indicator is concerned, respondents show a low indicator of financial resilience, which highlights the possibility of facing difficulties when facing predictable or unpredictable financial crises, such as unemployment or retirement. The worst scores were found in the areas of time to cover expenses and

Table 15. Testing the relationship between literacy, resilience, and financial well-being

	Global Financial Literacy Indicator	Mean value	Test	P-value	Correlation coefficient
Financial Resilience Indicator	[0; 6[	-	*Kruskal-Wallis Spearman*	0,000*** 0,030**	- 0,52
	[6; 11[	4,91			
	[11; 16[	6,05			
	[16; 21]	7,37			
Financial Well-being Indicator	[0; 6[	-	*Kruskal-Wallis Spearman*	0,000*** 0,040**	- 0,31
	[6; 11[	21,23			
	[11; 16[	22,67			
	[16; 21]	26,15			

Source: Own elaboration. Note: Significance level of ** p-value < 0,05; *** p-value < 0,01.

financial stress and concern. The groups that present less favourable results are men, respondents under 23 years of age, those attending a higher technical professional course, working students, and whose households with a monthly income of up to 705€. Statistically, it was possible to validate age and income as determinants of this indicator.

Also in the financial well-being indicator, respondents show lower results, with the worst results being verified in the group of women, respondents aged between 36 and 41 years old, attending a higher technical professional course, who are working students, and whose households with a monthly income of up to 705€. In this indicator, the influence of all socio-economic factors tested was corroborated, except gender and employment status.

Furthermore, and as a factor demonstrating the significance of promoting financial literacy, the considerable influence that financial literacy has on an individual's resilience and financial well-being was statistically validated.

These results allow competent entities (such as educational institutions or financial intermediaries) to define policies and actions that are more effective and appropriate to the identified needs. The segmentation of groups presented will also allow them to the socio-demographic profile of individuals. Our results make it clear that specific financial education initiatives must be put into place immediately, especially for Portuguese university students. Although the indices of attitude, behaviour, knowledge, and financial literacy are deemed rather adequate, our findings suggest that there exists potential for further enhancement. In particular, we advise creating and implementing educational initiatives that are adapted to the factors that have been found to influence financial literacy, including age, gender, educational attainment, and household income. Enhancing students' comprehension of financial concepts, encouraging responsible financial behaviour, and building resilience in the face of financial difficulties should be the goals of these programmes.

Furthermore, it is critical to incorporate financial education into higher education institutions' curricula given the substantial impact that financial literacy has on a person's resilience and financial well-being. Academic programmes can be enhanced by integrating financial literacy efforts, which provide students with fundamental financial information and skills from the beginning of their academic career. Also, in the current digital era, where knowledge of digital technology is essential for efficient money management, it is critical to promote digital financial literacy. Because they are so adept with technology, university students can act as advocates for digital financial literacy and are essential in encouraging the general public to adopt it. Moving forward, future research should aim to address the limitations of our study by conducting a more representative analysis across different geographical regions and educational levels. Despite the size of the sample, it is more representative of students from the north of the country, which does not allow the comparison between the different geographical areas. Although the pre-test was carried out to identify and correct difficulties in answering the questionnaire, a misinterpretation or an unclear or dishonest answer on the part of the students may bias the results obtained. The major limitation of this research is related to the questionnaire fact that the distribution was entirely carried out online, thus allowing respondents to answer the questions using external help. This limitation was overcome by changing the values present in the questions that measure financial knowledge.

For future research, it is proposed to apply the study to a representative sample of all regions of the country to understand whether the geographical location is also a determinant of financial literacy. It would also be important to replicate the study in a sample with greater representation of the various levels of education, namely PhDs. Additionally, it is proposed to analyse the contribution of educational institutions to students' financial education by measuring and comparing the level of students' financial literacy at the time of entry to higher education and later at the time of leaving.

As research has shown, the modern world presents even more challenges to all citizens in managing and planning their personal finances. In addition to a positive attitude, appropriate behaviour, and sound financial knowledge, a mastery of digital technologies is also required. Therefore, it is necessary to have citizens with high levels of digital financial literacy, and in this respect university students play a key role, as they are the generation with the greatest command of them.

REFERENCES

Azeez, N., & Akhtar, S. (2021). Digital financial literacy and its determinants: An empirical evidences from rural India. *South Asian Journal of Social Studies and Economics*, *11*(2), 8–22. doi:10.9734/sajsse/2021/v11i230279

Bilal, M., & Zulfiqar, M. (2016). Financial wellbeing is the goal of financial literacy. *Research Journal of Finance and Accounting*, *7*(11), 94–103.

Borg, M. E. (2017). Building Sustainable Businesses: The importance of Financial Literacy for Entrepreneurs. https://epale.ec.europa.eu/en/blog/building-sustainable-businesses-importance-financial-literacy-entrepreneurs

Carvalho, M. d. C. (2019). A Literacia Financeira: O caso dos alunos do ensino superior Universidade do Minho].

Consumer Financial Protection Bureau. (2015). *Financial Well-Being: The Goal of Financial Education*. Consumer Finance. https://files.consumerfinance.gov/f/201501_cfpb_report_financial-well-being.pdf

Coutinho, C. P. (2014). *Metodologia de investigação em ciências sociais e humanas.* Leya.

Dias, B. A. F. (2017). *O Financiamento, as Despesas e a Literacia Financeira dos Estudantes do Ensino Superior Instituto Politecnico do Porto.*

Direção-Geral de Estatísticas da Educação e Ciência. (2021). *Vagas e Inscritos (inclui inscritos em mobilidade internacional).* DGEEC. https://www.dgeec.mec. pt/np4/EstatVagasInsc/

Erdem, D., & Rojahn, J. (2022). The influence of financial literacy on financial resilience. New evidence from Europe during the COVID-19 crisis. *Managerial Finance.*

European Commission. (July 2023). *Monitoring the level of financial literacy in the EU.* EC. https://europa.eu/eurobarometer/surveys/detail/2953

Hallahan, T. A., Faff, R. W., & McKenzie, M. D. (2004). An empirical investigation of personal financial risk tolerance. *Financial Services Review-greenwich, 13*(1), 57–78.

Henriques, S. C. M. (2010). *Aspectos da literacia financeira dos portugueses.* [Estudo empírico, Universidade de Aveiro].

Jorgensen, B. L., & Savla, J. (2010). Financial literacy of young adults: The importance of parental socialization. *Family Relations, 59*(4), 465–478. doi:10.1111/j.1741-3729.2010.00616.x

Kadoya, Y., & Khan, M. S. R. (2020). What determines financial literacy in Japan? *Journal of Pension Economics and Finance, 19*(3), 353–371. doi:10.1017/S1474747218000379

Kempson, E., Collard, S., & Moore, N. (2005). *Measuring financial capability: an exploratory study, in Consumer Research Report 37.* University of Bristol: Financial Services Authority. https://www.bristol.ac.uk/media-library/sites/geography/migrated/documents/pfrc0510.pdf

Kempson, E., Collard, S., & Moore, N. (2006). Measuring financial capability: An exploratory study for the Financial Services Authority. *Consumer financial capability: Empowering European consumers, 39*, 44-76.

Klapper, L., & Lusardi, A. (2020). Financial literacy and financial resilience: Evidence from around the world. *Financial Management, 49*(3), 589–614. doi:10.1111/fima.12283

Lavoura, R. F. d. M. (2017). *O desenvolvimento de competências de literacia financeira em populações vulneráveis: um projeto de intervenção com alunos de cursos EFA em Odivelas* [Dissertação de mestrado, ISCTE-IUL].

Leary, E. (2017). *Best Investing Moves at Every Age*. Kiplinger. https://www.kiplinger.com/article/investing/t052-c000-s002-best-investing-moves-at-every-age.html

Luksander, A., Beres, D., Huzdik, K., & Nemeth, E. (2014). Analysis of the factors that influence the financial literacy of young people studying in higher education= A felsőoktatásban tanuló fiatalok pénzügyi kultúráját befolyásoló tényezők vizsgálata. PÉNZÜGYI SZEMLE. *Public Finance Quarterly*, *59*(2), 220–241.

Lusardi, A. (2019). Financial literacy and the need for financial education: Evidence and implications. *Swiss Journal of Economics and Statistics*, *155*(1), 1–8. doi:10.1186/s41937-019-0027-5

Lusardi, A., & Mitchell, O. S. (2014). The economic importance of financial literacy: Theory and evidence. American Economic Journal. *Journal of Economic Literature*, *52*(1), 5–44. doi:10.1257/jel.52.1.5 PMID:28579637

Mandell, L., & Klein, L. S. (2009). The impact of financial literacy education on subsequent financial behavior. *Financial Counseling and Planning*, *20*(1).

Mesquita, A., Oliveira, A., Sauer, P., Oliveira, L., & Sequeira, A. S. (2021). Financial Literacy and Its Importance: An Overall Picture from Portugal. In P. A. Robinson, K. V. Williams, & M. Stojanović (Eds.), *Global Citizenship for Adult Education: Advancing Critical Literacies for Equity and Social Justice* (1st ed.). Routledge. doi:10.4324/9781003050421-32

Messy, F.-A., & Monticone, C. (2016). *Financial education policies in Asia and the Pacific*. OECD. https://www.oecd-ilibrary.org/finance-and-investment/financial-education-policies-in-asia-and-the-pacific_5jm5b32v5vvc-en

Mitchell, O. S., & Lusardi, A. (2011). Financial literacy around the world: An overview. *Journal of Pension Economics and Finance*, *10*(4), 497–508. doi:10.1017/S1474747211000448 PMID:28553190

Monte, A. P., Galstian, N., Nobre, J. C. C., & Evseeva, O. A. (2018). Fatores influenciadores do nível de literacia financeira dos gestores das PME: comparação entre Portugal e Rússia. *XXVIII Jornadas Luso-Espanholas de Gestão Científica: Interioridade e Competitividade*. Desafios Globais da Gestão.

Monticone, C. (2010). How much does wealth matter in the acquisition of financial literacy? *The Journal of Consumer Affairs, 44*(2), 403–422. doi:10.1111/j.1745-6606.2010.01175.x

Morgan, P. J., Huang, B., & Trinh, L. Q. (2019). *The need to promote digital financial literacy for the digital age (The Future of Work and Education for the Digital Age.* T20 Japan. https://t20japan.org/policy-brief-need-promote-digital-financial-literacy/

Mouna, A., & Anis, J. (2017). Financial literacy in Tunisia: Its determinants and its implications on investment behavior. *Research in International Business and Finance, 39*, 568–577. doi:10.1016/j.ribaf.2016.09.018

Noctor, M., Stoney, S., & Stradling, R. (1992). *Financial literacy: a discussion of concepts and competences of financial literacy and opportunities for its introduction into young people's learning.* National Foundation for Educational Research.

OECD. (2013). *Financial Literacy Framework. In PISA 2012 Assessment and Analytical Framework - - Mathematics, Reading, Science, Problem Solving and Financial Literacy.* OECD Publishing. https://doi.org/10.1787/9789264190511-1-en

OECD. (2016). *OECD/INFE International Survey of Adult Financial Literacy Competencies.* OECD. https://www.oecd.org/daf/fin/financial-education/OECD-INFE-International-Survey-of-Adult-Financial-Literacy-Competencies.pdf

OECD. (2020). *OECD/INFE 2020 International Survey of Adult Financial Literacy.* OECD. https://www.oecd.org/financial/education/oecd-infe-2020-international-survey-of-adult-financial-literacy.pdf

OECD. (2023). *OECD/INFE 2023 International Survey of Adult Financial Literacy.* OECD.

Ouachani, S., Belhassine, O., & Kammoun, A. (2021). Measuring financial literacy: A literature review. *Managerial Finance, 47*(2), 266–281. doi:10.1108/MF-04-2019-0175

Philippas, N. D., & Avdoulas, C. (2020). Financial literacy and financial well-being among generation-Z university students: Evidence from Greece. *European Journal of Finance, 26*(4-5), 360–381. doi:10.1080/1351847X.2019.1701512

Pires, V. C. S. (2014). *O Nível de literacia entre os estudantes do ensino superior em Portugal* [PhD Dissertation, Instituto Superior de Contabilidade e Administração de Coimbra].

Pitsker, K., & Cross, M. (2016). *5 Keys to Building Wealth in Your 20s*. Kiplinger. https://www.kiplinger.com/article/saving/t065-c000-s002-build-wealth-for-a-lifetime.html

Potrich, A. C. G., Vieira, K. M., & Mendes-Da-Silva, W. (2016). Development of a financial literacy model for university students. *Management Research Review*, *39*(3), 356–376. doi:10.1108/MRR-06-2014-0143

Rai, K., Dua, S., & Yadav, M. (2019). Association of financial attitude, financial behaviour and financial knowledge towards financial literacy: A structural equation modeling approach. *FIIB Business Review*, *8*(1), 51–60. doi:10.1177/2319714519826651

Rainho, N., Santos, T. C. S. M. d., Sousa, M., & Tavares, D. (2017). *A literacia financeira e as necessidades de formação dos estudantes do ensino superior VI Conferência Internacional de Investigação, Práticas e Contextos em Educação 2017*. Instituto Politécnico de Leiria.

Santos, A. J. C. (2015). *Literacia Financeira: O caso dos alunos dos cursos da área financeira da Escola Superior de Ciências Empresariais (ESCE) do Instituto Politécnico de Setúbal*. IPS. [PhD Dissertation, Instituto Politécnico de Setúbal. Escola Superior de Ciências Empresariais]

Sarabando, P., Matias, R., Vasconcelos, P., & Miguel, T. (2023). Financial literacy of Portuguese undergraduate students in polytechnics: Does the area of the course influence financial literacy? *Journal of Economic Analysis*, *2*(2), 96–113. doi:10.58567/jea02020007

Sayinzoga, A., Bulte, E. H., & Lensink, R. (2016). Financial literacy and financial behaviour: Experimental evidence from rural Rwanda. *Economic Journal (London)*, *126*(594), 1571–1599. doi:10.1111/ecoj.12217

Schagen, S., & Lines, A. (1996). *Financial literacy in adult life: a report to the Natwest Group Charitable Trust*. NFER.

Scott, J., Williams, D., Gilliam, J., & Sybrowsky, J. (2013). Is an all cash emergency fund strategy appropriate for all investors. *Journal of Financial Planning*, *26*(9), 56–62.

Smyczek, S., & Matysiewicz, J. (2015). Consumers' financial literacy as tool for preventing future economic crisis. *Review of Business*, *36*(1), 19–33.

Tavares, F. O., & Almeida, L. G. d. (2020). A literacia financeira: Uma revisão da literatura. *Percursos & Ideias*, *11*(2), 73–88.

Trunk, A., & Dermol, V. (2015). EU integration through financial literacy and entrepreneurship Managing Intellectual Capital and Innovation for Sustainable and Inclusive Society, Management, Knowledge and Learning. *Joint International Conference*, Bari, Italy.

Türkmen, A., & Kılıç, Y. (2022). What matters for pension planning in Turkey: Financial literacy or perceived consumer risks? *International Journal of Social Economics*, *49*(1), 138–151. doi:10.1108/IJSE-03-2021-0140

Vieira, C. E. R. (2018). *A literacia financeira dos estudantes do ensino superior da rede APNOR* [PhD Dissertation, Instituto Politecnico de Braganca, Portugal].

Walstad, W. B., Rebeck, K., & MacDonald, R. A. (2010). The effects of financial education on the financial knowledge of high school students. *The Journal of Consumer Affairs*, *44*(2), 336–357. doi:10.1111/j.1745-6606.2010.01172.x

Wood, W. C., & Doyle, J. M. (2002). Economic literacy among corporate employees. *The Journal of Economic Education*, *33*(3), 195–205. doi:10.1080/00220480209595186

Chapter 9

Reading Development in the First Year:
Experimenting With Translanguaging to Connect Home Ways With University Texts

Simbayi Yafele
University of Johannesburg, South Africa

ABSTRACT

Literacy-as-social-practice urges inclusive, home-derived pedagogies for marginalised learners. Yet, many global-south universities remain locations of epistemological and monolingual biases that negate students' identities, raising inclusivity-praxis concerns. The study aimed to experiment with translanguaging literacy pedagogy for multilinguals' inclusivity and success by using students' home-based experiences to develop academic reading. Drawing from sociocultural and translanguaging fluidity theories, it seeks alternative localised translanguaging pedagogies to erase literacy-exclusion. Home-culture and language identities become extensions of university literacy learning in an experiment using mixed methods to tackle a reading problem by fluid, translingual, multilingual/cultural practices for inclusivity and success in a 1st-year academic-reading-mediation. Results show success when students' home-derived resources are activated and legitimated for inclusive literacy pedagogy.

INTRODUCTION

Reading proficiency at higher education levels is fundamental for students to engage fully with academic texts, obtain text gist, and participate in knowledge

DOI: 10.4018/979-8-3693-1777-8.ch009

co-construction, text-meaning negotiations, and understanding (Aldridge, 2019; Amir, 2019; Ballantyne, 2020). However, reading literacy itself is a world problem. The World Literacy Foundation identified illiteracy as a global difficulty since nearly 20% of the world's population cannot read or write. According to the latest UNESCO report on Literacy and Development, literacy gaps hinder academic and social progress. The chapter's research context of South Africa, too, has a significant reading problem (Spaull & Pretorius, 2019; Taylor et al., 2018; Yafele, 2021) characterised by reading and writing deficits and low literacy (Spaull & Pretorius, 2019; Yafele, 2021).

Makalela (2015) blames this reading crisis on educational establishments that promote a culture of silence through English monolithic, monocultural hegemony. He argues that monolingual/ cultural biases negatively impact the reading, writing, and learning abilities of many multilingual/ cultural students. Non-enactment of multilingual, multicultural, and inclusive literacy pedagogies has academically deprived speakers of local African languages, destroying their self-esteem and academic performance in HEIs. Sociocultural theorists (e.g., Blackledge & Creese, 2017; Makalela, 2016b; Street, 2016) locate the low literacy problem within the sociolinguistic and sociocultural frames. They link literacy education to language and society.

For example, the language of teaching and learning (LOLT) may be at odds with the learners' identities - languages and cultures - negatively impacting literacy education. This social viewpoint stresses that literacy learning must acknowledge, value, and exploit the literacy practices that participants and their communities are already involved in (Makalela, 2016). The argument is that culturally connected teaching methods in which students use their home repertoires in the literacy classroom are best for multilingual, multicultural contexts like South Africa (research context). Otheguy et al. (2019) call for elevating heritage languages and culture in literacy teaching and learning for inclusivity and epistemic access (Makalela, 2016b). Many researchers have heeded these calls for inclusive multilingualism in literacy pedagogies, which remains a burning issue in South Africa's linguistically and culturally diverse Higher Education landscape. Responding to the call, several South African scholars have contributed considerably to reading research and pedagogy targeting translingual, multicultural and linguistically diverse students across South African educational settings, e.g. Makalela (2015), Ngcobo et al. (2016), Mbirimi-Hungwe and McCabe (2020), Yafele (2021), and Motlhaka (2021). Hence, promising literacy research in multilingual settings increasingly recommend harnessing students' heritage home languages and their cultural power in reading and writing pedagogies targeting the multilingual/cultural learner. However, despite cited studies, translanguaging in academic reading or literacy instruction research remains thin on how students' sociocultural literacies of knowing, particularly communicative cultural tools, can be harnessed to develop academic reading engagement, grasp, and proficiency.

This chapter experiments with translanguaging as an alternative pedagogy to achieve inclusivity in literacy education. Translanguaging pedagogy - crisscrossing languages fluidly for meaning-making to learn and teach also encompasses various cultural dimensions, including cultural semiotics (Garcia & Kleigen, 2020). This chapter argues that translanguaging offers reading literacy education in multilingual/ multicultural contexts like South Africa and new, effective, viable, and inclusive reading solutions and pedagogical pathways. The participant academic readers in the reported study engaged in translanguaging (with an emphasis on culture) effectually, learning from the prescribed readings and drawing on all the features from their home repertoire flexibly and in an integrated way (Otheguy et al., 2019) to engage fully with academic texts.

Translanguaging Research in literacy pedagogy continues to gain momentum internationally, too (e.g., Otheguy et al., 2019; Daniel et al., 2019; Han et al., 2021). This chapter's proxy study showcases translanguaging as a cultural modality harnessing home-derived cultural tools or repertoire in collaborative, multilingual reading instruction. In a linguistically and culturally diverse society where the majority speaks African languages, the 1st-year academic readers and participants in the reported experimental study harnessed the features of translanguaging using localised cultural meaning-making modalities such as **proverbs** and **anecdotal axioms.**

The case study in the chapter adopts an inclusive translanguaging pedagogy, creating a learning space where students could mobilise their cultural and linguistic resources to negotiate text meanings, critically engage texts and gain a deep understanding of academic manuscripts. The case study explores how, even with English-only biases in place, first-year academic readers at a university in South Africa could utilise the features of translanguaging using cultural tools such as proverbs and sayings. The investigation draws from sociocultural and translanguaging fluidity theories to argue that cultural resources and other linguistic assets can be valuable tools in academic reading instruction, concept development, and critical thinking.

The investigation took a mixed-method research (MMR) design approach to explore translanguaging, home ways, and literacy. The data was first quantitatively collected through focus groups and individual interviews and second qualitatively collected via a quasi-experimental research design. Student's translingual collaborations using cultural tools allowed them to co-construct text meanings, understandings, and knowledge. – validating home identities for inclusivity. Results suggest that cultural repertoires are resources that support students by connecting their daily world to the words in academic texts and become resources for engagement. Hence, a culture-infused and collaborative translingual pedagogy approach is recommended for inclusiveness and cultural responsiveness to build literate academics and nations.

The chapter also intends to be a reference source for inclusive literacy education scholars investigating translanguaging practices in literacy instruction within multilingual, multicultural contexts. It uses a case study to raise translanguaging reading pedagogies' utility and viability profile, emphasising culture for engaged readers.

The objectives of this chapter are to:

- Demonstrate the value of translanguaging in inclusive reading literacy development and show how, in English-only biased institutions, first-year university students can harness features of translanguaging using cultural modalities such as proverbs and sayings.
- Demonstrate that translanguaging strategies (emphasising culture and home ways) can develop and improve academic reading.
- Endorse inclusive translanguaging reading pedagogy using an exemplar
- Advocate for an inclusive translanguaging stance in literacy research and pedagogy, particularly in the global south.
- Broaden the beneficial scope of inclusive translanguaging procedures and frameworks in enquiring into reading literacy scholarship.

Organisation of the Chapter

The rest of this chapter is organised as follows. The ensuing section starts with a brief background that presents the research problem, which requires a translanguaging reading development approach. Next is an elaboration of the theoretical and conceptual framework. The focus then shifts to a comprehensive exposition of translanguaging, providing examples, instances, and explanations. A section on reading models follows where the science of reading development gets considered because the study immersed student participants in a translanguaging reading development pedagogy. The case study's research methodology is now explicated before data analysis. The end sections present the research results as solutions to a reading problem, endorsing and recommending translanguaging interventions and strategies, particularly in the Global South. The discussion section encompasses translanguaging challenges and how to overcome transformation resistance. The final section is on future research directions.

BACKGROUND

As typical of Global South contexts, South Africa - a multilingual and multicultural country - has a colonial history of exclusion and disenfranchisement, which has handicapped literacy and educational development. An education history of predominantly race-based inequity means colonial cultures and languages persist. Transformative Literacy Pedagogies connected to community and cultural tools must now promote democracy rather than perpetuate inequality.

This chapter experiments with alternative pedagogies connected to home experiences as resources for literacy learning and teaching for marginalised learners with black, indigenous identities in higher education. It contributes to transformative conversations in literacy pedagogy by taking "a counter-hegemonic epistemic approach" (Chaka, 2020). It supports a more equitable and inclusive future by exploring how translanguaging African communities' languages and cultures can unlock new opportunities for inclusive literacy pedagogy. The investigation tests the efficacy of alternative translanguaging strategies and practices in an academic reading development intervention in HE.

English is the prime medium of instruction in South Africa. South African multilingual learners must not only grasp an additional language (English) but also learn and understand text content in that English colonial language. Many cannot do so under monolingual pedagogies in which students' languages and ways are viewed as problematic deficiencies and incompetence, not as resources (Makalela, 2022). Educational establishments promote a culture of exclusion and silence (Makalela, 2015), negatively impacting reading. Students have a reduced reading capacity, yet university education requires intensive reading. Makalela (2015) and Mojapelo (2023) also expose a reading problem in South Africa.

The Problem

South Africa has one of the lowest reading achievement rates (Mojapelo, 2023; Spaull & Pretorius, 2019). Its learners have performed poorly in international comparative literacy tests such as Primary International Reading Literacy Studies (PIRLS) (Howie et al., 2017). Spaull and Pretorius (2019) deduce that such low reading literacy implies that readers begin to read weakly and maintain a feeble reading trajectory. Rule and Land (2017) also bemoan shortfalls in 'reading for comprehension of meaning in a text' (p. 1). The latest PIRLS 2021 results, released in 2023, show that Grade 4 pupils who cannot read for meaning rose from 78% in

2016 to 82% in 2023 (Mojapelo, 2023). The current reading ratings remain low. Inclusive, localised interventions approaches and models must address this problem.

Developments in Reading Pedagogy and Research

Out of the several local reading research initiatives undertaken so far, Rose (2018) claims that the R2L (Read to Learn) model increases reading levels from double to four times the standard rates in a year. However, a study by Wildsmith-Cromarty and Steinke (2014) concedes that R2L does not erase academic reading difficulties, calling for future research exploring cultural or home/community-drawn elements. The researchers recommend that further research is still required to address critical academic reading adequately. The study in this chapter tries to do that.

There has been much research on bilingual, multilingual, and translanguaging methods in reading development and education – with emphasis on linguistic aspects (e.g. Otheguy et al., 2019; Mbirimi-Hungwe & MacCabe, 2020; Yafele, 2021). The current study focuses on leveraging and activating localised community resources to allow deep digestion of texts or academic content. Garcia and Kleifgen (2020) call for elevating heritage languages, cultures, and home ways. This study answers that call experimentally.

Alternative Translanguaging Pedagogy for Inclusivity

The research experiments with alternative translanguaging pedagogy using a culture-infused model that offers a reading comprehension pedagogy specifically targeting African multilingual learners. It entwines academic reading, a translanguaging pedagogy, and the role of culture (home literacies) in an academic reading classroom. Students' language(s) and culture(s), including proverbs and axioms (home ways), are valued and aligned to academic reading for literacy and academic success. The study thus adopts Ubuntu translanguaging, a "cultural competence" (p. 21). for Indigenous African multilingual communities in Southern Africa (Makalela 2016b). Ubuntu translanguaging mirrors everyday, regular, home, and community can release learners' home voices into the literacy classroom, facilitating text and epistemic access.

Embracing Home Ways of Knowing via Translanguaging Practices

Opting for alternative translanguaging pedagogy which accommodates community practices, knowledge systems, and ways of knowing makes sense, offering the following clear advantages:

- Recognises students' own linguistic and cultural discursive repertoires in literacy classrooms (Garcia & Lin, 2017)
- Makes full use of students' linguistic and cultural repertoire to make meaning (Lin, 2020; Otheguy et al., 2019)
- Involves the collaboration of all multilinguals' discursive, communicative, cultural, and linguistic resources in making sense of the word and the world (Garcia & Klifgen, 2020)
- Mediates meaning through multiple semiotic resources, multimodality and named languages as an integrated communicative system (Wei, 2018)

The proxy mixed-research study addresses marginalised learners with indigenous identities and embraces African communities' multilingualism practices, everyday life experiences, and philosophies in literacy pedagogy for inclusivity while addressing poor reading rates. The researcher hypothesised that translanguaging tactics (emphasising culture and involving community ways of speaking and thinking) could assist with reading comprehension skills for Higher Education students.

Study's Objective

The study's objective was to establish the efficacy of home ways utilised within an alternative, more inclusive translanguaging literacy pedagogy in scaffolding marginalised multilingual students' meaning-making of academic comprehension texts using fluid linguistic and cultural resources.

The research question was:

How effective is an inclusive translanguaging reading pedagogy (emphasising community ways) for gaining understanding and knowledge of academic texts through collaborative translingual reading (utilising home languages and cultural tools)?

Ethics Clearance

The research went through the required ethics clearance process.

THEORETICAL FRAMEWORK, CONCEPTS

This section discusses the concepts and theories informing and framing the study, comprising sociocultural theory, theory of funds of knowledge, cultural semiotic resources, translanguaging and its forms (including Ubuntu translanguaging), translanguaging pedagogic models and translanguaging's applications across educational settings.

Sociocultural Theory

The interventionist case study was framed around Vygotsky and Cole's (1978) sociocultural theory that learning is social. Street (2016) similarly analyses learning to read from a 'social practice' concept of literacy. This social viewpoint accentuates that literacy learning must acknowledge, value, and exploit the literacy practices in which participants and their communities are already involved (Prinsloo & Street 2014). Using sociocultural theory to promote communities' ways and capitals in teaching strategies in which students use their cultural and linguistic repertoires, community identities, knowledge systems, and literacies in the classroom was one way to investigate the research questions whilst fostering inclusivity in the literacy pedagogy. Sociocultural theory is suitable as the experimental intervention dovetails agreeably into this framework, which relies on interaction, including the home or cultural facet of a person or student.

Theory of Funds of Knowledge

Fundamental in the theoretical framework is Moll et al. (2006) theory of funds of knowledge, which values and reifies the cultural knowledge that learners bring to school as an opportunity and avenue to explore new learning situations, as in Vygotsky and Cole's (1978) scientific knowledge and everyday knowledge phenomena. The study believed that family, community, cultural, and literary aspects, including proverbs, are "the foundations of literacy development" (Herrera et al., 2011, p4). The challenge was mainly to get community resources - sociocultural literacies, languages, and pieces of knowledge - represented in the intervention and, therefore, official school discourses and pedagogy (Garcia& Lin 2017). The translingual intervention was situated in this theory and sociocultural framework, implying that the community significantly influences students' literacy practices. Adopting the theory in the study's framework strengthens the inclusive intentions of the intervention and the sociocultural stance - from whose lens the study was conducted.

Cultural Semiotic Resources

The study explicitly focused on aiding reading comprehension by tapping into students' community resources, cultural repertoire, and cultural, literary, or communicative tools like proverbs, anecdotes, languages, and multilingualism as cultural competence (Compton-Lilly et al., 2020). This aim became a way of constructing the home-to-school links in ways that reframe community literacy practices as assets (Heath, 1983). Proverbs form part of students' linguistic and cultural identities, mirroring the translingual African language speakers' ontological and epistemological orientations.

Communities' and learners' resources are regularly relegated in English-dominant universities. Community languages, knowledge, and sociocultural tools are scarcely official school discourses (Otheguy et al., 2019). The case study purposely employed proverbs as meaning-making cultural tools to enhance semiotics during reading tasks. The research participants' literacy practices and cultural assets were brought into the reading development project. The experimental study linked students' distinctive culture-based home experiences to school reading, respecting students' practices and literacies beyond school.

TRANSLANGUAGING

Translanguaging is central and refers to instructional practices in multilingual learning contexts where a student takes input in one language and gives output in another. The practices intentionally swap the input and output languages logically, resulting in information processing (Lewis, Jones, & Baker, 2012). Yafele and Makalela (2022) demonstrate translanguaging as moving fluidly between multiple languages. Makalela (2015) defines it as the directed interchange of languages in spoken, written, receptive and productive modes. The approach deliberately interchanges the languages of input and output in literacy lessons, allowing students to think about and express their thoughts about texts or academic content in any language they are comfortable with. In the current study, anecdotal axioms and proverbs from the students' communities became a springboard for student to use their home languages and community analytical kits via these cultural tools to tackle university texts.

Translanguaging leverages meaning-making by utilising two or more languages functionally and dynamically cohesive. Garcia and Kleifgen (2020) characterise translanguaging as a language alternation that encompasses cultural and linguistic repertoires for meaning-making without thinking about having numerous or diverse languages. Translanguaging literacy pedagogies can use all the linguistic, cultural, and social resources available to the students to learn, grasp, and express the domain-specific subject content of texts. Students can acquire or take text information in the Language of Learning and Teaching (LOLT) or the English of an academic text. Then, they make meaning in all their languages through dialogue or analytical discussions with the text and others during brainstorming, summary, paraphrasing or writing tasks in LOLT (see Mbirimi-Hungwe & McCabe, 2020; Yafele, 2021). The simultaneous use of multiple named languages in literacy and subject contents is acceptable in translanguaging literacy classes as a move from 'fixity to fluidity" (Yafele & Makalela, 2022).

The term denotes processes where bilinguals and multilinguals tactically negotiate complex social and cognitive activities using *multiple semiotic resources*, *including multimodality* and languages, as a cohesive, communicative scheme (Wei & Lin, 2019).

Translanguaging Applications Across Educational Settings

The present study alternated the participants' English and indigenous community African languages, including isiZulu, siSwati, isiXhosa Setswana, Sesotho, Sepedi, and Tshivenda. Translanguaging pedagogical strategies permit students to bring their literacies, languages, and communicative cultural tools, like proverbs or anecdotal axioms, to university settings where those acts are not inherently appreciated or prized (Compton-Lilly et al., 2020).

Local and international studies conducted in the past ten years on translanguaging and literacies inspired the current study. This section briefly describes this scholarship. It exemplifies translanguaging feasibility, offers application examples across different educational settings, and clarifies how translanguaging has contributed to reading development thus far and so is adapted in the current study.

Yafele (2021) used translanguaging for academic reading with Humanities students at the University of Johannesburg, while Mbirimi-Hungwe and McCabe (2020) and Mbirimi-Hungwe (2016) harnessed translanguaging in summarising and paraphrasing texts to enhance medical students' understanding of medical reading material at Sefako Makgatho Health Sciences University, South Africa. Wei and Lin (2019) indicate that translanguaging research is increasingly becoming established in literacy and content-focused instruction (including text content) in polyglot teaching contexts. Translanguaging models have unlocked new pedagogic possibilities for multilinguals' accomplishment in literacy education (Cummins, 2019; Garcia & Lin, 2017).

Yuksel et al. (2024) exemplify case studies of translingual models and practices enacted in higher education contexts across the globe – in Colombia, Indonesia, Iraq, Norway, Qatar, Spain, Turkey, United Arab Emirates, the UK and the USA. Translanguaging research in the last decade is full of evidence of translingual models in pedagogical aspects of assessments, courses or lessons taught in both students' languages and English. Simbolon and Sadiq (2024) use critical discourse analysis to foster a translanguaging pedagogy environment in Indonesian higher education settings where English is the medium of instruction, but most of the student population is not English. Tekin's (2024) case study focuses on translanguaging in English-medium instruction classrooms and explores teacher educators' practices in Turkish higher education contexts. Translanguaging models globally have effectively boosted learners' higher cognition proficiencies in reading, resulting in human growth and progression (Garcia & Lin, 2017; Garcia et al., 2017).

The cited empirical research reveals the endless possibilities of translanguaging in various education contexts, including the literacy classroom, and explains why it is adopted as a viable theory and practice in the current intervention. Yafele (2021) and Makalela (2015) have also demonstrated possibilities and strategies to offset English dominance by creating productive multilingual havens in literacy classrooms where languages work together harmoniously. Pacheco et al. (2019) exhibit the viability of several effective multilingual pedagogy techniques, including contextualising, invoicing, and recontextualising strategies. Additionally, Mbirimi-Hungwe and McCabe (2020) affirm that a method they coin *trans-collab* works well in multilingual university reading classes. Finally, Wei (2015) applauds the creation of 'translanguaging spaces' or classroom places and the freedom for translanguaging to thrive.

Recent studies on digital literacy within translanguaging contexts likewise offer a view of contemporary literacy practices. A few studies have tried to marry translanguaging and online learning. For example, Wimalasiri and Seals (2022) researched translanguaging in online language teaching. Ho and Tai (2021) explored how online teachers draw on translanguaging spaces to teach English vocabulary using role plays. Li and Wang (2024) investigated translanguaging strategies and online self-presentation through Internet slang.

Ubuntu Translanguaging

The study embraces Makalela's (2016a) framework of Ubuntu Translanguaging, an approach to translanguaging suited for inclusive literacy pedagogies for African university students and informed by African history, cultural values, and South African communities' linguistic realities. Makalela (2016b) pioneers a distinctly African worldview of Ubuntu Translanguaging, which is used to localise reading literacy pedagogy for South African communities in the current study. Ubuntu translanguaging, according to Yafele (2021), is "... a fluid approach to multilingualism, grounded in African cultural competencies", which "combines the South African idea of ubuntu (I am because we are; we are because I am) with translanguaging (p. 408)." It conveys that languages are not whole without other languages and that speakers cannot make complete sense of their environment without using multiple languages (Makalela, 2016b). The notion echoes that languages co-exist (Blackledge & Creese, 2017), leading to 'fuzzy languaging' (Makalela, 2016b, p. 188) for complete meaning-making, which typifies the relationship between African languages and is adaptable to the South African literacy classroom.

Makalela's (2016b) African, historically cultural Ubuntu translanguaging represents the complex language porousness in modern South African classrooms. According to Makalela (2019), language complexities, where languages seep into each other and work together for complete meaning-making, are historical and cultural to Africans. For the South African participants and their communities, multilingualism is cultural competence and a natural, 'wired' norm for the African learner. Makalela (2016b; 2019) emphasises the confluence of languages in the multilingual classroom and the infinite relations of dependency between these languages in enhancing identity construction and epistemic access for multilingual literacy students.

Makalela (2016b) asserts, as does this chapter, that the multilingualism of languages working simultaneously in meaning-making is part of African communities, culture, and history, disrupted by colonialism, which separated African multilingualism into distinct languages according to foreign colonial norms. Translanguaging literacy pedagogy, therefore, fits better with the African experience of multiple languages productively used simultaneously. Mapungubwe, a pre-colonial, powerful African civilisation and translingual kingdom that flourished in Southern Africa between 900 and 1,300 AD, linguistic and cultural confluence, as shown by archaeological artefacts, is an example emulated in the current inclusive literacy intervention. According to Makalela (2019), the colonial scramble and division bordering Africa handicapped the African fluid linguism by using poorly understood colonial languages in education and excluding indigenous African languages from positions of esteem. The current study tries to reverse that historical marginalisation by experimenting with an alternative Ubuntu translanguaging framework for complex multilingual communities that can be adopted for inclusive literacy education. Translanguaging is the appropriate framework for designing a reading literacy curriculum that embraces complex multilingual encounters typical in African settings and communities.

Ubuntu translanguaging pedagogy adopted in the experimental study becomes an inclusive literacy pedagogy meant to normalise the systematic inclusion of multiple languages creatively in the reading literacy classroom. The chapter argues that translanguaging approaches mirror the internal reality of South African multilingual learners, whose languages exist together and can improve literacy outcomes and home-school connections.

READING MODELS

A History and a Mismatch

Traditional reading models would have been adapted for the study but failed to address reading literacy problems in multilingual, multicultural contexts. Traditional monolingual-oriented reading approaches seemed unfit for purpose and incapable of catering to the translingual African academic reader.

History offers many reading models, including the Bottom-Up Model (e.g., Flesch, 1955; Gough et al., 1972), highlighting the importance of the written or printed text in reading. The Top-Down Reading Model (Primary idea-driven Model), e.g., Smith and Goodman (1973), utilises the senses and meanings the literary reader provides to the text in a "psycholinguistic guessing game" (Goodman & Goodman, 2014). The Interactive Reading Model - (e.g., Rumelhart, 2017) combines the top-down and the bottom-up models. It selects the strong points of both models and incorporates them in reading pedagogy. The schema theory and schemata (format and content) models and psychological, intertextuality, and sociolinguistic models are also in the fray. These mismatching monolingual-oriented models disappoint in multilingual contexts.

Hence, no model has resolved the reading problems in South Africa. Rumelhart's (2017) linear info-processing model is too direct and fails to accommodate the circumlocution in South African learners' rhetorical and cultural practices catered for by proverbs, axioms and anecdotes in the current study. The Psychological Model's "guessing game" is ineffective, unworkable, and perhaps unfeasible in making predictions about the reading when one reads foreign or intensely academic topics. Conclusively, these monoglossic models have restrictions and can harm the multilingual (Makalela, 2022), curtailing their creativity and transformative values. As demonstrated in the introduction, South Africa continues to witness low literacy rates and high levels of failure in reading and comprehension, sharply contrasting the results of the current intervention. Incongruities and resultant failures necessitate trying out fresh, community-derived reading models.

Devising a Translanguaging Reading Model

The researcher conceived a translanguaging model for polyglot literacy-teaching environments. The model blends relevant components from past reading models to generate one targeting multilingual/cultural students. Borrowing from new literacies and interactive models, it stresses promoting diversity to achieve equity and relevant education for all. New literacies emphasise shifting from traditional (often monolingual) to unique sociocultural practices. Unlike historical ones, it integrates pedagogical tactics emphasising the flexible use of English and students' diverse home languages. Language alternation is cultivated, with activities structured in ways that allow the concurrent usage of learners' languages. The originated model could work with any reading instructor, but it would be better if the facilitator shared languages with students for fluid interaction during the language interface. Students get translanguaging space to be themselves, use discursive resources they are comfortable with, and bring (discursive resources) to class from home.

THE CASE STUDY

Mixed Methods Research

The study used a mixed methods research (MMR) design approach, which accepts an interdependence of quantitative and qualitative methods for research rigour and uses the strands together for coherent, cohesive results, making for credible, rigorous, and reliable research. MMR suits the complex research phenomenon comprising translanguaging, cultural tools, semiotics, community capital, and reading literacy.

Population and Sampling

The case study utilised purposive and convenience sampling based on participants' qualities, e.g., being linguistically diverse from multilingual black townships. Townships in South Africa are poor, urban, or rural residential areas preserved throughout Apartheid for non-whites who lived near or were employed in white-only areas. The student-participants were also selected for their varying proficiencies in at least 3 South African languages and their willingness to provide the information based on their knowledge and experiences - in terms of relevance and depth - of the translanguaging phenomenon under study (Petty et al., 2012). The students were randomly assigned to control and experimental groups.

Sample

Strategic Communication PR students (Humanities) Sample population size	Experimental and Contol Grp each.	Age	Background	Home language
150	30	18-25	Township Rural /	isiZulu, siSwati, isiXhosa Setswana, Sesotho, Sepedi, and Tshivenda. English

Qualitative Case Study Approach

The *qualitative case study* utilised observation and interviews to explore the participants and evaluate their reading and pedagogic experiences through translanguaging strategies. Lesson and workshop observation transcripts were combined with interviews.

The *quantitative research* part took the form of a *Quasi-Experimental design*.

Figure 1. The originated translanguaging model

The pre-implementation phase of the Model
Mediator Plans- Prepare clear and concise translingual instructional strategies beforehand. Have an emphasis on Agenda: goals, plans, and knowledge to use formative and summative assessments to monitor student learning.
Select course readings guided by the appropriate reading levels, course, and discipline-related content.
A standard academic article can be covered easily thrice weekly for 1-2 hours per session.
Aim for explicit, clear and concise lesson plans and translingual instructional strategies. Numerous examples from empirical studies on Translangauging.

Activities and Roles	
Mediator, Intermediary, facilitator	**Academic reader**
Facilitates the reading pedagogy. Nudges. Mediates; Aims for students cantered class. Plans and uses - Explicit translanguaging teaching strategies	Collaborate in reading tasks and challenges. Talk, talk, and talk about the text using their languages or comfortable languages at their disposal. Use their own linguistic, cultural and discursive communicative resources, e.g., proverbs from their communities, to explain the content in a discussion.
The mediator models translanguaging reading strategies through action and allows students to discover answers for themselves. Engages in multiple linguistic repertoires with the students (if conditions permit). Introduces the concept of reading a text in one language and answering questions in a different one.	Keep multilingual vocabulary lists. Think- pair- share reading activities. The vocabulary inquiry across multiple voices and languages Make predictions and inferences from scanning headings and subheadings about the text they read in their languages.
Use formulated linguistically pluralistic instructional strategies that embody focused goals, plans, and monitoring feedback	Flexible use of English and different home languages in all their varieties Criss-cross between languages to extend meanings beyond the English language used in the text. Use both English and home language.

Figure 2.

The mediator identifies the main content points and concepts. Point out main and new disciplinary ideas in the reading texts to unpack them in indigenous (home languages). Provide the connection between the knowledge in the languages of students if possible. The mediator guides helping to scaffold the knowledge and skills they already possess — especially their rhetorical, cultural, and linguistic resources.	Read individually and Piecemeal – a few paragraphs at a time (one or two).
	Try to process and interrogate the information using different languages. Provide evidence-based reasoning.
	After reading – ask each other questions about what they have just read.
Sets up literature circles: Literature Circles have guidelines for learning tasks, assigned sections, and other reading activities, but students run them. The students get assigned reading material on course readings, and groups are formed based on the multiple languages and cultures they share. Homogenous bilinguals work together. Prompt students to discuss challenging or new content through think-pair-share activities	Meet regularly on a scheduled basis to discuss the readings given and the topics in multiple languages and voices.
Evaluations and monitoring & Sum up: Reinforce. Main concepts. USE students' local languages as much as possible.	

Implementation Phase of Model
Divide reading tasks and text according to Review, View, and Preview categories.
Prepare for and do group and pair reading functions that use multiple languages.
Focus on themes, main ideas, details, phrases, and words in translanguaged engagement with and discussion of the text — concept literacy development. Main and new disciplinary concepts in the selected comprehension reading texts unpacked in indigenous (home languages).
USE Constrictive elaboration allows students to criss-cross between languages, extend meanings beyond the language input, and enhance deeper understanding through translingual talk. Have a whole class or small group share meaning-making using multiple languages and other discursive repertoires. Meaning-making changes as students share and interact with each other, the teacher, and the text. Ensure ALL languages get used. Ensure students use the languages and discursive communicative repertoire that are most comfortable for them.
Simultaneous use of more than one language in the classroom for either language or content subject teaching and learning, including writing, summaries, paraphrasing, and comprehension reading practised. Reviews and paraphrasing activities are done in any language using new vocabulary in context.
Translingual dialogues and conversations about academic texts and so personal connections are made.
Be creative and ensure optimal translanguaging conditions for the best results.
When groups finish sections, chapters, or articles assigned, the readers share in their multiple voices and languages with their classmates about their reading topics, and then new groups are formed based on further reading selections. Homework attempted as modelled increases the independent reading time.
A monolingual mediator can conduct these translanguaging classes. What is just required is willpower to implement the Model according to the unique needs of participants and the dictates of a sociocultural translanguaging framework. FLEXIBLE MODEL

Figure 3.

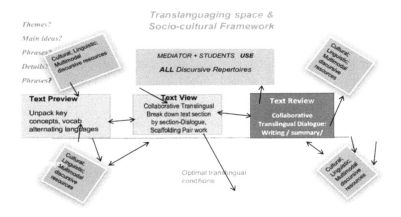

Translanguaging Academic Reading Model for multilingual at first-year tertiary level

How Translanguaging Strategies Got Used

Participants were randomly divided into control and experimental groups.

The Control Group

30 (n=30) participant students were taught using English as the medium of instruction in typical monolingual/monocultural university classes, where the use of languages other than the target language (English) or students' cultural resources is severely limited. They were given typical university lectures and tutorials.

The Experimental Group

The 30 (n=30) participants used pedagogical strategies emphasising English's flexible use and their different home languages in all their varieties. The principle of language alternation was cultivated in this class, with activities structured to enable the simultaneous use of these languages. The experimental class used their everyday home languages, collaborative translingual dialogue, and other cultural, literary meaning-making tools like proverbs in their communities. They participated in multilingual comprehension text-reading discussions in their home languages and English.

Strategies

They collaboratively brainstormed and discussed text content matters in any language they knew but reported to the group in English. They read texts in English, retold text content in their home languages, and then wrote summarised ideas in English. They used relevant proverbs to unpack and engage text ideas and content.

Translanguaging Activities

- Lecturer and students crisscrossed between home languages
- interpreted, summarised articulated text ideas using proverbs and idioms
- Students took reading notes in any home language
- Annotations used students' languages
- Brainstorming and idea outlines in any natural language
- "Transcollab" (Mbirimi-Hungwe & McCabe, 2020) - translingual collaborative dialogues in students' home and English languages for group work
- Summarising in any home language shared with other multilingual students.
- Multilingual dictionary and vocabulary work using Google.

Test Design

The Quantitative data collection first was a pre-test assessment focused on critical reading and appreciation of an academic text of both the control and experimental groups. This assessment was a diagnostic baseline test. Second, a post-translanguaging-intervention critical reading assessment approximated the first test measures. Test results were compared to gauge intervention effectiveness.

Data Analysis

Theories within sociocultural frameworks were used to examine and deductively analyse data. The aim was to demonstrate the inclusiveness and efficacy of translanguaging strategies (emphasising culture and home ways) to develop and improve academic reading. The observation and interview data transcripts were inductively coded using thematic analysis for emerging trends, categories and supported ideas. The researcher condensed these into themes and sub-themes in the analysis. The quantitative data – scores - were analysed using descriptive statistical approaches.

RESULTS AND DISCUSSION

An overarching theme emerging from data is the efficacy and potency of translingual engagements utilising community resources or cultural tools (e.g., community proverbs or axiomatic sayings). The participants were fascinating observations. They demonstrated active involvement in collaborative translingual reading tasks, freedom of participation, and inclusiveness. They had fun and became self-confident and motivated to learn more from texts.

Four themes that emerge from the study are now introduced, illustrated, analysed, interpreted, and discussed: Proverbs as powerful cultural tools for translingual text-tackling; Leveraging critical thinking with proverbial natural bridges; Democratisation, active involvement and inclusion and Translanguaging driving critical thinking.

FROM OBSERVATION DATA

Proverbs: Powerful Cultural Tools for Translingual Text-Tackling

Observation data exemplifies proverbs as powerful cultural tools to access academic text concepts translingually. They facilitated engagements in cognitive processes of making sense of text ideas. Excerpt 1 below is a prototypical illustration of this emerging theme. The reading referred to was a chapter article on "*Communication Barriers*." The main text concepts covered in the article included ethnocentrism, in-group, out-group, xenophobia, and stereotyping in the context of communication barriers.

Excerpt One

Field notes: (The group is observed discussing an article on communication barriers in a translingual reading. Group members crisscross between languages (IsiZulu, IsiXhasa, Sepedi, and Setwana), suggesting relevant proverbs for the concepts read. Andi contributes a Zulu proverb and chooses to explain the relevance of text concepts in English)

Andi:

*Another Zulu proverb goes, "*__Hamba Juba bayacuthapha mbili__*." This proverb's story warns a dove, saying, "Go dove, but they will pluck your feathers off wherever you go." The interpretation is that - if one fraternises with outsiders against the* *wishes of one's people, family, or parents, it ends badly. The saying captures mistrust of foreigners, which is xenophobia.*

Field notes*: The students then go into lively and detailed translanguaging collaborative dialogue, unpacking how the runaway dove's proverb captures the concept of ethnocentricism.*

According to the field notes, the group members crisscross fluidly between at least four documented languages in translingual class discussions using fluid linguistic resources of the learners and cultural tools in the form of proverbs in meaning-making. In this example, Andi appropriated proverbs to explain and enhance her understanding of *xenophobic barriers* to communication explored in the readings. Community proverbs typically scaffold and enhance understanding through cognitive engagements (Honeck, 2013). The students' strategies typically involved the process of metaphorical mapping using proverbs and then relating to the constituents of the conceptual domain to understand text meaning or concepts (Mutonyi, 2016). Andi explains later that she used proverbs as an avenue to the analytical understanding of the concepts of *in-group* and *out-group* in the *ethnocentrism* text. Analogies in proverbs became a process of understanding concepts in domain-specific texts.

FROM INTERVIEW DATA

Leveraging Critical Thinking With Proverbial Natural Bridges

In the interview data in Excerpt 2 below, Anami demonstrates how home-derived proverbs helped her engage intellectually with the text material. She can now fluidly express and explicate topics in readings and opinionated using proverbs.

Excerpt Two

Anami

Our grandparents and parents usually use proverbs with us at home. Using proverbs and idioms and linking or associating these with ideas and concepts from the text helped give us a clear picture of ethnocentrism. Take, for example, the **proverb of the rebellious dove**. *We could relate this proverb to concepts of ethnocentrism and mistrust of strangers and foreigners or people of different ethnicities. It helped me understand ethnocentrism.*

The statement shows that proverbs formed part of the communicative and literacy practices that students were already familiar with, and they became natural bridges leveraging critical thinking and text and concept comprehension. Proverbs offer a familiar pathway to the "strange" academic rhetoric of the text (Honeck, 2013, p31) via cultural tools that guide learners from what they know toward the unknown (Mutonyi, 2016). Using familiar stories embedded in proverbs became powerful mnemonics and tools for accessing and understanding academic text information and concepts, especially during the follow-up translingual group dialogues.

Students could review, clarify, discuss, and explain topics/texts using proverbs in the home language(s) and then revert to the new language through translanguaging. This step helped them to solidify their understanding of the text content. Karabuga & Kaya (2013 p621) regard this reading type as problem-solving. Academic readers actively engaged with the text, extrapolating meanings, including the writers' cues and implications (Hafernik & Wiant 2012 p79). They inferred and evaluated main ideas like xenophobia and in-group and out-group politics via translingual thought processes, the comprehension procedure characteristic of reading (Yusmalinda and Astuti, 2020). Translingual and culturally familiar ways developed reading in university (English) and home (indigenous language via proverbs) systems.

Democratisation, Active Involvement, and Inclusion

No one got left behind in the inclusive translanguaging reading intervention, as illustrated by the evidence in Excerpt 3 below.

Excerpt Three

Andile declares,

I can now speak and partake in the class.

Siyanda testifies:

The translanguaging academic reading lessons permitted us to voice our thoughts in our languages and to explain ourselves. We could engage in different ways. We were able to participate in group discussions, mixing our languages. You are no longer good-for-nothing stooges with nothing to contribute because of language difficulties. You can always offer something.

Students positively evaluate translanguaging home ways in literacy education and academia, as medical students do in Mbirimi Hungwe and McCabe's (2020) summary writing studies. The chapter thus endorses translanguaging pedagogies.

Translanguaging Driving Critical Thinking

Excerpt 4 is from a reading class session reviewing an assigned reading. Student 1 contributes to a lively group evaluative talk on text notions of *ethnocentrisms*. In this example, the student insightfully reformulates the meanings of ethnocentrism.

Excerpt Four (Observation)

Student One

It [ethnocentrism] can be positive and negative simultaneously. It can be patriotism - loving one's culture. [*Swings fluidly and naturally into isiZulu] noma ufuna ukukhombwa ukuthi iculture yako uyithanda kangakani kodwa Uma usubuka ngendlele enegative ukuthi uyibeka phambili;* **at the expense of others**. *Mawungaqala ukujaja amanye amacultere kungaba* **detrimental and positive at the same time**.

*('**Ethnocentrism, like love for one's culture, has good connotations. However, it discriminates against other people's cultures and is detrimental, but it has positives, too.**')*

Yingakho omunye engathi harmful and positive Kanye Kanye. Isphetho sisekwe itextual evidence, nginga quote if kunesdingo sokwenza njalo.

*('**It is both harmful and positive. I can support my ideas with textual evidence!**')*

Here, the student displays critical thinking by reevaluating textual definitions of ethnocentrism. He converses (in a mixture of IsiZulu and English) with the text to reach conclusions based on *interdependent languages*. He fluidly traverses Isizulu and English in his translingual appreciation of the text concepts. He generates debate and justifications by abstractly identifying positive aspects not necessarily in the text. His output utterances naturally shift between languages, supporting Carroll and Sambolín Morales (2016), who found that translanguaging aided students in higher-order reasoning functions such as conjecturing, discussing, and solving problems.

TRANSLANGUAGING IN ACTION: A SUMMARY

Students used proverbs, axioms, and anecdotes expressed in their home languages – as output - in dialogic pedagogy to tackle academic texts. The text content was received (via reading) as input in English. The students crisscrossed between their languages and English in analytical and probing translingual dialogue, hence translanguaging in vocabulary and concept inquiries. The following interview extract is a prototypical instance.

Andi

I had a problem with the concept **of prejudice**. *I was like,* **'Aah**. *What is this about?' I asked Palesa. While discussing the meanings in IsiIXhosa and IsiZulu, we agreed that the concept links well with the saying, "U***kuthathela or Ukubukela Bantu pansi.***" This IsiZulu saying is about looking down on other people or having negative biases, targeting those who do not belong to your in-group.*

This student has had a problem with the textual construct of "prejudice," which later links with the saying "***ukuthathela or ukubukela Bantu pansi***" in isiZulu. She seeks help from a reading and dialogue partner, the lecturer, and the other students. After some translingual dialogic engagements and self-monitoring, she modifies her original definition and reaches confident conclusions of contextual connotations and denotations of "prejudice," as the text uses. In this way, translanguaging discussions bridged the perceived distance between English and other students' languages and melted the vocabulary barrier that may have hindered a critical understanding of concepts in word texts. Metalinguistic awareness of two languages created pathways to sematic awareness and knowledge of text content. The engagement of traversing languages in seeking semantic insights helped students grasp other connotative associations. Moving between languages helped students infer specialised terminology in disciplinary contexts.

They perceived the concept of ***"prejudice"*** explored in the English source text juxtaposed with the famous axiomatic saying, "***ukuthathela or ukubukela Bantu pansi***", and it extended the students' understanding of the English-text concepts. Students developed flexible linguistic ways of giving mirror meanings to the texts' concepts, words, jargon, or meanings. Hence, when confronted with complex texts and unfamiliar vocabulary, students resorted to engagements in collaborative translingual dialogue (fuelled by community *sayings*).

Contrastive Elaboration

The students' elucidated nuances revealed reading content through all their languages at play, including English, using contrastive elaboration. Explication was done simultaneously with languages working together, in line with Makalela's (2016b) Ubuntu translanguaging, where meaning cannot be achieved without using all the languages at our disposal. The languages of output and input were deliberately and fluidly juxtaposed (Makalela, 2015). Blackridge and Creese (2017) explain that meaning in one language cannot exist without the meanings in another.

Fluid Translingual Dialogic Pedagogy

Fluid dialogic situations during reading sessions provided the undergraduate participants multiple contacts with textual, domain-specific notions or vocabulary items. Translingualism allowed for the appreciation of diverse textual connotations and senses for text understanding. When they moved between languages in discussion, students could preview, view, and review academic readings in their home languages to help them understand the texts. Reviewing the topic/text in the home language and back to English and discussing, summarising, or analysing the text/topic again in the home language and via the use of translanguaging resulted in text grasp. Readers clarified and negotiated what they learned from English texts, solidifying their understanding of the text words, concepts and content.

QUANTITATIVE RESULTS

The quantitative results also proved the efficacy and inclusivity of cultural-educational tools used translingually in academic reading intervention. The control group experienced a slight decline in marks from the pre- to post-test, while there was a definite increase in scores from the pre- to post-test for the experimental group. The experimental translingual collaborative groups outperformed the control group in the second reading comprehension post-tests. The quantitative findings complemented the qualitative results, and the better reading achievement highlights the success of a translanguaging academic reading model as initially hypothesised. The test results are portrayed graphically in Figure 4. below:

Figure 4.

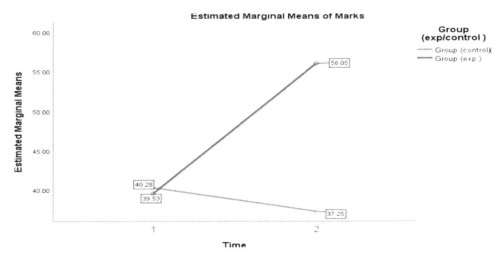

DISCUSSION

The results indicated that the culturally-infused translanguaging learning approach in academic reading with the Experimental Group led to higher achievement than the traditional monolingual/monocultural teaching approaches of the Control Group. Moreover, the readers in the control group who received zero translanguaged reading treatment had a regression. The results demonstrated that students in the experimental translingual group showed statistically more significant academic gains in the written comprehension post-test than in the control group. The increase in students' academic reading achievement (with the experimental group) could have resulted from combining and optimising all the inclusive translanguaging techniques, including home-derived cultural tools, employed in the research. The inclusiveness of language alternations gave the academic readers an edge.

Translanguaging reading pedagogy scaffolds students into understanding text content, facilitates participation in the reception and production of text content and is practical and inclusive. The home-ways in the translanguaging secured the participant students' academic reading citizenry. One implication is that if we can help students raise their consciousness about their cultural and linguistic discursive resources in academic reading processes, they might be able to mediate their reading competencies with many resources strategically. Moreover, extrapolate accurate meaning from course readings, explore text meanings through engagement, co-construct text meanings, understanding, and knowledge, and gradually develop into better academic readers. Using home-derived discursive resources like proverbs and other linguistic and cultural tools in a translingual reading of academic texts brought together home and school's linguistic and cultural worlds to significantly improve academic reading success and inclusivity in literacy pedagogy.

TRANSLANGUAGING CHALLENGES AND OVERCOMING RESISTANCE

Although the results prove the viability of translanguaging literacy pedagogies, implementation is complex, as cited in numerous studies. Educators worldwide face many challenges in implementing translanguaging pedagogies, especially in monolingual and monocultural educational systems.

Resource Constraints

Resource constrictions exist, whereby resources and support for carrying out translanguaging pedagogies are either not provided, limited or missing. Cele (2021) highlights failures to model translingual pedagogies as problematic and a lack of fitting learning materials or textbooks to support multi/translingual education. Omidire (2020) pinpoints educators' ill-readiness in managing multilinguals and the need for training and support for translingual pedagogies to accommodate polyglots. From a different angle, Portolés and Martí (2020) and Clegg and Simpson (2016) invite the necessary support with content knowledge, resources and skills. They call for translingual educational support services through continuing professional development. There is a real need not only to overcome institutional resistance and train educators in translanguaging practices but also to evaluate the impact of translanguaging on student engagement and academic performance. Kaschula and Kretzer (2019) conclude that if insufficient support and resources are NOT provided to back trans/multilingual literacy pedagogies, educators become incapacitated, lacking pedagogical guidelines or training in multilingual pedagogy settings.

Hangover Effect of Monolingual Teacher Educational Programmes

According to Dhokotela and Makalela (2022), a barrier to translanguaging implementation is that some educators have internalised monolingual biases and pedagogies. They distance themselves from students' languages and choose to use English only. They perceive English as the only vehicle of text and other education dissemination. Such views among educators show a carry-over effect (Dhokotera & Makalela, 2022) from the training they received from the monolingual universities they attended and now perpetuate. Such educators silence other languages within education spaces. Dhokotera and Makalela (2022) characterise these hanging-onto-past English-only ways as a hangover effect of monolingual teacher educational programmes—such remnants of monoglossic perceptions detach educators from students' languages and cultures and are harmful.

Pacheco et al.'s (2019) solution is to cultivate accommodative attitudes, recognising students' languages and leveraging them in English-centred classrooms to support students' meaningful engagement with academic text content. There is also a need to combat embedded nihilism about the workability of translanguaging in academia. Catalano and Hamann (2016) encourage us to shift from the viewpoint of multiple languages as problematical to diverse languages as community capital. Similarly, Gorter and Cenoz (2021) maintain that a theoretical shift from monolingual perceptions to trans/multilingualism is essential. Conceptual and mindset shifts are required to permit multi/translingual practices in inclusive literacy pedagogies.

Multilingualism Management Woes: Multilingual Proficiency Problems

McNamara (2015) and Wang and Li (2020) also acknowledge the challenge of implementing pluralistic literacy pedagogies because both educators and student bodies may feel they lack proficiency in other's different language. These scholars show the difficulties of managing multilingual literacy classes. Teachers lack multilingualism management, and predominant monolingual institutions and beliefs have a stopping power.

The Demand for English

Another obstacle is the demand for English- a principal lingua franca of choice globally (Jenkins, 2019) — education systems, units and modules privilege English in academia. (Jenkins (2019) believes numerous universities have shifted to English more because of internationalisation drives. Internationalisation accompanies 'Englishisation'. Oddly, universities are increasingly concentrating on English, on the one hand, and, on the other, becoming more lingua-culturally diverse.

Hornberger (2003) has long warned that any monolingualism prejudices are against developmental evidence that learners learn best from the starting point of their languages and cultures. She demands that educational institutions neutralise deep-seated ideologies, preferring English only. Offsetting English monolingualism dogmata may entail rethinking literacy pedagogy to include fluid translingual models in which English complements learners' languages.

TRANSLANGUAGING AS INCLUSIVE LITERACY AND ACADEMIC EDUCATION

Nonetheless, the current exemplary case study should still offer valuable lessons for embracing translanguaging pedagogy in academic literacy research and practices for inclusivity in the developing world or the Global South. There is a justified growing push for literacy education practitioners and other fields to develop more competencies in inclusive translanguaging pedagogy and practices. Practitioners ought to become translanguaging enthusiasts who are innovative strategists. They must implement this knowledge successfully in literacy development to open education to all for sustainable development and poverty eradication.

Research and teaching in academic and other literacies in education must harness translanguaging practices and theories to champion "multiple ways of seeing and hearing" (Greene, 2007, p. 20) as we forge a future of inclusivity, social justice and equity in educational opportunities and success.

FUTURE RESEARCH DIRECTIONS

Research combining translanguaging, literacy development, and pedagogy for inclusivity remains limited. The full potential of inclusive translanguaging pedagogies in academia and literacy development is unknown. Future studies must fully exploit various translanguaging frameworks and models to open educational opportunities and resolve social justice, equity, inclusivity, and pedagogical and literacy development problems. This chapter's experimental exemplary case study should catalyse more robust translanguaging research and practices in inclusive literacy pedagogy.

CONCLUSION

The case study reported in this chapter addresses the problem of inclusiveness in literacy education and low reading achievement in the South African Higher Education context. It expands on translanguaging research and practice, emphasising the culture/community factor. The students' linguistically and culturally fluid discursive resources were harnessed to leverage academic reading-literacy development and open literacy educational access to all in South Africa. The study thus resolved the problem of poor reading within higher education via a cultural translanguaging stance and inclusive pedagogy using mixed methods. Translanguaging theory and practice are endorsed.

The translanguaging turn in which students' identities, culture and communities that shape those identities are validated, accommodated, and affirmed in academic literacy and reading pedagogy should continue to gain momentum. The case-study example described in this chapter demonstrates the viability of translanguaging as a theory and practice for inclusive and community-partnership representation in literacy education.

REFERENCES

Aldridge, D. (2019). Reading, engagement, and higher education. *Higher Education Research & Development*, *38*(1), 38–50. doi:10.1080/07294360.2018.1534804

Amir, A. (2019). The effect of reading strategies and speed reading on students' reading comprehension skill in higher education. *Paper presented at the Advances in Social Science, education, and Humanities research. Proceedings of the Seventh International Conference on Languages and Arts (ICLA 2018)*. IEEE. 10.2991/icla-18.2019.68

Ballantyne, E. (2020). Book Review: Critical Reading in Higher Education. *The Canadian Journal for the Scholarship of Teaching and Learning*, *11*(1). doi:10.5206/cjsotl-rcacea.2020.1.8241

Blackledge, A., & Creese, A. (2017). Translanguaging in mobility. In S. Canagarajah (Ed.), *The Routledge Handbook of Migration and Language* (pp. 31–46). Taylor & Francis. doi:10.4324/9781315754512-2

Carroll, K. S., & Sambolín Morales, A. N. (2016). Using university students' L1 as a resource: Translanguaging in a Puerto Rican ESL classroom. *Bilingual Research Journal*, *39*(3-4), 248–262. doi:10.1080/15235882.2016.1240114

Catalano, T., & Hamann, E. T. (2016). Multilingual pedagogies and pre-service teachers: Implementing "language as a resource" orientations in teacher education programs. *Bilingual Research Journal*, *39*(3-4), 263–278. doi:10.1080/15235882.2016.1229701

Cele, N. (2021). Understanding language policy as a tool for access and social inclusion in South African higher education: A critical policy analysis perspective. *South African Journal of Higher Education*, *35*(6), 25–46. doi:10.20853/35-6-3730

Cenoz, J., & Gorter, D. (2021). *Pedagogical translanguaging*. Cambridge University Press.

Chaka Chaka, C. (2020). Translanguaging, Decoloniality, and the Global South: An Integrative Review Study. *Scrutiny, 2,* 6-42. doi:10.1080/18125441.2020.1802617

Clegg, J., & Simpson, J. (2016). Improving the effectiveness of English as a medium of instruction in sub-Saharan Africa. *Comparative Education, 52*(3), 359–374. doi:10.1080/03050068.2016.1185268

Compton-Lilly, C. F., Rogers, R. L., & Lewis Ellison, T. (2020). A meta-ethnography of family literacy scholarship: Ways with metaphors and silence. *Reading Research Quarterly*, *55*(2), 271–289. doi:10.1002/rrq.272

Cummins, J. (2019). Should schools undermine or sustain multilingualism? An analysis of theory, research, and pedagogical practice. *Darnioji daugiakalbystė 15*(1), 1–26. doi:10.2478/sm-2019-0011

Daniel, S. M., Jiménez, R. T., Pray, L., & Pacheco, M. B. (2019). Scaffolding to make translanguaging a classroom norm. *TESOL Journal, 10*(1), e00361. doi:10.1002/tesj.361

Dhokotera, C., & Makalela, L. (2022). The Carry-over Effect of Monolingual Teacher Education Programmes: Towards a Decolonized University. In L. Makalela (Ed.), *Language and Institutional Identity in the Post-Apartheid South African Higher Education. Language Policy* (Vol. 27). Springer. doi:10.1007/978-3-030-85961-9_5

Flesch, R. (1955). *Why Johnny can't read—and what you can do about it.* Harper & Brothers.

Garcia, O. (2009). Education, multilingualism and translanguaging in the 21st century. *Social justice through multilingual education*, 140-158.

García, O., Johnson, S. I., Seltzer, K., & Valdés, G. (2017). *The translanguaging classroom: Leveraging student, for learning.* Caslon.

García, O., & Kleifgen, J. A. (2020). Translanguaging and literacies. *Reading Research Quarterly*, *55*(4), 553–571. doi:10.1002/rrq.286

García, O., & Lin, A. M. (2017). Translanguaging in Bilingual Education. In O. García, A. M. Lin, & S. May (Eds.), *Bilingual and Multilingual Education* (pp. 117–130). Springer. doi:10.1007/978-3-319-02258-1_9

Goodman, K. S., & Goodman, Y. (2014). Reading: A psycholinguistic guessing game. In *Making Sense of Learners Making Sense of Written Language* (pp. 103–112). Routledge. doi:10.4324/9780203366929

Gough, P. B., Kavanagh, J. F., & Mattingly, I. G. (1972). *One second of reading.* MIT Press.

Greene, J. C. (2007). *Mixed methods in social inquiry* (Vol. 9). John Wiley & Sons.

Hafernik, J. J., & Wiant, F. M. (2012). *Integrating multilingual students into college classrooms.* Multilingual Matters. doi:10.21832/9781847698216

Han, M., Van Duinen, D. V., & Weng, A. (2021). Interactive Read-Alouds as Translanguaging Spaces. *The Reading Teacher*, 75(3), 389–394. doi:10.1002/trtr.2059

Heath, S. B. (1983). *Ways with words: Language, life, and work in communities and classrooms.* Cambridge University Press. doi:10.1017/CBO9780511841057

Herrera, S. G., Perez, D. R., & Escamilla, K. (2011). Teaching reading to English language learners: Differentiating literacies: Pearson Higher Ed.

Ho W.Y.J, Tai K.W.H (2021) Translanguaging in digital learning: The making of translanguaging spaces in online English teaching videos. *International Journal of Bilingual Education and Bilingualism.* . doi:10.1080/13670050.2021.2001427

Honeck, R. P. (2013). *A proverb in mind: The cognitive science of proverbial wit and wisdom.* Psychology Press. doi:10.4324/9780203771556

Hornberger, N. H. (Ed.). (2003). *Continua of biliteracy: An ecological framework for educational policy, research, and practice in multilingual settings.* Multilingual Matters. doi:10.21832/9781853596568

Howie, S. J., Combrinck, C., Roux, K., Tshele, M., Mokoena, G., & McLeod Palane, N. (2017). *PIRLS Literacy 2016: Progress in international reading literacy study (PIRLS) 2016: South African children's reading literacy achievement.* Centre for Evaluation and Assessment (CEA).

Jenkins, J. (2019). English medium in higher education: The role of English as a lingua franca. In X. Gao (Ed.), *Second Handbook of English Language Teaching* (pp. 1–17). Springer. doi:10.1007/978-3-030-02899-2_7

Karabuga, F., & Kaya, E. S. (2013). Collaborative strategic reading practice with adult EFL learners: A collaborative and reflective approach to reading. *Procedia: Social and Behavioral Sciences*, 106, 621–630. doi:10.1016/j.sbspro.2013.12.071

Kaschula, R. H., & Kretzer, M. M. 2019, 'The Politics of Language Education in Africa'., Oxford Research Encyclopedia of Politics. Oxford. Oxford University Press. doi:10.1093/acrefore/9780190228637.013.750

Lewis, G., Jones, B., & Baker, C. (2012). Translanguaging: Origins and development from school to street and beyond. *Educational Research and Evaluation, 18*(7), 641–654. doi:10.1080/13803611.2012.718488

Li, Z., & Wang, L. (2024). *Investigating translanguaging strategies and online self-presentation through internet slang on Douyin (Chinese TikTok)*. Applied Linguistics Review. doi:10.1515/applirev-2023-0094

Lin, A. M. (2020). *Translanguaging and translanguaging pedagogies Translanguaging in Multilingual English Classrooms*. Springer.

Makalela, L. (2015). Translanguaging as a vehicle for epistemic access: cases for reading comprehension and multilingual interactions. *Per Linguam: a Journal of Language Learning= Per Linguam. Tydskrif vir Taalaanleer, 31*(1), 15–29.

Makalela, L. (2016a). *Translanguaging Practices in a South African Institution of Higher Learning: A Case of Ubuntu Multilingual Return Translanguaging in higher education*. Multilingual Matters.

Makalela, L. (2016b). Ubuntu translanguaging: An alternative framework for complex multilingual encounters. *Southern African Linguistics and Applied Language Studies, 34*(3), 187–196. doi:10.2989/16073614.2016.1250350

Makalela, L. (2019). Uncovering the universals of Ubuntu translanguaging in classroom discourses. *Classroom Discourse, 10*(3-4), 237–251. doi:10.1080/194 63014.2019.1631198

Makalela, L. (2022). Introduction: Language, Identity and African Universities. In L. Makalela (Ed.), *Language and Institutional Identity in the Post-Apartheid South African Higher Education. Language Policy* (Vol. 27, pp. 1–10). Springer., doi:10.1007/978-3-030-85961-9_1

Mbirimi-Hungwe, V., & McCabe, R.-M. (2020). Translanguaging during collaborative learning: A 'transcollab' model of teaching. *Southern African Linguistics and Applied Language Studies, 38*(3), 244–259. doi:10.2989/16073614.2020.1847670

Mcnamara, T. (2015). Applied linguistics: The challenge of theory. *Applied Linguistics, 36*(4), 466–477. doi:10.1093/applin/amv042

Mojapelo, S. M. (2023). Whopping low reading literacies in South Africa. *South African Journal of Library and Information Science, 89*(1), 1–14.

Moll, L., Amanti, C., Neff, D., & Gonzalez, N. (2006). Funds of knowledge for teaching: Using a qualitative approach to connect homes and classrooms. In *Funds of knowledge* (pp. 71–87). Routledge.

Motlhaka, H. (2021). Translanguaging in Collaborative Reading Activity: A Multilingual Perspective of Meaning Making. *Psychology and Education Journal*, *58*(5), 2683–2691.

Mutonyi, H. (2016). Stories, proverbs, and anecdotes as scaffolds for learning science concepts. *Journal of Research in Science Teaching*, *53*(6), 943–971. doi:10.1002/tea.21255

Ngcobo, S., Ndaba, N., Nyangiwe, B., Mpungose, N., & Jamal, R. (2016). Translanguaging as an approach to address language inequality in South African higher education: Summary writing skills development. [CriSTaL]. *Critical Studies in Teaching and Learning*, *4*(2), 10–27.

Omidire, F. (2020). Derived knowledge and lived experiences of teachers working in resource-constrained multilingual classrooms. [TETFLE]. *Teacher Education Through Flexible Learning in Africa*, *2*(1), 156–171. doi:10.35293/tetfle.v2i1.92

Otheguy, R., Garcia, O., & Reid, W. (2019). A translanguaging view of the linguistic system of bilinguals. *Applied Linguistics Review*, *10*(4), 625–651. doi:10.1515/applirev-2018-0020

Pacheco, M. B., Daniel, S. M., Pray, L. C., & Jiménez, R. T. (2019). Translingual practice, strategic participation, and meaning-making. *Journal of Literacy Research*, *51*(1), 75–99. doi:10.1177/1086296X18820642

Petty, N. J., Thomson, O. P., & Stew, G. (2012). Ready for a paradigm shift? Part 2: Introducing qualitative research methodologies and methods. *Manual Therapy*, *17*(5), 378–384. doi:10.1016/j.math.2012.03.004 PMID:22480949

Portolés, L., & Martí, O. (2020). 'Teachers' beliefs about multilingual pedagogies and the role of initial training'. *International Journal of Multilingualism*, *17*(2), 248–264. doi:10.1080/14790718.2018.1515206

Prinsloo, M., & Street, B. (2014). Literacy, language, and development: a social practices perspective. *Language Rich Africa Policy Dialogue, 65*.

Rose, D. (2018). Languages of schooling: Embedding literacy learning with genre-based pedagogy. *European Journal of Applied Linguistics*, *6*(1), 59–89. doi:10.1515/eujal-2017-0008

Rule, P., & Land, S. (2017). Finding the plot in South African reading education. *Reading and Writing*, *8*(1), 1–8.

Rumelhart, D. E. (2017). Schemata: The building blocks of cognition. In R. J. Spiro, B. C. Bruce, & W. F. Brewer (Eds.), *Theoretical issues in reading comprehension* (pp. 33–58). Routledge. doi:10.4324/9781315107493-4

Sadiq, N., & Simbolon, N. E. (2024). Fostering Translanguaging Pedagogy Environment in Indonesian Higher Education EMI Settings: A Critical Discourse Analysis. *Multilingual and Translingual Practices in English-Medium Instruction: Perspectives from Global Higher Education Contexts*, 51.

Smith, F., & Goodman, K. S. (1973). On the psycholinguistic method of teaching reading. In F. Smith (Ed.), *Psycholinguistics and Reading* (pp. 177–182). Holt, Rinehart and Winston.

Spaull, N., & Pretorius, E. (2019). *Still falling at the first hurdle: Examining early grade reading in South Africa South African Schooling: The Enigma of Inequality*. Springer.

Street, B. (2016). Learning to read from a social practice view: Ethnography, schooling, and adult learning. *Prospects*, *46*(3), 335–344. doi:10.1007/s11125-017-9411-z

Taylor, S., Cillier, J., Prinsloo, C., & Reddy, J. (2018). *Improving early grade reading in South Africa*. Research Gate.

Vygotsky, L. S., & Cole, M. (1978). *Mind in society: Development of higher psychological processes*. Harvard University Press.

Wang, Y., & Li, S. (2020). Issues, challenges, and future directions for multilingual assessment. *Journal of Language Teaching and Research*, *11*(6), 914–919. doi:10.17507/jltr.1106.06

Wei, L. (2015). Complementary classrooms for multilingual minority ethnic children as a translanguaging space. In J. Cenoz & D. Gorter (Eds.), *Multilingual education: Between language learning and translanguaging* (pp. 177–198). Cambridge Applied Linguistics. doi:10.1017/9781009024655.010

Wei, L. (2018). Translanguaging as a practical theory of language. *Applied Linguistics*, *39*(1), 9–30. doi:10.1093/applin/amx039

Wei, L., & Lin, A. M. (2019). *Translanguaging classroom discourse: Pushing limits, breaking boundaries* (Vol. 10). Taylor & Francis.

Wildsmith-Cromarty, R., & Steinke, K. (2014). The write approach: Can R2L help at tertiary level? *Per Linguam*, *30*(1), 38–54. doi:10.5785/30-1-570

Wimalasiri, A., & Seals, C. A. (2022). Translanguaging in online language teaching: A case study of a multilingual English language teacher in New Zealand. *Journal of Multilingual Theories and Practices*, *3*(1), 127–145. doi:10.1558/jmtp.20849

Yafele, S. (2021). Translanguaging for academic reading at a South African university. *Southern African Linguistics and Applied Language Studies*, *39*(4), 404–424. doi: 10.2989/16073614.2021.1981767

Yafele, S., & Makalela, L. (2022). From Fixity to Fluidity: A Critique of Higher Education Language Policy. In L. Makalela (Ed.), *Language and Institutional Identity in the Post-Apartheid South African Higher Education. Language Policy* (Vol. 27). Springer. doi:10.1007/978-3-030-85961-9_8

Yuksel, D., Altay, M., & Curle, S. (Eds.). (2024). *Multilingual and translingual practices in English-medium instruction: Perspectives from global higher education contexts*. Bloomsbury Publishing. doi:10.5040/9781350373273

Yusmalinda, A., & Astuti, P. (2020). English teachers' methods in teaching reading comprehension of procedure text. *Journal of English Language Teaching*. 10.15294/elt.v9i1.38676

Chapter 10
Towards a Literate Community:
An Action Plan Using Microsoft's Reading Progress and Immersive Reader

Lemuel-Kim A. Garcia
(iD) https://orcid.org/0000-0003-1533-7012
Department of Education, San Leonardo, Philippines

Ramil Gutierrez Ilustre
Department of Education, San Fernando, Philippines

ABSTRACT

The researchers implemented Microsoft Reading Progress and Immersive Reader to address the reading problems of students in terms of reading speed and oral reading miscues. Using a true experimental design, it was found that the digital intervention and traditional way of teaching have shown significant improvement on the reading skills of the students. The Reading Progress and Immersive Reading can be considered by the teachers who have numerous workloads because the application can let the students learn reading independently. However, traditional instruction where the teacher is physically guiding the students can not be replaced by the software intervention, despite of its time-consuming-issue. This means that both reading pedagogies have their pros and cons. This enabled the researchers to craft an action plan focused on implementing the application and engaging the stakeholders and parents to address the learning gaps in reading as an education community.

DOI: 10.4018/979-8-3693-1777-8.ch010

INTRODUCTION

Reading plays an indispensable part in every plane of life. From knowing the nutritional contents of the food that we eat to understanding book that we read, reading has always been a need, thus considering as vital in opening the doors for everything especially in learning.

Reading has many benefits. According to the National Institute of Child Health and Human Development (2000), Cunningham and Stanovich (1997), and Krashen (1993), reading develops the vocabulary, communication, imagination, and creativity of an individual, aside from reducing stress, improving concentration and building good self-image.

Considering reading as a necessity for learning, the basic education curriculum, particularly the language education, was aligned to developing the literacy of the students, from direct instruction to skill integration. However, reading has been a boulder shouldered by DepEd for a long time, driving them to develop numerous strategies and interventions to address the learning gaps and catch the needs of the students today.

As per the report of the Program for International Student Assessment (PISA) in 2018, the Philippines ranked as the low in reading comprehension. Recently, although the results have improved a bit, the recent PISA 2022 still shows that the country is still ranked low. According to the interpretation of the said international assessment, the country's learners are still below the threshold of understanding the text that they read. This result also reflects to the performance of the students in domestic large-scale assessments where the students get below average scores (i.e., National Achievement Test).

These findings are also in agreement with the data of the United Nations Children's Fund in 2022 where the Philippines also ranked last in reading (UNICEF Philippines, 2021) while in the Southeast Asia – Primary Learning Metrics, the Philippines was ranked low in reading, and writing literacy (De Vera, 2021).

The cited challenges made the Department of Education enhance its drives in fighting reading difficulties and illiteracy among its learners. This made the DepEd implement the National Reading program, and enhance *Every Child a Reader Program* (ECARP).

The National Reading Program is a program that promotes literacy development in Key Stages 1 to 3. This program has two tiers: a core reading program and a supplemental reading program. The core reading program focuses on developing the necessary skills of the students in comprehending texts at their level. It involves the use of textbooks, workbooks and other instructional materials. The supplemental reading program, on the other hand, is designed to support students who are struggling readers. Examples of this are the remedial programs, reading camps and other interventions that target to meet the individual needs of the students (Department of Education, 2014; Maipot, 2019; and Chi, 2023).

Another is *Every Child a Reader Program* (ECARP) that integrates the strengthened initiatives on ELLN (Early Language, Literacy and Numeracy Program), MTB-MLE (Mother Tongue-based of Multilingual Education) and PRIMALS (Pedagogical Retooling in Mathematics, Language, and Sciences) (Montemayor, 2021). The program focuses on developing the multidisciplinary knowledge of the students, but reading is the primary skill that has the most concentrated focus since it is the key on accessing the knowledge in different learning areas.

For the language teachers, remediating the learning gaps is not an easy task because of their workloads. Usually, a teacher has six teaching loads thus spending six hours in the classroom, and two hours in the preparation of instructional materials and recording of activities and academic tasks. This affects the remedial sessions that are supposed to be conducted to struggling readers.

The Department of Education, in response to the reading challenges, has been implementing the Philippine Informal Reading Inventory (Phil-IRI) in schools to diagnose the struggling readers and remediate them. This is a comprehensive learning material in reading that guides the teachers how they will assess their students, and what interventions can be given to them based on the teacher's diagnosis. Despite of the comprehensiveness of the Phil-IRI, there is an issue on the required effort in implementing it. As it is being conducted, teachers sit with their students to track their progress individually. An intervention usually lasts for an hour to teach a struggling reader how to enunciate words correctly. If a language teacher has 10 or more struggling readers for instance, it will be difficult for the teacher to address their needs one-by-one. This makes the conduct of learning interventions slow thus not addressing all the needs of the students.

Because of this, the Department of Education released a statement in 2021 about one of the tools that the teachers can use in efficiently developing and diagnosing the reading skills of the students, Microsoft Reading Progress and Immersive Reader. These applications can be maximized by teachers because they are given Microsoft o365 accounts for instructional purposes.

Reading Progress is free software tool that aids students in practicing their reading fluency. It allows the students to read a passage out loud while recording video and audio (Microsoft Learn Educator Center, n.d.). This helps the teachers develop the reading skills of the students while having a less classroom disruption. Moreover, the application can give more time for the teacher to check the reading of their students since the students' activities can be recorded.

The Immersive Reader, on the other hand, is a free tool built in different Microsoft applications such as OneNote, Word, and MS Teams that implements techniques to improve reading and writing. It has a text-to-speech features, picture dictionary, translation and more. The fonts can be adjusted based on the needs and preferences of the students. This can be integrated to the Reading Progress so that the students can be developed through self-directed learning (e.g., the software checks the students' errors and helps them to correct them).

Despite the promising feature of the applications, challenges are still present in the education field such as lack of access to computers and challenging internet connection. Uneven distribution of educational resources particularly in rural and marginalized areas are still present (UNICEF, 2021). This means that even teachers have their o365 accounts, they might find it difficult to implement Reading Progress and Immersive Reader in their respective schools.

On the end of the DepEd, it currently addresses the problem through the continuous implementation of DCP or DepEd Computerization Program, and Digital Rise Program. In the second component of Digital Rise Program, schools are being provided with equipment, software content and skills for their daily classroom teaching such as providing them laptops, smart TVs and lapels (DepEd, 2022). The DepEd continued to partner with Microsoft and Google to enhance the country's practice in implementing ICT. Though the bureau has a long way to go, the country's education ministry is still on the go. Meaning, introducing and engaging teachers to innovations such as Immersive Reader and Reading Progress should not be hindered by the cited challenges because there are schools who have received computers and have the capacity to implement the said software in their areas. On the researcher's end, they aim to train and encourage the teachers to use the said software to somewhat lighten their load, which this study aims to understand.

In support to the drive of the Department of Education, the researchers implemented the Reading Progress and Immersive Reader of Microsoft as the Phil-IRI is being used in schools. The end goal of this study is to test whether the said tools are effective in diagnosing and developing the reading skills of the students. This research may open new doors of knowledge in improving the instructional efficiency of the nation's education bureau in terms of teaching reading to students.

With a true experimental research design, the researchers carefully examined whether there was a significant improvement on the learners who used Reading Progress and Immersive Reader as compared to the ones who do the conventional way of implementing the Phil-IRI.

The study was able to come up with an action plan that suggests the integration of the said applications in implementing Phil-IRI to DepEd – Region III. The action plan is planned to be disseminated in the different schools division offices in Central Luzon, engaging the teachers, learners and the learning support providers such as the parents and stakeholders.

This study could also open more gates for future research, such as the experience of the teachers as they use the applications and the convenience that it brings as they diagnose their students. Moreover, the Department of Education can add the findings of this study to their archives of knowledge for future policy recommendations, and stakeholders' engagement particularly those members of the education community.

To gather the necessary data for the achievement of the aim of the study, the researchers have chosen two schools as a research locale. These schools have their reading programs being implemented wherein non-decoders and struggling readers are the ones that they cater.

The researchers determined the reading speed, oral reading miscues and comprehension level of the students before and after the application of Reading Progress and Immersive Reader. These results were then compared to the results of the control group who received traditional instruction in learning reading. The researchers also sought the feedback from the facilitators as they use Immersive Reader and Reading Progress.

With the data that were gathered and interpreted, the researchers were able to develop an action plan that targets to engage the education community in DepEd – Central Luzon.

Methodology

Using a true experimental design, the researchers determined the reading performance of grade 7 students in terms of their reading speed, oral reading miscues and comprehension level through the Philippine Informal Reading Index assessment tools.

With the two schools that were used as research locale, the study was able to form a control and an experimental group; the first group receives traditional instruction while the latter receives an instruction using Reading Progress and Immersive Reader. With the pretest and posttest design, the researchers were able to gauge the reading performance of the students before and after the different independent variables were applied.

In implementing the study, the researchers applied two strategies: implementation of Reading Progress and Immersive Reader, and the traditional way of teaching reading.

Reading Progress and Immersive Reader were the independent variables that were applied in the experimental group. They have been remediated with the software. Here, they were oriented how to use the application and the teacher-facilitators let them use the software.

The said programs allowed the students to read texts and identify their errors. Once their errors are identified, the software asks them to pronounce it again. In case that a student needs assistance, Reading Progress and Immersive Reader though the Reading Coach, can read the word for him/ her so that the student may know how to pronounce certain words.

Traditional reading, on the other hand, is a way of teaching where students learn how to read through direct instruction. They are assisted by a teacher who is physically present during the intervention process. It is the teacher who assists them in knowing the correct pronunciation of the words, and their meaning.

The data that were gathered were analyzed using weighted mean, percentage, and mean difference through t-test.

To interpret the data that were from the adapted tests from the Phil-IRI, the study adapted its data analysis. They are as follow:

Oral Reading Speed and Rate in Oral Reading. To compute the speed of the respondents in reading, the study adopted Phil-IRI's evaluation of reading speed. Below is the sample computation of the reading speed as cited in the Phil-IRI:

Computation of Student Comprehension. To compute the comprehension of the participants, the researchers adopted the computation of the Phil-IRI. The sample of the computation can be seen below:

Analysis and Interpretation of Word Reading and Comprehension Level. In profiling the students, the study used the Oral Reading Profile and Student's Reading Profile Per Passage of the Phil-IRI:

Table 1. Oral reading score computation as per Phil-IRI 2018

Oral Reading Score: the number of words – number of miscues X100
$$\text{number of words}$$

Example: Pedro's Performance in Oral Reading
No. of words in the passage: 65
No. of miscues: 15

$$\frac{65-15 = 50}{65} \text{ x100} = \textbf{76.9\%}$$

Pedro's rating in oral reading is 76.9%

Table 2. Reading speed computation as per Phil-IRI 2018

Reading speed = No. of words read X 60
$$\text{Reading time in seconds}$$
No. of words in the passage: 103
No. of minutes it took Karlo to read it: 1.5mins. (90 seconds)

$$\frac{103 \text{ words read}}{90 \text{ seconds}} = 69 \text{ words per minute}$$

Pedro's reading rate: 69 words per minute

Table 3. Comprehension score computation as per Phil-IRI 2018

C= <u>No. of correct answers</u> X100= % of comprehension 　　No. of questions No. of correct answers: 4 Total no. of questions: 7 　4/7 = 57 **Pedro's comprehension: 57%**

Table 4. Oral reading and student reading profile as per Phil-IRI 2018

Oral Reading Level	Word Reading Score (in %)	Comprehension Score (in %)
Independent	97% – 100%	80% - 100%
Instructional	90% - 96%	59% - 79%
Frustration	89% and below	58% and below

Table 5. Example of computing the oral reading profile

Word reading score: **Comprehension score:** **Reading Rate:**	15 miscues = 76.9%: *Frustration* 4 out of 7= 57%: *Frustration* 69.5 words per minute
Karlo's Oral Reading Profile: **Frustration**	

Table 6. Reading profile per passage

Word Reading	Reading Comprehension	Reading Profile per Passage
Independent	Independent	Independent
Independent	Instructional	Instructional
Instructional	Independent	Instructional
Instructional	Frustration	Frustration
Frustration	Instructional	Frustration
Frustration	Frustration	Frustration

RESULTS AND DISCUSSION

This section presents the data gathered by the researchers. It contains reading performance of control group and experimental group in terms of their reading speed, oral reading score, and comprehension level, the test of significance of the pretest and post test results of the control and experimental group, the feedback of the teacher-facilitators, and the proposed action plan based on the gathered results.

Pretest Results of the Experimental and Control Group

The table presents the sex, reading speed, oral miscues and comprehension level of the students and the respective interpretation of their reading level.

Based on the table, there are 15 participants in the experimental group, all of them are male students. On the other hand, the controlled group has 25 participants in which 13 are male and 12 female.

The reading speed of the experimental group in their pretest is 66 words per minute while 77 words per minute for the controlled group.

In terms of the experimental group's oral reading miscues, they had 95% which is verbally interpreted as frustration while the controlled group had 7% thus being an independent reader.

For their comprehension level, the experimental group had a reading level of frustration with a 25% comprehension score while the controlled group had a comprehension level of 36% thus being a frustration reader.

It can be observed that the experimental group is mostly male students. This means that the students who suffer from learning gaps in reading. This is in contrary to the number of male and female of the controlled group which has the same of number.

Also, the controlled group performed better in comprehension level, reading speed and number of miscues than the experimental group.

Table 7. Pretest results of the experimental and control group

Group	N	Sex		Reading Speed	Oral Reading Miscues	Int	Comprehension Level	Int
		M	F					
Experimental	15	15	0	66 wpm	95%	Frus	25%	Frus
Control	25	13	12	77 wpm	7%	Ind	36%	Frus

Table 8. Posttest results of the experimental and control group

Group	N	Sex		Reading Speed	Oral Reading Miscues	Int	Comprehension Level	Int
		M	F					
Experimental	15	15	0	55 wpm	49%	Frus	35.83%	Frus
Control	25	13	12	91 wpm	6%	Ind	61%	Ins

Post Test Results of Experimental and Control Group

The table presents the post test results of the experimental and controlled group after undergoing different treatments.

The data shows that the experimental group had a reading speed of 55 words per minute while the control group had a reading speed of 91 words per minute. It can be observed that the experimental group got slower by 11% in reading as compared to their pretest results.

According to the teachers who conducted the treatment of using Immersive Reading and Reading Progress, the students became conscious in reading words because of the drills provided by the software (e.g. showing their mistakenly read words for them to practice). Moreover, the slowness in reading can be attributed to the focus of the students in comprehending the text.

The control group, on the other hand, got faster in reading by 14%. This is because of the focus given by the teachers in reading as they decode and read the words. This means that the physical presence of the teacher is a factor in developing the reading performance of the students.

For the oral reading miscues, the experimental group had an improvement, from 95% to 49% decrease as compared to the controlled group which improved by only 1%. This is because the Reading Progress and Immersive Reader practice the students in recognizing the words. The students master the unfamiliar words to them by repeatedly pronouncing them in the software since it has a feature that makes the reader master a word before letting them proceed to the next text or word that they are going to read.

For the comprehension level of the participants, the experimental group had a score of 35.38%, being interpreted as frustration level while the controlled group had a comprehension score of 61% thus making them instructional reader.

Although the Reading Progress and Immersive Reader does not focus on developing the comprehension of the students, it is noticeable that both groups improved: 10.83% for the experimental, and 25% for the control group.

Significant Difference on the Reading Speed, Oral Reading Miscues and Comprehension Level of Experimental Group During Pretest and Posttest

The table presents the test of hypothesis on the reading speed, oral miscues and reading comprehension of the experimental group before and after the treatment.

It can be gleaned from the data that there is a significant difference between the reading speed, oral miscues and reading comprehension of the respondents since the p-value $<= 0.05$ thus rejecting the null hypotheses.

Table 9. Paired samples test on reading speed, oral reading miscues and comprehension level of the experimental group during their pretest and posttest

		Paired Samples Test								
		Paired Differences						**t**	**df**	**Sig. (2-tailed)**
		Mean	**Std. Deviation**	**Std. Error Mean**	**95% Confidence Interval of the Difference**					
					Lower	**Upper**				
Pair 1	ExperimentalPretestReadingSpeed - ExperimentalPostTestReadingSpeed	13.88898	12.90303	3.33155	6.74351	21.03444	4.169	14	.001
Pair 2	ExperimentalPretestOralMiscues - ExperimentalPostTestOralMiscues	.44419	.17720	.04575	.34606	.54232	9.708	14	.000
Pair 3	ExperimentalPretestComprehension - ExperimentalPostTestComprehension	-.11167	.10559	.02726	-.17014	-.05319	-4.096	14	.001

Table 10. Paired samples test on reading speed, oral reading miscues and comprehension level of the control group during their pretest and posttest

		Paired Samples Test							
		Paired Differences							
					95% Confidence Interval of the Difference		t	df	Sig. (2-tailed)
		Mean	Std. Deviation	Std. Error Mean	Lower	Upper			
Pair 1	ControlPretestReadingSpeed - ControlPostTestReadingSpeed	-13.38231	21.69970	4.33994	-22.33950	-4.42512	-3.084	24	.005
Pair 2	ControlPretestOralMiscues - ControlPostTestOralMiscues	.03555	.02710	.00542	.02437	.04674	6.560	24	.000
Pair 3	ControlPretestComprehension - ControlPostTestComprehension	-.24571	.07737	.01547	-.27765	-.21378	-15.879	24	.000

This means that the reading level of the students is influenced by the use of Immersive Reader and Reading Progress.

Significant Difference on the Reading Speed, Oral Reading Miscues and Comprehension Level of Control Group During Their Pretest and Posttest

The table presents the test of hypothesis on the difference of the control group's reading speed, oral reading miscues and reading comprehension before and after the treatment.

The data shows that there is a significant difference on the reading speed, oral reading miscues and reading comprehension of the respondents before and after the treatment since p-value $<= 0.05$.

This means that despite the traditional approach in teaching the students how to read, it has an impact to their learning in recognizing words.

Feedback of the Teacher-Facilitators in Using Reading Progress and Immersive Reader

Table 11 presents the thematic results of the interview of the researchers with the teacher-facilitators who spearheaded the implementation of the Reading Progress and Immersive Reader.

According to the respondents, the software can be learned easily, especially by the students. The software can be accessed on phones and laptops. This means that the software can be handy to the students especially those who do not have computers at home.

Since the Reading Progress and Immersive Reader are integrated in Microsoft Teams, updates and instructions can be easily transmitted to the students. The teacher

Table 11. Feedback of the teacher-facilitators in the experimental group

Theme	Description
Convenient	The software is easy to be used. The students can independently learn reading.
Flexible	They can teach the students at any time and any place.
Requires Online	The software requires internet.
Challenges the students to learn	There are features of the program that prohibits the students from proceeding to the next word that they have to learn unless they complete the present word that they find difficult
Perfect for the students today	Students are digital natives, they find this interesting.

can post the assignments and the students will be notified. Another is that students can engage themselves in formative and summative assessment in any place and at any time of the day.

However, the software requires an internet connection. The internet speed should be fast so that their video recording can be transmitted fast to MS Teams.

Despite being handy, the software can provide challenges to the students because of its feature of challenging the students to read every word correctly before proceeding to another word.

Lastly, the teacher-facilitators believe that Reading Progress and Immersive Reader are perfect to the digital natives today.

Feedback of the Teacher-Facilitators in the Control Group

One of the biggest advantages of traditional reading is the physical presence of the teacher who is conducting the intervention. With him/ her around, the miscues and challenges of the students can be easily determined. Moreover, an accurate description can be recorded thus being able to provide effective interventions.

The student can realize his/ her errors because of the immediate feedback that the students can receive from the teacher. For instance, if a student mispronounces a word, the teacher can give the student the correct pronunciation of that word and its meaning.

However, teaching the students how to read requires time. In the field, the teachers are having a hard time doing this because of their hectic schedule. For example, if the teacher has six teaching loads, s/he has to teach 6 hours then in his/ her two hours break, s/he can teach his/ her students. In a usual scenario, teachers are to report and do other clerical tasks that are also a priority thus compromising the reading schedule of the students.

Table 12. Feedback of the teacher-facilitators in the control group

Theme	Description
Focused	The teacher can concentrate to the students. The miscues and other reading errors can be easily determined.
Accurate Diagnosis	The mistake of the students can be accurately described.
Immediate Feedback	The teacher can immediately give feedback to the students such as telling the student's error and area of improvement.
Time consuming	It requires time to assess the students. It requires more time in giving intervention to the students
Assistance in Decoding Words	The teacher can have an opportunity in assisting the students in decoding words

Table 13. Proposed action plan in Department of Education – Region III based on results of the study

Timeline	Objective	Activity	Responsible Person/s	Success Indicators
July 2024	• To present the results of the study to the language Education Program Supervisors in Central Luzon • To explain the influence of Reading Progress and Immersive Reader, and in developing the reading speed and oral miscues of the students • To show to the language Education Program Supervisors the advantages and disadvantages of using traditional instruction, and Reading Progress and Immersive Reader in developing the reading skills of the students	• Consultative conference on the reading practices among the different school division offices in Central Luzon	• Researchers • Education Program Supervisors in language education • Master Teachers	• 100% attendance from the different school division offices in Central Luzon
July 2024	• To assess the schools in Central Luzon in terms of their capability to implement the Reading Progress and Immersive Reader • To pilot test the applications in selected schools to develop a concrete guideline on implementing the interventions	• Equipment Assessment: A Preparation for Pilot-testing the Reading Progress and Immersive Reader	• Researchers • Language Education Program Supervisors • Curriculum Implementation Division Units • School Principals • School ICT Coordinators	• List of schools who can implement the Reading Progress and Immersive Reader • Secured list of functioning computers and internet speed • Accomplishment report
August 2024	• Design a training-workshop for the different divisions in Central Luzon on using Reading Progress and Immersive Reader • Conduct a training-workshop on Reading Progress and Immersive Reader	• Training-workshop on the use of Reading Progress and Immersive Reader in Addressing the Reading Gaps of the Students in Central Luzon	• Language Education Program Supervisors • ICT Teachers • Reading Teachers	• Accomplishment report • 100% attendance across divisions
August 2024	• To develop an action plan for the different divisions focused engaging the parents and stakeholders in developing the reading skills of the students • To develop an action plan on addressing the reading gaps of the students	• Consultative meeting on crafting an action plan for the engagement of parents and stakeholders in developing the reading skills of the students	• Language Program Supervisors • School Principals • Reading Teachers • Advisers	• Transformative action plan

continued on following page

Table 13. Continued

Timeline	Objective	Activity	Responsible Person/s	Success Indicators
August 2024	• To consolidate the status of the reading skills of the students in Central Luzon through the Phil-IRI assessment	• Consolidation of the Phil-IRI Status in Central Luzon	• Language Program Supervisors • School Principals • Reading Teachers • Advisers	• Consolidated results of the Phil-IRI pretest report
September 2024 – March 2025	• To implement the action plans focused on Reading Progress and Immersive Reader in schools	• Implementation of Reading Progress and Immersive Reader in schools	• Language Program Supervisors • School Principals • Language Department Heads • Reading Teachers • Advisers	• Attendance of the students • Progress reports • Accomplish report
April 2025	• To assess the participating students using the Phil-IRI evaluation tool	• Posttest of participating learners using Phil-IRI	• Language Program Supervisors • School Principals • Language Department Heads • Reading Teachers	• Consolidated assessment reports based on Phil-IRI

LIMITATIONS

The study utilized a true experimental design thus utilizing a random sampling method, disabling the researchers to form groups that have the same characteristics. This limitation is due to the limited number of schools that are available to be a subject of the study during the time of the conduct of the study.

CONCLUSION AND RECOMMENDATIONS

With the data gathered, the study concludes that that the learners in the experimental group are more challenged than those from the control group because of their pre-conditions. This shows that students who are in the reading programs are in the frustration level are not only those who are struggling from pronouncing words per se but also those who have problems in comprehension.

It was also found that the students in the control group are struggling in comprehension but not in word forms. This is contrary to the experimental group who have difficulty in all the indicators of reading levels. This can be considered as a limitation of the study since it used a true experimental design of research.

In terms of the reading speed of the students, it was observed that the students have a low speed of words-per-minute, lower than the standard 150-200 wpm for junior high school students. However, both variables have an influence on the reading performance of the students. Between the two groups, the independent variable applied in the experimental group, the application of Reading Progress and Immersive Reader, had a more impact to the students since it decreased the miscues of 95% to 49% [as compared to the controlled group that only decreased 1%].

In terms of comprehension, the traditional method of teaching in reading influenced the comprehension score of the students while the Reading Progress and Immersive Reader remained the students into "frustration" level. This means that the traditional approach in teaching reading has a more influence in developing the comprehension skills of the students than using the Immersive Reader and Reading Progress. This can be attributed to the physical presence of the teacher as s/he teaches reading.

Based on the data, traditional reading is deemed to be more holistic than the Reading Progress and Immersive Reader in teaching the students how to read. However, it requires focus and time on the part of the teacher.

In the test of difference, there is a significant difference between the pretest and post test results of both groups. Hence, the study concludes that both strategies in teaching reading are still applicable to today's students.

With the data gathered, the developed action plan for the dissemination and application of this study's results focuses on consultative conferences, crafting of the action plan, engagement of the stakeholders and parents, assessment of the students and implementation of the reading interventions.

Armed with the conclusions of the study, the study came up with different recommendations.

The Department of Education may consider cascading the Immersive Reader and Reading Progress in the schools so that teachers can add it to their arsenal of strategies in teaching reading. This will be beneficial to the teachers who have other workloads aside from teaching. With the application, the teachers can teach the students how to read words in their correct forms without compromising their classes or other tasks.

The Teachers can consider Reading Progress and Immersive Reader as a way of remediating the students' learning gaps especially in high school where the students are *reading to learn* than *learning to read*. This will be helpful in addressing reading miscues and challenges in the reading speed of the students.

Those schools that have computers and internet connection can consider maximizing the o365 accounts so that computers can be their allies in fighting illiteracy and learning gaps in reading. This can also be a way for the students technology skills to be developed, which is also an essential factor in taking up large-scale assessments such as PISA.

In terms of the design of the present study, a quasi-experimental design can be considered by future researchers to further study the impact of Reading Progress and Immersive Reader to the reading skills of the students.

Because of the developing reading gaps in the country, the proposed action plan may be implemented in a year so that an efficient guideline or handbook may be developed. This can enable the Department of Education to create a resource for addressing the reading gaps of the students in terms of reading speed and oral reading miscues efficiently. Also, once the action plans are implemented, a brighter light for stakeholders and parents' engagement will be discovered, which might be a great help in combating learning loss in reading.

ACKNOWLEDGMENT

The researchers acknowledge the invaluable efforts and support of different individuals who have enabled them to finish this study: Department of Education Regional Director May B. Eclar, PhD, CESO III; Curriculum, Learning and Management Division of Region III, Librada M. Rubio, PhD; Danica Guevarra and Mark Nathaniel G. Pascual, the department heads of the schools where the research was conducted.

Funding: The research received no funding grant from any agency in the public, private or non-profit entities.

REFERENCES

Cunningham, A. E., & Stanovich, K. E. (1997). Early reading acquisition and its relation to reading experience and ability 10 years later. *Developmental Psychology*, *33*(6), 934–945. doi:10.1037/0012-1649.33.6.934 PMID:9383616

DeCarlo, M., Cummings, C., & Agnelli, K. (n.d.). True Experimental Design. *Graduate Research Methods in Social Work*. Research Gate.

Department of Education. (2014). The effects of remedial reading among elementary students. Department of Education. http://www.udyong.gov.ph/index. php?option=com_content&view=article&id=5787:the-effects-of-remedial-reading-among-elementary-students&catid=90&Itemid=1368

Department of Education. (2021, December 6). *DepEd encourages teachers, parents to use Reading Progress Tool to assess learners' reading skills*. Department of Education. https://www.deped.gov.ph/2021/12/06/deped-encourages-teachers-parents-to-use-reading-progress-tool-to-assess-learners-reading-skills/

Flippo, R. (2014). *Assessing readers qualitative diagnosis and instruction* (2nd ed.). Copublished with Routledge/Taylor & Francis. http://www.reading.org/Libraries/books/assessing-readers--second-ed--chapter3.pdf doi:10.4324/9780203118825

Inquirer News. (2022, June 1). PH ranks last in reading, second to last in science, math among 79 countries in Pisa. *News Info*. https://newsinfo.inquirer.net/1502996/ph-ranks-last-in-reading-second-to-last-in-science-math-among-79-countries-in-pisa

Krashen, S. D. (1993). *The power of reading: Insights from the research* (2nd ed.). Libraries Unlimited.

Manila Bulletin. (2019, December 25). DepEd orders schools to 'intensify' reading advocacy. *Manila Bulletin*. https://mb.com.ph/2019/12/25/deped-orders-schools-to-intensify-reading-advocacy/

Microsoft Learn Educator Center. (n.d.). *Immersive Reader*. Microsoft. https://learn.microsoft.com/en-us/training/educator-center/product-guides/immersive-reader/

Microsoft Learn Educator Center. (n.d.). *Reading progress product guide*. Microsoft. https://learn.microsoft.com/en-us/training/educator-center/product-guides/reading-progress/

National Institute of Child Health and Human Development. (2000). *Teaching children to read: An evidence-based assessment of the scientific research literature on reading and its implications for reading instruction*. Report of the National Reading Panel. (NIH Publication No. 00-4769). U.S. Government Printing Office.

Philstar.com. (2023, July 7). *DepEd to launch reading, math and science programs in learning recovery plan*. PhilStar. https://www.philstar.com/headlines/2023/07/07/2279406/deped-launch-reading-math-and-science-programs-learning-recovery-plan

Philstar.com. (2023, July 7). *DepEd to launch reading, math and science programs in learning recovery plan*. PhilStar. https://www.philstar.com/headlines/2023/07/07/2279406/deped-launch-reading-math-and-science-programs-learning-recovery-plan

UNICEF. (2021). *Alternative learning system in the Philippines: A review of the evidence*. UNICEF.

UNICEF Philippines. (2021). *Southeast Asia Primary Learning Metrics 2019 National Report of the Philippines*. UNICEF Philippines. https://www.unicef.org/philippines/reports/sea-plm-metrics-2019-national-report-philippines

APPENDIX

*Figure 1. The head teacher and language teacher of the control group, Telabastagan
Integrated School, as they remediate students with traditional way of teaching reading*

Figure 2. The head teacher and teacher of Parada National High School with the experimental group as they implement Reading Progress and Immersive Reading

Compilation of References

Aabø, S., & Audunson, R. (2012). Use of library space and the library as place. *Library & Information Science Research*, *34*(2), 138–149. doi:10.1016/j.lisr.2011.06.002

Abiodun-Oyebanji, O. J. (2019). Emerging issues in the school-community relations. In D. A. Adeyemo, D. A. Oluwole, & A. O. Busari (Eds.), *Counselling and contemporary social issues in multicultural settings*.

Abreu, P. M., Fricke, S., & Wealer, C. (2020). Effects of an early literacy intervention for linguistically diverse children: A quasi-experimental study. *Frontiers in Psychology*, *11*, 569854.

Ahmad, F. K. (2015). Use of assistive technology in inclusive education: Making room for diverse learning needs. *Transcience*, *6*(2), 62–77.

Ahmad, Z., Soroya, M. S., Tariq, M., & Chaudhry, M. S. (2021). An empirical analysis of parental involvement in leisure reading development of the children. *Library Philosophy and Practice*, *5012*, 1–20.

Akyol, H. (2012). *Türkçe ilk okuma yazma öğretimi*. Pegem Akademi.

Aldridge, D. (2019). Reading, engagement, and higher education. *Higher Education Research & Development*, *38*(1), 38–50. doi:10.1080/07294360.2018.1534804

Allen, N. (2009). Making a difference – Better beginnings family literacy program. *The Australian Library Journal*, *58*(4), 369–376. doi:10.1080/00049670.2009.10735925

AlWadi, H. (2020). Bahrain's Secondary EFL Teacher' Belief of English Language National Examination: 'How it made teaching different?' *International Journal of Instruction. 13*: 1, 197-214. chrome-extension://efaidnbmnnnibpcajpcglclefindmkaj/https://www.e-iji.net/dosyalar/iji_2020_1_13.pdf

Amaria, K. H., & Hafidz, N. (2021). Upaya pemberdayaan masyarakat oleh rumah kreatif wadas kelir melalui penguatan literasi. *Jurnal AKRAB*, *12*(2), 12–19. doi:10.51495/jurnalakrab.v12i2.405

Amir, A. (2019). The effect of reading strategies and speed reading on students' reading comprehension skill in higher education. *Paper presented at the Advances in Social Science, education, and Humanities research. Proceedings of the Seventh International Conference on Languages and Arts (ICLA 2018)*. IEEE. 10.2991/icla-18.2019.68

Anagurthi, C. (2017). *Applying an ecological model to predict adolescent academic achievement.* [Doctoral thesis, Wayne State University]. https://digitalcommons.wayne.edu/oa_dissertations/1684

Anand, P., & Ackley, S. (2021). Assessment of 21 Century Skills & Academic Literacies: From Theory to Practice. Senior Editor: Paul Robertson, 119.

Anani, G. E., Lamptey, H. K., & Frempong, C. O. (2021). Redefining literacy in a digital age: The role of instructors in promoting digital literacy. *Journal of English Language Teaching and Applied Linguistics, 3*(8), 20–25. doi:10.32996/jeltal.2021.3.8.3

Anaxagorou, George. (2023). Teachers' and community stakeholders' perceptions about school-community relations in Cyprus. *International Journal about Parents in Education, 1.* https://doi. doi:10.54195/ijpe.18249

Anderson-Butcher, D., Bates, S., Lawson, H. A., Childs, T. M., & Lachini, A. L. (2022). The community collaboration model for school improvement: A scoping review. *Education Sciences, 12*(918), 1–20. doi:10.3390/educsci12120918

Anderson-Butcher, D., Lachini, A. L., Ball, A., Barke, S., & Martin, L. D. (2016). A university–school partnership to examine the adoption and implementation of the Ohio community collaboration model in one urban school district: A mixed-method case study. *Journal of Education for Students Placed at Risk, 21*(3), 190–204. doi:10.1080/10824669.2016.1183429

Anderson-Butcher, D., Paluta, L., Sterling, K., & Anderson, C. (2018). Ensuring healthy youth development through community schools: A case study. *Children & Schools, 40*(1), 7–16. doi:10.1093/cs/cdx026

Anderson-Yockel, J., & Haynes, O. W. (1994). Joint book-reading strategies in working-class african american and white mother-toddler dyads. *Journal of Speech and Hearing Research, 37*(3), 583–593. doi:10.1044/jshr.3703.583 PMID:8084190

Aram, D., Most, T., & Mayafit, H. (2006). Contributions of mother-child storybook telling and joint writing to literacy development in kindergartners with hearing loss. *Language, Speech, and Hearing Services in Schools, 37*(3), 209–223. doi:10.1044/0161-1461(2006/023) PMID:16837444

Arbarini, M., Jutmini, S., Djoyoatmojo, S., & Sutarno, S. (2015). Implementation of functional literacy education by participatory learning as effort of lifelong learning. In *Proceeding of the International Conference on Teacher Training and Education, 2*(1), 734-745. https://jurnal.uns.ac.id/ictte/article/view/7630 accessed March 10, 2024.

Arbarini, M., Jutmini, S., Joyoatmojo, S., Jutmini, S., & Joyoatmojo, S. (2017). Participatory learning model on adults literacy education of rural communities. *International Journal of Education, Psychology and Counseling, 2*(6), 153-164. http://www.ijepc.com/PDF/IJEPC-2017-06-12-09.pdf

Arendale, D. R., & Lee, N. L. (2018). Bridge Programs. In R. F. Flippo & T. W. Bean (Eds.), *Handbook of College Reading and Study Strategy Research* (3rd ed., pp. 281–292). Routledge. doi:10.4324/9781315629810-20

Arslan, M. L. (2018). Sivil toplum kuruluşlarında gönüllülük: Sorunlar ve çözüm yolları. *İlke Politika Notları, 4*, 1-16. https://kurumsalyonetim.org/images/sivil-toplum-kuruluslarinda-gonulluluk-sorunlar-cozum-yollari-pdf-ilke-org-tr.pdf

Arthur, J., Harrison, T., Taylor-Collins, E., & Moller, F. (2017). *A habit of service: The factors that sustain service in young people (Report).* Jubilee Centre for Character and Virtues, University of Birmingham.

Atlar, H., & Uzuner, Y. (2018). Okul oncesi donemdeki isitme kayıplı bir cocugun gelisen okuryazarlık yasantılarının incelenmesi [Examining the emergent literacy experiences of a preschool child with hearing loss]. *Journal of Qualitative Research in Education, 6*(1), 54–89. doi:10.14689/issn.2148-2624.1.6c1s3m

Auerbach, S. (2011). Conceptualizing leadership for authentic partnerships: A continuum to inspire practice. In S. Auerbach (Ed.), *School leadership for authentic family and community partnerships: Research perspectives for transforming practice* (pp. 29–51). Routledge.

Australian Curriculum, Assessment and Reporting Authority. (2021, August 25). *NAPLAN 2021 summary results data: No major impacts on learning from COVID-19 evident - long-term trends positive* [Press release]. ACARA. https://www.acara.edu.au/docs/default-source/media-releases/20210813-naplan-results-med-rel.pdf

Ayaz, H. (2021). Dijital Melezlerin Dijital Yurttaşlık Seviyelerinin Haber Yayılımı Bağlamında İncelenmesi. *Trt Akademi, 6*(12), 364-395. https://dergipark.org.tr/en/pub/trta/article/901959

Aydoğan Boschele, F. (2021). Dijital Tekolojilerin Vatandaşı ve Politikası. *Middle Black Sea Journal of Communication Studies, 6*(2), 58-63. https://dergipark.org.tr/tr/pub/mbsjcs/issue/67099/1009899

Azeez, N., & Akhtar, S. (2021). Digital financial literacy and its determinants: An empirical evidences from rural India. *South Asian Journal of Social Studies and Economics, 11*(2), 8–22. doi:10.9734/sajsse/2021/v11i230279

Baccal, V. S., & Ormilla, R. C. G. (2021). The implementation of alternative learning system in public schools in Isabela, Philippines. *EDUCATUM Journal of Social Sciences, 7*(1), 19–29. doi:10.37134/ejoss.vol7.1.3.2021

Bachman, L. F. (1990). *Fundamental considerations in language testing.* Oxford University Press.

Bachman, L. F., & Palmer, A. S. (2010). *Language assessment in practice: Developing language assessments and justifying their use in the real world.* Oxford University Press.

Badgett, K. (2016). School-business partnerships: Understanding business perspectives. *School Community Journal, 26*(2), 83–105. https://files.eric.ed.gov/fulltext/EJ1123994.pdf

Bahrain Teachers College [@btc]. (2024, February 21). *Artificial intelligence day as a* [Video]. Instagram. https://www.instagram.com/reel/C3m2ak1svWJ/?igsh=NjZiM2M3MzIxNA==

Balaban, A. Y., & İnce, İ. Ç. (2015). Gençlerin sivil toplum kuruluşlarındaki gönüllülük faaliyetleri ve gönüllülük algısı: türkiye eğitim gönüllüleri vakfı (tegv) örneği. *Dokuz Eylül University Journal of Faculty of Economics and Administrative Sciences, 30*(2), 149-169. https://dergipark.org.tr/en/pub/deuiibfd/issue/22713/242424

Ballantyne, E. (2020). Book Review: Critical Reading in Higher Education. *The Canadian Journal for the Scholarship of Teaching and Learning, 11*(1). doi:10.5206/cjsotl-rcacea.2020.1.8241

Barratt-Pugh, C., Hill, S., Johnson, N. F., Barblett, L., & Parker, A. (2022). Designing and implementing a family literacy program through smartphones: How does recruitment method influence uptake and attrition? *Early Childhood Education Journal*, 1–12. Advance online publication. doi:10.1007/s10643-022-01433-z PMID:36597553

Becker, K. (2012). 24 hours in the children's section: An observational study at the public library. *Early Childhood Education Journal, 40*(2), 107–114. doi:10.1007/s10643-011-0499-0

Beers, S. (2011). *21st century skills: Preparing students for their future*. U Maine. https: https://cosee.umaine.edu/files/coseeos/21st_century_skills.pdf

Beetham, H., & Sharpe, R. (Eds.). (2019). *Rethinking pedagogy for a digital age: Principles and practices of design*. Routledge. doi:10.4324/9781351252805

Bekar, S., & Sağlam, M. (2023). Siber âlem: Yeni medya ve dijital yurttaşlık. *Niğde Ömer Halisdemir Üniversitesi İletişim Fakültesi Akademik Dergisi, 2*(2), 133-144. https://dergipark.org.tr/en/pub/nohuifad/issue/81919/1374065

Benavides, K. R. (2022*). Leading for sustainability in school- community partnerships*. [Thesis, ACU].

Benner, A. D., Boyle, A. E., & Sadler, S. (2016). Parental involvement and adolescents' educational success: The roles of prior achievement and socioeconomic status. *Journal of Youth and Adolescence, 45*(6), 1053–1064. doi:10.1007/s10964-016-0431-4 PMID:26847424

Bennett, R. E. (2011). Formative assessment: A critical review. *Assessment in Education: Principles, Policy & Practice, 18*(1), 5–25. doi:10.1080/0969594X.2010.513678

Bentahar, A., & O'Brien, J. (2019). Raising students' awareness of social justice through civic literacy. *Journal of social studies education research, 10*(1), 193-218. https://dergipark.org.tr/en/pub/jsser/issue/45447/570410

Bergeron, J. P. (2013). *Effectiveness of parent training on shared reading practices in families with children who are deaf and hard of hearing*, [Phd Dissertation, Atlanta Georgia State University, USA].

Berkowitz, R., Astor, R. A., Pineda, D., DePedro, K. T., Weiss, E. L., & Benbenishty, R. (2021). Parental involvement and perceptions of school climate in California. *Urban Education, 56*(3), 393–423. doi:10.1177/0042085916685764

Bers, M. U. (2010). Beyond computer literacy: Supporting youth's positive development through technology. *New Directions for Youth Development*, *2010*(128), 13–23. doi:10.1002/yd.371 PMID:21240949

Better Beginnings report: Making a difference: the evaluation of the better beginnings birth to three family literacy program 14 years (2017). Australia: School of Education Early Childhood Research Group Edith Cowan University. https://www.better-beginnings.com.au/research/research-about-better-beginnings/making-difference

Bhatia, V., Anthony, L., & Noguchi, J. (2011). ESP in the 21st century: ESP theory and application today. *Proceedings of the JACET 50th Commemorative International Convention, Aug. 30-Sept.2,* (pp. 143-150). Seinan Gakuin University.

Bhatia, V. (2017). *Critical genre analysis: Investigating interdiscursive performance in professional practice*. Routledge.

Bilal, M., & Zulfiqar, M. (2016). Financial wellbeing is the goal of financial literacy. *Research Journal of Finance and Accounting*, *7*(11), 94–103.

Billington, C. (2016). *How digital technology can support early language and literacy outcomes in early years settings: A review of the literature*. National Literacy Trust.

Bincan, S. (2020). E-Devlet Uygulamaları Üzerine Bir İnceleme: Polonya ve Slovakya Örneği. *ASSAM Uluslararası Hakemli Dergi*, *7*(16), 41-57. https://dergipark.org.tr/en/pub/assam/issue/53879/626341

Blackledge, A., & Creese, A. (2017). Translanguaging in mobility. In S. Canagarajah (Ed.), *The Routledge Handbook of Migration and Language* (pp. 31–46). Taylor & Francis. doi:10.4324/9781315754512-2

Black, P., & Wiliam, D. (1998). Assessment and classroom learning. *Assessment in Education: Principles, Policy & Practice*, *5*(1), 7–74. doi:10.1080/0969595980050102

Blaiser, K. M., Edwards, M., Behl, D., & Munoz, K. F. (2012). Telepractice services at sound beginnings at Utah State University. *The Volta Review*, *112*(3), 365–372.

Bodrova, E., & Leong, J. D. (2010). *Zihnin araçları erken çocukluk eğitiminde Vygotsky yaklaşımı* (T. Güler, F. Şahin, A. Yılmaz, & E. Kalkan, Eds.). Anı Publishing.

Bookstart report: An evaluation of the bookstart corner programme parents' survey. (2014). UK: BookTrust/ActionPoint Marketing Solutions. https://www.buchstart.at/data/bookstart-corner-evaluation.pdf

Boonk, L., Gijselaers, H. J., Ritzen, H., & Brand-Gruwel, S. (2018). A review of the relationship between parental involvement indicators and academic achievement. *Educational Research Review*, *24*, 10–30. doi:10.1016/j.edurev.2018.02.001

Borg, M. E. (2017). Building Sustainable Businesses: The importance of Financial Literacy for Entrepreneurs. https://epale.ec.europa.eu/en/blog/building-sustainable-businesses-importance-financial-literacy-entrepreneurs

Boyalı, H. (2023). Türkiye'de Vatandaş Odaklı İdare: E- Devlet Ötesi Dijitalleşen Kamu. *Bucak İşletme Fakültesi Dergisi, 6*(2), 172–190. doi:10.38057/bifd.1325556

Bracken, S. S., & Fischel, J. E. (2008). Family reading behavior and early literacy skills in preschool children from low-income backgrounds. *Early Education and Development, 19*(1), 45–67. doi:10.1080/10409280701838835

Brice Heath, S. (1983). *Ways with words language, life and work in communities and classrooms.* Cambridge University Press. doi:10.1017/CBO9780511841057

Britt, N., Bates, S., Anderson-Butcher, D., Edwards, R., Noteman, N., Bardy, C., DuMond, L., & Childs, T.M. (2022). University-assisted community schools as partners in neighborhood revitalization efforts. *Child. Sch.*

Bronfenbrenner, U. (1994). Ecological models of human development. *International encyclopedia of education, 3*(2), 37-43.

Bronfenbrenner, U. (1999). *Environments in developmental perspective: Theoretical and operational models.*

Bronfenbrenner, U. (1979). *The ecology of human development.* Harvard University Press. doi:10.4159/9780674028845

Bronfenbrenner, U. (2005). Making human beings human: Bioecological perspectives on human development. *Sage (Atlanta, Ga.).*

Bronfenbrenner, U., & Ceci, S. J. (1994). Nature-nurture reconceptualized in developmental perspective: A bioecological model. *Psychological Review, 101*(4), 568–586. doi:10.1037/0033-295X.101.4.568 PMID:7984707

Brookhart, S., & Nitko, A. (2008). *Assessment and grading in classrooms.* Pearson Publishing.

Brooks Young, S. (2016). *ISTE Standarts for Young Students.* ISTE Publising.

Brouwer, K., Downing, H., Westhoff, S., Wait, R., Entwisle, L. K., Messersmith, J. J., & Hanson, E. K. (2017). Effects of clinician-guided emergent literacy intervention using interactive tablet technology for preschool children with cochlear implants. *Communication Disorders Quarterly, 38*(4), 195–205.

Browns, F. (1979). Beginning reading instruction with hearing-impaired children. *The Volta Review, 100*–108.

Bruner, J. (1972). Child's play. J. Bruner (Ed.),(2006), In search of pedagogy volume I: The selected works of Jerome S. Bruner içinde (s. 162-166). Oxon: Routledge.

Bryk, A., & Schneider, B. (2002). *Trust in schools: A course resource for improvement*. Russell Sage.

Buchholz, B., DeHart, J., & Moorman, G. (2020). Digital citizenship during a global pandemic: Moving beyond digital literacy. *Journal of Adolescent & Adult Literacy, 64*(1), 11 17. doi: https:// doi.org/ doi:10.1002/jaal.1076

Burnett, C., & Merchant, G. (2013). Learning, literacies and new technologies: The current context and future possibilities. The Sage handbook of early childhood literacy, 2, 575-586.

Burnett, C., Dickinson, P., Myers, J., & Merchant, G. (2006). Digital connections: Transforming literacy in the primary school. *Cambridge Journal of Education, 36*(1), 11–29. doi:10.1080/03057640500491120

Cabunilas, A. J. A., Gabutero, A. O., & Baluno, A. B. (2023). Enhanced implementation of community learning center based on the reading level of the learners of San Roque elementary school during pandemic. *AIDE Interdisciplinary Research Journal, 4*, 51–62. doi:10.56648/ aide-irj.v4i1.43

Cairney, T. H., & Munsie, L. (1995). Parent participation in literacy learning. *The Reading Teacher, 48*(5), 392–403.

Campbell, D. E. (2010). *Why we vote*. Princeton University Press. doi:10.1515/9781400837618

Can, S., & Eke, E. (2020). E-Devlet Kullanıcılarının Bilgi ve Memnuniyet Düzeylerine Yönelik Bir Araştırma. *Dumlupınar Üniversitesi Sosyal Bilimler Dergisi* (64), 19-37. https://dergipark. org.tr/tr/pub/dpusbe/issue/53850/621551

Canale, M., & Swain, M. (1980). Theoretical bases of communicative approaches to second language teaching and testing. *Applied Linguistics, 1*(1), 1–47. doi:10.1093/applin/1.1.1

Carroll, K. S., & Sambolín Morales, A. N. (2016). Using university students' L1 as a resource: Translanguaging in a Puerto Rican ESL classroom. *Bilingual Research Journal, 39*(3-4), 248–262. doi:10.1080/15235882.2016.1240114

Cartelli, A. (2009). Frameworks for digital literacy and digital competence assessment. In *Proceedings of the 8th European Conference on e-Learning* (pp. 116-123). IEEE.

Carvalho, M. d. C. (2019). A Literacia Financeira: O caso dos alunos do ensino superior Universidade do Minho].

Castro, M., Expósito-Casas, E., López-Martín, E., Lizasoain, L., Navarro-Asencio, E., & Gaviria, J. L. (2015). Parental involvement on student academic achievement: A meta-analysis. *Educational Research Review, 14*, 33–46. doi:10.1016/j.edurev.2015.01.002

Catalano, T., & Hamann, E. T. (2016). Multilingual pedagogies and pre-service teachers: Implementing "language as a resource" orientations in teacher education programs. *Bilingual Research Journal, 39*(3-4), 263–278. doi:10.1080/15235882.2016.1229701

Ceci, S. J. (2006). Urie Bronfenbrenner (1917- 2005). *The American Psychologist*, 61. PMID:16478360

Cele, N. (2021). Understanding language policy as a tool for access and social inclusion in South African higher education: A critical policy analysis perspective. *South African Journal of Higher Education*, *35*(6), 25–46. doi:10.20853/35-6-3730

Cenoz, J., & Gorter, D. (2021). *Pedagogical translanguaging*. Cambridge University Press.

Chaka Chaka, C. (2020). Translanguaging, Decoloniality, and the Global South: An Integrative Review Study. *Scrutiny*, *2*, 6-42. doi:10.1080/18125441.2020.1802617

Chalhoub-Deville, M. (2003). Second language interaction: Current perspectives and future trends. *Language Testing*, *20*(4), 369–383. doi:10.1191/0265532203lt264oa

Chapelle, C. A., & Plakans, L. (2013). Assessment and testing: Overview. In C. A. Chapelle (Ed.), *The encyclopedia of applied linguistics* (pp. 240–244). Blackwell/Wiley. doi:10.1002/9781405198431

Cheng, L., & Curtis, A. (2004). Washback or backwash: A review of the impact of testing on teaching and learning. In L. Cheng & Y. Watanabe (Eds.), *Washback in language testing: research contexts and methods* (pp. 3–17). Lawrence Erlbaum. doi:10.4324/9781410609731-9

Chen, P. H., & Liu, T. W. (2017). A pilot study of telepractice for teaching listening and spoken language to Mandarin-speaking children with congenital hearing loss. *Deafness & Education International*, *19*(3-4), 134–143.

Chong, S. W., & Isaacs, T. (2023). An Ecological Perspective on Classroom-Based Assessment. *TESOL Quarterly*, *57*(4), 1558–1570. doi:10.1002/tesq.3201

Chong, S. W., Isaacs, T., & McKinley, J. (2023). Ecological systems theory and second language research. *Language Teaching*, *56*(3), 333–348. doi:10.1017/S0261444822000283

Clary, D. M. (2008). *Literacy learning communities in partnership*, 1-11.

Clay, M. M. (1975). *What did I write? beginning writing behaviour*. Heinemann Educational Books.

Clay, M. M. (2015). *Becoming literate the construcition of inner control*. The Mary Clay Literacy Trust.

Clegg, J., & Simpson, J. (2016). Improving the effectiveness of English as a medium of instruction in sub-Saharan Africa. *Comparative Education*, *52*(3), 359–374. doi:10.1080/03050068.2016 .1185268

Cleveland, B. (2023). A framework for building schools as community hubs: If it were simpler would it happen everywhere? In B. Cleveland, S. Backhouse, P. Chandler, I. McShane, J. M. Clinton, & C. Newton (Eds.), Schools as community hubs building 'more than a school' for community benefit (p. 11-28). Springer. doi:10.1007/978-981-19-9972-7_3

Coley, R. J., & Sum, A. (2012). *Fault Lines in Our Democracy: Civic Knowledge, Voting Behavior, and Civic Engagement in the United States*. Educational Testing Service.

Collins, A., & Halverson, R. (2018). *Rethinking education in the age of technology: The digital revolution and schooling in America*. Teachers College Press.

Compton-Lilly, C. F., Rogers, R. L., & Lewis Ellison, T. (2020). A meta-ethnography of family literacy scholarship: Ways with metaphors and silence. *Reading Research Quarterly*, *55*(2), 271–289. doi:10.1002/rrq.272

Connell, S. L., Lauricella, A. R., & Wartella, E. (2015). Parental co-use of media technology with their young children in the USA. *Journal of Children and Media*, *9*(1), 5–21. doi:10.1080/17482798.2015.997440

Constantine, J. L. (2004). *Relationships among early lexical and literacy skills and language-literacy environments at home and school*. [Phd Dissertation, A.B.D: South Florida Collage of Education].

Consumer Financial Protection Bureau. (2015). *Financial Well-Being: The Goal of Financial Education*. Consumer Finance. https://files.consumerfinance.gov/f/201501_cfpb_report_financial-well-being.pdf

Conway, D. (1985). Children recreating writing: A preliminary look at the purposes of free-choice writing of hearing impaired kindergarteners. *The Volta Review*, *87*, 91–107.

Cook, S. (2016). *Integrating Technology in Early Literacy: A Snapshot of Community Innovation in Family Engagement*. New America.

Cooper, L. Z., & Pace, J. (2004). Early literacy in a collaborative community service project. *Knowledge Quest*, *33*(2).

Cope, B., & Kalantzis, M. (2000). *Multiliteracies: Literacy learning and the design of social futures*. Routledge.

Coutinho, C. P. (2014). *Metodologia de investigação em ciências sociais e humanas*. Leya.

Cruzat, M., Cruzat, A. P., & Javillonar, M. G. (2022). The school and its stakeholders: Partners in building a strong school community. *International Journal of Multidisciplinary Research and Growth Evaluation*, *3*(4), 314–418.

Cummins, J. (2019). Should schools undermine or sustain multilingualism? An analysis of theory, research, and pedagogical practice. *Darnioji daugiakalbystė 15*(1), 1–26. doi:10.2478/sm-2019-0011

Cunningham, A. E., & Stanovich, K. E. (1997). Early reading acquisition and its relation to reading experience and ability 10 years later. *Developmental Psychology*, *33*(6), 934–945. doi:10.1037/0012-1649.33.6.934 PMID:9383616

Dahlgren, P. (2013). *The political web: Media, participation and alternative democracy*. Springer. doi:10.1057/9781137326386

Dalton, E. M. (2017). Beyond universal design for learning: Guiding principles to reduce barriers to digital & media literacy competence. *The Journal of Media Literacy Education*, 9(2), 17–29. doi:10.23860/JMLE-2019-09-02-02

Damber, U. (2015). Read-alouds in preschool–A matter of discipline? *Journal of Early Childhood Literacy*, 15(2), 256–280. doi:10.1177/1468798414522823

Daniel, S. M., Jiménez, R. T., Pray, L., & Pacheco, M. B. (2019). Scaffolding to make translanguaging a classroom norm. *TESOL Journal*, 10(1), e00361. doi:10.1002/tesj.361

Darling-Hammond, L., Holtzman, D. J., Gatlin, S. J., & Heilig, J. V. (2005). Does teacher preparation matter? Evidence about teacher certification, Teach for America, and teacher effectiveness. *Education Policy Analysis Archives*, 13(42), 42. doi:10.14507/epaa.v13n42.2005

DeCarlo, M., Cummings, C., & Agnelli, K. (n.d.). True Experimental Design. *Graduate Research Methods in Social Work*. Research Gate.

Decree Law No 573, MoNe [Ministry of National Education]. (1997). Decree law on special education no. 573, Official Gazette dated 06.06.1997 and numbered 23011.

Dei, G. J., James, I. M., Karumanchery, L. L., James-Wilson, S., & Zine, J. (2000). *Removing the margins: The challenges & possibilities of inclusive schooling*. Canadian Scholars' Press.

Department of Education. (2014). The effects of remedial reading among elementary students. Department of Education. http://www.udyong.gov.ph/index.php?option=com_content&view=article&id=5787:the-effects-of-remedial-reading-among-elementary-students&catid=90&Itemid=1368

Department of Education. (2021, December 6). *DepEd encourages teachers, parents to use Reading Progress Tool to assess learners' reading skills*. Department of Education. https://www.deped.gov.ph/2021/12/06/deped-encourages-teachers-parents-to-use-reading-progress-tool-to-assess-learners-reading-skills/

Desjardin, J. L., Doll, E. R., Stika, C. J., Eisenberg, L. S., Johnson, K. C., Hammus Gangully, D. M., Colson, B. G., & Henning, S. C. (2014). Parental support for language development during joint book reading for young children with hearing loss. *Communication Disorders Quarterly*, 35(3), 167–181. doi:10.1177/1525740113518062 PMID:25309136

Desjardin, J. L., Stika, C. J., Eisenberg, L. S., Johnson, K. C., Hammus Gangully, D. M., Henning, S. C., & Colson, B. G. (2017). A longitudinal investigation of the home literacy environment and shared book reading in young children with hearing loss. *Ear and Hearing*, 38(4), 441–454. doi:10.1097/AUD.0000000000000414 PMID:28234669

Detlor, B., Julien, H., La Rose, T., & Serenko, A. (2022). Community-led digital literacy training: Toward a conceptual framework. *Journal of the Association for Information Science and Technology*, 73(10), 1387–1400. doi:10.1002/asi.24639

Dhokotera, C., & Makalela, L. (2022). The Carry-over Effect of Monolingual Teacher Education Programmes: Towards a Decolonized University. In L. Makalela (Ed.), *Language and Institutional Identity in the Post-Apartheid South African Higher Education. Language Policy* (Vol. 27). Springer. doi:10.1007/978-3-030-85961-9_5

Dias, B. A. F. (2017). *O Financiamento, as Despesas e a Literacia Financeira dos Estudantes do Ensino Superior Instituto Politecnico do Porto.*

Dias, L., & Victor, A. (2022). Teaching and learning with mobile devices in the 21st century digital world: Benefits and challenges. *European Journal of Multidisciplinary Studies*, *7*(1), 26–34.

Dickinson, D. K., & Caswell, L. (2007). Building support for language and early literacy in preschool classrooms through in-service professional development: Effects of the literacy environment enrichment program. *Early Childhood Research Quarterly*, *22*(2), 243–260. doi:10.1016/j.ecresq.2007.03.001

Didiharyono, D., & Qur'ani, B. (2019). Increasing community knowledge through the literacy movement. To Maega. *Jurnal Pengabdian Masyarakat*, *2*(1), 17–24. doi:10.35914/tomaega. v2i1.235

D'Ignazio, C., & Bhargava, R. (2016). *DataBasic: Design principles, tools and activities for data literacy learners.*

Direção-Geral de Estatísticas da Educação e Ciência. (2021). *Vagas e Inscritos (inclui inscritos em mobilidade internacional).* DGEEC. https://www.dgeec.mec.pt/np4/EstatVagasInsc/

Dirks, E., & Wauters, L. (2018). It takes two to read: Interactive reading with young deaf and hard-of-hearing children. *Journal of Deaf Studies and Deaf Education*, *23*(3), 261–270.

Dogan, S. (2018). *Bir ogretmenin okul oncesi donemdeki isitme kayıplı bir cocukla kitap okuma uygulamalarinin incelenmesi.* [Md Dissertation. Eskisehir: Anadolu University].

Domingue, B. W., Dell, M., Lang, D., Silverman, R., Yeatman, J., & Hough, H. (2022). The effect of COVID on oral reading fluency during the 2020–2021 academic year. *AERA Open*, *8*. Advance online publication. doi:10.1177/23328584221120254

Dorn, E., Hancock, B., Sarakatsannis, J., & Viruleg, E. (2020, June 1). *COVID-19 and student learning in the United States: The hurt could last a lifetime.* Apucis. https://www.apucis. com/frontend-assets/porto/initial-reports/COVID-19- and-student-learning-in-the-United-StatesFINAL.pdf.pagespeed.ce.VHbS948yF4.pdf

Dudley, R. L., & Gitelson, A. R. (2010). Political Literacy, Civic Education, and Civic Engagement: A Return to Political Socialization? *Applied Developmental Science*, *6*(4), 175–182. doi:10.1207/S1532480XADS0604_3

Duke, B., Harper, G., & Johnston, M. (2013). Connectivism as a digital age learning theory. *The International HETL Review*, *2013*(Special Issue), 4–13.

Duman, E., & Aktel, M. (2021). Türkiye'nin e-Devlet kapısı (Dijital Türkiye Portalı). *Süleyman Demirel Üniversitesi Hukuk Fakültesi Dergisi, 11*(2), 613–641. doi:10.52273/sduhfd..957529

Durak, A., & Kaygin, H. (2020). Parental mediation of young children's internet use: Adaptation of parental mediation scale and review of parental mediation based on the demographic variables and digital data security awareness. *Education and Information Technologies, 25*(3), 2275–2296. doi:10.1007/s10639-019-10079-1

Durrant, C., & Green, B. (2000). Literacy and the new technologies in school education: Meeting the l(IT)eracy challenge? *Australian Journal of Language and Literacy, 23*(2), 89–108.

Dyson, H. A. (2005). Children out of bounds: the power of case studies in expanding visions of literacy development. J. Flood, S.B. Heath ve D. Lapp (Eds.), Handbook of research on teaching literacy through the communicative and visual arts içinde (s.167-180). New Jersey: Lawrance Erlbalum Associates Publishers.

Eady, M. J. (2015). Eleven design-based principles to facilitate the adoption of internet technologies in Indigenous communities. *International Journal of Social Media and Interactive Learning Environments, 3*(4), 267–289. doi:10.1504/IJSMILE.2015.074010

Easterbrooks, R. S., Lederberg, R. A., Miller, M. E., Bergeron, P. J., & Connor McDonald, C. (2008). Emergent literacy skills during early childhood in children with hearing loss: Strengths and weaknesses. *The Volta Review, 108*(2), 91–114. doi:10.17955/tvr.108.2.608

Ebrahim, P., Al-Moumni, M., Al-Hattami, A., & Ali, A. (2021). A study of student attrition in the foundation year program of a teachers' college. *International Journal of Lifelong Education, 40*(3), 198–214. doi:10.1080/02601370.2021.1931973

Education & Training Quality Assurance. (2022). *Annual Reports*. Bahrain: BQA. https://www.bqa.gov.bh/En/Publications/Pages/AnnualReports.aspx

Education and Training Quality Authority. (2016). *Programmes-within-College Review Report: Bachelor of Education, Bahrain Teachers College*. Bahrain: BQA. https://www.bqa.gov.bh/En/Reports/UniReports/HigherEducationReport/BTC%20UOB%20edu%20en-after%20FA%20corrections%208Mar2017%20-%20V2.pdf

Education and Training Quality Authority. (2020). *Annual Report 2020: Education in a Changing World*. Bahrain: BQA. https://www.bqa.gov.bh/En/Publications/Pages/AnnualReports.aspx

Eliot, S. (2016). National bookstart week england evaluation 2016. UK: BookTrust. https://www.booktrust.org.uk/globalassets/resources/research/national-bookstart-week-2016-report-final.pdf

Elmahdi, I., Al-Hattami, A., & Fawzi, H. (2018). Using technology for formative assessment to improve students' learning. *Turkish Online Journal of Educational Technology—TOJET, 17*(2), 182-188. https://www.learntechlib.org/p/189651/

Epstein, J. (2011). *School, family, and community partnerships: Preparing educators and improving schools* (2nd ed.). Routledge.

Epstein, J. L., Sanders, M. G., Sheldon, S. B., Simon, B. S., Salinas, K. C., Jansorn, N. R., & Williams, K. J. (2018). *School, family, and community partnerships: Your handbook for action* (4th ed.). Corwin Press.

Erdem, D., & Rojahn, J. (2022). The influence of financial literacy on financial resilience. New evidence from Europe during the COVID-19 crisis. *Managerial Finance*.

Ergul, C., Akoglu, G., Dolunay Sarıca, A., & Karaman, G. (2016). *Etkilesimli kitap okuma programı (EKOP)*. Egiten Kitap.

Erturk Mustul, E., Turan, Z., & Uzuner, Y. (2016). İsitme kayıplı cocugu olan bir annenin etkilesim davranıslarının aile egitimi baglamında incelenmesi [Investigation of interaction behaviors of a mother with a child with hearing loss in the context of family education]. *Ankara Universitesi Egitim Bilimleri Fakultesi Ozel Egitim Dergisi, 17*(1), 1–22. doi:10.1501/Ozlegt_0000000236

Eschenfelder, K. R., Beachboard, J. C., McClure, C. R., & Wyman, S. K. (1997). Assesing U.S. Federal Goverment Websites. *Government Information Quarterly, 14*(2), 173–189. doi:10.1016/S0740-624X(97)90018-6

European Commission. (July 2023). *Monitoring the level of financial literacy in the EU*. EC. https://europa.eu/eurobarometer/surveys/detail/2953

Eveland, W. P. Jr, & Hively, M. H. (2009). Political discussion frequency, network size, and "heterogeneity" of discussion as predictors of political knowledge and participation. *Journal of Communication, 59*(2), 205–224. doi:10.1111/j.1460-2466.2009.01412.x

Ewoldt, C. (1985). A descriptive study of the developing literacy of young hearing impaired children. *The Volta Review, 87*, 109–125.

Faiz, M. (2018). Chapter: Yurttaşlık Okuryazarlığı. (Teaching Social Studies in Primary School). Eğiten Kitap Publishing, Ankara.

Fakhruddin, I. S. (2019). The impact of non-formal education in community development: A case study in pati, indonesia. *International Journal of Innovation. Creativity and Change, 5*(5), 339–352.

Fang, M. L., Canham, S. L., Battersby, L., Sixsmith, J., Wada, M., & Sixsmith, A. (2019). Exploring privilege in the digital divide: Implications for theory, policy, and practice. *The Gerontologist, 59*(1), e1–e15. PMID:29750241

Fatonah, N. (2020). Parental involvement in early childhood literacy development. *In International Conference on Early Childhood Education and Parenting 2019 (ECEP 2019)* (pp. 193-198). Atlantis Press. 10.2991/assehr.k.200808.038

Fauzi, A., Ridwan, T., & Sholihah, P. (2020, March). Digital Literacy as a Media to Introduce Technology for Elementary School Children. *In International Conference on Elementary Education* (Vol. 2, No. 1, pp. 1507-1518).

Fein, G. G., Ardila-Rey, A. E., & Groth, L. A. (2000). The narrative connection: Stories and literacy. In K. A. Roskos & J. F. Christie (Eds.), *Play and literacy in early childhood research from multiple perspectives* (pp. 27–44). Lawrance Erlbaum Associates.

Ferreiro, E., & Teberosky, A. (1983). *Literacy before schooling*. Heinemann Publishing.

FitzGerald, A. M., & Quiñones, S. (2018). Working in and with community: Leading for partnerships in a community school. *Leadership and Policy in Schools*, *18*(4), 511–532. doi:10.1080/15700763.2018.1453938

Flesch, R. (1955). *Why Johnny can't read—and what you can do about it*. Harper & Brothers.

Flewitt, R., Messer, D., & Kucirkova, N. (2015). New directions for early literacy in a digital age: The iPad. *Journal of Early Childhood Literacy*, *15*(3), 289–310. doi:10.1177/1468798414533560

Flippo, R. (2014). *Assessing readers qualitative diagnosis and instruction* (2nd ed.). Copublished with Routledge/Taylor & Francis. http://www.reading.org/Libraries/books/assessing-readers--second-ed--chapter3.pdf doi:10.4324/9780203118825

Foster, J. E., & Loven, R. G. (1992). The need and directions for parent involvement in the 90's: Undergraduate perspectives and expectations. *Action in Teacher Education*, *14*(3), 13–18. doi:10.1080/01626620.1992.10463127

Fox, J. D. (2004). Test decisions over time: Tracking validity. *Language Testing*, *21*(4), 437–465. doi:10.1191/0265532204lt292oa

Friesen, A., Butera, G., Kang, J., Horn, E., Lieber, J., & Palmer, S. (2014). Collaboration and consultation in preschool to promote early literacy for children: Lessons learned from the CSS curriculum. *Journal of Educational & Psychological Consultation*, *24*(2), 149–164.

Fulcher, G. (2010). *Practical language testing*. Routledge.

Fung, P. C., Chow, B. W. Y., & McBride-Chang, C. (2005). The impact of a dialogic reading program on deaf and hard-of-hearing kindergarten and early primary school–aged students in Hong Kong. *Journal of Deaf Studies and Deaf Education*, *10*(1), 82–95. doi:10.1093/deafed/eni005 PMID:15585750

Garcia, O. (2009). Education, multilingualism and translanguaging in the 21st century. *Social justice through multilingual education*, 140-158.

Garcia, D. C., & Hasson, D. J. (2004). Implementing family literacy programs for linguistically and culturally diverse populations: Key elements to consider. *School Community Journal*, *14*(1), 113–137.

García, O., Johnson, S. I., Seltzer, K., & Valdés, G. (2017). *The translanguaging classroom: Leveraging student, for learning*. Caslon.

García, O., & Kleifgen, J. A. (2020). Translanguaging and literacies. *Reading Research Quarterly*, *55*(4), 553–571. doi:10.1002/rrq.286

García, O., & Lin, A. M. (2017). Translanguaging in Bilingual Education. In O. García, A. M. Lin, & S. May (Eds.), *Bilingual and Multilingual Education* (pp. 117–130). Springer. doi:10.1007/978-3-319-02258-1_9

Gelen, İ. (2017). P21-Program ve öğretimde 21. yüzyıl beceri çerçeveleri (ABD Uygulamaları). *Disiplinlerarası Eğitim Araştırmaları Dergisi*, *1*(2), 15–29.

George, M. J., & Odgers, C. L. (2015). Seven fears and the science of how mobile technologies may be influencing adolescents in the digital age. *Perspectives on Psychological Science*, *10*(6), 832–851. doi:10.1177/1745691615596788 PMID:26581738

Gerek, A., Karasu, H. P., & Girgin, U. (2018). İsitme kayipli bir cocugun okul oncesi donemde okumaya hazirlik becerilerinin paylasilan okuma etkinligi ile desteklenme surecinin incelenmesi. *Akdeniz Egitim Arastırmaları Dergisi*, *12*(25), 203–229.

Gil de Zúñiga, H., & Diehl, T. (2019). News finds me perception and democracy: Effects on political knowledge, political interest, and voting. *New Media & Society*, *21*(6), 1253–1271. doi:10.1177/1461444818817548

Girgin, U. (1999). *Eskisehir ili ilkokul 4. ve 5. sınıf isitme engelli ogrencilerinin okumayi ogrenme durumlarının cozumleme ve anlama duzeylerine gore degerlendirilmesi.* Anadolu University.

Girgin, U. (2003). İsitme engelli cocuklar icin erken donem okuma yazma egitimi. In U. Tufekcioglu (Ed.), *İsitme, konusma ve gorme sorunları olan cocukların egitimi* (pp. 139–163). Anadolu University Publishing.

Gold, E., Simon, E., & Brown, C. (2002). *Strong neighborhoods, strong schools: The indicators project on education organizing.* Cross City Campaign for Urban School Reform.

Gonzales, A., Zappler AuD, A., Coco AuD, L., & Julie, C. (2016). The future of healthcare delivery: IPE/IPP audiology and nursing student/faculty collaboration to deliver hearing aids to vulnerable adults via telehealth. *Journal of Nursing & Interprofessional Leadership in Quality & Safety*, *1*(1), 1–11.

Goodman, K. S., & Goodman, Y. (2014). Reading: A psycholinguistic guessing game. In *Making Sense of Learners Making Sense of Written Language* (pp. 103–112). Routledge. doi:10.4324/9780203366929

Goodman, Y. (1984). The development of initial literacy. In H. Goelman, A. Oberg, & F. Smith (Eds.), *Awakening to literacy* (pp. 102–109). Heinemann.

Goranova, E. (2019). Creation of electronic learning objects for the high cognitive levels of Bloom's digital taxonomy. *KNOWLEDGE-International Journal*, *31*(2), 585–590. doi:10.35120/kij3102585g

Gough, P. B., Kavanagh, J. F., & Mattingly, I. G. (1972). *One second of reading.* MIT Press.

Gözüm, A. İ. C., & Kandır, A. (2021). Digital games pre-schoolers play: Parental mediation and examination of educational content. *Education and Information Technologies*, *26*(3), 3293–3326. doi:10.1007/s10639-020-10382-2

Grabill, J. T. (2001). *Community literacy programs and the politics of change*. SUNY Press.

Greene, J. C. (2007). *Mixed methods in social inquiry* (Vol. 9). John Wiley & Sons.

Güler, M., & Döventaş, E. (2009). Elektronik Devletten Mobil Devlete Geçişte Türkiye'de Yerel Yönetim Uygulamaları. *Hitit University Journal of Institute of Social Sciences, 1* (2), 25-48. https://dergipark.org.tr/en/pub/hititsosbil/issue/7708/100965

Gutiérrez, K. D., Cortes, K., Cortez, A., DiGiacomo, D., Higgs, J., Johnson, P., Ramón Lizárraga, J., Mendoza, E., Tien, J., & Vakil, S. (2017). Replacing representation with imagination: Finding ingenuity in everyday practices. *Review of Research in Education*, *41*(1), 30–60. doi:10.3102/0091732X16687523

Gutiérrez-Porlán, I., Prendes-Espinosa, P., & Sánchez-Vera, M. D. M. (2022). Digital technologies for the assessment of oral English skills. *Applied Sciences (Basel, Switzerland)*, *12*(22), 11635. doi:10.3390/app122211635

Hafernik, J. J., & Wiant, F. M. (2012). *Integrating multilingual students into college classrooms*. Multilingual Matters. doi:10.21832/9781847698216

Hall, N. (1987). The emergence of literacy. (1.Ed.). Portsmouth: Heinemann Publishing.

Hallahan, T. A., Faff, R. W., & McKenzie, M. D. (2004). An empirical investigation of personal financial risk tolerance. *Financial Services Review-greenwich*, *13*(1), 57–78.

Hall, C. M., & Bierman, K. L. (2015). Technology-assisted interventions for parents of young children: Emerging practices, current research, and future directions. *Early Childhood Research Quarterly*, *33*, 21–32. doi:10.1016/j.ecresq.2015.05.003 PMID:27773964

Ham, C. D., Lee, J., Hayes, J. L., & Bae, Y. H. (2019). Exploring Sharing Behaviors Across Social Media Platforms. *International Journal of Market Research*, *61*(2), 157–177. doi:10.1177/1470785318782790

Hammer, M., Scheiter, K., & Stürmer, K. (2021). New technology, new role of parents: How parents' beliefs and behavior affect students' digital media self-efficacy. *Computers in Human Behavior*, *116*, 106642. doi:10.1016/j.chb.2020.106642

Hamp-Lyons, L. (2011). English for academic purposes. In *Handbook of research in second language teaching and learning* (pp. 89–105). Routledge.

Hanemann, U. (2015). *The evolution and impact of literacy campaigns and programmes, 2000-2014*. Hamburg [Germany]: Unesco, Institute for Lifelong Learning, 2015. https://redined.educacion. gob.es/xmlui/bitstream/handle/11162/118504/234154e.pdf?sequence=1&isAllowed=y

Han, M., Van Duinen, D. V., & Weng, A. (2021). Interactive Read-Alouds as Translanguaging Spaces. *The Reading Teacher*, *75*(3), 389–394. doi:10.1002/trtr.2059

Hannon, P., Morgan, A., & Nutbron, C. (2006). Parents' experiences of a family literacy programme. *Journal of Early Childhood Research*, *4*(1), 19–44. doi:10.1177/1476718X06059788

Harvard Family Research Project. (2010). *Partnerships for learning: Promising practices in integrating school and out-of-school time program supports*. HFRP. https://www.hfrp.org/publications-resources/browse-our-publications/partn

Harvard University Graduate School of Education. (2022). *Project Zero*. Harvard. https://pz.harvard.edu/

Hattaka, M., Smaal, J., van der Merve, R. I., & Ainane, S. (2017). Addressing retention at an English-medium Engineering College: A case study of freshman students in the Middle East. In J.C. Quadrado, J, Bernardino, & J. Rocha (Eds), *Proceedings of SEFI 2017 annual conference* (pp. 903-910). European Society for Engineering Education SEFI.

Hauge, C., & Rowsell, J. (2020). Child and youth engagement: Civic literacies and digital ecologies. *Discourse (Abingdon)*, *41*(5), 667–672. doi:10.1080/01596306.2020.1769933

Hawkins, J. (1991). Technology-mediated communities for learning: Designs and consequences. *The Annals of the American Academy of Political and Social Science*, *514*(1), 159–174. doi:10.1177/0002716291514001013

Head, E. (2020). Digital technologies and parental involvement in education: The experiences of mothers of primary school-aged children. *British Journal of Sociology of Education*, *41*(5), 593–607. doi:10.1080/01425692.2020.1776594

Henderson, M. J. (1976). Learning to read: A case study of a deaf child. *American Annals of the Deaf*, *121*(5), 502–506. PMID:983909

Henriques, S. C. M. (2010). *Aspectos da literacia financeira dos portugueses*. [Estudo empírico, Universidade de Aveiro].

Herrera, S. G., Perez, D. R., & Escamilla, K. (2011). Teaching reading to English language learners: Differentiating literacies: Pearson Higher Ed.

Hines, M., & Brooks, G. (2005). *Sheffield babies love books: an evaluation of the sheffield bookstart Project*. The University of Sheffield.

Hiniker, A., Schoenebeck, S. Y., & Kientz, J. A. (2016, February). Not at the dinner table: Parents' and children's perspectives on family technology rules. In *Proceedings of the 19th ACM conference on computer-supported cooperative work & social computing* (pp. 1376-1389).

Ho W.Y.J, Tai K.W.H (2021) Translanguaging in digital learning: The making of translanguaging spaces in online English teaching videos. *International Journal of Bilingual Education and Bilingualism*. . doi:10.1080/13670050.2021.2001427

Hofstadler, N., Babic, S., Lämmerer, A., Mercer, S., & Oberdorfer, P. (2021). The ecology of CLIL teachers in Austria – an ecological perspective on CLIL teachers' wellbeing. *Innovation in Language Learning and Teaching, 15*(3), 218–232. doi:10.1080/17501229.2020.1739050

Holdaway, D. (1979). *The foundations of literacy.* Ashton.

Honeck, R. P. (2013). *A proverb in mind: The cognitive science of proverbial wit and wisdom.* Psychology Press. doi:10.4324/9780203771556

Hopkins, K., Keefe, B., & Bruno, A. (2012). Telepractice: Creating a statewide network of support in rural maine. *The Volta Review, 112*(3), 409–416.

Hornberger, N. H. (Ed.). (2003). *Continua of biliteracy: An ecological framework for educational policy, research, and practice in multilingual settings.* Multilingual Matters. doi:10.21832/9781853596568

Hourihan, M. (2005). *Deconstructing the hero: Literary theory and children's literature.* Routledge. doi:10.4324/9780203974100

Howard, S. K., & Mozejko, A. (2015). Teachers: technology, change, and resistance. In M. Henderson & G. Romeo (Eds.), Teaching and Digital Technologies: Big Issues and Critical Questions (pp. 307-317). Cambridge University Press. https://www.researchgate.net/publication/292971267_Teachers_technology_change_and_resistance

Howat, H. (2006). Maximizing family involvement in early literacy. *Contemporary Issues in Communication Science and Disorders, 33*(Fall), 93–100. doi:10.1044/cicsd_33_F_93

Howie, S. J., Combrinck, C., Roux, K., Tshele, M., Mokoena, G., & McLeod Palane, N. (2017). *PIRLS Literacy 2016: Progress in international reading literacy study (PIRLS) 2016: South African children's reading literacy achievement.* Centre for Evaluation and Assessment (CEA).

Huang, E., Jiang, L., & Yang, M. (2021). The affordances of a technology-aided formative assessment platform for the assessment and teaching of English as a foreign language: An ecological perspective. *Educational Technology Research and Development, 69*(6), 3391–3412. doi:10.1007/s11423-021-10047-y

Hughes, J., Thomas, R., & Scharber, C. (2006, March). Assessing technology integration: The RAT–replacement, amplification, and transformation-framework. *In Society for Information Technology & Teacher Education International Conference* (pp. 1616-1620). Association for the Advancement of Computing in Education (AACE).

Hunt, P. (Ed.). (2006). *Understanding children's literature.* Routledge. doi:10.4324/9780203968963

Hylton, M. E. (2015). Civic Engagement and Civic Literacy Among Social Work Students: Where Do We Stand? *Journal of Policy Practice, 14*(3-4), 292–307. doi:10.1080/15588742.2015.1004396

Ihmeideh, F. M. (2014). The effect of electronic books on enhancing emergent literacy skills of pre-school children. *Computers & Education, 79*, 40–48.

Inquirer News. (2022, June 1). PH ranks last in reading, second to last in science, math among 79 countries in Pisa. *News Info.* https://newsinfo.inquirer.net/1502996/ph-ranks-last-in-reading-second-to-last-in-science-math-among-79-countries-in-pisa

International Bureau of Education. (2011) Bahrain. *World Data of Education, 7th Edition, 2010/11.* UNESCO. https://www.ibe.unesco.org/

International Reading Association. (2008). Partnerships for improving literacy in urban schools. *The Reading Teacher, 61*(8), 678–680.

Invernizzi, M., Rosemary, C., Juel, C., & Richards, H. C. (2021). At-risk readers and community volunteers: A 3-year perspective. In *Components of Effective Reading Intervention* (pp. 277–300). Routledge. doi:10.4324/9781315046365-6

Jamil, M. I. M., & Almunawar, M. N. (2021). Importance of digital literacy and hindrance brought about by digital divide. In *Encyclopedia of Information Science and Technology* (5th ed., pp. 1683–1698). IGI Global. doi:10.4018/978-1-7998-3479-3.ch116

Jenkins, J. (2019). English medium in higher education: The role of English as a lingua franca. In X. Gao (Ed.), *Second Handbook of English Language Teaching* (pp. 1–17). Springer. doi:10.1007/978-3-030-02899-2_7

Jeynes, W. (2010). *Parental involvement and academic success.* Routledge. doi:10.4324/9780203843444

Jiajing, G. (2007 April). Designing an ESP course for Chinese students of business. *The Asian ESP Journal, 3*(1), 97-106. https://www.asian-esp-journal.com/wp-content/uploads/2016/01/AESp-Volume-3-Issue-1-Apri-2007.pdf

Johnson, L. (2015). Rethinking parental involvement: A critical review of the literature. *Urban Education Research & Policy Annuals, 3*(1).

Jones, C. (2018). SPARK early literacy: Testing the impact of a family–school–community partnership literacy intervention. *School Community Journal, 28*(2).

Jordan, J. (1998). Constructing school partnerships with families and community groups. http://www.ncrel.or^sdrs/areas/issues/envrnmnt/farnnncmrn/pa400.htm.retrieved.

Jordan, G. E., Snow, C. E., & Porche, M. V. (2000). Project EASE: The effect of a family literacy project on kindergarten students' early literacy skills. *Reading Research Quarterly, 35*(4), 524–546. doi:10.1598/RRQ.35.4.5

Jorgensen, B. L., & Savla, J. (2010). Financial literacy of young adults: The importance of parental socialization. *Family Relations, 59*(4), 465–478. doi:10.1111/j.1741-3729.2010.00616.x

Joshi, P. (2017). *Collaboration to improve literacy: making learning sustainable in schools [Paper presentation].* 42nd Association for Teacher Education in Europe (ATEE) *Annual Conference*, Brussels, Belgium.

Jung, I. (2019). Connectivism and networked learning. In Open and distance education theory revisited: Implications for the digital era (pp. 47-55). Springer. doi:10.1007/978-981-13-7740-2_6

Justice, M. L. (2006). Emergent literacy: Development, domains and intervention approaches. In L. M. Justice (Ed.), *Clinical approaches to emergent literacy intervention* (pp. 3–27). Plural Publishing Inc.

Justice, M. L., & Sofka, E. A. (2010). *Engaging children with print building early literacy skills through quality read-alouds*. The Guilford Press.

Kadoya, Y., & Khan, M. S. R. (2020). What determines financial literacy in Japan? *Journal of Pension Economics and Finance, 19*(3), 353–371. doi:10.1017/S1474747218000379

Karabuga, F., & Kaya, E. S. (2013). Collaborative strategic reading practice with adult EFL learners: A collaborative and reflective approach to reading. *Procedia: Social and Behavioral Sciences, 106*, 621–630. doi:10.1016/j.sbspro.2013.12.071

Karabulut, B. (2015) Bilgi Toplumu Çağında Dijital Yerliler, Göçmenler ve Melezler, *Pamukkale Üniversitesi Sosyal Bilimler Enstitüsü Dergisi,* (21), 11-23. https://dergipark.org.tr/en/pub/pausbed/issue/34743/384200

Karasu, P. H. (2014). İsitme engelli cocuklara okul oncesi donemde uygulanan okuma yazmaya hazirlik grup etkinlikleri. *Egitim ve Bilim., 39*(174), 297–312. doi:10.15390/EB.2014.2602

Kaschula, R. H., & Kretzer, M. M. 2019, 'The Politics of Language Education in Africa'., Oxford Research Encyclopedia of Politics. Oxford. Oxford University Press. doi:10.1093/acrefore/9780190228637.013.750

Kaye, L. (Ed.). (2016). *Young children in a digital age: Supporting learning and development with technology in early years*. Routledge. doi:10.4324/9781315752709

Keith, N. Z. (1999). Whose community schools? New discourses, old patterns. *Theory into Practice, 38*(4), 225–234. doi:10.1080/00405849909543858

Kellner, D. (2004). Technological transformation, multiple literacies, and the re-visioning of education. *E-Learning and Digital Media, 1*(1), 9–37. doi:10.2304/elea.2004.1.1.8

Kempson, E., Collard, S., & Moore, N. (2005). *Measuring financial capability: an exploratory study, in Consumer Research Report 37*. University of Bristol: Financial Services Authority. https://www.bristol.ac.uk/media-library/sites/geography/migrated/documents/pfrc0510.pdf

Kempson, E., Collard, S., & Moore, N. (2006). Measuring financial capability: An exploratory study for the Financial Services Authority. *Consumer financial capability: Empowering European consumers, 39*, 44-76.

Kerimoğlu, C., & Keleşoğlu, S. (2023). Covid-19 Pandemisinde İnternet Kullanımı ve Dijital Yurttaşlık. [JFES]. *Ankara University Journal of Faculty of Educational Sciences, 56*(2), 495–545. doi:10.30964/auebfd.1148787

Kervin, L. (2016). Powerful and playful literacy learning with digital technologies. *Australian Journal of Language and Literacy*, *39*(1), 64–73. doi:10.1007/BF03651907

Kildare, C. A., & Middlemiss, W. (2017). Impact of parents mobile device use on parent-child interaction: A literature review. *Computers in Human Behavior*, *75*, 579–593. doi:10.1016/j.chb.2017.06.003

King, A., & Xu, Y. (2021). Caregiver coaching for language facilitation in early intervention for children with hearing loss. *Early Child Development and Care*, *191*(10), 1507–1525.

Kirkpatrick, R., & Barnawi, O. Z. (2017). Introduction: English Language Education Policy in MENA. In R. Kirkpatrick (Ed.), *English language Education Policy in the Middle East and North African* (Vol. 13, pp. 1–8). Springer International Publishing. doi:10.1007/978-3-319-46778-8_1

Klapper, L., & Lusardi, A. (2020). Financial literacy and financial resilience: Evidence from around the world. *Financial Management*, *49*(3), 589–614. doi:10.1111/fima.12283

Koch, L. A. (2018). *Parent Involvement in Early Childhood Education and Its Impact on the Development of Early Language and Literacy Skills: An Exploration of One Head Start Program's Parent Involvement Model*. Drexel University. doi:10.17918/D84D49

Koehler, M., & Mishra, P. (2009). What is technological pedagogical content knowledge (TPACK)? *Contemporary Issues in Technology & Teacher Education*, *9*(1), 60–70.

Krashen, S. D. (1993). *The power of reading: Insights from the research* (2nd ed.). Libraries Unlimited.

Kress, G., & van Leeuwen, T. (2001). *Multimodal discourse: The modes and media of contemporary communication*. Bloomsburry.

Kretschmer, R. R., Kretschmer, W. L., & Truax, R. T. (1978). *Language development and intervention with the hearing impaired*. University Park Press.

Kristanto, N. (2020). Model penyelenggaraan program pendidikan keaksaraan dasar melalui pelibatan pemerintah kampung dan tokoh agama. *Jurnal Akrab*, *11*(2), 1–9. doi:10.51495/jurnalakrab.v11i02.335

Kucirkova, N. (2017). New literacies and new media: The changing face of early literacy. In *The Routledge international handbook of early literacy education* (pp. 40–54). Routledge. doi:10.4324/9781315766027-5

Kurt, A. A. ve Odabaşı, F. (2021). Pandemi döneminde sınanan dijital vatandaşlık [Digital citizenship tested during the pandemic]. Anı Yayıncılık.

Laksono, K., & Retnaningdyah, P. (2018). Literacy infrastructure, access to books, and the implementation of the school literacy movement in primary schools in Indonesia. In IOP Conference Series: Materials Science and Engineering (Vol. 296, No. 1, p. 012045). IOP Publishing. doi:10.1088/1757-899X/296/1/012045

Laksono, B. A., & Wahyuni, S. (2018). An investigation of local wisdom to support adult literacy program. *PEOPLE: International Journal of Social Sciences*, *4*(2), 1320–1336. doi:10.20319/pijss.2018.42.13201336

Lalios, A. P. (2012). ConnectHear teleintervention program. *The Volta Review*, *112*(3), 357–364.

Lankshear, C., & Knobel, M. (2003). *New literacies: Changing knowledge and classroom learning.* Open University Press.

Laranjeiro, D., Antunes, M. J., & Santos, P. (2018). Tablets in kindergarten for learning and parental involvement. In *EDULEARN18 Proceedings* (pp. 5089-5096). IATED. 10.21125/edulearn.2018.1245

Lauwo, H., & Gerold Mkulu, D. (2021). Challenges facing community involvement in ensuring quality education in public secondary schools in Meru district, Arusha Region-Tanzania. [IJELS]. *International Journal of English Literature and Social Sciences*, *6*(1), 074. https://journal-repository.theshillonga.com/index.php/ijels/article/view/3021. doi:10.22161/ijels.61.8

Lavoura, R. F. d. M. (2017). *O desenvolvimento de competências de literacia financeira em populações vulneráveis: um projeto de intervenção com alunos de cursos EFA em Odivelas* [Dissertação de mestrado, ISCTE-IUL].

Lea, M. R. (2017). Academic literacies in theory and practice. In B. V. Street & S. May (Eds.), *Literacies and language education: Encyclopedia of language and education* (pp. 147–158). Springer. doi:10.1007/978-3-319-02252-9_19

Lea, M. R., & Street, B. V. (1998). Student writing in higher education: An academic literacies approach. *Studies in Higher Education*, *23*(2), 157–172. doi:10.1080/03075079812331380364

Lea, M. R., & Street, B. V. (2006). The" academic literacies" model: Theory and applications. *Theory into Practice*, *45*(4), 368–377. doi:10.1207/s15430421tip4504_11

Leary, E. (2017). *Best Investing Moves at Every Age.* Kiplinger. https://www.kiplinger.com/article/investing/t052-c000-s002-best-investing-moves-at-every-age.html

Lee, C. D. (2017). Integrating Research on How People Learn and Learning Across Settings as a Window of Opportunity to Address Inequality in Educational Processes and Outcomes. *Review of Research in Education*, *41*(1), 88–111. doi:10.3102/0091732X16689046

Lemke, J. L. (2001). The Long and the Short of It: Comments on Multiple Timescale Studies of Human Activity. *Journal of the Learning Sciences*, *10*(1), 17–26. https://www.learntechlib.org/p/165494/. doi:10.1207/S15327809JLS10-1-2_3

Lestari, H., Siskandar, R., & Rahmawati, I. (2020, March). Digital Literacy Skills of Teachers in Elementary School in The Revolution 4.0. *In International Conference on Elementary Education* (Vol. 2, No. 1, pp. 302-311). IATED.

Lev-On, A., Steinfeld, N., Abu-Kishk, H., & Pearl Naim, S. (2021). The long-term effects of digital literacy programs for disadvantaged populations: Analyzing participants' perceptions. *Journal of Information. Communication and Ethics in Society*, *19*(1), 146–162. doi:10.1108/JICES-02-2020-0019

Levy, T., & Gertler, H. (2015). Harnessing technology to assess oral communication in Business English. *Teaching English with Technology*, *15*(4), 52–59.

Lewis, G., Jones, B., & Baker, C. (2012). Translanguaging: Origins and development from school to street and beyond. *Educational Research and Evaluation*, *18*(7), 641–654. doi:10.1080/13803611.2012.718488

Li, D. (2022). A review of academic literacy research development: from 2002 to 2019. *Asian-Pacific Journal of Second and Foreign Language Education*, *7*(1), 1–22. doi:10.1186/s40862-022-00130-z

Lin, A. M. (2020). *Translanguaging and translanguaging pedagogies Translanguaging in Multilingual English Classrooms*. Springer.

Lin, Y.-T. (2023). Learning performances towards the BookRoll e-book system for flipped classrooms in software engineering education. *Journal of Educational Technology & Society*, *26*(3), 190–202. https://www.jstor.org/stable/48734330

Li, Z., & Wang, L. (2024). *Investigating translanguaging strategies and online self-presentation through internet slang on Douyin (Chinese TikTok)*. Applied Linguistics Review. doi:10.1515/applirev-2023-0094

Long, E. (2008). *Community literacy and the rhetoric of local publics*. Parlor Press LLC.

Luksander, A., Beres, D., Huzdik, K., & Nemeth, E. (2014). Analysis of the factors that influence the financial literacy of young people studying in higher education= A felsőoktatásban tanuló fiatalok pénzügyi kultúráját befolyásoló tényezők vizsgálata. PÉNZÜGYI SZEMLE. *Public Finance Quarterly*, *59*(2), 220–241.

Lusardi, A. (2019). Financial literacy and the need for financial education: Evidence and implications. *Swiss Journal of Economics and Statistics*, *155*(1), 1–8. doi:10.1186/s41937-019-0027-5

Lusardi, A., & Mitchell, O. S. (2014). The economic importance of financial literacy: Theory and evidence. American Economic Journal. *Journal of Economic Literature*, *52*(1), 5–44. doi:10.1257/jel.52.1.5 PMID:28579637

Lutz, L. (2013). *Early reading development in young deaf children supportive family context*. [Md Dissertation, University of Virginia: USA].

Lyons, C. D., & Tredwell, C. T. (2015). Steps to implementing technology in inclusive early childhood programs. *Computers in the Schools*, *32*(2), 152–166.

Lyons, J., Jaeger, W. P., & Wolak, J. (2012). The roots of citizens' knowledge of state politics. *State Politics & Policy Quarterly*, *13*(2), c, 183–202. doi:10.1177/1532440012464878

Machado, J. M. (2012). Early chilhood experiences in language arts: early literacy (10. Ed.). USA: Wadsworth.

Machen, S. M., Wilson, J. D., & Notar, C. E. (2005). Parental involvement in the classroom. *Journal of Instructional Psychology*, *32*(1), 13–17.

Makalela, L. (2015). Translanguaging as a vehicle for epistemic access: cases for reading comprehension and multilingual interactions. *Per Linguam: a Journal of Language Learning= Per Linguam. Tydskrif vir Taalaanleer*, *31*(1), 15–29.

Makalela, L. (2016a). *Translanguaging Practices in a South African Institution of Higher Learning: A Case of Ubuntu Multilingual Return Translanguaging in higher education*. Multilingual Matters.

Makalela, L. (2016b). Ubuntu translanguaging: An alternative framework for complex multilingual encounters. *Southern African Linguistics and Applied Language Studies*, *34*(3), 187–196. doi:10.2989/16073614.2016.1250350

Makalela, L. (2019). Uncovering the universals of Ubuntu translanguaging in classroom discourses. *Classroom Discourse*, *10*(3-4), 237–251. doi:10.1080/19463014.2019.1631198

Makalela, L. (2022). Introduction: Language, Identity and African Universities. In L. Makalela (Ed.), *Language and Institutional Identity in the Post-Apartheid South African Higher Education. Language Policy* (Vol. 27, pp. 1–10). Springer., doi:10.1007/978-3-030-85961-9_1

Malcolm, D., & Majed, M. (2013). Foundation-level Gulf Arab student response to self-access learning. *Studies in Self-Access Learning Journal*, *4*(4), 323–338. doi:10.37237/040408

Mandell, L., & Klein, L. S. (2009). The impact of financial literacy education on subsequent financial behavior. *Financial Counseling and Planning*, *20*(1).

Manila Bulletin. (2019, December 25). DepEd orders schools to 'intensify' reading advocacy. *Manila Bulletin.* https://mb.com.ph/2019/12/25/deped-orders-schools-to-intensify-reading-advocacy/

Marschark, M., Lang, H. G., & Albertini, J. A. (2002). Reading, writing and literacy. In M. Marschark, G. L. Harry, & J. A. Albertini (Eds.), *Educating deaf students. From research to practice* (pp. 157–186). Oxford University Press.

Marsh, J., Hannon, P., Lewis, M., & Ritchie, L. (2017). Young children's initiation into family literacy practices in the digital age. *Journal of Early Childhood Research*, *15*(1), 47–60. doi:10.1177/1476718X15582095

Maxwell, M. (1984). A deaf child's natural development of literacy. *Sign Language Studies*, *44*(1), 191–224. doi:10.1353/sls.1984.0001

Mayer, C., & Trezek, B. J. (2015). *Early literacy development in deaf children*. Oxford University Press. doi:10.1093/acprof:oso/9780199965694.001.0001

Mayger, L. K., & Hochbein, C. D. (2021). Growing connected: Relational trust and social capital in community schools. *Journal of Education for Students Placed at Risk*, *26*(3), 210–235. doi: 10.1080/10824669.2020.1824676

Mbirimi-Hungwe, V., & McCabe, R.-M. (2020). Translanguaging during collaborative learning: A 'transcollab'model of teaching. *Southern African Linguistics and Applied Language Studies*, *38*(3), 244–259. doi:10.2989/16073614.2020.1847670

McCarthy, M., Leigh, G., & Arthur-Kelly, M. (2020). Children's hearing and speech centre telepractice programs. *The Volta Review*, *112*(3), 429–433.

McDaniel, B. T. (2019). Parent distraction with phones, reasons for use, and impacts on parenting and child outcomes: A review of the emerging research. *Human Behavior and Emerging Technologies*, *1*(2), 72–80. doi:10.1002/hbe2.139

McDaniel, B. T., & Radesky, J. S. (2018). Technoference: Longitudinal associations between parent technology use, parenting stress, and child behavior problems. *Pediatric Research*, *84*(2), 210–218. doi:10.1038/s41390-018-0052-6 PMID:29895837

McKee, H., & Blair, K. (2007). Older adults and community-based technological literacy programs: Barriers & benefits to learning. *Community Literacy Journal*, *1*(2), 2. https://www.semanticscholar.org. doi:10.25148/CLJ.1.2.009516

McKnight, J. L., & Russell, C. (2018). *The four essential elements of an asset-based community development process: What Is Distinctive about Asset-Based Community Process*. Nurture Development.

Mcnamara, T. (2015). Applied linguistics: The challenge of theory. *Applied Linguistics*, *36*(4), 466–477. doi:10.1093/applin/amv042

Mendelshon, A. L., Mogilner, L. N., Preyer, B. P., Forman, J. A., Weinstein, S. C., Broderick, M., Cheng, K. J., Magloire, T., Moore, T., & Napier, C. (2001). The impact of a clinic-based literacy intervention on language development in inner-city preschool children. *American Academy of Pediatrics*, *107*(1), 130–134. PMID:11134446

Menon, R., Nedungadi, P., & Raman, R. (2017). Technology enabled teacher training for low-literate, remote and rural multi-grade education centers. 2017 *International Conference on Advances in Computing, Communications and Informatics (ICACCI)*, (pp. 1594-1599). Semantic Scholar. https://www.semanticscholar.org

Mesquita, A., Oliveira, A., Sauer, P., Oliveira, L., & Sequeira, A. S. (2021). Financial Literacy and Its Importance: An Overall Picture from Portugal. In P. A. Robinson, K. V. Williams, & M. Stojanović (Eds.), *Global Citizenship for Adult Education: Advancing Critical Literacies for Equity and Social Justice* (1st ed.). Routledge. doi:10.4324/9781003050421-32

Messick, S. (1996). Validity and washback in language testing. *Language Testing*, *13*(3), 241–256A. doi:10.1177/026553229601300302

Messier, J., & Wood, C. (2015). Facilitating vocabulary acquisition of children with cochlear implants using electronic storybooks. *Journal of Deaf Studies and Deaf Education, 20*(4), 356–373.

Messy, F.-A., & Monticone, C. (2016). *Financial education policies in Asia and the Pacific.* OECD. https://www.oecd-ilibrary.org/finance-and-investment/financial-education-policies-in-asia-and-the-pacific_5jm5b32v5vvc-en

Microsoft Learn Educator Center. (n.d.). *Immersive Reader.* Microsoft. https://learn.microsoft.com/en-us/training/educator-center/product-guides/immersive-reader/

Microsoft Learn Educator Center. (n.d.). *Reading progress product guide.* Microsoft. https://learn.microsoft.com/en-us/training/educator-center/product-guides/reading-progress/

Mills, K. A. (2010). A review of the "digital turn" in the new literacy studies. *Review of Educational Research, 80*(2), 246–271. doi:10.3102/0034654310364401

Ministry of Education of Indonesia. (2010). *Country Paper: Status and Major Challenges of Literacy in Indonesia. United Nations Educational, Scientific, and Cultural Organization.* UNESDOC. https://unesdoc.unesco.org/ark:/48223/pf0000191512 accessed February 29, 2024.

Mitchell, O. S., & Lusardi, A. (2011). Financial literacy around the world: An overview. *Journal of Pension Economics and Finance, 10*(4), 497–508. doi:10.1017/S1474747211000448 PMID:28553190

Moeller, M. P. (2000). Early intervention and language development in children who are deaf and hard of hearing. *Pediatrics, 106*(3). Advance online publication. https://doi.org/10.1542/peds.106.3.e43

Mojapelo, S. M. (2023). Whopping low reading literacies in South Africa. *South African Journal of Library and Information Science, 89*(1), 1–14.

Moll, L., Amanti, C., Neff, D., & Gonzalez, N. (2006). Funds of knowledge for teaching: Using a qualitative approach to connect homes and classrooms. In *Funds of knowledge* (pp. 71–87). Routledge.

Monte, A. P., Galstian, N., Nobre, J. C. C., & Evseeva, O. A. (2018). Fatores influenciadores do nível de literacia financeira dos gestores das PME: comparação entre Portugal e Rússia. *XXVIII Jornadas Luso-Espanholas de Gestão Científica: Interioridade e Competitividade.* Desafios Globais da Gestão.

Monticone, C. (2010). How much does wealth matter in the acquisition of financial literacy? *The Journal of Consumer Affairs, 44*(2), 403–422. doi:10.1111/j.1745-6606.2010.01175.x

Moore, M., & Wade, B. (2003). Bookstart: A qualitative evaluation. *Educational Review, 55*(1), 1, 3–13. doi:10.1080/00131910303250

Moretti, G. A. S. (2016). Youth and adult literacy and education: a good practice analysis (No. 56). International Policy Centre for Inclusive Growth. *Econ Papers.* https://econpapers.repec.org/RePEc:ipc:pbrief:56

Morgan, P. J., Huang, B., & Trinh, L. Q. (2019). *The need to promote digital financial literacy for the digital age (The Future of Work and Education for the Digital Age.* T20 Japan. https://t20japan.org/policy-brief-need-promote-digital-financial-literacy/

Morrow, C. (2017). Assessing entry-level academic literacy with IELTS in the UAE. *Revisiting EFL assessment: Critical perspectives*, 151-169.

Morrow, M. L. (2009). Literacy development in the early years. (6.Ed.). U.S.A: Pearson.

Motlhaka, H. (2021). Translanguaging in Collaborative Reading Activity: A Multilingual Perspective of Meaning Making. *Psychology and Education Journal*, *58*(5), 2683–2691.

Mouna, A., & Anis, J. (2017). Financial literacy in Tunisia: Its determinants and its implications on investment behavior. *Research in International Business and Finance*, *39*, 568–577. doi:10.1016/j.ribaf.2016.09.018

Mualo, Y. (2020). Pembelajaran keaksaraan dasar berbasis kearifan lokal sebagai upaya pemberantasan buta aksara. *Jurnal AKRAB*, *11*(2), 62–79. doi:10.51495/jurnalakrab.v11i02.354

Mulya, Y. H., Putra, Z. H., & Hermita, N. (2023). The Correlation between Parents' Digital Literacy Knowledge and Parents' Perception of Digital Literacy Knowledge of Elementary School Students. AL-ISHLAH. *Jurnal Pendidikan*, *15*(2), 1965–1978.

Mulyono, B., Affandi, I., Suryadi, K., & Darmawan, C. (2022). Online civic engagement: Fostering citizen engagement through social media. *Jurnal Civics: Media Kajian Kewarganegaraan*, *19*(1), 75–85. doi:10.21831/jc.v19i1.49723

Murray, M. C., & Pérez, J. (2014). Unraveling the digital literacy paradox: How higher education fails at the fourth literacy. *Issues in Informing Science and Information Technology*, *11*, 85. doi:10.28945/1982

Murray, N. (2016). An academic literacies argument for decentralizing EAP provision. *ELT Journal*, *70*(4), 435–443. doi:10.1093/elt/ccw030

Murray, N. (2018). University gatekeeping tests: What are they really testing and what are the implications for EAP provision? *JACET Journal*, *62*, 15–27.

Muthoni, K. C. (2015). *The impact of community involvement in public secondary schools management: A case of Machakos County, Kenya* [Masters Dissertation, Kenyatta University]. https://pdfs.semanticscholar.org/ffe8/0734efc2151ac327bb410a7c309b6ff7dbe9.pdf

Mutonyi, H. (2016). Stories, proverbs, and anecdotes as scaffolds for learning science concepts. *Journal of Research in Science Teaching*, *53*(6), 943–971. doi:10.1002/tea.21255

Myende, P. E. (2018). Creating functional and sustainable school-community partnerships: Lessons from three South African cases. *Educational Management Administration & Leadership*, *47*(6), 1001–1019. doi:10.1177/1741143218781070

Nar, M. Ş. (2021). Eğitim, İdeoloji, Demokrasi ile Oy Verme Davranışı Arasındaki İlişki: Türkiye Örneği. *Mecmua*, (12), 199-212. https://dergipark.org.tr/en/pub/mecmua/issue/65116/990437

National Institute of Child Health and Human Development. (2000). *Teaching children to read: An evidence-based assessment of the scientific research literature on reading and its implications for reading instruction.* Report of the National Reading Panel. (NIH Publication No. 00-4769). U.S. Government Printing Office.

Nazirjonovich, K. Z. (2021). The use of modern educational technologies in the organization of physical education is a guarantee to increase the effectiveness of education. *ACADEMICIA: An International Multidisciplinary Research Journal*, *11*(10), 477–480.

Nedungadi, P. P., Menon, R., Gutjahr, G., Erickson, L., & Raman, R. (2018). Towards an inclusive digital literacy framework for digital India. *Education + Training*, *60*(6), 516–528. doi:10.1108/ET-03-2018-0061

Needlman, R., Fried, L. E., Morley, D. S., Taylor, S., & Zuckerman, B. (1991). Clinic-based intervention to promote literacy: A pilot study. *American Journal of Diseases of Children*, *145*(8), 881–884. doi:10.1001/archpedi.1991.02160080059021 PMID:1858725

NELP. (2008). *National early literacy panel report.* USA: National Institute for Literacy. https://lincs.ed.gov/publications/pdf/NELPReport09.pdf

Nelson, J., & Braafladt, K. (2012). *Technology and literacy: 21st century library programming for children and teens.* American Library Association.

Neumann, M. M., & Neumann, D. L. (2017). The use of touch-screen tablets at home and pre-school to foster emergent literacy. *Journal of Early Childhood Literacy*, *17*(2), 203–220. doi:10.1177/1468798415619773

Neupane, K., & Dhakal, H. R. (2023). School-community partnership: A model of participatory governance for students' learning improvement. *ISAR Journal of Arts. Humanities and Social Sciences*, *1*(5), 1–9.

Ngcobo, S., Ndaba, N., Nyangiwe, B., Mpungose, N., & Jamal, R. (2016). Translanguaging as an approach to address language inequality in South African higher education: Summary writing skills development. [CriSTaL]. *Critical Studies in Teaching and Learning*, *4*(2), 10–27.

Ngobeni, S. T. (2022). Establishing and maintaining school-community partnerships: A challenge for school management teams. *International Journal of Leadership in Education*, 1–26. doi:10.1080/13603124.2022.2117414

Nickbakht, M., Meyer, C., Scarinci, N., & Beswick, R. (2020). Exploring factors influencing the use of an eHealth intervention for families of children with hearing loss: An application of the COM-B model. *Disability and Health Journal*, *13*(4), 1–8.

Niezen, R. (2020). *HumanRights: The technologies and politics of justice claims in practice.* Stanford University Press. doi:10.1515/9781503612648

Noble, C., Cameron-Faulkner, T., Jessop, A., Coates, A., Sawyer, H., Taylor-Ims, R., & Rowland, C. F. (2020). The impact of interactive shared book reading on children's language skills: A randomized controlled trial. *Journal of Speech, Language, and Hearing Research: JSLHR*, *63*(6), 1878–1897.

Noctor, M., Stoney, S., & Stradling, R. (1992). *Financial literacy: a discussion of concepts and competences of financial literacy and opportunities for its introduction into young people's learning*. National Foundation for Educational Research.

Nodelman, P. (2008). *The hidden adult: Defining children's literature*. JHU Press. doi:10.56021/9780801889790

Novianti, R., & Garzia, M. (2020). Parental engagement in children's online learning during covid-19 pandemic. *Journal of Teaching and Learning in Elementary Education (Jtlee)*, *3*(2), 117–131. doi:10.33578/jtlee.v3i2.7845

Nur, A., & Abdullah, M. S. (2022). Barru literacy community as the alternative literacy movement: A study on cultivating reading literacy toward society in Barru Regency, South Sulawesi Province. *Salus Cultura: Jurnal Pembangunan Manusia Dan Kebudayaan*, *2*(1), 11–25. doi:10.55480/saluscultura.v2i1.41

Nutbrown, C., Clough, P., Levy, R., Little, S., Bishop, J., Lamb, T., & Yamada-Rice, D. (2017). Families' roles in children's literacy in the UK throughout the 20th century. *Journal of Early Childhood Literacy*, *17*(4), 551–569. doi:10.1177/1468798416645385

OECD. (2013). *Financial Literacy Framework. In PISA 2012 Assessment and Analytical Framework - - Mathematics, Reading, Science, Problem Solving and Financial Literacy*. OECD Publishing. https://doi.org/10.1787/9789264190511-1-en

OECD. (2016). *OECD/INFE International Survey of Adult Financial Literacy Competencies*. OECD. https://www.oecd.org/daf/fin/financial-education/OECD-INFE-International-Survey-of-Adult-Financial-Literacy-Competencies.pdf

OECD. (2019). *Programme for International Student Assessment (PISA) Results from PISA 2018*. OECD. https://www.oecd.org/pisa/publications/PISA2018_CN_PHL.pdf

OECD. (2020). *OECD/INFE 2020 International Survey of Adult Financial Literacy*. OECD. https://www.oecd.org/financial/education/oecd-infe-2020-international-survey-of-adult-financial-literacy.pdf

OECD. (2023). *OECD/INFE 2023 International Survey of Adult Financial Literacy.* OECD.

Omidire, F. (2020). Derived knowledge and lived experiences of teachers working in resource-constrained multilingual classrooms. [TETFLE]. *Teacher Education Through Flexible Learning in Africa*, *2*(1), 156–171. doi:10.35293/tetfle.v2i1.92

Organization for Economic Cooperation and Development (OECD). (2023). *PISA 2022 Results: Factsheets*. OECD. https://www.oecd.org/publication/pisa-2022-results/country-notes/indonesia-c2e1ae0e/

Otheguy, R., Garcia, O., & Reid, W. (2019). A translanguaging view of the linguistic system of bilinguals. *Applied Linguistics Review*, *10*(4), 625–651. doi:10.1515/applirev-2018-0020

Ouachani, S., Belhassine, O., & Kammoun, A. (2021). Measuring financial literacy: A literature review. *Managerial Finance*, *47*(2), 266–281. doi:10.1108/MF-04-2019-0175

Özen, Z., Körükmez, L., & Demirel, C. A. (2021). Dijital Çağda Sivil Toplum: İmkânlar ve Kısıtlılıklar. *İnsan hakları okulu raporu, 1.*

Pacheco, M. B., Daniel, S. M., Pray, L. C., & Jiménez, R. T. (2019). Translingual practice, strategic participation, and meaning-making. *Journal of Literacy Research*, *51*(1), 75–99. doi:10.1177/1086296X18820642

Palaiologou, I. (2016). Children under five and digital technologies: Implications for early years pedagogy. *European Early Childhood Education Research Journal*, *24*(1), 5–24. doi:10.1080/1350293X.2014.929876

Pangrazio, L., & Sefton-Green, J. (2020). The social utility of 'data literacy.'. *Learning, Media and Technology*, *45*(2), 208–220. doi:10.1080/17439884.2020.1707223

Parodi, G. (2010). Discourse genres, academic and professional discourses. In G. Parodi (Ed.), *Academic and professional discourse genres in Spanish* (pp. 7–16). John Benjamins. doi:10.1075/scl.40.05par

Paşaoğlu, D. (2017). Dünyada E-Devlet Uygulamaları. Güney, Y. ve Okur, M.R. (Ed.). Bilgi Toplumu Ve E-Devlet içinde (Ünite 4). Eskişehir: Anadolu Üniversitesi Yayınları.

Patrikakou, E. N. (2016). Parent Involvement, Technology, and Media: Now What? *School Community Journal*, *26*(2), 9–24.

Patterson, R., & Weideman, A. (2013). The Refinement of a construct for tests of academic literacy. *Tydskrif vir Taalonderrig*, *47*(1), 125–151. doi:10.4314/jlt.v47i1.6

Pearson, L. C., & Moomaw, W. (2005). The relationship between teacher autonomy and stress, work satisfaction, empowerment, and professionalism. *Educational Research Quarterly*, *29*(1), 38–54.

Pellegrino, J. W. (2002). Knowing what students know. *Issues in Science and Technology*, *19*(2), 48–52.

Petty, N. J., Thomson, O. P., & Stew, G. (2012). Ready for a paradigm shift? Part 2: Introducing qualitative research methodologies and methods. *Manual Therapy*, *17*(5), 378–384. doi:10.1016/j.math.2012.03.004 PMID:22480949

Pharness, G., & Weinstein, L. (2004). Community literacy: from home to work and back. In J. Flood, S. B. Heath, & D. Lapp (Eds.), *Handbook of research on teaching literacy through the communicative and visual arts* (pp. 386–393). Routledge.

Philippas, N. D., & Avdoulas, C. (2020). Financial literacy and financial well-being among generation-Z university students: Evidence from Greece. *European Journal of Finance*, *26*(4-5), 360–381. doi:10.1080/1351847X.2019.1701512

Philstar.com. (2023, July 7). *DepEd to launch reading, math and science programs in learning recovery plan*. PhilStar. https://www.philstar.com/headlines/2023/07/07/2279406/deped-launch-reading-math-and-science-programs-learning-recovery-plan

Phuong, N., & Hegelheimer, V. (2021). New Technologies in Second Language Spoken Assessment. In T. Haug, W. Mann, & U. Knoch (Eds.), *The Handbook of Language Assessment Across Modalities* (pp. 403–416). Academic., doi:10.1093/oso/9780190885052.003.0035

Piasta, S. B., Logan, J. A., Zettler-Greeley, C. M., Bailet, L. L., Lewis, K., & Thomas, L. J. (2023). Small-group, emergent literacy intervention under two implementation models: Intent-to-treat and dosage effects for preschoolers at risk for reading difficulties. *Journal of Learning Disabilities*, *56*(3), 225–240.

Pires, V. C. S. (2014). *O Nível de literacia entre os estudantes do ensino superior em Portugal* [PhD Dissertation, Instituto Superior de Contabilidade e Administração de Coimbra].

Pitsker, K., & Cross, M. (2016). *5 Keys to Building Wealth in Your 20s*. Kiplinger. https://www.kiplinger.com/article/saving/t065-c000-s002-build-wealth-for-a-lifetime.html

Popham, W. J. (2009). Assessment literacy for teachers: Faddish or fundamental? *Theory into Practice*, *48*(1), 4–11. doi:10.1080/00405840802577536

Portolés, L., & Martí, O. (2020). 'Teachers' beliefs about multilingual pedagogies and the role of initial training'. *International Journal of Multilingualism*, *17*(2), 248–264. doi:10.1080/14790718.2018.1515206

Potrich, A. C. G., Vieira, K. M., & Mendes-Da-Silva, W. (2016). Development of a financial literacy model for university students. *Management Research Review*, *39*(3), 356–376. doi:10.1108/MRR-06-2014-0143

Poveda, D. (2019). Researching digital literacy practices in early childhood: Challenges, complexities and imperatives. In *The Routledge handbook of digital literacies in early childhood* (pp. 45–63). Routledge. doi:10.4324/9780203730638-4

Prabhakar, A. (2022). Digital citizenship for 21st century children. *Bhavaveena*, *19*(6), 6476. https://www.researchgate.net/publication/361614925_Digital_Citizenship_For_21st_Century

Prensky, M. (2001). Digital natives, digital immigrants. *On the Horizon MCB University Press*, *9*(5), 1-6. https://www.marcprensky.com/writing/Prensky%20-%20Digital%20Natives,%20Digital%20Immigrants%20-%20Part1.pdf

Prew, M. S. (2012). *Community involvement in school development: Modifying school improvement concepts to the needs of South African township schools*. SAGE Publishers.

Pribudhiana, R. (2013). *Case Study of Post-Literacy Program in Indonesia.* Scholar Works. https://scholarworks.umass.edu/cie_capstones/78/

Primavera, J. (2000). Enhancing family competence through literacy activities. *Journal of Prevention & Intervention in the Community, 20*(1-2), 85–101. doi:10.1300/J005v20n01_07

Prinsloo, M., & Street, B. (2014). Literacy, language, and development: a social practices perspective. *Language Rich Africa Policy Dialogue, 65.*

Puentedura, R. (2013). SAMR: Moving from enhancement to transformation. Hippasus. http://www.hippasus.com/rrpweblog/archives/2013/05/29/SAMREnhancementToTransformation.pdf

Purinton, T. (2024, March 2). *Ted Purinton Bio.* Google Sites. https://sites.google.com/view/tedpurinton/bio

Pushor, D. (2007). *Parent engagement: Creating a shared world.* In the Ontario Education Research Symposium [Symposium]. Toronto, Ontario, Canada.

Putnam, R. (2001). Social capital: Measurement and consequences. *Canadian Journal of Policy Research, 2*(1), 41–51.

Quick, K. S., & Bryson, J. M. (2022). Public participation. In *Handbook on Theories of Governance* (pp. 158–168). Edward Elgar Publishing. doi:10.4337/9781800371972.00022

Rai, K., Dua, S., & Yadav, M. (2019). Association of financial attitude, financial behaviour and financial knowledge towards financial literacy: A structural equation modeling approach. *FIIB Business Review, 8*(1), 51–60. doi:10.1177/2319714519826651

Rainho, N., Santos, T. C. S. M. d., Sousa, M., & Tavares, D. (2017). *A literacia financeira e as necessidades de formação dos estudantes do ensino superior VI Conferência Internacional de Investigação, Práticas e Contextos em Educação 2017.* Instituto Politécnico de Leiria.

Rasyad, A., Wiyono, B. B., & Rahma, R. A. (2020). An analysis of workshop program implementation and competency improvement for adult education facilitators in Indonesia. *Int. J. Innov, 10*(10), 15. https://www.researchgate.net/profile/Bambang-Wiyono-2/publication/345038849_An_Analysis_of_Workshop_Program_Implementation_and_Competency_Improvement_for_Adult_Education_Facilitators_in_Indonesia/links/5f9cd4ff299bf1b53e546aa8/An-Analysis-of-Workshop-Program-Implementation-and-Competency-Improvement-for-Adult-Education-Facilitators-in-Indonesia.pdf

Rex, L. A., & McEachen, D. (1999). If Anything Is Odd, Inappropriate, Confusing, or Boring, It's Probably Important":" The Emergence of Inclusive Academic Literacy through English Classroom Discussion Practices. *Research in the Teaching of English, 34*(1), 65–129. doi:10.58680/rte19991685

Rhyner, P. M. (2009). *Emergent literacy and language development.* The Guilford Press.

Rinawati, N. K. A. (2020). Meningkatkan motivasi belajar dengan bermain kartu pada program keaksaraan dasar. *Jurnal Akrab, 11*(2), 52–61. doi:10.51495/jurnalakrab.v11i02.352

Rix, J., Perry, J., Durry, R., Messer, D. & Hancock, R. (2015). The family experience of bookstart corner an evaluation of bookstart corner. *The Open University Bookstart*, 1-43.

Roche, T. B. (2017). Assessing the role of digital literacy in English for Academic Purposes university pathway programs. *Journal of Academic Language and Learning*, *11*(1), A71–A87.

Roque, V. J., Teodoro, L. A., Cunanan, B. M., & Evangelista, M. T. (2017, June). Using animated e-storybooks to develop Filipino vocabulary and story comprehension among preschool children. In *De La Salle University Congress*.

Rose, D. (2018). Languages of schooling: Embedding literacy learning with genre-based pedagogy. *European Journal of Applied Linguistics*, *6*(1), 59–89. doi:10.1515/eujal-2017-0008

Rottenberg, J. C., & Searfoss, W. L. (1992). Becoming literate in a preschool class: Literacy development of hearing impaired children. *Journal of Reading Behavior*, *24*(4), 463–479. doi:10.1080/10862969209547791

Rowe, D. W. (2000). Bringing books to life: The role of book-related dramatic play in young children's literacy learning. In K. A. Roskos & J. F. Christie (Eds.), *Play and literacy in early childhood research from multiple perspectives* (pp. 3–45). Lawrance Erlbaum Associates Inc.

Rowsell, J., & Walsh, M. (2011). Rethinking literacy education in new times: Multimodality, multiliteracies, & new literacies. *Brock Education*, *21*(1), 53–61. doi:10.26522/brocked.v21i1.236

Ruiz, T. N. (1995). A young deaf child learns to write: Implications for literacy development. *The Reading Teacher*, *49*(3), 206–217.

Rule, P., & Land, S. (2017). Finding the plot in South African reading education. *Reading and Writing*, *8*(1), 1–8.

Rumelhart, D. E. (2017). Schemata: The building blocks of cognition. In R. J. Spiro, B. C. Bruce, & W. F. Brewer (Eds.), *Theoretical issues in reading comprehension* (pp. 33–58). Routledge. doi:10.4324/9781315107493-4

Rundgren, C.-J., Rundgren, S.-N. C., Tseng, Y.-H., Lin, P.-L., & Chang, C.-Y. (2010). Are you SLiM? Developing an instrument for civic scientific literacy measurement (SLiM) based on media coverage. *Public Understanding of Science (Bristol, England)*, *21*(6), 759–773. doi:10.1177/0963662510377562 PMID:23832159

Rusydiyah, E. F. (2023). Literacy policy in southeast Asia: A comparative study between Singapore, Malaysia, and Indonesia. *Center for Educational Policy Studies Journal*, *13*(2), 79–96. doi:10.26529/cepsj.1214

Sadiq, N., & Simbolon, N. E. (2024). Fostering Translanguaging Pedagogy Environment in Indonesian Higher Education EMI Settings: A Critical Discourse Analysis. *Multilingual and Translingual Practices in English-Medium Instruction: Perspectives from Global Higher Education Contexts*, *51*.

Sadoski, M., & Paivio, A. (2013). *Imagery and text: A dual coding theory of reading and writing.* Routledge.

Samsuddin, S. F., Shaffril, H. A. M., Mohamed, N. A., & Bolong, J. (2021). Into the unknown: Do people in low literacy rate areas practise digital reading? *Malaysian Journal of Library and Information Science, 26*(2), 23–36. doi:10.22452/mjlis.vol26no2.2

Sánchez-Cruzado, C., Santiago Campión, R., & Sánchez-Compaña, M. T. (2021). Teacher digital literacy: The indisputable challenge after COVID-19. *Sustainability, 13*(4), 1858.

Sanders, M. G., & Galindo, C. (2014). Communities, schools, and teachers. *Professional Development in Today's Schools.* https://llc.umbc.edu/wp-content/uploads/sites/15/2014/05/2014_Sanders-Galindo1.pdf

Sanders, M. G. (1999). Schools' program and progress in the national network of partnership schools. *The Journal of Educational Research, 92*(4), 220–232. doi:10.1080/00220679909597599

Sanders, M. G. (2001). The role of "community" in comprehensive school, family, and community programs. *The Elementary School Journal, 102*(1), 19–34. doi:10.1086/499691

Sanders, M. G. (2003). Community involvement in schools: From concept to practice. *Education and Urban Society, 35*(2), 161–180. doi:10.1177/0013124502239390

Sanders, M. G. (2018). Crossing boundaries: A qualitative exploration of relational leadership in three full-service community schools. *Teachers College Record, 120*(4), 1–36. doi:10.1177/016146811812000403

Sandvik, M. J., Daal, V., & Ader, J. H. (2014). Emergent literacy:preschool teachers' beliefs and practices. *Journal of Early Childhood Literacy, 14*(1), 28–52. doi:10.1177/1468798413478026

Santos, A. J. C. (2015). *Literacia Financeira: O caso dos alunos dos cursos da área financeira da Escola Superior de Ciências Empresariais (ESCE) do Instituto Politécnico de Setúbal.* IPS. [PhD Dissertation, Instituto Politécnico de Setúbal. Escola Superior de Ciências Empresariais]

Sarabando, P., Matias, R., Vasconcelos, P., & Miguel, T. (2023). Financial literacy of Portuguese undergraduate students in polytechnics: Does the area of the course influence financial literacy? *Journal of Economic Analysis, 2*(2), 96–113. doi:10.58567/jea02020007

Saracho, O. N. (2019). Literacy in the twenty-first century: children, families and policy. In Research in Young Children's Literacy and Language Development (pp. 332-345).

Sari, B. T., van de Vijver, F. J., Chasiotis, A., & Bender, M. (2019). Contextualized bilingualism among adolescents from four different ethnic groups in Indonesia. *The International Journal of Bilingualism, 23*(6), 1469–1482. doi:10.1177/1367006918803678

Sayinzoga, A., Bulte, E. H., & Lensink, R. (2016). Financial literacy and financial behaviour: Experimental evidence from rural Rwanda. *Economic Journal (London), 126*(594), 1571–1599. doi:10.1111/ecoj.12217

Schagen, S., & Lines, A. (1996). *Financial literacy in adult life: a report to the Natwest Group Charitable Trust*. NFER.

Schirmer, R. B. (2005). Language and literacy development in children who are deaf. (2.Ed.) MA: Allyn and Bacon.

Schmidt, P. R., & Lazar, A. M. (Eds.). (2019). *Practicing what we teach: How culturally responsive literacy classrooms make a difference*. Teachers College Press.

Schriever, V. (2018). Digital technology in kindergarten: Challenges and opportunities. Handbook of research on mobile devices and smart gadgets in K-12 education, 57-76.

Schutz, A. (2006). Home is a prison in the global city: The tragic failure of school-based community engagement strategies. *Review of Educational Research*, *76*(4), 691–743. doi:10.3102/00346543076004691

Sciacca, B., Laffan, D. A., Norman, J. O. H., & Milosevic, T. (2022). Parental mediation in pandemic: Predictors and relationship with children's digital skills and time spent online in Ireland. *Computers in Human Behavior*, *127*, 107081. doi:10.1016/j.chb.2021.107081 PMID:34720386

Scott, A., & Gillon, G. (2022). The evolution of an innovative online task to monitor children's oral narrative development. *Frontiers in Psychology*, *13*, 903124. https://doi.org/10.3389/fpsyg.2022.903124

Scott, J., Williams, D., Gilliam, J., & Sybrowsky, J. (2013). Is an all cash emergency fund strategy appropriate for all investors. *Journal of Financial Planning*, *26*(9), 56–62.

Sharif, I., Rieber, S., Ozuah, P. O., & Reiber, S. (2002). Exposure to reach out and read and vocabulary outcomes in inner city preschoolers. *Journal of the National Medical Association*, *94*(3), 171. https://www.ncbi.nlm.nih.gov/pmc/articles/PMC2594107/pdf/jnma00320-0069.pdf PMID:11918387

Shatkin, G., & Gershberg, A. I. (2007). Empowering parents and building communities: The role of school-based councils in educational governance and accountability. *Urban Education*, *42*(6), 582–615. doi:10.1177/0042085907305044

Shepard, L. A., Penuel, W. R., & Pellegrino, J. W. (2018). Using learning and motivation theories to coherently link formative assessment, grading practices, and large-scale assessment. *Educational Measurement: Issues and Practice*, *37*(1), 21–34. doi:10.1111/emip.12189

Sheridan, S. M., Knoche, L. L., Kupzyk, K. A., Edwards, C. P., & Marvin, C. A. (2011). A randomized trial examining the effects of parent engagement on early language and literacy: The Getting Ready intervention. *Journal of School Psychology*, *49*(3), 361–383. doi:10.1016/j.jsp.2011.03.001 PMID:21640249

Shrestha, S., & Krolak, L. (2015). The potential of community libraries in supporting literate environments and sustaining literacy skills. *International Review of Education*, *61*(3), 399–418. https://eric.ed.gov/?id=EJ1071442. doi:10.1007/s11159-014-9462-9

Silbert, P. & Bitso, Constance (2015). Towards functional school libraries: supporting library assistants in under-resourced schools through a university-community-school partnership. *SA Jnl Libs & Info Sci, 81*(1), 53-62. https://doi:. doi:10.7553/81-1-1553

Simpson, S. (2010). *Learning systems: An ecological perspective on advanced academic literacy practices of multilingual writers*. [Doctoral thesis, University of New Hampshire]. University of New Hampshire Scholars Repository. https://scholars.unh.edu/dissertation/530

Simpson, A., El-Refaie, A., Stephenson, C., Chen, Y. P. P., Deng, D., Erickson, S., Tay, D., Morris, M. E., Doube, W., & Caelli, T. (2015). Computer-based rehabilitation for developing speech and language in hearing-impaired children: A systematic review. *Deafness & Education International, 17*(2), 111–119. https://doi.org/10.1179/1557069X14Y.0000000046

Sindoni, M. G., & Moschini, I. (Eds.). (2021). *Multimodal literacies across digital learning contexts*. Routledge. doi:10.4324/9781003134244

Smith, L. (2011, January). Applying the bioecological theory of human development to learning. Enhancing student engagement in online learning. In *Proceedings of the 10th Teaching Matters Annual Conference* (pp. 1-8). Springer.

Smith, F., & Goodman, K. S. (1973). On the psycholinguistic method of teaching reading. In F. Smith (Ed.), *Psycholinguistics and Reading* (pp. 177–182). Holt, Rinehart and Winston.

Smyczek, S., & Matysiewicz, J. (2015). Consumers' financial literacy as tool for preventing future economic crisis. *Review of Business, 36*(1), 19–33.

Snow, C. E. (2017). Early literacy development and instruction: An overview. The Routledge international handbook of early literacy education, 5-13.

Snow, C. E., Burns, M. S., & Griffin, P. (1998). *Preventing reading difficulties in young children*. National Academy Press.

Song, Y., & Ma, Q. (2021). Affordances of a mobile learner-generated tool for pupils' English as a second language vocabulary learning: An ecological perspective. *British Journal of Educational Technology, 52*(2), 858–878. doi:10.1111/bjet.13037

Soyoof, A., Reynolds, B. L., Neumann, M., Scull, J., Tour, E., & McLay, K. (2024). The impact of parent mediation on young children's home digital literacy practices and learning: A narrative review. *Journal of Computer Assisted Learning, 40*(1), 65–88.

Spaull, N., & Pretorius, E. (2019). *Still falling at the first hurdle: Examining early grade reading in South Africa South African Schooling: The Enigma of Inequality*. Springer.

Star, J. (2022). *Application of Adult Education in Indonesia*. Kompasiana. https://www.kompasiana.com/bintangjayezvara/6399130408a8b552e75f4d42/penerapan-pendidikan-orang-dewasa-adult-education-dalam-pendidikan-di-indonesia

Statti, A., & Torres, K. M. (2020). Digital literacy: The need for technology integration and its impact on learning and engagement in community school environments. *Peabody Journal of Education*, *95*(1), 90–100. https://eric.ed.gov/?id=EJ1247203. doi:10.1080/0161956X.2019.1702426

Street, B. (2016). Learning to read from a social practice view: Ethnography, schooling, and adult learning. *Prospects*, *46*(3), 335–344. doi:10.1007/s11125-017-9411-z

Suleymanova, S., & Hysaj, A. (2022, June). Undergraduate Emirati Students' Challenges of Language Barrier in Meeting Expectations of English Medium University in the UAE. In *International Conference on Human-Computer Interaction* (pp. 199-209). Cham: Springer International Publishing. 10.1007/978-3-031-05064-0_15

Sulzby, E., & Teale, W. H. (1987). *Young children's storybook reading: Longitudinal study of parent-child interaction and children's independent functioning.* Spencer Foundation, The University of Michigan.

Sung, Y. Y. C., & Chiu, D. K. (2022). E-book or print book: Parents' current view in Hong Kong. *Library Hi Tech*, *40*(5), 1289–1304. doi:10.1108/LHT-09-2020-0230

Swanwick, R., & Watson, L. (2005). Literacy in the homes of young deaf children: Common and distinct features of spoken language and sign bilingual environments. *Journal of Early Childhood Literacy*, *5*(1), 53–78. doi:10.1177/1468798405050594

Talay, Ö. (2018). *Mobil Ortam Reklamlarında Dijital Gözetim Algısı: Dijital Göçmenler ve Dijital Yerlilerin Karşılaştırılmalı Analizi.* Yüksek Lisans Tezi Akdeniz Üniversitesi Sosyal Bilimler Enstitüsü.

Tamer, M. G. (2010). Tarihsel süreçte sivil toplum. *Hacettepe Üniversitesi Edebiyat Fakültesi Dergisi, 27*(1), 89-105. https://dergipark.org.tr/en/download/article-file/615583

Tavares, F. O., & Almeida, L. G. d. (2020). A literacia financeira: Uma revisão da literatura. *Percursos & Ideias, 11*(2), 73–88.

Taylor, S., Cillier, J., Prinsloo, C., & Reddy, J. (2018). *Improving early grade reading in South Africa.* Research Gate.

Teale, W. H., & Sulzby, E. (1986). Introduction: Emergent literacy as a perspective for examining how young children become writers and readers. In W. H. Teale & E. Sulzby (Eds.), *Emergent literacy* (pp. vii–xxii). Ablex Publishing.

The 1987 Constitution of the Republic of the Philippines – Article XIV (n.d.). *Education, science and technology, arts, culture and sports.* https://www.officialgazette.gov.ph/constitutions/the-1987-constitution-of-the-republic-of-the-philippines/the-1987-constitution-of-the-republic-of-the-philippines-article-xiv/

The Jakarta Post. (2020). HAI 2020: Indonesia's literacy programs show great success. *The Jakarta Post.* https://www.thejakartapost.com/adv/2020/09/07/hai-2020-indonesias-literacy-programs-show-great-success.html

The National Council of Teachers of English. (2019). *Definition of literacy in a digital age.* NCTE. https://ncte.org/statement/nctes-definition-literacy-digital-age/

The World Bank. (2022). *70% of 10-year-olds now in learning poverty, unable to read and understand a simple text.* World Bank. https://www.worldbank.org/en/news/press- release/2022/06/23/70-of-10-year-olds-now-in-learning-poverty-unable-to-read-and- understand-a-simple-text

Theriot, J. A., Franco, S. M., Sisson, B. A., Metcalf, S. C., Kennedy, M. A., & Bada, H. S. (2003). The impact of early literacy guidance on language skills of 3-year-olds. *Clinical Pediatrics, 42*(2), 165–172. doi:10.1177/000992280304200211 PMID:12659391

Thompson, B. C., Mazer, J. P., & Flood Grady, E. (2015). The changing nature of parent–teacher communication: Mode selection in the smartphone era. *Communication Education, 64*(2), 187–207. doi:10.1080/03634523.2015.1014382

Troseth, G. L., Strouse, G. A., Flores, I., Stuckelman, Z. D., & Johnson, C. R. (2020). An enhanced eBook facilitates parent–child talk during shared reading by families of low socioeconomic status. *Early Childhood Research Quarterly, 50*, 45–58. doi:10.1016/j.ecresq.2019.02.009

Truax, R. R. (1978). Reading and language. In R. R. Kretschmer, L. W. Kretschmer, & R. R. Truax (Eds.), *Language development and intervention with the hearing impaired* (pp. 279–309). University Park Press.

Trunk, A., & Dermol, V. (2015). EU integration through financial literacy and entrepreneurship Managing Intellectual Capital and Innovation for Sustainable and Inclusive Society, Management, Knowledge and Learning. *Joint International Conference*, Bari, Italy.

Tufekcioglu, U. (2007). Cocuklarda isitme kaybının etkileri. U. Tufekcioglu (Ed.), İsitme konusma, gorme sorunu olan cocukların egitimi icinde (pp.1-45). Eskisehir: Anadolu University Publishing.

Turan, Z. KucukOncu D., Cankuvvet, N. & Yolal, Y. (2012). Koklear implant ve isitme cihazı kullanan isitme kayıplı cocukların dil ve dinleme becerilerinin degerlendirilmesi [Evaluation of language and listening skills of the children with hearing loss who use cochlear implants and hearing aids]. *Gulhane Tip Dergisi, 4*, 142-150. https://cms.gulhanemedj.org/Uploads/Article_33377/GMJ-54-142-En.pdf

Turan, Z., Koca, A., & Uzuner, Y. (2019). İsitme kayıplı cocugu olan bir annenin aile egitimi surecinin incelenmesi. *Ankara Universitesi Egitim Bilimleri Fakultesi Ozel Egitim Dergisi, 20*(1), 93–117. doi:10.21565/ozelegitimdergisi.417177

Türkmen, A., & Kılıç, Y. (2022). What matters for pension planning in Turkey: Financial literacy or perceived consumer risks? *International Journal of Social Economics, 49*(1), 138–151. doi:10.1108/IJSE-03-2021-0140

Uğurlu, H. Y. (2019). *Sivil Toplum çalışmalarına katılımı Motive Eden faktörler ve gönüllü üniversite öğrencileri arasında Bir araştırma* [Doctoral dissertation, Marmara University, Turkey].

Ullah, A., & Anwar, S. (2020). The effective use of information technology and interactive activities to improve learner engagement. *Education Sciences, 10*(12), 349. doi:10.3390/educsci10120349

Undheim, M. (2022). Children and teachers engaging together with digital technology in early childhood education and care institutions: A literature review. *European Early Childhood Education Research Journal*, *30*(3), 472–489. doi:10.1080/1350293X.2021.1971730

UNESCO Institute of Learning. (February 26, 2016). *AKRAB! Literacy Creates Power, Indonesia.* UNESCO. https://uil.unesco.org/case-study/effective-practices-database-litbase-0/akrab-literacy-creates-power-indonesia#:~:text=Aksara%20Agar%20Berdaya%20(AKRAB!),local%20languages%20and%20Bahasa%20Indonesia

UNICEF Philippines. (2021). *Southeast Asia Primary Learning Metrics 2019 National Report of the Philippines*. UNICEF Philippines. https://www.unicef.org/philippines/reports/sea-plm-metrics-2019-national-report-philippines

UNICEF. (2021). *Alternative learning system in the Philippines: A review of the evidence*. UNICEF.

United Nations (UN). (2018). *E-government survey: Gearing E-government to support transformation towards sustainable and resilient societies*. UN. https://publicadministration.un.org/egovkb/Portals/egovkb/Documents/un/2018-Survey/E-Government%20Survey%202018_FINAL%20for%20web.pdf

Uzuner, Y. (1993). *An investigation of a hearing mother's reading aloud efforts to her preschool age hearing and hearing impaired children before bedtime*. [Phd Dissertation. A.B.D: Cincinnati University].

Valli, L., Stefanski, A., & Jacobson, R. (2014). *School-community partnerships: A typology for guiding systemic educational reform. Policy Brief*. College of Education. University of Maryland.

Van Dijk, J. A. (2017). Digital divide: Impact of access. The International Encyclopedia of Media Effects, 1-11.

van Steensel, R., McElvany, N., Kurvers, J., & Herppich, S. (2011). How effective are family literacy programs? results of a meta-analysis. *Review of Educational Research*, *81*(1), 69–96. doi:10.3102/0034654310388819

VÁSquez, O. A. (2007). Technology out of school: What schools can learn from community-based technology. *Teachers College Record*, *109*(14), 182–206. doi:10.1177/016146810710901410

Vélez, A. P., Olivencia, J. J. L., & Zuazua, I. I. (2017). The role of adults in children digital literacy. *Procedia: Social and Behavioral Sciences*, *237*, 887–892. doi:10.1016/j.sbspro.2017.02.124

Vezzoli, Y., Kalantari, S., Kucirkova, N., & Vasalou, A. (2020, April). Exploring the design space for parent-child reading. *In Proceedings of the 2020 CHI Conference on Human Factors in Computing Systems* (pp. 1-12). 10.1145/3313831.3376696

Vieira, C. E. R. (2018). *A literacia financeira dos estudantes do ensino superior da rede APNOR* [PhD Dissertation, Instituto Politecnico de Braganca, Portugal].

Vontz, T. S., Metcalf, K. K., & Patrick, J. J. (2000). *Project Citizen and the civic development of adolescent students in Indiana, Latvia, and Lithuania.* The ERIC Clearinghouse for Social Studies/Social Science Education.

Vygotsky, L. S. (1978). *Mind in society the development of higher psychological processes.* Harvard University Press.

Vygotsky, L. S., & Cole, M. (1978). *Mind in society: Development of higher psychological processes.* Harvard University Press.

Wade, B., & Moore, M. (1993). *Bookstart in Birmingham: a description and evaluation of an exploratory British project to encourage sharing books with babies.* Book Trust.

Waldbart, A., Meyers, B., & Meyers, J. (2006). Invitations to families in an early literacy support program. *The Reading Teacher, 59*(8), 774–785. doi:10.1598/RT.59.8.5

Walker, L. O., & Avant, K. C. (2011). *Strategies for Theory Construction in Nursing* (5th ed.). Prentice Hall.

Walstad, W. B., Rebeck, K., & MacDonald, R. A. (2010). The effects of financial education on the financial knowledge of high school students. *The Journal of Consumer Affairs, 44*(2), 336–357. doi:10.1111/j.1745-6606.2010.01172.x

Wang, Y., & Li, S. (2020). Issues, challenges, and future directions for multilingual assessment. *Journal of Language Teaching and Research, 11*(6), 914–919. doi:10.17507/jltr.1106.06

Warschauer, M. (2006). Literacy and technology: Bridging the divide. *Cyberlines, 2,* 163–174.

Wason-Ellam, L., Ward, A., Fey, C., King, A.-L., Gilchrist, B., & Townsend, L. (2004). Community literacy: Commodifying children's spaces. *Language and Literature, 6*(1). doi:10.20360/G2MS4H

Wei, L. (2015). Complementary classrooms for multilingual minority ethnic children as a translanguaging space. In J. Cenoz & D. Gorter (Eds.), *Multilingual education: Between language learning and translanguaging* (pp. 177–198). Cambridge Applied Linguistics. doi:10.1017/9781009024655.010

Wei, L. (2018). Translanguaging as a practical theory of language. *Applied Linguistics, 39*(1), 9–30. doi:10.1093/applin/amx039

Wei, L., & Lin, A. M. (2019). *Translanguaging classroom discourse: Pushing limits, breaking boundaries* (Vol. 10). Taylor & Francis.

Weiss, Y., Yeatman, J. D., Ender, S., Gijbels, L., Loop, H., Mizrahi, J. C., Woo, B. Y., & Kuhl, P. K. (2022). Can an online reading camp teach 5-year-old children to read? *Frontiers in Human Neuroscience, 16,* 52.

Wenger, E. (2000). Communities of practice and social learning systems. *Organization, 7*(2), 225–246. doi:10.1177/135050840072002

Whitehurst, G. J., & Lonigan, C. J. (1998). Child development and emergent literacy. *Child Development*, *69*(3), 848–872. doi:10.1111/j.1467-8624.1998.tb06247.x PMID:9680688

Wickham, C. A., & Carbone, E. T. (2018). "Just Say It Like It Is!" Use of a Community-Based Participatory Approach to Develop a Technology-Driven Food Literacy Program for Adolescents. *International Quarterly of Community Health Education*, *38*(2), 83–97. doi:10.1177/0272684X17749572 PMID:29283040

Wie, O. B., Falkenberg, O. T., & Tomblin, B. (2007). Children with a cochlear implant: Characteristics and determinants of speech recognition, speech recognition growth rate, and speech production. *International Journal of Audiology*, *46*(5), 232–243. doi:10.1080/14992020601182891 PMID:17487671

Wildsmith-Cromarty, R., & Steinke, K. (2014). The write approach: Can R2L help at tertiary level? *Per Linguam*, *30*(1), 38–54. doi:10.5785/30-1-570

William, A. (2004). Civic Education and Political Participation. Political Science Online. http://www.apsanet.org/imgtest/CivicEdPoliticalParticipation.pdf

Williams, C. (2004). Emergent literacy of deaf children. *Journal of Deaf Studies and Deaf Education*, *9*(4), 352–365. doi:10.1093/deafed/enh045 PMID:15314011

Willingham, D. T. (2006). The effectiveness of brief instruction in reading comprehension strategies. *American Educator*, (Winter), 39–45.

Wilson, K. K. (2002). *Promoting civic literacy*. (ERIC Document Reproduction Service No. ED466924).

Wimalasiri, A., & Seals, C. A. (2022). Translanguaging in online language teaching: A case study of a multilingual English language teacher in New Zealand. *Journal of Multilingual Theories and Practices*, *3*(1), 127–145. doi:10.1558/jmtp.20849

Windisch, H. C. (2015). *Adults with low literacy and numeracy skills: A literature review on policy intervention*. doi:10.1787/19939019

Wingate, U. (2015). *Academic literacy and student diversity: The case for inclusive practice*. Multilingual Matters. doi:10.21832/9781783093496

Wingate, U. (2018). Academic literacy across the curriculum: Towards a collaborative instructional approach. *Language Teaching*, *51*(3), 349–364. doi:10.1017/S0261444816000264

Wood, W. C., & Doyle, J. M. (2002). Economic literacy among corporate employees. *The Journal of Economic Education*, *33*(3), 195–205. doi:10.1080/00220480209595186

Xanthopoulou, D., & Papagiannidis, S. (2012). Play online, work better? Examining the spillover of active learning and transformational leadership. *Technological Forecasting and Social Change*, *79*(7), 1328–1339. doi:10.1016/j.techfore.2012.03.006

Yafele, S. (2021). Translanguaging for academic reading at a South African university. *Southern African Linguistics and Applied Language Studies*, *39*(4), 404–424. doi:10.2989/16073614.2021.1981767

Yafele, S., & Makalela, L. (2022). From Fixity to Fluidity: A Critique of Higher Education Language Policy. In L. Makalela (Ed.), *Language and Institutional Identity in the Post-Apartheid South African Higher Education. Language Policy* (Vol. 27). Springer. doi:10.1007/978-3-030-85961-9_8

Yaribakht, M., & Movallali, G. (2020). The effects of an early family-centered tele-intervention on the preverbal and listening skills of deaf children under tow years old. *Iranian Rehabilitation Journal*, *18*(2), 117–124.

Yaşar, İ. H., & Altıncık, H. (2018). Türkiye Cumhuriyeti bakanliklarinin web sitelerinin halkla ilişkiler bağlamında değerlendirilmesi. *Dumlupinar University Journal of Social Sciences, 2*(55), 224-236. https://dergipark.org.tr/en/pub/dpusbe/issue/35683/333941

Ychart. (2020). *Indonesia Adult Literacy Rate (I:IALRUY).* y Charts. https://ycharts.com/indicators/indonesia_adult_literacy_rate#:~:text=Indonesia%20Adult%20Literacy%20Rate%20is%20at%2096.00%25%2C%20compared,higher%20than%20the%20long%20term%20average%20of%2090.51%25.

Yıldırım Kaptan, B. (2023). *Kamu Yönetimi Kuramlari ve E-Devlet Olgusu Arasında Bir İnceleme* [Doctoral dissertation].

Yılmaz, V. (2019). E-Devlet Uygulamasının güvenilirliği ve kullanım düzeyinin ölçülmesi: Bitlis ili örneği. *Assam Uluslararası Hakemli Dergi, 6(14),* 226-239. https://dergipark.org.tr/tr/pub/assam/issue/48907/577924

Yoshinaga-Itano, C., Sedey, A. L., Wiggin, M., & Chung, W. (2017). Early hearing detection and vocabulary of children with hearing loss. *Pediatrics*, *140*(2).

Yuksel, D., Altay, M., & Curle, S. (Eds.). (2024). *Multilingual and translingual practices in English-medium instruction: Perspectives from global higher education contexts*. Bloomsbury Publishing. doi:10.5040/9781350373273

Yulaelawati, E. (2016). *AKRAB! Literacy Creates Power, Indonesia*. UNESCO. https://uil.unesco.org/case-study/effective-practices-database-litbase-0/akrab-literacy-creates-power-indonesia

Yunas, M., Dad, R., Shakoor, A., & Wahid, F. (2021). Dimensions of school community relationship: Issues and concerns. *Psychology and Education*, *58*(4), 4587–4591. http://psychologyandeducation.net/pae/index.php/pae/article/view/5815/4990

Yurttadur, M. ve Süzen, E. (2016). Türkiye'de Banka Müşterilerinin İnternet Bankacılığına Yaklaşımlarının İncelenmesi Üzerine Bir Uygulama, *Tüketici ve Tüketim Araştırmaları Dergisi, 8* (1), 93-120. http://hdl.handle.net/11363/1039

Yusmalinda, A., & Astuti, P. (2020). English teachers' methods in teaching reading comprehension of procedure text. *Journal of English Language Teaching*. 10.15294/elt.v9i1.38676

Compilation of References

Zarnowski, M. (2009). The Thought Experiment: An Imaginative Way into Civic Literacy. *Social Studies*, *100*(2), 55–62. doi:10.3200/TSSS.100.2.55-62

Zuckerman, S. J. (2022). Beyond the school walls: Collective impact in micropolitan school-community partnerships. *Peabody Journal of Education*, *97*(1), 1–14. doi:10.1080/016195 6X.2022.2026724

About the Contributors

Al Ryanne Gabonada Gatcho is an Associate Professor at the School of Foreign Languages and Literature at Hunan Institute of Science and Technology. He supervises PhD students and teaches English and Literacy Education at both undergraduate and graduate levels. A PhD graduate in Reading Education from Philippine Normal University and a research fellow at International Islamic University Malaysia. His research, which he has presented and published internationally, explores the nexus between technology and literacy education in ESL/EFL contexts, focusing on support for learning-disabled readers, the integration of technology in literacy education, and the future of literacy in digital societies. He contributes to the editorial boards of two international journals, is an active member of several professional organizations, and has been involved in significant research projects, including developing a national framework for literacy programs in the Philippines. Additionally, he consults on reading program development and module evaluation in the Philippines' Department of Education and serves as a course evaluator for SEAMEO INNOTECH.

Cecille Marie Titar Improgo is a faculty of Bukidnon State University, Philippines. Her teaching career started with teaching English to adolescents. She later began teaching in the college department, mentoring English major students in the College of Education. She has been involved in extension services along her field of specialization - English language teaching - where she had the opportunity to work with teachers in the field and instructors/trainers in the military. Driven by her passion for reading, she later proceeded to this more specific field and pursued advance studies at PNU-Manila where she earned her PhD in Reading Education as a grantee of CHED Scholarship under the K to 12 Transition Program. With the challenges in delivering continued instruction during the pandemic, she served as the university coordinator of instructional design and development. This opened yet another opportunity for her to further practice her interest in instructional materials construction and explore instructional design. Currently, she is serving as the director of the university's Center for Innovative Teaching and Learning.

Merry Ruth Morauda Gutierrez is a full time faculty of CGSTER, PNU-Manila. She is the graduate college representative to the University Curriculum and Instructional Materials Management Office. She earned her PhD in Reading Education under the CHED Scholarship Grant for Dissertation Writing.

***

Poonam Anand is an Assistant Professor in the English Language Education program at Bahrain Teachers College, University of Bahrain. Her PhD is in Applied Linguistics and Discourse Studies from Carleton University, Canada. She has several years of teaching experience in Bahrain and Canada as a teacher trainer as well as an ESL/EAP teacher. Currently, she teaches Assessment Methods in Education, Language Testing, and ESL content and pedagogy courses to pre-service and in-service teacher candidates. Her research interests lie in Genre-based teaching methods, assessment of English for academic purposes literacies, and assessment of Young Language Learners. She is keen on questions arising from the social impact of high stakes examinations, issues of validity in test use, and various assessment models of second languages.

Hilal Atlar-Yildirim graduated from Anadolu University, Department of Special Education, Teaching of the Hearing Impaired in 2008. She taught children with hearing loss until 2014. She received her MS in Education of the Hearing Impaired from Anadolu University in 2017. She completed her master's thesis with a study examining the emergent literacy experiences of a child with hearing loss in Turkey. She conducted a pilot implementation of a program that supports the early literacy experiences of children with hearing loss by empowering their families in Turkey under the consultancy of Yıldız Uzuner.

Aniesa Samira Bafadhal is a senior lecturer in the Tourism Study Program, Faculty of Administrative Science, at the University of Brawijaya, Indonesia. Since 2018, she has served as vice head of the Tourism Research Laboratory and has been involved in the Tourism Research Center at the University of Brawijaya. Her research interests currently focus on a number of areas, including virtual tourism, heritage tourism, visual culture, and health tourism.

Parween Ebrahim is a faculty member in the English Language Education Department at the Bahrain Teacher College. She served as the chairperson of English Language Department from 2018-2022. She holds a Ph.D. in English from Princeton University, USA. Dr Ebrahim has taught foundation and bachelor's degree students at the teachers' college in addition to supervising pre- and in-service teachers. Her research and teaching interests include bilingual and multi-cultural literacy, World Englishes, teaching writing to ESL students, children's literature, and teaching English literature to second language learners of English.

Lemuel-Kim A. Garcia is a graduate of Bachelor of Secondary Education major in English at Nueva Ecija University of Science and Technology where he also finished his Master of Arts in English with an academic excellence award. He served as an instructor at College for Research and Technology, and as a senior high school teacher at Honorato C. Perez Memorial Science High School. Currently, he is serving as an English and ICT teacher at Magpapalayok National High School. He is also Board Licensure for Professional Teachers reviewer at ChainRinivarts Educational Training Center, teaching foundations and legal bases of education. As he goes on with his career as a teacher, he was engaged and appointed to hold different tasks in the Department of Education such as being a resource speaker in research, assessment, and pedagogy. He is sought after in developing diagnostic tests, session guides, reading materials for struggling readers, learning activity sheets, video lessons, layout and language consultation from division up to regional level. He is the associate editor of "The Reading Teacher", the official reading journal of DepEd – Region III. He is also one of the consultants in the developed modules for struggling readers in Grade 4 used in DepEd Region III. In the field of research, he was able to publish and acknowledged in the following journals: International Journal on Scientific Advancement, International Journal for Applied and Basic Subjects, International Journal of Scientific and Research Publication, American Journal of Educational Research, Researchers' World of Arts, Science and Commerce and North Asian International Research Journal of Science and Engineering and IT. Locally, he published 2 action researches in the DepEd-Schools Division of Nueva Ecija for policy recommendations and pedagogical improvement, both were also published in indexed journals. Because of his consistent engagement in the field of research, he was selected to be a member of the DepEd-Nueva Ecija's Project ARM, a research council that was formed to quality assure the action researches, and innovations in the provincial division. In the teaching field, he was awarded as the Most Outstanding Teacher Implementer in English, ICT and LRMDS in 2019. He was also a Gawad ng Tagapamanihala Gintong Butil Awardee in 2020. He believes that competence is not measured by achievement, but by the number of inspired lives which he perceives that only teachers can do.

Muhammad Rosyihan Hendrawan is an assistant professor in the Department of Library and Information Science at the Faculty of Administrative Science, University of Brawijaya, Indonesia. He was a vice head of university archives at the University of Brawijaya from 2016–2020 and a vice head of institutional memory for the Faculty of Administrative Science at the University of Brawijaya since 2020. His involvement extends to the Indonesian Library and Information Science Scholars Association, where he serves on the board. His research interests include cultural heritage information management, knowledge organization systems, information governance, and knowledge management. The email address at which to contact him is mrhendrawan@ub.ac.id

Ramil G. Ilustre is Regional Education Program Supervisor II in English, Journalism, and Foreign Language in DepEd Regional Office III-Curriculum and Learning Management Division. As Regional English Supervisor, his main tasks include periodic curriculum monitoring and evaluation of the K-12 English curriculum towards enhancing the management of delivery of the basic education curriculum as enunciated in RA 10533. In addition, he is a qualitative researcher, resource speaker, writer, and international paper presenter. Dr. Ilustre obtained his MAEd in English Language Education and PhD in Education both at Bulacan State University. He completed with flying colors his Diploma in TESOL at Concordia International College, Vancouver, Canada. He has written action researches for DepEd and presented in division, regional, and international research conferences. In addition, he is handling PhD and MAED subjects at Bulacan State University-Graduate School and Nueva Ecija University of Science and Technology-Graduate School as Professional Lecturer. Presently, he is finishing his dissertation writing for his second doctorate degree, Doctor of Education in English Language Teaching, at Filamer Christian University in Roxas City. Just recently he is selected to be a Chief Trainer in the Upskilling of English Teachers on Language Instruction by DepEd Central Office- Bureau of Learning Delivery.

Jeremiah Paul G. Manuel boasts over twenty years of experience as an educator, impacting the literacy development of countless children worldwide. Currently pursuing advanced studies at the Philippine Normal University, he aspires to earn a Doctor of Philosophy in Reading Education. Previously, Jeremiah served as an instructor of Pedagogy and English disciplines at the College of Education of Pamantasan ng Lungsod ng Muntinlupa. Presently, he contributes as an associate researcher at the National Research Council of the Philippines, delving into areas such as early and adult literacy, technology-integrated education, brain-based learning, and Physical Education and sports. Currently, Jeremiah imparts knowledge and guidance to students at Sekolah Pelita Harapan Kemang Village in Jakarta, Indonesia, where children benefit from his expertise and instruction.

Xing Geng Mao serves as an Associate Professor at Nanhu College and the School of Foreign Languages and Literature at Hunan Institute of Science and Technology, China, where he specializes in translation theory and literature, as well as English language teaching in EFL contexts. His research spans the fields of Juvenile and Adult Literature, emphasizing the profound impact of literary studies across age groups. With a keen focus on how literature bridges cultural divides and fosters deeper linguistic understanding, his work enriches the academic discourse on language acquisition and the transformative power of literature in education. His commitment to exploring the intersections of language, culture, and literature aims to inspire both young learners and adults, making significant contributions to the understanding and appreciation of English literature in a global context.

Ana Pinto Borges holds a PhD in Economics, Faculty of Economics, University of Porto from 2009. Since 2010 She is Coordinating Professor at ISAG - European Business School specializing on the areas of Economics, Management, and Finance, and since 2015 Coordinator of the Master's Degree in Business Management and President of the Pedagogical Council of ISAG. She is Scientific Coordinator of Research Centre in Business Sciences and Tourism (CICET – FCVC) since 2021 and coordinated the ISAG Research Centre (NIDISAG) between 2015 and 2021. Since 2018, she is researcher of the Centre for Research in Organizations, Markets and Industrial Management (COMEGI). She supervised 2 PhD theses and is now supervising other 2, in addition to having supervised more than 40 master's theses. She published more than 180 publications (around 120 indexed in Scopus/WoS databases) in journals/book chapters/proceedings and 5 books (3 indexed in Scopus). She is associate editor at the Eurasian Business Review (indexed by Scopus/WoS – Q1) and editor and one of the founding members of the European Journal of Applied Business and Management (EJABM). She founded, integrated the organizer and scientific committees and did the co-editor of the proceedings of International Conference in Applied Business and Management (ICABM – 5 eds since 2016), International Workshop in Tourism and Hospitality Management (IWTHM – 3 eds since 2017), and in Accounting and Taxation (IWAT – 3 eds since 2021). All these academic events have been indexed or are in evaluation by WoS and by EBSCO, among others. Furthermore, she is the coordinator and co-author of several applied projects financed by external entities (companies, municipalities, among others). She is Economist at the Portuguese Health Regulatory Authority since 2010 with the main function of carrying out sectoral studies and issuing opinions in the scope of access, quality and competition.

Fu Ting holds the position of Deputy Director at the International Exchange Office of Hunan Institute of Science and Technology, China, and is currently pursuing her PhD at the University of Science Malaysia. Her research focuses on leadership and management within the realm of Higher Education, exploring the dynamics and strategies that influence the effective governance and advancement of academic institutions. With a keen interest in how leadership practices shape educational outcomes and organizational cultures, her work contributes to a deeper understanding of the complexities involved in managing and leading higher educational establishments in today's global and rapidly evolving academic landscape.

Yıldız Uzuner received her Ph.D. in Special Education Division of Hearing Impairment from the University of Cincinnati in the United States. In 1993, she completed her doctoral dissertation titled " An Investigation of A Hearing Mother's Reading Aloud Efforts to Her Preschool Age Hearing And Hearing Impaired Children Before Bedtime ". She works as a lecturer (also researcher) at Anadolu University, Faculty of Education, Department of Special Education, Department of Hearing Impaired Education. In addition to her thirty-eight years of experience in the language development and education of children with hearing loss, she is also an expert in qualitative research methods.

Elvira Vieira holds a PhD in Applied Economics at the University of Santiago de Compostela (2007). Since 2012, she is Dean of ISAG – European Business School, where's she is also Principal Coordinating Professor and Member of the Technical-Scientific Council. Invited Adjunct Professor at the Polytechnic Institute of Viana do Castelo - School of Business Sciences. Integrated Member at the Applied Management Research Unit (UNIAG) since 2010, and Collaborative Member of the Research Centre in Business Sciences and Tourism (CICET - FCVC), since 2021. Coordinated the ISAG Research Centre (NIDISAG) between 2009 and 2021. Author of more than 160 publications, between books, book chapters and papers in scientific journals with peer review, indexed in the various international databases. Her professional profile and career path can be described as inter and multidisciplinary – between teaching and researching experience starting on early stages of her life, alongside business and institutional responsibilities and top management positions, she embeds an experience that enables specialization and general expertise to coexist – from economics, to management, tourism, regional and cross-border development, innovation and entrepreneurship, information and communication technologies and corporate governance. Started as a Professor in the private sector, and soon joined public higher education institutions. Throughout this career, common effects and outcomes can be highlighted: whenever possible, joined bodies concerning pedagogic and/or scientific matters, enrolled in the organization of several events (scientific and/or pedagogical), established new partnerships and projects based on cooperation, created new divisions/departments to enhance students' experiences or to promote scientific performance (she is the founder of ISAG's first research center – NIDISAG). In relation to the professional path, a similar course can be traced. Invited as the first Director of the European Grouping for Territorial

Cooperation Galicia-Norte Portugal (GNP-EGTC), she was able to place into policies and cooperation strategies her scientific-research experience concerning economic, regional and cross-border development, corporate governance and innovation and entrepreneurship areas. Later, assumed the position as Dean of ISAG, until today, where she preconized a profound restructure of the institution.

Simbayi Yafele, is a Senior Lecturer in the Department of Languages, Cultural Studies and Applied Linguistics (LanCSAL) at the University of Johannesburg, South Africa. His PhD in Applied Language and Literacy Education from Wits University combined applied linguistics, literacy, and education specialisations. He is theoretically grounded in translanguaging (fluidly using more than one language for pedagogy), and his research centres on working with literacies and inclusive literacy pedagogies for multilingual education contexts and social justice. His research areas thus include translanguaging, multilingual education, and academic literacies. His work has explored academic reading development and epistemic access for marginalised bi/multilingual learners at 1st-year university levels. His interest is in inclusive, fluidly multilingual literacy pedagogy, which draws on students' literacies from their communities and applies them to the classroom and educational contexts.

Index

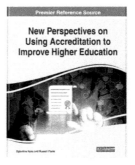

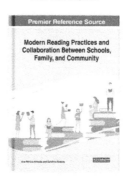
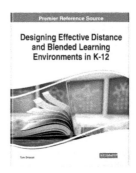

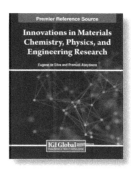
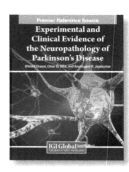
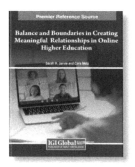

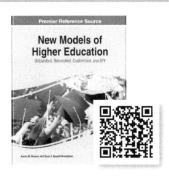

Are You Ready to
Publish Your Research ?

IGI Global
PUBLISHER of TIMELY KNOWLEDGE

IGI Global offers book authorship and editorship opportunities across 11 subject areas, including business, computer science, education, science and engineering, social sciences, and more!

Benefits of Publishing with IGI Global:

- Free one-on-one editorial and promotional support.

- Expedited publishing timelines that can take your book from start to finish in less than one (1) year.

- Choose from a variety of formats, including Edited and Authored References, Handbooks of Research, Encyclopedias, and Research Insights.

- Utilize IGI Global's eEditorial Discovery® submission system in support of conducting the submission and double-blind peer review process.

- IGI Global maintains a strict adherence to ethical practices due in part to our full membership with the Committee on Publication Ethics (COPE).

- Indexing potential in prestigious indices such as Scopus®, Web of Science™, PsycINFO®, and ERIC – Education Resources Information Center.

- Ability to connect your ORCID iD to your IGI Global publications.

- Earn honorariums and royalties on your full book publications as well as complimentary content and exclusive discounts.

Join Your Colleagues from Prestigious Institutions, Including:

Australian National University

MIT
Massachusetts Institute of Technology

JOHNS HOPKINS UNIVERSITY

HARVARD UNIVERSITY

COLUMBIA UNIVERSITY
IN THE CITY OF NEW YORK

Milton Keynes UK
Ingram Content Group UK Ltd.
UKHW050755230424
441593UK00007B/282